W9-BMZ-236

Cooking Light.

way to
cook

Oxmoor
House.

ISBN-13: 978-0-8487-3739-9
ISBN-10: 0–8487-3739–3
Library of Congress Control Number: 2013934190
Printed in the United States of America
Third printing 2013

Be sure to check with your health-care provider before making any changes in your diet.

Oxmoor House, Inc.

VP, Publishing Director: Jim Childs
Brand Manager: Allison Long Lowery
Managing Editor: L. Amanda Owens

Cooking Light® Way to Cook

Editor: Rachel Quinlivan, R.D.
Senior Designer: Emily Albright Parrish
Director, Test Kitchens: Elizabeth Tyler Austin
Assistant Director,
Test Kitchens: Julie Christopher
Test Kitchens Professionals: Kathleen Royal Phillips,
Catherine Crowell Steele,
Ashley T. Strickland
Photography Director: Jim Bathie
Senior Photo Stylist: Kay E. Clarke
Associate Photo Stylist: Katherine Eckert Coyne
Production Manager: Terri Beste-Farley

Contributors

Designers: Teresa Cole, Joline Rivera
Copy Editor: Norma Butterworth-McKittrick
Proofreader: Jacqueline B. Giovanelli
Indexer: Mary Ann Laurens
Interns: Emily Chappell,
Anne-Harris Jones,
Shea Staskowski,
Christine Taylor,
Angela Valente
Photographer: Beau Gustafson

To order additional publications, call 1-800-765-6400.

For more books to enrich your life, visit **oxmoorhouse.com**

To search, savor, and share thousands of recipes, visit **myrecipes.com**

Cooking Light®

Editor in Chief: Mary Kay Culpepper
Executive Editor: Billy R. Sims
Creative Director: Susan Waldrip Dendy
Managing Editor: Maelynn Cheung
Deputy Editor: Phillip Rhodes
Senior Food Editor: Ann Taylor Pittman
Projects Editor: Mary Simpson Creel, M.S., R.D.
Associate Food Editors: Timothy Q. Cebula;
Kathy Kitchens Downie, R.D.;
Julianna Grimes
Associate Editors: Cindy Hatcher,
Brandy Rushing
Test Kitchens Director: Vanessa Taylor Johnson
Assistant Test Kitchens
Director: Tiffany Vickers
Senior Food Stylist: Kellie Gerber Kelley
Test Kitchens Professionals: Mary Drennen Ankar,
SaBrina Bone, Deb Wise
Art Director: Maya Metz Logue
Associate Art Directors: Fernande Bondarenko,
J. Shay McNamee
Senior Designer: Brigette Mayer
Senior Photographer: Randy Mayor
Senior Photo Stylist: Cindy Barr
Photo Stylists: Jan Gautro, Leigh Ann Ross
Copy Chief: Maria Parker Hopkins
Assistant Copy Chief: Susan Roberts
Copy Editor: Johannah Gilman Paiva
Copy Researcher: Michelle Gibson Daniels
Production Manager: Liz Rhoades
Production Editor: Hazel R. Eddins
Cookinglight.com Editor: Kim Cross
Cookinglight.com Intern: Maggie Gordon
Administrative Coordinator: Carol D. Johnson
Editorial Assistant: Jason Horn
Interns: Caroline Ford, Emily Kaple

Cooking Light®
way to
cook

Oxmoor
House®

Contents

5

Welcome

Every cook, beginner to expert, knows that there is always something more to learn in the kitchen, and that learning is enormously satisfying because it pays off almost immediately—when you take the first bite.

If there is a more expeditiously gratifying experience than perfecting a simple cooking technique—such as searing fish or making a correctly balanced vinaigrette for a summer salad—I'm not sure what it is. Yet it's easy to fall into habits and assumptions in the kitchen. For example, I made perfectly acceptable but uninspired scrambled eggs for many years until I learned to slow things down, lower the heat, mind the curd, and remove the eggs from the pan a bit earlier. So utterly simple! Suddenly, scrambled eggs became a sort of specialty—everyone I serve them to loves them. There's no "trick." It's about easy, accessible technique. Every single dish has within it an ideal expression, and a less-than-ideal expression, and it's the former we're all seeking as cooks: ideals of taste and texture. The best news is that achieving this is open to all of us, because cooking is such a personal, domestic art.

New techniques and better techniques keep the cook fresh and everyone who eats the food happy. Healthy cooking, in particular, requires attention to method, because you're usually working with less fat, salt, and sugar (which hide a multitude of sins). The healthy cook also seeks to preserve the vibrant, often subtle flavors of fresh ingredients through the seasons. That requires a light touch. There are hundreds of techniques adapted for healthy recipes in this book, none of them difficult, and each one will improve the cooking of every cook, beginner to expert.

Scott Mowbray
Editor

the Cooking Light

way to cook

way to cook
healthy

For more than 20 years of recipe testing and food development, *Cooking Light*'s goal has always been to provide healthy, flavorful recipes. While some of our principles for creating these recipes have remained the same—such as heeding the Academy of Nutrition and Dietetics' guidelines—we've created or adapted others, and the concept of what makes a nutritious recipe continues to evolve. Here we share our nine most important cooking principles.

Incorporate healthful fats

healthy eating principle 1

Using less fat is only part of the solution when it comes to healthy, balanced eating. Over the years, health experts' knowledge and recommendations have changed as we've learned more about the effect fats have on health and disease. In the late 1980s, the idea that some fatty food might be healthful was a fairly new concept. Now, monounsaturated and polyunsaturated fats, found in foods like salmon, avocado, nuts, and many oils, are considered an essential part of good health. When these fats replace saturated and trans fats in the diet, they can help reduce harmful LDL cholesterol levels and may lower risk for heart disease and stroke. We often incorporate foods with these beneficial fats into our recipes.

Oils

Cooking oils are indispensable. They lubricate food, distribute heat, facilitate browning, create tenderness in baked goods, and provide a smooth, rich mouthfeel. Many also impart their own unique flavors to dishes. Other oils—notably regular olive oil and canola oil—taste more neutral, allowing the flavors of the food to shine.

Light, oxygen, and heat cause oil to spoil rapidly, so store in tightly sealed, colored-glass or opaque containers in a cool, dark place; a cabinet or pantry is ideal.

Anatomy of Oil
• Oils are liquid fats (as opposed to solid fats, such as butter or shortening)—so 100 percent of any oil's calories come from fat.
• Oils are derived from plant sources—nuts (such as walnuts), seeds (such as sesame seeds), plants (such as rapeseed), and fruits (such as olives or avocados).
• Many oils are low in saturated fat and high in heart-healthy monounsaturated and polyunsaturated fats.

Oils and Nutrition
Several comprehensive studies have revealed that overall fat consumption isn't as much of a concern to our health as the types of fat we consume. Substituting monounsaturated and polyunsaturated fats (like those found in cooking oils) for saturated and trans fats (found mostly in fatty meats and processed foods, respectively) may actually reduce harmful LDL, and monounsaturated fat may raise beneficial HDL cholesterol, helping to lower your risk of heart disease.

Oil Glossary

Extra-virgin olive oil: Extra-virgin olive oil has a rich range of flavors, from pungent and bold to smooth and buttery. Because the flavor of extra-virgin olive oil can diminish with heat, it's often used to finish a dish, drizzled over pasta, or whisked into a vinaigrette (though many chefs cook with it, too).

Regular olive oil: Also called "pure" or "light" olive oil, which are simply marketing tags and not an indication of nutritional qualities, this olive oil is a blend of refined olive oil and extra-virgin olive oil. It costs less and has a mild flavor. Use it when you want to preserve the flavors of the food rather than impart the character of the oil to it. We often use it for sautés or stir-fries.

Canola oil: Derived from a strain of rapeseed in Canada in the 1970s that yields oil with lower acidity than traditional rapeseed, this oil's name is an amalgam of the words "Canada" and "oil." Canola oil continues to be a major export crop for its namesake country. It's high in both polyunsaturated and monounsaturated fats and very low in saturated fat. Its neutral flavor makes it a good choice when you don't want to detract from the flavors of the food.

Sesame oil: This oil is pressed from crushed sesame seeds. The lighter-colored oil comes from raw seeds and has a mild, neutral taste. Dark sesame oil, also called toasted sesame oil, has been pressed from toasted sesame seeds and has an intense, nutty flavor and aroma. Both are considered a seasoning.

Walnut oil: Unrefined walnut oil tastes just like the nut from which it comes. It's rich and flavorful (especially if made from toasted walnuts) and perfect as a finishing drizzle on salads, rice, pasta, or even desserts like tarte tatin or rice pudding.

All foods have a place in a healthful diet

We've never declared certain foods off-limits, but years ago, we avoided high-fat ingredients, particularly those high in saturated fat like butter, cream, and bacon. We started using butter in 1998 after scientific evidence showed that small amounts of higher-fat foods, including those that contain saturated fat, can be included in a nutritious diet. The keys are moderation and balance. As long as your overall diet is healthful, what you eat at one meal isn't as important as the balance of what you eat over a few days or a week. This means all foods—beef, butter, cheese, and even salt—have a place in your diet, and we strive to show you how to use and enjoy them judiciously.

Milk

Milk is crucial to many cooking applications, from velvety custards to creamy casseroles. Over the years, we've learned that all types of milk products have a place in the pages of *Cooking Light*. Depending on the role milk plays in a particular dish, we may call for low-fat milk or perhaps a higher-fat product such as whipping cream or half-and-half.

Anatomy of Milk

• Raw cow's milk is about 87 percent water, about 5 percent sugar, about 3½ percent protein, and just under 4 percent fat.
• Because fat is lighter than water, unhomogenized milk separates so the cream rises to the top; when skimmed off, the milk that's left is almost fat free.
• One cup of milk contains about 102 milligrams of sodium.
• Ninety-eight percent of milk in the United States is vitamin D-fortified; one cup of fortified milk contains 25 percent of the Daily Value for vitamin D.
• When fat is removed from milk, vitamin A is removed, too. That's why 2 percent, 1 percent, and fat-free milk are most often fortified with this vitamin. One cup of fortified milk contains 10 percent of the Daily Value for vitamin A.

Milk Glossary

Whole milk: With none of its inherent fat removed, whole milk is thick and rich. Each 8-ounce glass has 146 calories, 7.9 grams of fat, and 276 milligrams of calcium. Whole milk is recommended for children under the age of two, but in most cases it is considered too high in fat for adults and older children to drink regularly. It can, however, play an important role in cooking. It adds silky texture to sauces and soups, contributes flavor and texture to baked goods, and lends golden gloss to doughs and crusts.

Two percent milk: An 8-ounce glass of 2 percent (reduced-fat) milk contains 121 calories, 4.7 grams of fat, and 297 milligrams of calcium. The higher fat content makes it creamier than 1 percent milk or fat-free milk, which can be beneficial in cooking.

One percent milk: An 8-ounce glass of 1 percent, or low-fat, milk has 102 calories, 2.6 grams of fat, and 300 milligrams of calcium. Some dishes rely on other ingredients or techniques for texture and are dependent on milk mostly for flavor and liquidity. So a lower-fat milk works fine in these cases.

Fat-free milk: Fat-free milk is many people's milk beverage of choice. Also called skim milk, it contains no fat, only 83 calories, and 306 milligrams of calcium per 8-ounce glass. Lower-fat milks have more calcium per cup than whole milk because in whole milk some of the volume is displaced by milk fat, which has no calcium. Use fat-free milk on cereal, in coffee, as a drink—and to make certain dishes, such as puddings and cheese sauces, where the milk provides background flavor, and other ingredients, such as flour or cornstarch, lend texture.

Whipping cream: Whipping cream (or heavy whipping cream) has 51 calories and 5.6 grams of fat per tablespoon. When beaten, whipping cream doubles in volume to create a classic dessert topping. (Neither light whipping cream nor light cream contains enough fat to hold its shape when whipped.) Whipping cream is the only type of milk that is heat stable—it won't curdle when brought to a boil. Use it to enrich sauces and soups, adding just a bit at a time—as little as a tablespoon can add the right amount of body and rich taste.

Half-and-half: A mixture of equal parts milk and cream, half-and-half weighs in with only 20 calories and 1.7 grams of fat per tablespoon. Use it to finish sauces and soups, but add it off the stove or over lower heat to prevent it from curdling.

Buttermilk: Traditionally, buttermilk was the liquid that remained after butter was churned from cream. Today, buttermilk is made by adding bacteria cultures to fat-free, low-fat, or whole milk. Buttermilk has a thick consistency and tart flavor. It's often used for cakes, biscuits, pancakes, and quick breads.

Acidophilus milk: Acidophilus milk is whole, reduced-fat, or fat-free milk with friendly *Lactobacillus acidophilus* bacteria added to it. The bacteria is believed to benefit the digestive tract, much the same way yogurt does.

Butter

Although made up completely of fat—which accounts for almost all its calories—butter has a place in a healthful diet. This is partly because fat is satisfying, but mostly because when it comes to flavor, there's simply no substitute.

The key to cooking with butter in light recipes is to use techniques that stretch it so you enjoy its benefits. Small amounts add richness to sauces, keep baked goods tender, and enhance the flavor of other ingredients. So go ahead and dab some on—just do so sparingly. Your cooking, like butter itself, will be golden.

Anatomy of Butter

• By law, butter must contain at least 80 percent milk fat, but premium and imported brands may have as much as 85 percent. (The more milk fat butter has, the creamier the flavor.) It's also made up of 16 to 17 percent water and 1 to 2 percent milk solids, or proteins.
• One tablespoon of butter packs 100 calories and 11 grams of fat, the vast majority from saturated fats.
• One tablespoon of butter contains 30 milligrams of cholesterol.

Storage Savvy

Air and bright light break down fat molecules and eventually turn butter rancid, which is why butter is best stored in cool, dark places—like refrigerators. Since refrigerator door temperatures vary considerably, skip the butter compartment and store butter near the back. In a cold refrigerator, a stick of salted butter in its original wrapping will keep for about two months (the salt acts as a preservative); unsalted butter, for one and a half months. Butter freezes well for up to six months.

Salted vs. Unsalted

The difference between salted and unsalted butter is simple: about 80 milligrams of sodium per tablespoon. Salt acts as a preservative and prolongs the shelf life of butter. Most people use salted butter, and most of our recipes were tested with that variety. Some cooks prefer unsalted butter because it allows them to control the amount of salt in a dish and preserves the mellow sweetness of butter. If you want unsalted butter, look for the phrase "sweet butter" or "unsalted." The term "sweet cream butter" is used for both salted and unsalted butter.

kitchen how-to: make clarified butter

Clarified butter contains no water or milk solids, and it can withstand temperatures as high as 400° without burning (regular butter burns at around 250°). To make clarified butter, simply melt butter, and remove the solids. What remains is pure milk fat that can be used to brown meats and seafood or enrich sauces. Just don't use it as a spread: It's grainy when it cools. Ghee is similar to clarified butter, but the butter is browned to develop a nutty taste before the solids are skimmed off. It's popular in Indian cuisine for enriching sauces, finishing soups, or as a general cooking oil.

1. Melt the butter over medium-low heat.
2. Skim the milk solids from the top of the melted butter.
3. Slowly pour the butter out of the pan, leaving the remaining solids in the bottom of the pan.

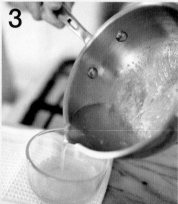

Butter Glossary

Cultured cream butter: Cultured cream butter is made by adding lactic acid to butter. Before the advent of large-scale commercial butter production, farmers made butter from cream collected over several days of milking. During this time, the cream soured from the natural formation of lactic acid and made a pleasingly tart butter. Some people prefer its sharper taste.

Organic butter: Organic butter is made from organic milk. By law, the cream used to produce it must be free of antibiotics, synthetic growth hormones, and pesticides.

Whipped butter: Whipped butter is standard butter pumped with air or nitrogen gas to create a light, fluffy texture. (Oxygen hastens rancidity.) This is a good choice to serve at the table because it has a spread-able texture even when cold.

European-style butter: European-style butter contains more milk fat than the standard 80 percent for American butters, and as a result, it has a creamier taste and a smoother texture. Because of its lower water content, this type of butter makes rich sauces, pastries, and frostings, but you can use it in any application for which you would use regular butter.

Stick butter: Stick butter, the most widely available form, comes salted or unsalted; both are often termed "sweet cream butter." Light butter, made by combining butter with skim milk, has half the fat and calories of regular butter. It's fine as a spread, but its lower fat content makes it a poor choice for baking or frying.

Cheese

No matter how tasty a dish may be, it's almost always better with cheese. Because cheese is naturally high in fat (particularly saturated fat), it's important to use it wisely.

Anatomy of Cheese

• Milk is the main ingredient in cheese; cow's, goat's, and sheep's milk are most commonly used.

• Milk is allowed to thicken (often with the addition of rennin or rennet, an enzyme) and separate into curds and whey. The whey is drained, and the curds are used to make cheese.

• Because cheese is made from milk, it's a good source of calcium. It's also high in fat and sodium.

Cheese Glossary

There are hundreds of specific cheese varieties, ranging in flavor from sweet and nutty to bitter and acidic, so we focus here on the ones we use most often.

Saint André: This French cheese is made from cow's milk and is surrounded in a soft white rind. Inside the rind, the creamy center is about 75 percent buttermilk fat. Saint André has a buttery texture and rich flavor similar to Brie.

Feta: Feta is a fresh Greek cheese that is tangy and salty as a result of the brine in which it's cured. It's traditionally made from sheep's milk, but it can also be made from goat's or cow's milk. Its crumbly yet creamy texture lends it to a variety of culinary applications. A choice addition to salads, feta is also good for fillings, sauces, and pasta dishes.

Brie: Brie's soft texture oozes at peak ripeness. Creamy, buttery, rich, and slightly sweet, it is spreadable and completed by its edible white rind. The soft-ripened French cheese is best enjoyed as an appetizer or dessert at room temperature, or it can be baked with an array of savory or sweet toppings.

Goat cheese: Goat cheese—or chèvre, French for "goat"—is a fresh, unripened goat's milk cheese that has a fruity flavor early on but develops a sharper and slightly tart quality as it ages. Crumble it over salads,

Saint André

feta

Brie

goat
cheese

mascarpone

chevrot
(goat cheese)

or serve it with herbs as a spread on crusty bread. You can also use it as a topping for pizzas, quesadillas, or open-faced sandwiches.

Mascarpone: This Italian cheese has a silky texture and a rich, creamy flavor. It's a very spreadable cheese, but, depending on how it's processed, the texture can range from very soft to more stiff, like butter. It's a traditional dessert cheese that's used in classic Italian desserts such as tiramisu and zabaglione.

Gruyère: Produced in Switzerland, Gruyère has a smooth yet pliable texture with a mild nutty or toasty flavor. This semifirm cheese also has fruity or sweet hints and should have a pale yellow interior and slightly browned edges. Flavorful and moist, it's a popular dessert cheese and also melts well for sauces or fondues. Gruyère is traditional in veal dishes and chicken cordon bleu and is excellent for gratins and soufflés.

Fontina: Semisoft but dense with small holes, fontina is encased by a dark gold, crusty rind. With a fruity overtone, its buttery qualities make it a natural for dessert. Fontina is a good melting cheese, often used in sauces and on pizzas or casseroles.

Cheddar: The salty tang of Cheddar cheese can range from mild to sharp, making it versatile for both cooking and snacking. It can be white or dyed orange; both deliver a robust quality that can stand alone or incorporates well into soups, casseroles, and sandwiches.

Parmesan: Parmesan cheese is perhaps the most widely used hard cheese. Parmigiano-Reggiano is considered the finest of Parmesan. It has an appealing grainy texture and a rich and strong nutty flavor. This grade of Parmesan must be aged at least 12 months and is specific to the Italian province bearing its name—Parma. Its piquant quality makes it a versatile cheese that can be grated and incorporated into soups, salads, and pasta dishes.

Gorgonzola: Among blues, Gorgonzola is moist, creamy, savory, earthy, and slightly spicier than its relatives. A pleasing addition to salads, it's excellent paired with apples, pears, figs, and peaches, and it works well with pastas, sauces, and meat and poultry dishes.

Gruyère

fontina

Cheddar

Parmigiano-Reggiano

blue cheeses

Eggs

We love this humble ingredient. Eggs are low in calories and provide an excellent source of protein. Although they're high in dietary cholesterol, researchers believe eggs can be a part of a heart-healthy diet. The American Heart Association says that as long as a person's diet limits cholesterol from other sources, he or she can enjoy up to one egg a day.

Eggs are also very versatile. In baking, eggs contribute structure, color, flavor, and richness. They lighten and leaven, bind, thicken, add moisture, and glaze. To keep fat concerns in check, we often use a combination of whole eggs and egg whites to great success.

Anatomy of an Egg

• The yolk holds all the egg's fat (about 5 grams in a large egg yolk); cholesterol; vitamins A, D, and E; and nearly half its protein. The color of the yolk varies with the bird's diet and doesn't affect nutritional content.
• A large egg contains 75 calories, 5 grams of fat, and 6.3 grams of protein.
• The American Heart Association recommends that people limit their dietary intake of cholesterol to 300 milligrams a day. A large egg contains about 213 milligrams of cholesterol.

Storage Savvy

Buy the freshest eggs available (check the sell-by date) and always from a refrigerated case. At home, refrigerate immediately in the original carton, which prevents moisture loss and absorption of odors from other foods in the refrigerator. Discard any with cracks. Store eggs on an inside shelf—not in the egg "cups" on the door where the temperature is not as cold—for three to five weeks from the day they're purchased. The sell-by date may pass within this period, but the eggs are still safe.

Pasteurized Eggs

Eggs can be pasteurized to eliminate salmonella and other bacteria, making them safe for low-temperature or uncooked applications. The pasteurization process uses heat to kill the bacteria without cooking the egg.

Size Wise

Eggs are sized from peewee to jumbo. The terms refer to the weight of the eggs per dozen, not the dimensions of an individual egg. You can readily make size substitutions in dishes such as omelets and scrambles. However, for best results when baking, use the size of egg called for in the recipe. If no size is specified, assume it's large.

kitchen how-to:
crack & separate eggs

If you need pristine egg whites for meringues, cakes, and omelets, or yolks for sauces and soufflés, follow these steps. You'll need: Two bowls—one for the whites and one for the yolks. Choose fresh eggs, and make sure they appear clean and the shells are intact. Stored in a tightly sealed container, egg whites will keep in the fridge for up to four days, and yolks for two days.

1. Lightly tap the middle of the egg—the widest portion—against the rim of the bowl. You'll hear a slight pop when the egg has cracked. At that point, one more tap will do the trick. The egg should crack evenly with a slightly larger hole at the point of impact. Use this hole to separate the shell.

2. Hold a cupped hand over one bowl. With the other, gently separate the shell along the crack, letting the yolk and whites drip into your waiting hand. Keeping the solid yolk in your hand, allow the whites to fall through your fingers into the bowl below. Place the yolk in the second bowl, and throw away the shell.

3. Check to make sure your whites are clean, and remove any bits of the shell that may have fallen in.

kitchen how-to:
scramble eggs

To make light and fluffy scrambled eggs, use a fork to beat the eggs together in a bowl. Pour the mixture in a nonstick skillet, and cook over medium-low heat. The key to large, fluffy curds is to allow the eggs to set in the pan for about 30 seconds without stirring. Then, using a rubber spatula, gently pull the cooked edges away from the pan, creating an almost folded effect. Continue moving them fairly regularly until they form plump curds that appear slightly wet, not dry. Remove them from the pan immediately because they will continue to cook.

Egg Substitute

Nutritionally, egg substitute and egg whites are the same because egg substitutes are made from egg whites, corn oil, water, flavorings, and preservatives. Egg substitutes are great to use in recipes that call for just egg whites, particularly in those where the eggs aren't fully cooked, because they're pasteurized. This means they have a low risk of containing bacteria and don't have to be heated to 160° to be safe to eat. Don't use egg substitute in place of whole eggs in baking because they don't perform the same.

kitchen how-to:
make an omelet

Omelets are easy to make and fun to fill. Dress one up with leftover vegetables, such as mushrooms, cherry tomatoes, and green onions; or add ham or turkey, plus a little cheese for calcium. The omelet cooks swiftly, so precook meats and dice vegetables beforehand because you'll have to work quickly. Before beginning, preheat a nonstick pan over medium-high heat. It's important that the pan be hot. To test, add a few drops of water; they should sizzle.

1. Whisk the eggs until slightly frothy, about 20 to 30 seconds. Be careful not to overbeat them. Spray pan with cooking spray, and then pour in eggs.
2. Gently shake the pan to distribute the eggs. Use a nonstick spatula to lift the edges and allow any uncooked egg to flow underneath. Cook until the egg appears set, not runny.
3. Add ingredients to half of the omelet, and then use the spatula to lift and fold the other half over the fillings. Allow the omelet to cook for another 30 seconds.

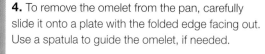

4. To remove the omelet from the pan, carefully slide it onto a plate with the folded edge facing out. Use a spatula to guide the omelet, if needed.

Fish

With the enormous variety of fresh fish available at supermarkets today, there's a fish to suit anyone's palate—from assertive salmon to subtle tilapia, from buttery, delicate halibut to meaty tuna and swordfish and beyond.

Buying Fish

Often the fresh fish you buy to prepare at home has been frozen. Fish sold as fresh can be anywhere from one day to two weeks out of the water. Large fishing vessels may stay at sea for two weeks, keeping their catch on ice to sell fresh. For top quality, look for "Frozen-at-Sea" (FAS)—fish that has been flash-frozen at extremely low temperatures in as little as 3 seconds onboard ship. When thawed, sea-frozen fish are almost indistinguishable from fresh fish.

Whole Fresh Fish
• Look for shiny skin; tightly adhering scales; bright, clear eyes; firm, taut flesh that springs back when pressed; and a moist, flat tail.
• Gills should be cherry-red, not brownish.
• Saltwater fish should smell briny; freshwater fish should smell like a clean pond.

Fresh Fillets or Steaks
• When buying white-fleshed fish, choose translucent-looking fillets with a pinkish tint.
• When buying any color fish, the flesh should appear dense without any gaps between layers.
• If the fish is wrapped in plastic, the package should contain little to no liquid.
• Ask the fishmonger to remove any pin bones, which run crosswise to the backbone.

Frozen Fish
• Look for shiny, rock-hard frozen fish with no white freezer-burn spots, frost, or ice crystals.
• Choose well-sealed packages from the bottom of the freezer case that are at most three months old.

Storing Fish

Buy fish on your way out of the store, take it directly home, and cook (or freeze) it within 24 hours. Keep the fish as cold as possible until you're ready to cook it by storing it in the coldest part of your refrigerator.

Fish Nutrition

Fish contains 17 to 25 percent protein and is generally a good source of B vitamins. Fatty fish are good sources of vitamins A and D. The small, soft, edible bones of fresh sardines and smelts and canned bone-in fish like salmon are valuable sources of calcium.

Some fish also contain heart-healthy omega-3s. Darker-fleshed fish that swim in cold, open waters, such as tuna, herring, and mackerel, store fat in their flesh and are high in omega-3s. Freshwater fish from cold waters, such as lake herring, lake trout, salmon, and whitefish, are also high in omega-3s. In general, white-fleshed fish, such as cod, tilapia, or flounder, are low in all types of fat, including omega-3s. That's because they store fat in their livers (as in cod-liver oil).

amberjack

arctic char

catfish

cod

Fish Glossary

Amberjack: Full flavor and firm flesh make amberjack, which stands up to more assertive flavors, ideal to grill, pan-fry, or broil. Amberjack is available in fillets and steaks year-round.

Arctic char (farmed freshwater): Arctic char, most often sold in fillets, has a distinctive pink flesh with a rich flavor similar to salmon and steelhead trout. You can substitute arctic char for salmon in almost any recipe, and vice versa. Like salmon, this fish lends itself to most any cooking method.

Catfish (farmed freshwater): Farmed catfish is available fresh year-round. Its sweet flavor and firm texture make it ideal for grilling, roasting, pan-frying, and braising. It can also substitute for other firm-flesh fish, such as pompano.

Cod: Cod is a flaky white fish with mild, sweet flavor—so mild, in fact, those who are wary of seafood tend to gravitate to it. Cod (along with pollock) is often used to make fish cakes and fish sticks and frequently appears in chowders and stews.

Halibut: Popular because of its mild flavor, this flaky white fish should be prepared with subtle flavors that won't overwhelm its delicacy. Fresh halibut is plentiful and available fresh from March to November. It's sold frozen the rest of the year.

Mahimahi: Originally called dolphinfish, the Hawaiian name mahimahi was adopted to alleviate confusion that this fish is related to the aquatic mammal. Popular because of its versatility, mahimahi pairs well with fruits and spicy sauces. It grills, broils, pan-fries, and braises beautifully.

Pompano: Pompano has a delicate, sweet flavor. Catfish makes a suitable substitute when pompano is scarce. Grill, broil, or pan-fry it.

Red snapper: The most prized member of the large snapper family is American red snapper, which has a pronounced sweet flavor, similar to shrimp. Many varieties of snapper are available year-round, and though they may not be quite as sweet as American red snapper, they're excellent substitutions.

Salmon: Most of what we get at the market is farmed Atlantic salmon. While wild Atlantic salmon is virtually extinct, wild Pacific salmon is still available. The high fat content of salmon keeps it moist when cooked by

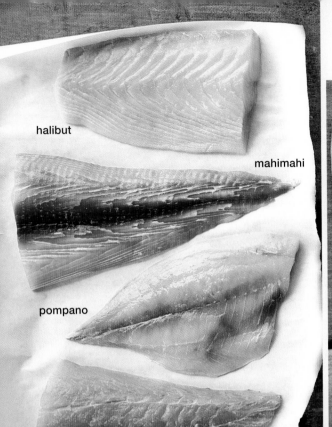

halibut

mahimahi

pompano

red snapper

sole/flounder

salmon

tilapia

swordfish

tuna

trout

almost any method—you can pan-fry, grill, roast, steam, poach, or smoke it.

Sole/Flounder: Although sole are actually members of the flounder family, the words sole and flounder are often used interchangeably. (You're likely to see flounder at the fish market, and sole on restaurant menus.) You can substitute turbot, plaice, or fluke (sometimes called summer flounder) for flounder/sole.

Swordfish: Popular for its mild flavor and meaty texture, swordfish appears in markets year-round, usually as steak, and it's best pan-fried or grilled.

Tilapia (farmed freshwater): Tilapia has a firm texture and mild flavor (some argue that it has almost none) that make it an ideal canvas on which to paint layers of flavor. Like cod, this is a great fish for people who say they don't like fish. Readily available year-round, tilapia can be pan-fried, broiled, baked, or braised.

Trout (farmed freshwater): The flavor of trout ranges from subtle and mild to sweet. Most of the trout sold at markets is rainbow trout, although you'll also see other varieties such as brook trout. At its best, trout is subtle; prepare it simply to avoid masking its flavor.

Tuna: The many species of tuna vary in flavor and texture. Costly sashimi-grade tuna—so named because this is the best quality for sushi and sashimi—has a clean, subtle flavor and a delicate texture, and it's higher in fat. The tuna most widely available in grocery stores tends to be meatier, with a more assertive flavor. Tuna is ideal for grilling or searing, which caramelizes the outside and leaves the interior moist. It is less forgiving than other fish, and when overcooked it can be dry and tough. Tuna is sold fresh and frozen year-round.

Shellfish

There are two main categories of shellfish: crustaceans and mollusks. Crustaceans include crabs, crawfish, lobster, and shrimp. Mollusks are invertebrates with soft bodies covered by a shell of one or more pieces. Mollusks with two shells hinged together are called bivalves and include clams, mussels, and oysters. Here's our guide to selecting and cooking these different types of shellfish.

Clams

Clams are found in two main varieties: soft-shell and hard-shell. Both types vary in size from clams that are no bigger than a thumbnail to large ones that weigh hundreds of pounds. Generally, the smaller the clam, the more tender the meat. Soft-shell clams, so named because they have a thin, brittle exterior, are usually fried or steamed in the shell. The clams most often sold in markets are the hard-shells.

Buying and Storing Clams

When purchasing clams, look for firm, gray, tightly closed shells with no signs of yellowing. The clams are still alive and should be until you cook them. You can tell if a soft-shell clam is alive because it will retract further into its shell if it's poked. The shell of a live hard-shell clam will be clamped tight so that it's very difficult to pry it apart. Dead clams smell bad and are unsafe to eat. If you can move the shell easily, the clam is probably dead.

Store clams in a single layer on a flat tray; cover with damp paper towels, and refrigerate for up to two days. Do not overcrowd clams, submerge them in liquid, or store them in a sealed plastic bag or on ice because they will die.

For chowders and other dishes that use only the meat of the clams, we often call for canned clams. You can buy them whole or chopped. As with most canned seafood, the canned versions are higher in sodium than the fresh.

kitchen how-to: clean clams

Cleaning clams is an important process that you need to be familiar with. If you don't properly clean clams before cooking them, you can end up eating salty, sandy clams. It's a quick and easy process—just follow these steps.

1. Scrub the clams under cold running water with a stiff brush to remove sand and dirt.
2. Shuck the clams; release the meat from bottom shell.

Mussels

There are two varieties of mussels generally available in the United States: the blue (or common) mussel and the New Zealand mussel. The blue mussel has a shiny black exterior and an iridescent blue interior shell. The New Zealand mussel is also called the green-shelled mussel because of its color.

Buying and Storing Mussels

Always buy fresh mussels, and use them within a day. Choose tightly closed shells or those that are slightly open and snap shut when tapped. This indicates the mussel is alive; an open shell means it's dead or dehydrated. Avoid broken and chipped shells. Once you're home, remove the mussels from the packaging, and store them wrapped in a moist towel in the fridge to keep them fresh. Don't store mussels in plastic—it prevents them from breathing.

kitchen how-to:
scrub & debeard mussels

It will take just a few seconds to scrub and debeard each mussel.

1. When ready to cook, scrub each mussel to remove any sand or dirt on the shell. Holding it under cool water, scrub each mussel's shell with a stiff-bristled brush, such as those used for cleaning vegetables.
2. Next, debeard to remove the byssal threads (or beard), which connect the mussel to rocks or pilings in the sea. Grab the fibers with your fingers, and pull them out, tugging toward the hinged point of the shell.

1

2

Oysters

Not only are oysters remarkably versatile in how they can be prepared, but they're also packed with minerals such as zinc and iron, as well as heart-healthy omega-3 fatty acids. There are many kinds of oysters, and they usually take the name of the place where they grow.

Buying and Storing Oysters

All the many oyster varieties are at their best in the winter since they spawn in the summer and become fat and sweet later in the year. Choose plump oysters packed in clear liquid (reject any whose liquid seems cloudy or milky), and refrigerate them for up to two days. If you decide to purchase fresh live oysters in the shell, choose ones with tightly sealed shells and no fishy odor. To store, arrange them in a single layer on a flat tray, cover with damp paper towels, and refrigerate for up to two days. They need space to breathe, so don't overcrowd them, submerge them in liquid, or store them in a sealed plastic bag or on ice.

Best Time to Eat Oysters

You may have heard the old saying that you should only eat oysters during months with an "R" in them, which leaves out the warm-weather months of May through August. This idea may have started in the days when oysters were shipped without adequate refrigeration and could spoil. Today, thanks to regular safety monitoring for microbes and rapid refrigeration that prevents spoilage, this proscription no longer applies to most of us—especially if oysters are cooked.

Vibrio vulnificus, a type of bacteria commonly found in warm seawater, can contaminate raw oysters. Though the risk of illness from bacteria is rare in healthy people, anyone with a compromised immune system should eat thoroughly cooked oysters. And because of that bacteria, you may want to avoid warm-water oysters—such as those from the Gulf of Mexico—in summer months.

kitchen how-to:
shuck an oyster

Before shucking, scrub the shell with a stiff vegetable brush and rinse under cold water. This will keep loose dirt from getting on the meat. To protect your hands, wear a rubber shucking glove (available at specialty food shops), or use a towel to hold the oyster steady in case the knife slips or the shell cracks.

1. With the flat shell on top and the hinged point of the oyster shell toward you, work a short, sturdy oyster knife with a round pointed tip into the hinge. Using lots of pressure, pry the top and bottom shell apart until you hear the hinge pop.

2. Carefully slide the knife horizontally across the roof of the oyster to release it from the top shell. Then run the knife under the oyster to release it from the bottom shell. Be careful not to spill the translucent liquid; it's flavorful and an ingredient on its own in oyster stew.

Crabs

Crabs are protein-rich and low in calories and fat. There's also a wide selection—the type you'll see in the supermarket most often depends on where you live. Use this guide to help you decide which variety will suit your tastes.

Buying and Storing Crabs

When selecting hard-shelled crabs, look for those that move their claws when poked. They should look moist and soft, and the shell should not look like it's hardening. If a crab's claws droop when you lift it, don't buy it. While it's best to use fresh crabs on the day you buy them, you can store them in the refrigerator for up to two days if they're properly packed. Lay them in a shallow bowl, and place that bowl in a larger bowl filled with ice. Cover the crabs with a damp towel, and replace the ice as needed. Before you cook them, discard any crabs that are no longer alive. You can store freshly cooked crabmeat in the refrigerator for two days.

When buying soft-shell crabs, live ones are the best, but they're not always easy to find. The freshest soft-shells smell clean and astringent and are usually only available from spring until early autumn. But you can also find them frozen, and these have usually already been cleaned. Store cleaned crabs wrapped in plastic wrap in the coldest part of the refrigerator for up to two days.

You can also buy delicious crabmeat that is freshly cooked, unpasteurized, and packed in plastic tubs. Lump crabmeat (also called backfin or jumbo) is the most desirable. It's taken from the center of the body and is in large pieces. Flake crabmeat is light and dark meat from the center and the legs, and it comes in smaller pieces.

kitchen how-to:
clean soft-shell crabs

Put live crabs on ice until they're almost immobilized before you clean them.

1. To clean soft-shell crabs, hold the crab in one hand, and using a pair of kitchen shears, cut off the front of the crab, about ½ inch behind the eyes and mouth. Squeeze out the contents of the sack located directly behind the cut you just made.

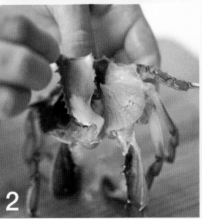

2. Lift one pointed end of the crab's outer shell.
3. Remove and discard the gills. Repeat on the other side.
4. Turn the crab over and snip off the small flap known as the apron. Rinse the entire crab well and pat dry. Once they're cleaned, the crabs should be cooked or stored immediately.

blue crab

dungeness crab

Crab Glossary

Blue (hard-shell/soft-shell):
Two types of blue crab are harvested: hard-shell and soft-shell. The meat within the hard-shelled body of the crab is thick and whitish in color, while the leg meat is smaller and flakier. Meat from the two large claws is solid and more abundant. Soft-shell crabs are those that have recently molted, which occurs when the crab has outgrown its shell and sheds it to be replaced by a new, soft shell. When cooked, soft-shell crabs have a sweet flavor and crisp texture—they're meant to be eaten whole, shell and all. Peak season runs from May through August.

Dungeness: One of the Pacific Northwest's delicacies, dungeness crab is harvested from Alaska to California. In peak harvest during winter and spring months, fresh crabs are readily available at supermarket seafood counters and specialty seafood markets, and they can be delivered overnight nation-wide. Although not as abundant, fresh cooked crab is available during the summer months. Frozen market forms are accessible year-round. The meat is sweet, sharp, and has a firm texture. The season for the Pacific variety begins in mid-November and runs through April; the season for Alaskan Dungeness is late spring and early summer.

Alaskan King: Three species of king crab grow in Alaska—red, blue, and golden—and they're found in different areas of Alaskan waters. Red king crab is the most prized species. Alive, red king crabs are actually dark burgundy, and they only turn their characteristic red hue

when cooked. Blue king crabs are known for their proportionally giant claws. When they're alive, blue king crabs are brown with royal blue highlights, but they turn a bright orange-red when cooked. This is why blue king crabs are generally marketed as red king crabs. Golden king crabs have golden-orange shells. Alaskan king crabs are the largest of all crab varieties and have a meaty, solid texture; they taste sweet but also slightly salty. They're available year-round, but the biggest and best run for the season is for

Alaskan
king crab

10 days in October, usually around the second week of the month.

Stone: The only part of this crab that is eaten is the claws. When caught, only one of the claws—the pincher claw—is removed and the crab is then thrown back. The claw is harvested again 18 to 24 months later when it has regenerated to at least 2¾ inches in length. Each crab can regenerate its large claw three or four times. Female stone crabs filled with eggs aren't harvested. Stone crabs are sweet and dense and have a more leathery texture than other varieties. They're available year-round.

Snow: Snow crabs are found in cold waters. They have a finer, lighter, sweeter meat than others. They're available year-round.

stone crab

snow crab

Crawfish

Crawfish season begins each December and peaks in April or May, when the crawfish are the fattest and most lively. If live crawfish aren't available in your area, you can order them by telephone or online for next-day delivery. Most sources sell live crawfish by the 30- or 40-pound sack. Some also sell fresh boiled crawfish, crawfish tail meat, and parboiled crawfish. (Most sources also sell shrimp, which you can substitute, if you prefer.) You can find frozen crawfish tail meat in some supermarkets. See page 253 for information about how to peel crawfish.

crawfish

Lobster

The best locale to eat a lobster dinner is on the Maine coast, but you can prepare a great lobster dinner in your home. Buy only live lobsters. The more active they are—legs, claws, and tails moving—the better. Once you get the lobsters home, it's best to cook them immediately. If you can't cook them immediately, you can refrigerate lobsters with hard shells, covered with a damp cloth, for up to 24 hours. See pages 118 and 255 for information about how to cook and extract meat from lobster.

For recipes where you need only the meat of the lobster (such as lobster salad), it's fine to use frozen lobster tails. To get 1 cup of chopped lobster meat, use 3 (6-ounce) tails, and steam them for about 8 minutes.

lobster

Shrimp

Besides their succulent flavor, the culinary versatility and largely year-round availability of shrimp are likely what makes them so popular. And despite the fact that shrimp contain more cholesterol than some other types of seafood, the total fat and saturated fat (the real culprit in heart disease) content is very low. So we think it's fine to include shrimp in a heart-healthy diet.

How Much to Buy?

To save prep time, instead of peeling and deveining your own shrimp, you can buy peeled and deveined raw shrimp at the seafood counter of most supermarkets.

The chart below shows how much peeled and deveined shrimp to buy when the recipe calls for unpeeled shrimp.

Unpeeled Raw Shrimp		Peeled & Deveined Raw Shrimp
⅔ pound	=	½ pound
1 pound	=	¾ pound
1⅓ pounds	=	1 pound
2 pounds	=	1½ pounds
2⅔ pounds	=	2 pounds
4 pounds	=	3 pounds

Storing Shrimp

Fresh uncooked shrimp is very perishable, so use it within two days of purchase. After bringing it home, rinse thoroughly under cold running water, and pat dry with paper towels. Cover shrimp loosely with wax paper so that air can circulate around it; store in the coolest part of the refrigerator, preferably on a bed of ice. Shrimp can be frozen, but they lose some of their texture after thawing. When you want to use refrozen shrimp, just thaw them in a bowl or sink filled with tap water.

kitchen how-to:
butterfly shrimp

Butterflying, in cooking terms, means to split a food down the center, cutting almost through the food. The halves are then opened flat, hence the butterfly shape. To butterfly shrimp, pull a sharp knife along the back of the shrimp, and cut almost through the shrimp to split it open.

kitchen how-to:
peel & devein shrimp

Recipes often call for shrimp to be peeled and deveined. Except for the largest shrimp, however, there's neither danger nor distaste in leaving the thin black line (vein) right where it is. (If you're butterflying shrimp, deveining occurs anyway.)

1. Peel the shell off the shrimp.
2. Cut a shallow slit along the back using a sharp paring knife.
3. Remove the dark vein using a sharp knife or deveining tool. Rinse under cold water, and drain.

Meats

Meats, such as beef, pork, lamb, and veal, contain many essential nutrients that are necessary for good health. Although concerns have been raised in recent years about the saturated fat and cholesterol content found in meats, they can be part of a healthy diet, especially when you choose lean cuts and use healthy cooking methods to prepare them.

Beef

Beef Nutrition
The USDA defines "lean beef" as having less than 10 grams of total fat, 4.5 grams or less of saturated fat, and less than 95 milligrams of cholesterol per 3½-ounce serving (100g) of cooked beef. Half of the fat is saturated, and half is heart-healthy monounsaturated. In our Test Kitchens, we generally use naturally lean cuts of beef, such as tenderloin, flank steak, and sirloin, as well as some other lesser-known cuts shown on page 32. Others, such as ribeye or chuck roast, naturally contain more fat, although it's similarly divided between saturated and monounsaturated.

Doneness: A Matter of Taste
Doneness is an issue of personal preference. According to the U.S. Department of Agriculture, beef steaks and roasts should be cooked to a minimum of 145°. For ground beef, the minimum is 160°. *Cooking Light* follows the USDA temperature guidelines. If you like your beef rare, cook it to a lower temperature than the recipes direct, but remember that ground beef should always be cooked to 160°. See page 385 for more information about determining doneness.

Storing Beef

Tightly wrapped and refrigerated, raw beef will last three to four days (ground beef, one to two days). At that point, it should be cooked or frozen. Cooked, it will keep in the refrigerator three to four days longer; frozen, it's best used within two months.

Buying the Best Beef: What to Look for

Any bones should have a pinkish tint

Marbling to help retain moisture during cooking and improve flavor

Fine-textured, firm, cherry-red beef

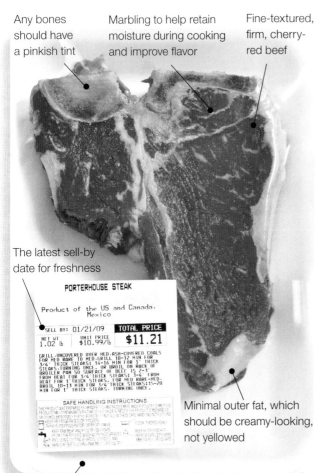

The latest sell-by date for freshness

PORTERHOUSE STEAK

Product of the US and Canada, Mexico

SELL BY: 01/21/09   **TOTAL PRICE**
NET WT   UNIT PRICE   **$11.21**
1.02 lb $10.99/lb

Minimal outer fat, which should be creamy-looking, not yellowed

Cold, tightly wrapped packages with a minimum of liquid; the longer the beef stays in its package, the more it drips.

Our Favorite Cuts of Beef

Two cuts show up repeatedly in our recipes: tenderloin and flank steak. Tenderloin is the most tender, luxurious cut you can buy, and it's very lean. Roasted whole, it's the ideal entrée for a celebratory dinner. Cut into filets and pan-seared, it's a superb supper for two. Cut into cubes, it makes outstanding kebabs on the grill.

Flank steak is one of those tough-but-flavorful cuts, and it has a little more fat than tenderloin. Its flat shape and coarse grain absorb flavors quickly, making it a good candidate for marinades.

Here are four lesser-known budget-friendly lean cuts:

Bottom round steak, aka Western griller. Boneless and quick cooking; best marinated to help tenderize.

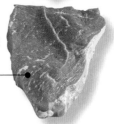

Shoulder tender, aka butcher's steak, petite filet, chuck shoulder steak. Resembles pork loin; slice into medaillons and grill.

Shoulder center steak, aka ranch steak, shoulder grill steak. Moderately tender; serve whole or sliced.

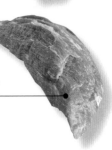

Tri-Tip steak, aka sirloin triangle tip, Santa Maria barbecue. Comes from the bottom sirloin; rich flavor; affordable. Roast or grill whole, and then slice.

Ground Beef

To accurately gauge the amount of fat in ground beef, look at the percentages. If the package is labeled "80% lean," that means it's 20% fat. In addition to ground chuck (20% fat), round (15% fat), and sirloin (10% fat), you may also find ground beef simply labeled "lean ground beef." At 7% fat, it's the leanest ground beef available.

*We most frequently use ground sirloin in recipes calling for ground beef. Our staff considers 10% fat ideal.

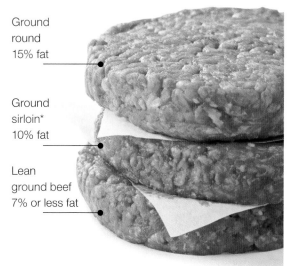

Ground round 15% fat

Ground sirloin* 10% fat

Lean ground beef 7% or less fat

Veal

Veal is the meat of a calf up to three months of age. Good veal is pale pink; the redder the color, the older the veal. Any visible fat should be very pale.

• Milk-fed veal is the most tender and flavorful. It has a creamy pink color and fine-grained texture.

• Formula-fed veal is also tender and pale, but it doesn't have as much flavor as milk-fed veal.

• Free-range veal is from a calf that has been weaned and fed on grass and grains. This veal has a redder color and meatier flavor.

Cooking Veal

The lack of fat can cause veal to become tough and dry if not cooked properly. Veal roasts and shanks are best cooked by moist-heat methods such as braising and stewing. Cutlets and scallops are best when quickly pan-fried or sautéed; chops are good when pan-fried, broiled, or grilled.

Lamb

Lamb is a lean meat so it's very important that you watch the cooking time and temperature carefully to make sure the meat isn't tough and overcooked. For the best flavor and tenderness, cook lamb only until it's pink: medium-rare (145°) or medium (160°). Most of the fat on lamb is on the outside; if you cook the lamb to 180° or 185° (well done), the meat will be tough and dry.

For the leanest cuts of lamb, look for "loin" or "leg" on the label. Some lean cuts of lamb include the leg loin, chops, arm chops, and foreshanks. Ground lamb is also fairly lean and can be used in the same way as ground beef.

Pork

People have enjoyed pork for ages because it's both delicious and versatile—from the dinner-party elegance of succulent roast tenderloin to the down-home appeal of bone-in chops. The gamut also extends to fresh cuts such as loin and shoulder. Aged with salt, pork becomes the cured meats we love in the form of bacon, ham, pancetta, prosciutto, and sausage.

Pork Glossary

Pork Chops: Chops come from the loin and can be bone-in or boneless. They're usually named for the section of the loin from which they're cut. Buy chops that are at least 1 to 1¼ inches thick; they tend to brown nicely without overcooking.

Pork Loin: For a more forgiving cut, choose pork loin; it's slightly higher fat content makes it harder to overcook than the tenderloin. Loin is sold both on the bone and boneless, usually in 2- to 4-pound roasts, and it's also cut into chops. The meat is tender but lean.

Pork Shoulder Roast (Boston Butt): Often labeled "pork shoulder butt," this large, inexpensive chunk of meat is a well-marbled, square cut from the upper part of the shoulder. The arm part of the shoulder, called "picnic shoulder," is quite fatty and gristly, and thus best avoided.

Pork Tenderloin: Pork tenderloin, which comes from the sirloin (the back part of the loin), is the leanest and most tender cut of pork. It's a narrow, cylinder-shaped cut about 1 foot long and 3 inches wide. Its small size means it cooks quickly; don't overcook it because this lean cut can dry out easily.

Ham: Regular hams can contain added water, and phosphates are added to keep that water in the hams during cooking. The best hams have the least water.

The most expensive hams are simply labeled "ham." They contain no added water, and because of shrinkage, they will weigh less than they did before smoking or curing (their "green weight").

You're more likely to find hams labeled "ham with natural juices" in grocery stores. These hams have been pumped with brine before smoking and cooking so that they will weigh the same as they did before they were injected (green weight).

Cheaper hams are labeled "ham—water added." Their weights after smoking and cooking are actually heavier than their green weights, which means you're buying mostly water. The cheapest hams of all say "ham and water product." These hams can include as much water as the manufacturer wishes, but the label must state the percentage of extra water in the ham.

Ham Hocks: Ham hocks, from the meaty portion of the lower leg bone, come cured and smoked (though you occasionally find fresh hocks). Hocks have a rich, smoky flavor. Usually sold with the skin still attached,

pork chops

pork tenderloin

ham hocks provide flavor, and the gelatin released when the skin cooks gives body and richness to whatever the hocks cook with. Because they're tough, ham hocks take up to 3 hours to cook completely; they're best when the meat is almost falling off the bone.

Bacon: Bacon comes from the belly of the pig and is usually cured and smoked. It's generally about 50 percent fat. As bacon cooks, the fat separates from the meat and can be poured off and discarded or used for sautéing. Because bacon has such an intense smoky flavor, a little goes a long way. Look for thick center-cut bacon; applewood-smoked bacon is particularly flavorful.

Pancetta: This Italian bacon is cured but unsmoked pork belly—the same cut from which bacon is made. Think of it as unsmoked bacon. It has a subtle salty pork flavor but lacks the characteristic smokiness of American smoked bacon.

Canadian bacon: This lean alternative is actually cured and smoked pork loin. Choose it when you need a punch of flavor without much additional fat.

Prosciutto: This specialty Italian ham (pronounced pro-SHOO-toe) isn't smoked like American ham—it's air-cured with salt and seasonings and refrigerated for several weeks. The aging gives it a unique flavor and silky texture when cut into very thin slices. In Italy, prosciutto is labeled with the name of the city or region in which it's produced. Prosciutto di Parma is considered the ultimate indulgence.

bacon

pancetta

prosciutto

kitchen how-to:
prepare pork tenderloin

When preparing pork tenderloin, remove the silver skin, which is the thin, shiny membrane that runs along the surface of the meat. Leaving it on can cause the tenderloin to toughen and lose shape during cooking.

1. Stretch the membrane with one hand so it's tight, and use your other hand to slip the tip of the knife underneath the silver skin.

2. Slowly slice back and forth, angling the sharp edge of the blade up, rather than down, through the meat. Continue until all the silver skin is removed; discard the skin.

Cooking Lean Pork

Lean pork has a fat content so low that it compares favorably to chicken. The leanest cuts, such as loin chops, loin roasts, and tenderloins, have less overall fat, saturated fat, and cholesterol than equal amounts of skinless chicken thighs.

Except for fattier cuts like Boston butt, spare ribs, and blade shoulder chops, pork has little or no marbling; it must be cooked carefully so it won't dry out. Cook pork to 150° to 155°. Perfect pork will have a faint pink blush (see photo above). Let it stand for 10 to 15 minutes after cooking to reabsorb juices and allow the meat to finish cooking (raising the internal temperature by 5° to 10°; the USDA recommends cooking pork to 160°).

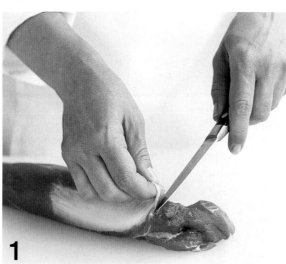

1

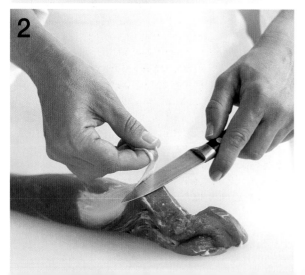

2

Poultry

Poultry offers a lean and flavorful source of protein. The dark meat of the thighs and drumsticks are the areas most heavily exercised and therefore have more fat stored in them, which is the reason it's both more flavorful and less healthy than the white meat of the breast.

The skin is another source of fat. If you remove it from a whole bird before cooking, you reduce the fat by about half. However, the skin adds moisture and protects lean meat from drying out. You'll get the best results by cooking the poultry with the skin on, and then removing it before serving—the fat savings are substantial.

roaster

Poultry Safety

Storing: Refrigerate raw poultry for up to two days and cooked poultry for up to three days. Raw skinless, boneless poultry can marinate in the refrigerator for up to 8 hours; raw poultry pieces with skin and bone can marinate for up to one day. Freeze uncooked poultry up to six months and cooked poultry up to three months.

Thawing: The best way to defrost poultry is to set the bird in a shallow pan in the refrigerator for 24 hours per every 5 pounds. This process will take several days—almost three days for a 12-pound bird—so plan accordingly. If you lack the refrigerator space, submerge the poultry—still in its wrapping—in a sink or pot of cold water, and change the water every 30 minutes until it's thawed. In an emergency, you can thaw the bird in the microwave, but you'll have to refer to your manufacturer's instructions for the proper way to do this. Whatever way you thaw the bird, you'll know it's fully thawed when a meat thermometer inserted into a thick part of the meat registers 40°. Store the thawed bird in the refrigerator until you're ready to cook it.

Handling: Wash your hands well with hot water and plenty of soap before and after handling poultry. Use hot water and soap to wash the cutting board and any utensils that come in contact with the meat.

Cooking: To prevent food-borne illnesses, poultry must be cooked to 165°. For whole birds, use an instant-read thermometer inserted in the thickest part of the thigh to confirm the temperature. Pierce poultry parts with the tip of a knife—when it's done, the flesh should be opaque, and the juices clear.

Chicken

Chicken is versatile and dependable. You'll often find it in the ingredient lists of our recipes.

Chicken Glossary

Broiler-fryers: Broiler-fryers are about seven weeks old, and they weigh 3 to 4 pounds. They're good for making stock (they're not as meaty as roasters) and will work in any recipe that calls for a cut-up fryer.

Roasters: At three to five months old, roasters weigh 4 to 7 pounds. If you want to bake a whole chicken, look for a roaster—they have the highest meat-to-bone ratio.

Stewing hens: At 10 months to 1½ years old, stewing hens are literally tough old birds. They're best used for chicken and dumplings or soup; when roasted, they're almost jaw-exhausting.

Cornish game hen: The term Cornish game hen is a misnomer. These small birds are actually a cross between Cornish game roosters and White Rock hens; despite the gender-specific name, both male and female birds are sold. At a month old, they weigh about 1½ to 2 pounds. Roasting works best for these petite birds.

Boneless, skinless chicken breasts: We often use this cut in our Test Kitchens because chicken breasts are lean and versatile. You can buy them with the skin on, but be sure to remove the skin before eating it—you can easily remove the skin and fat with kitchen shears.

Chicken thighs: Either bone-in or skinless, chicken thighs are higher in fat than breasts, but they have a succulent and hearty flavor and a firmer flesh that work well in dishes with a longer cook time.

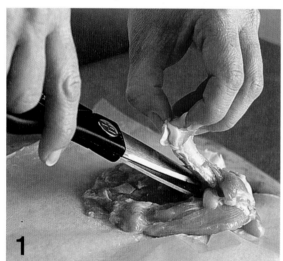

kitchen how-to:
bone a chicken thigh

You can usually find boneless, skinless chicken thighs, but, if you can't, follow these steps to debone your own.

1. Work from the inside of the thigh, and cut along both sides of the thigh bone, separating it from the meat.
2. Cut around the cartilage at the joint, and remove the thigh bone and cartilage.

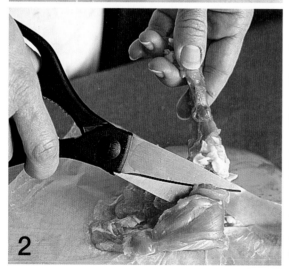

Turkey

Turkey is not just for Thanksgiving. It's lean, versatile, and has great flavor, which makes it ideal all year long.

Turkey Glossary

Whole turkeys: Whole turkeys are often sold by the sex of the bird. Hens weigh up to 16 pounds, while toms weigh more. There is no flavor difference; buy the size that suits your needs, figuring about 1 pound (including skin and bones) per person to allow for seconds and leftovers.

White meat: White-meat turkey cuts come from the breast. Skinless, boneless turkey breast halves; bone-in breast halves; turkey cutlets, also known as turkey scaloppine; and turkey tenderloins are all lean cuts. Keep a close eye on them to avoid overcooking.

Dark meat: Economical and tasty dark meat parts include drumsticks, wings, and thighs. Poultry skin contains plenty of fat, and removing it reduces the fat by about one-third, but these cuts aren't always skinless. It's easy to remove the skin from drumsticks and thighs. Taking the skin off raw turkey wings is virtually impossible.

Ground turkey: You'll find a variety of ground turkey options in the grocery store so read the label to make sure you get exactly what you want. The leanest—labeled "ground turkey breast"—is white meat only and about 3 percent fat. Regular ground turkey is a combination of white and dark meat with some skin and about 10 percent fat, which is nutritionally similar to ground sirloin. Frozen ground turkey is a mix of white and dark meat and includes skin. It's about 15 percent fat, which is about the same nutritionally as ground round.

Turkey sausage: Fresh turkey sausages are pork-free since the casings are made from vegetable cellulose. They're made from ground turkey seasoned in various ways. Cooked turkey sausages can be lower in fat than traditional sausages, but they can be smoked and relatively high in sodium—be sure to check the label.

Turkey: Fresh vs. Frozen

Both fresh and frozen turkeys have their own advantages. Frozen turkey is the cheapest and most widely available option, but thawing it properly will occupy some valuable real estate in the refrigerator. Fresh turkey costs slightly more, and you need to order it in advance. But because the meat has not undergone the freezing and thawing process, which can damage its cell structure, the flavor and texture of fresh turkey are generally considered superior. Either way, for the best results, it's important not to overcook the turkey. The USDA recommends cooking it to an internal temperature of 165°. Let the turkey rest for 30 minutes before carving it to allow the juices to redistribute, ensuring moist, flavorful meat.

turkey

quail

Quail

These dainty birds weigh only about 8 ounces each and have mild flesh that's well suited to bold flavors. Whole birds used to be the norm, but semiboned birds are now available. Look for quail in your supermarket's freezer section or at specialty butcher shops.

duck

Duck

For a sophisticated meal, it's hard to surpass the rich flavor of duck. Like turkey, the bird is now frequently sold in parts. Your gourmet market, for example, may carry boned duck breast and leg quarters. Duck skin is thick and fatty, but duck meat has little marbling and is only about 2 percent fat. You can usually find whole duck or duck parts in the freezer case.

Salt

From a culinary perspective, salt is indispensable. It enhances and rounds out the flavors of almost every other ingredient it touches, even sweets. Salt brightens flavors, balances the bitterness of certain foods, acts as a preservative, and tenderizes. In essence, salt makes food taste more like itself.

Due to a proven link between eating too much salt and high blood pressure, many people have to watch their sodium intake. We've found that it doesn't take a lot of salt to achieve its many culinary benefits. Using a small amount of salt in a strategic way helps flavors bloom without overloading on sodium. Learn how thoughtful use of this ingredient can truly enhance many of the favorite foods you cook.

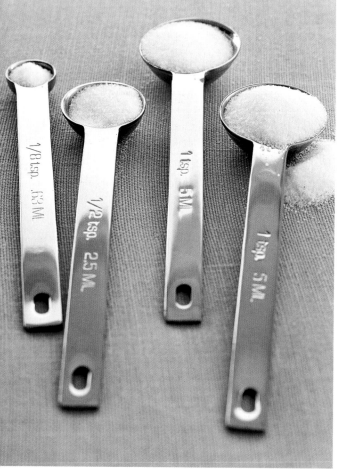

Salt by the Numbers

The sodium level of salt varies by type. Some types are coarser than others, so you actually get more or fewer grains per teaspoon. Sodium content varies by brand, as well, so be sure to check the label.

The Institute of Medicine, American Heart Association, and USDA all recommend we consume less than 2,300 milligrams of sodium each day, but many people far exceed this amount. Packaged, processed, and take-out foods are notoriously high in sodium and contribute heavily to the problem. Fortunately, cooking for yourself makes it much easier to control the amount of sodium you consume.

How Your Daily Sodium Intake Measures Up

• Daily sodium needed for basic physiological functions: scant ⅛ tsp salt = 250mg sodium
• Daily sodium limit for seniors: ½ tsp salt = 1,200mg sodium
• Daily sodium limit for adults: scant 1 tsp salt = 2,300mg sodium
• Daily sodium the average American consumes: heaping 1½ tsp salt = 4,000mg sodium

Low-sodium Alternatives

For cooks who seek to minimize sodium in their recipes, there are ways to play up flavors without extra salt. Highlight a dish's savory notes with a finishing spritz of lemon or lime juice or a flavored vinegar. Fresh herbs or homemade blends of dried spices also enhance taste.

Salt Storage

Salt doesn't spoil, but if it comes into contact with humidity, it can cake. Add toothpicks or roasted grains of rice to table salt in saltshakers to help absorb the humidity. Open salt cellars (great for kosher salt, which cooks pinch into often) left out near the stovetop benefit from the drying effects of any residual heat. In the pantry, large quantities of salt of any sort are best kept in airtight containers, such as glass jars with rubber-lined lids, to lock out humidity. If, however, moisture causes your salt to cake, it can simply be dried out in a cool oven and easily repulverized with a mortar and pestle.

Salt Glossary

Kosher salt: For chefs and many home cooks, this cousin of table salt has become the standard. Kosher salt, named as such because it's used by Jewish butchers, is chemically identical to table salt. But it has fewer additives and comes in coarser particles, which make it easy to pinch and sprinkle.

Fleur de sel: The crystalline "flower of salt," skimmed from the tops of marshes in northwestern France, may be the most special and sought-after sea salt. It's considered a comparably pure sea salt, free of most trace elements that define many other varieties. Its clean, well-balanced bite makes it nice for finishing simple dishes, such as grilled vegetables or pasta tossed in olive oil and garlic.

Sea salt: These salts come from all over the world in a variety of textures and colors. Sea salt doesn't contain additives, but it does contain more minerals than table salt. Because their taste nuances become almost untraceable once absorbed in food and they tend to be pricier, sea salts are often used as finishing touches.

Rock salt: In culinary terms, rock salt generally refers to the large-crystal salt sprinkled on the ice used in the making of ice cream. (Salt lowers the freezing point of water, making ice cold enough to freeze sugared cream.) Also, since salt is a potent and quick conductor of heat, rock salt can be packed around foods such as fish or shrimp for fast baking.

Table salt: This fine-grain salt has been a staple of American pantries for more than 100 years. In 1924, iodine was added to address what was then an epidemic of thyroid disorders. World health organizations continue to implore table salt producers to add it. But the supplement's presence—and that of anticaking agents—slightly alters the salt's flavor, so table salt has fallen out of favor with many food-lovers.

Sugar

Sugar is essential to cooking. At the simplest level, it imparts sweetness. But it often performs more than one role in a recipe, and it can be key in dishes other than desserts because it balances bitter and sour tastes.

Anatomy of Sugar

• Two sugars that occur naturally in many fruits and honey are glucose and fructose.
• The scientific name for granulated table sugar is sucrose.
• Each sucrose molecule is made up of one glucose and one fructose molecule joined together.
• Most of the sugar in the world is derived from either sugar cane or sugar beets.
• Sugars are carbohydrates—they contain no fat or protein.
• Because of variations in processing, moisture level, and the size of the grains, the same amount of different sugars contains different caloric values.

Measure for Measure

For the greatest accuracy when measuring granulated, superfine, powdered, or turbinado sugar, we recommend treating it as you do flour: Lightly spoon the sugar into a dry measuring cup, and level off the excess with the flat side of a knife. Brown sugar's moist texture requires that it be measured differently from other sugars. Because it can trap air, you need to firmly pack it into measuring cups or spoons when doling it out; the sugar should hold the shape of the cup or spoon when it's turned out.

Storage Savvy

To help granulated sugar stay dry and pourable, keep it in an airtight container or moisture-proof heavy-duty plastic bag. Properly stored, it keeps indefinitely. If humidity causes it to clump, place it in a heavy-duty zip-top plastic bag, and give it a few whacks with a mallet or the flat side of a meat cleaver. You can also whirl it in a food processor or blender or use a mortar and pestle or a spice grinder.

Powdered sugar is harder to salvage if humidity strikes. If it becomes lumpy try sifting it.

Brown sugar, which needs to retain its moisture, should also be stored in an airtight container. There are a number of tricks to bring dried-out brown sugar back to life. Let it stand overnight in a zip-top plastic bag with a damp paper towel or an apple slice from which the sugar can absorb moisture (see photo above). Or warm it for a few minutes in a 250° oven or in the microwave for about 1 minute per cup, but be careful—the sugar will be hot, and it should be measured and mixed quickly before it rehardens.

Sugar Glossary

Granulated sugar: Granulated sugar, chemically designated "sucrose," is bright white, dry, and free-flowing. All-purpose granulated sugar is the most commonly used sugar—for everything from sweetening coffee to being mixed into cake and cookie batters. Its flavor is pure sweetness, with no other taste.

Superfine granulated sugar: Called caster sugar in Britain, superfine granulated sugar is more finely ground granulated sugar, often used in applications where it's important for the sugar to dissolve quickly (such as in meringues, angel food cakes, and iced tea).

Brown sugar: Brown sugar is either partially refined sugar with traces of molasses remaining or refined white sugar to which molasses has been added. Molasses gives these varieties their unique flavors and textures. **Light brown sugar** (often called just "brown sugar") possesses a subtle caramel taste, while **dark brown sugar** has more molasses and thus a fuller, more robust molasses flavor. Light and dark brown sugar can be used interchangeably in recipes, but the final product will taste more subtle or more assertive depending on which you use. Brown sugar is often used for cookies and savory applications (such as barbecue sauce or rubs) where a richer taste is desired.

Powdered sugar: Also known as confectioners' sugar, powdered sugar is granulated sugar ground to a fine powder with an anticaking agent such as cornstarch added. The "X" designation on powdered sugar products denotes how finely the sugar has been ground—the more Xs, the finer (10X is the finest); they can be used interchangeably in recipes. Because it dissolves quickly, it's often used for uncooked cake frostings. It's also a pretty decoration when dusted over cookies or cakes.

Turbinado sugar: Turbinado sugar is a dry, pourable sugar (as opposed to many brown-colored sugars, which are moist) that has been only partially refined and steam cleaned. Blond in color and made up of large, coarse crystals, it has subtler molasses flavor than brown sugar. It derives its name from the part of the sugar-making process where raw cane is spun in a turbine. It's often sprinkled atop cakes, cookies, and other baked goods to add crunch.

Cook from a global pantry

In the early years of *Cooking Light,* ethnic fare seemed a foreign concept to most cooks, even though we often spotlighted other cuisines as ways to relish flavorful, low-fat food. Now, once-exotic dishes like pad thai, Indian curries, and Mexican moles have become mainstream, thanks to broader availability of ingredients for these dishes. Today's pantry staples like fish sauce, chipotle chiles, and even cilantro were largely unavailable in the early years of the magazine. Our Test Kitchens staff uses these ingredients on a regular basis. One great benefit of the availability of global ingredients is you can learn to use them in everyday applications. These concentrated sauces and robust herbs and spices offer ways to add flavor with minimal effort and little or no fat.

Garlic

Garlic is widely used around the world for its characteristic pungent, spicy flavor, including serving as a fundamental component in dishes from Asia, the Middle East, North Africa, Europe, and the Americas. The edible bulb is made up of sections called cloves that are surrounded by a thin, paper-like exterior. The flavor varies in intensity depending on the cooking method that's used.

kitchen how-to: peel, mince & crush garlic

Garlic can be used whole, crushed, or minced in dishes. Choose plump, firm heads of garlic that are free from sprouts or spots. Garlic will stay fresh for months when stored in a cool, dry place but not in the refrigerator.

1. To loosen the papery skin, place the flat side of a chef's knife on an unpeeled garlic clove. To crush, press down using the heel of your hand.
2. Peel off the skin. Remove the tough end with a knife.
3. To mince, make lengthwise cuts through the clove, and then cut the strips crosswise for chopped or minced pieces.
4. You can also use a garlic press to crush or mince garlic. Place a peeled clove in the press, and force it through the tiny holes.

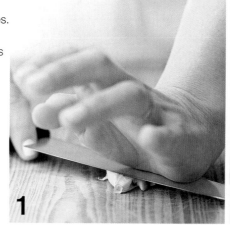

Ginger

Ginger's warm, slightly woody flavor makes it one of the world's favorite spices. Virtually all of the plant possesses ginger's signature spicy fragrance, although cooks look solely to the pungent root for their purposes. Fresh ginger, with its gnarled root and papery brown skin, is available in almost any grocery's produce department. Chopped or grated, fresh ginger gives subtle sweetness to many dishes.

Processed versions of this ingredient, like ground and powdered ginger, work well in applications that require ginger's peppery flavor to infuse every bite of a dish—cookies, cakes, or quick breads. It also perks up spice rubs for meats or mixtures for mulled wine and hot chocolate. As with dried herbs, use less ground ginger than fresh in recipes—as much as six to eight times less. Because powdered ginger loses its potency quickly, buy only a small quantity and use it within two or three months. Keep it tightly sealed in a cool, dry, dark place.

kitchen how-to:
prepare fresh ginger

Choose fresh, young-looking ginger. Old ginger is fibrous, tough, and flavorless. Store it tightly wrapped in plastic wrap in the vegetable crisper section of your refrigerator for up to three weeks.

1. Use a vegetable peeler to remove the tough skin and reveal the yellowish flesh.
2. For chopped or minced ginger, place a peeled piece on a cutting board. Cut with the grain into thin strips; stack the slices. Cut across the pile into small pieces.
3. For grated ginger, rub a peeled piece of ginger across a fine grater, such as a microplane.

Herbs

Using both fresh and dried herbs is an easy way to add lots of flavor without adding significant amounts of fat, calories, or sodium.

Herb Glossary

Basil: Basil, a member of the mint family, is one of the most important culinary herbs. Sweet basil, the most common type, tastes like a cross between licorice and cloves.

Cilantro: Also called coriander or Chinese parsley, cilantro has a pungent flavor. The leaves are often mistaken for flat-leaf parsley, so read the tag to verify that you're buying the correct herb. Since cilantro is susceptible to heat, add it at the end of the cooking process.

Mint: This versatile herb can be used in both sweet and savory dishes. Mint comes in many varieties, but spearmint is the preferred choice for cooking. Its bright green leaves are fuzzy, making them very different from the darker stemmed, rounded leaves of peppermint.

Oregano: Oregano has an aromatic, warm flavor. It's commonly used in Greek and Italian cooking.

Parsley: This versatile herb can go in just about every dish you cook because its mild, grassy flavor allows the flavors of other ingredients to come through. Curly parsley is less assertive than its brother, flat-leaf parsley (often called Italian parsley). Reach for either when a dish needs a little burst of color.

Rosemary: Rosemary is one of the most aromatic and pungent of all herbs. Its needlelike leaves have a pronounced lemon-pine flavor. Use a light hand because its flavor is strong.

Sage: Sage's long, narrow leaves have a distinctively fuzzy texture and a musty flavor redolent of eucalyptus, cedar, lemon, and mint. Use it with discretion; it can overwhelm a dish.

Thyme: This congenial herb pairs well with many other herbs—especially rosemary, parsley, sage, savory, and oregano. Because the leaves are so small, they often don't require chopping. Add thyme during cooking; its powerful taste develops best at high temperatures.

basil

cilantro

mint

oregano

parsley

rosemary

sage

thyme

Keep Herbs Fresh

When storing a bunch of fresh herbs, wrap the stems in a damp paper towel, and store them in a zip-top plastic bag. Wash herbs just before using; pat them dry with a paper towel (see photo above).

kitchen how-to:
use fresh & dried herbs

The flavor of fresh herbs is generally much better than that of dried because most herbs (excluding rosemary, thyme, and dill) lose significant flavor when dried. However, using fresh isn't always practical, so it's important to keep quality dried herbs on hand, especially when it comes to convenience and last-minute meal preparation. Because fresh herbs are not as strong or concentrated as their dried counterparts, substitute one part dried herbs to three parts fresh. This translates into 1 teaspoon dried for 1 tablespoon fresh. The exception is rosemary; use equal amounts of fresh and dried.

1

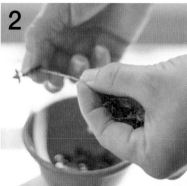

2

3

1. Don't worry about stemming cilantro, dill, or parsley; their stems are tender and can be chopped and used with the leaves. Simply place the bunch on a cutting board, and chop with a sharp knife.
2. Strip rosemary and thyme leaves from their tough, inedible stems by holding the top of a stem in one hand, and then pulling in the opposite direction of the way the leaves grow.
3. The stems of mint, oregano, tarragon, and sage are also unusable, but the leaves are large enough that they can be easily pinched off one at a time.

Spices

Spices are derived from the bark, pods, fruit, roots, seeds, or stems of plants and trees. They appeal to our senses, and they're key in healthy cooking. You often don't need fat to enhance the flavor of a dish because spices alone can add intrigue, zest, and depth to food without increasing calories.

Spice Glossary

1. Allspice: As the name suggests, the flavor and aroma of allspice are a mixture of cinnamon, nutmeg, and a touch of clove. It's a delicious spice that adds deep, warm flavor to dishes. Buy whole rather than ground allspice. Whole allspice stores almost indefinitely in an airtight jar and will grind in a pepper mill. Cooking brings out its sunny flavor.

2. Cinnamon: Although cinnamon may be more familiar in sweet dishes, its distinctive notes blend with meats and fish and perk up grains and vegetables in a surprising way. Buy it as sticks (or quills) or ground. Cinnamon sticks have a sweeter, subtler flavor and a

longer shelf life than ground. Whole cinnamon is best ground in a clean coffee mill.

3. Caraway: Caraway has a pungent aroma and a slightly lemony, anise flavor. The caraway seed is soft and easy to grind, but it loses its scent quickly once it's ground. Buy it whole, and warm or lightly toast the seeds to bring out the flavor before using them.

4. Ground cumin: Cumin has a pungent, nutty flavor. It's common in Mediterranean cuisines and is also featured in Indian curries and garam masala, Mexican chile powders and salsas, and Thai marinades. Cumin is typically found ground, but you can also purchase whole seeds.

5. Cloves: Cloves have an intensely sharp, slightly bitter taste. Use sparingly because they can overpower other flavors. Use whole or ground, but if you use whole cloves to flavor a dish, be sure to remove them before serving. Cloves don't need toasting before use.

6. Anise: Two spices give us anise flavor. The first is sweet anise; warm it gently before use to release its aroma. The second and more familiar spice is star

anise, probably the world's prettiest spice. Buy star anise whole. One or two "stars" usually impart sufficient flavor to infuse an entire dish. To substitute star anise for aniseed in a recipe, reduce the quantity to half or a third of the recipe's recommendation.

7. Five-spice powder: Chinese five-spice powder is a fragrant blend of cinnamon, cloves, fennel seed, star anise, and Szechuan peppercorns. The licorice-like anise and fennel melded with the sweet, pungent cloves and cinnamon contrast the woodsy flavor of peppercorn.

8. Cardamom: The best pods will be pale sage green and have sticky black seeds inside. They're intensely aromatic and have an orangy flavor. Since cardamom's essential oils are volatile, the flavor of ground cardamom dissipates quickly. Bruise whole pods before using them to allow the flavor to escape. If the seeds are dry and light brown, they're old and have lost their flavor and aroma; discard those pods.

9. Cumin seeds: These small seeds have a nutty, peppery flavor and are an essential component of curry powders and chile powders. They add a punch of flavor when added to a

dish, particularly when toasted. Keep them in a tightly sealed glass container in a cool, dark, dry place. Whole seeds will stay fresh for about a year.

10. Paprika: Paprika is made from grinding sweet red bell peppers into a fine powder. Most paprikas are mild and slightly sweet, but you'll also find hot paprikas that are made from more intense peppers. Paprika can be used to add flavor and color to a variety of dishes, but remember that it only releases its flavor when heated; so while sprinkling some on a dish may help improve its color, it won't do much for the flavor.

11. Black peppercorns: The strongest in flavor and bite, black peppercorns are the world's most popular spice. They're picked when slightly underripe and then air-dried, which results in their dark color.

12. Nutmeg: Each kernel of nutmeg comes wrapped in a lacy covering that we use separately as the spice mace. They both share a warm, sweet, musky flavor suited to desserts, cookies, and cakes. Use nutmeg freshly grated or milled. Except in cakes, add nutmeg toward the end of cooking to retain its evanescent aroma and warm, spicy flavor.

13. Saffron: Saffron has always been the world's most expensive spice, but you need only a few dried stigmas to color a dish golden yellow and impart a warm, aromatic, and slightly bitter quality. For most dishes, saffron is best soaked in a few tablespoons of warm liquid to allow the color and flavor to develop fully before adding it to the rest of the ingredients.

14. Turmeric: Turmeric gives food a golden color and a peppery, slightly pungent flavor. While it's best known as one of the ingredients used to make curry, it also gives ballpark mustard its signature bright yellow color.

Buying and Storing Spices

Purchase small quantities, particularly those that you won't use often, from a store that has frequent turnover. You don't want to buy spices that have been sitting on the shelf for a long time. Ground spices tend to lose their flavor after a year. They won't spoil, but they won't add much flavor to your dishes either. The best way to tell if your spices are past their prime is to smell them—they should still be vibrant when you use them and have a strong, aromatic scent.

Light, heat, and humidity all can diminish the color and potency of spices. The best place to store spices is in airtight containers in a cool, dry, dark place, such as a drawer or pantry. If stored properly, they'll last up to 18 months, but for maximum flavor, it's best to use them within six months to a year. If you don't think you'll use certain spices in that time frame, store them in the freezer to keep them fresher longer.

Spice Blends

The unique tastes of a region's cuisine often begin with a particular blend of spices, and bottled spice blends are a convenient way to get the same flavors without having to mix your own.

Ground chipotle chile powder: Chipotle chiles are dried, smoked jalapeño peppers, previously available only in cans with adobo sauce. The powder is much easier to use, and you can get the pure taste of the chile without the flavor of the tomato-based adobo sauce, which can sometimes take over. Blend it with other ingredients to give a pure smoky chipotle flavor.

Garam masala: This Indian spice blend's ingredients typically include black pepper, cardamom, cinnamon, cloves, and cumin. Commercial varieties are usually milder than homemade, but they certainly save time.

Wasabi powder: This intensely hot green powder, made from a ground root, can be used anywhere horseradish would be used. Like red curry powder, wasabi powder is milder than the pure wasabi you buy in Asian markets, and it's also more versatile.

Red curry powder: This spice mix is the basis of many Thai and Malaysian dishes. The mainstream version is milder than its ethnic counterpart. It has a softer edge, making it more versatile and easier to incorporate into a variety of dishes.

Ground ancho chile powder: Ancho chiles are dried poblano peppers. Most chili (with an "i") powders are a blend of spices, including ancho chiles, cumin, garlic, and oregano. Chile (with an "e") powders are finely ground dried chiles and nothing else. Tex-Mex dishes use chili powder; true Mexican dishes uses chile powder for pure flavor with mild heat.

Sauces

Sauces help make life in the kitchen a little easier. They are a quick and convenient way to add a punch of flavor to any dish.

Chipotles in adobo sauce: Chipotle chile peppers in adobo sauce are smoked jalapeños canned in a sauce of tomatoes, onions, garlic, spices, and vinegar. Taking a cue from Mexican cooks, we often reach for these to add complex, smoky flavor to a dish. If these fiery chiles are new to you, start easy—a little goes a long way. Chipotles are a natural in barbecue recipes, braised and stewed meats and poultry, and chili. Add minced chipotles to turkey burgers, bean dips, soups, salsas, and even scrambled eggs.

Coconut milk: The "cream" of the tropics is produced by blending freshly grated coconut with hot water. A "lite" coconut milk is also available—it's great to use in healthy Caribbean cooking.

Fish sauce: Widely used in southeast Asia as a condiment and flavoring for various dishes, fish sauce is a salty, light-brown liquid made from fermented fish, water, and salt. It's best used sparingly—just a spoonful makes a world of difference in many dishes. Combine fish sauce with sugar and lime juice to make a dipping sauce for vegetables and spring rolls, or use it as a base to add pungent flavor.

Hoisin sauce: This sauce is made with soybeans, sugar, vinegar, and spices. Sweet and fairly thick, it's often used in marinades for barbecuing and roasting and also in dipping sauces.

Oyster sauce: This Cantonese staple, usually sold in bottles, is made from oysters, salt, and seasonings. It's often used in sauces for seafood, meat, and vegetable dishes. You can substitute an equal amount of soy sauce.

Sambal oelek (chile paste with garlic): This Chinese condiment is often added to stews as a flavoring. It's essentially pureed fresh chiles, but some varieties have bean paste or garlic added. We prefer the basic variety. This somewhat thin sauce has intense heat. Stir it into sauces and marinades.

Soy sauce: Made from fermented soybeans and wheat, the flavor of soy sauce varies by manufacturer and aging process. Regular soy sauce contains approximately 900 milligrams of sodium per tablespoon; light or low-sodium versions have 500 to 600 milligrams.

Vinegars

Vinegar can add depth and brightness to dishes without adding fat. Use it to deglaze pan drippings and add a little acidity to balance a sauce; reduce it into a syrup for drizzling over fruit or vegetables; add it to cooking liquid, and then braise the food to subdue the bite; or simply use it in a vinaigrette.

Vinegar Glossary

Red and white wine vinegar: These two versatile vinegars work well in just about any dish. Wine vinegars, like wine itself, vary in flavor according to the type of grape from which they're made, where the grapes are grown, and how the vinegar is stored and aged. Generally, the more expensive the vinegar, the better. Wine vinegars that don't refer to a particular wine on the label are often made from undistinguished wine blends or grape juice. These are what you'll usually find at the supermarket, and they are fine for most recipes.

Balsamic vinegar: Some traditionally produced balsamic vinegars are aged for decades and become increasingly concentrated and syrupy over time. They're phenomenally expensive—sometimes more than $100 per bottle. Reserve these for drizzling over berries and vegetables since they stand on their own. The commercially produced balsamics found in supermarkets aren't as well rounded or deep but are perfectly fine for cooking. Try balsamics in marinades, vinaigrettes, tomato sauces, and soups.

Cider vinegar: Before gourmet vinegars came around, cider vinegar was the choice for most recipes and is common in many traditional American dishes. Made from the juice of apples (or apple cider), it's light brown in color and has sweet fruit flavor and gentler acidity than most white wine vinegars, although it is still quite sharp. It's an excellent everyday vinegar to use in pickling, salad dressings, and barbecue sauces.

Rice vinegar: Colorless and very mild, vinegar made from fermented white rice is essential to many Asian recipes. The sweet-and-sour mildness makes it suitable for Asian dipping sauces and salad dressings. Because it's not harsh, rice vinegar is excellent for making quick pickles. **Rice wine vinegar** is made from fermented rice wines, like sake and mirin, and it's sweeter than rice vinegar. It's a good choice when you want a combined sweet-and-sour flavor without the acidic "heat" of a stronger vinegar, such as white wine vinegar.

Sherry vinegar: Sherry makes a strong but mellow concentrated vinegar with powerful acidity and great depth of taste. The best ones age in oak barrels and have a sour-sweet flavor and deep notes of oak. Read the label to see how long the vinegar has aged; some are aged six years, others for as long as 30 years. The longer the aging, the more complex the flavor. It's a great everyday vinegar for salad dressings and marinades or drizzling over cooked vegetables. It's also good for deglazing the pan after cooking poultry or game.

Use quality ingredients

Splurging on top-notch ingredients can boost taste. A light shaving of the highest quality Parmesan, Parmigiano-Reggiano, imparts maximum flavor. And using a splash of authentic, aged balsamic vinegar makes a world of difference, providing intense yet sweet sharpness. The same goes for coarse or exotic sea salts; they add a burst of flavor that makes a dish stand out.

Maximize flavor

Often, how you cook food is as important as the ingredients you use. For example, we've found that toasting spices and nuts heightens their flavor, as does browning meat before braising. Toasting nuts intensifies their nuttiness so you can use fewer. The same principle works for meat—browning creates a caramelized crust that builds flavor in the overall dish.

Balance ingredients

When there's less fat to smooth out the taste in a recipe, other salty, sour, or sweet flavors may come to the forefront and overpower the dish. Consider low-fat salad dressings. In traditional vinaigrettes, the ratio of oil to acid might be two to one. In a light vinaigrette, though, the ratio is much lower. If we didn't compensate for that loss of oil with, say, a sweet touch of honey or maple syrup, the dressing would be too tart. Adjusting the sweet component in the dressing rounds out the flavors so the vinaigrette tastes balanced.

Use a combo fat approach

For many recipes, using fat-free products exclusively doesn't work—the flavor and the texture may be off. For example, a cheesecake made with egg substitute and fat-free cream cheese has a too-tangy taste as well as a slick appearance and mouthfeel. Using a combination of fat-free and reduced-fat cream cheese, along with a whole egg or two, yields a more luscious, creamy dessert that's still much lower in calories and fat than traditional versions.

Embellish convenience products

Our readers are busier than ever. We're always mindful of this, and so we now include well-chosen convenience products to help speed preparation. But there are limitations for some of these products. For a soup made with canned beans and canned tomatoes, for example, we're likely to add fresh herbs, a squeeze of fresh lemon juice, or a sprinkling of freshly grated cheese. That way, you reap the benefits of time-saving ingredients as well as the spark of the fresh ones.

Add healthful ingredients

We look for smart ways to enhance a dish's nutritional benefits, such as adding whole wheat flour to muffins or wheat germ to a piecrust. Such additions don't alter the overall texture or taste of the finished dish, but they add fiber, vitamins, antioxidants, or other nutrients.

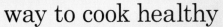

way to cook healthy
kitchen essentials

Home cooks everywhere prepare meals every day with less than all the "necessary" equipment in kitchens that are often much smaller than they'd like. No matter where you live, if you have less space and tools than you'd like, you know how complicated it can seem to prepare the meals you want. Of course, it's possible. You can do it. We'll provide a basic list of the tools you'll need to get any meal on the table. If you're one of the lucky ones to have adequate storage space or a larger kitchen, we've provided an expanded list of tools that will make life in your kitchen easier.

Pots, Pans, and Small Appliances

Skillets

A one-pan dish requires a really big pan—at least 12 inches in diameter—that can hold a meal for four. There are two types: nonstick and those without a nonstick coating. Both are useful for different cooking methods and results.

For healthy cooking, a nonstick skillet is essential because it requires little added fat. But sometimes, foods need to stick. If you want to leave browned bits behind for deglazing or achieve a dark browned surface on meats, use a heavy skillet without a nonstick coating, such as one made of copper, cast iron, or stainless steel. Is there one perfect skillet for everything? Not really. It depends on what you want to achieve when cooking; see the Nonstick and Heavy Skillet Comparisons chart on page 57.

Nonstick Skillets

Nonstick skillets don't have to be expensive. They need to be replaced more frequently than just about anything else in your kitchen, however, because the nonstick surface will wear down over time. Here's what to look for when selecting a nonstick skillet.
• Start out with a medium- to heavy-gauge skillet. This provides a sturdy base for the nonstick coating and helps prevent overheating, which can cause the coating to lose its nonstick properties.
• Check the packing box or manufacturer's pamphlet for a nonstick finishing process involving multiple-step application. Multiple coats suggest the base metal has been carefully prepared and the nonstick layer is thick enough to be durable.

• Manufacturers of nonstick coatings say their finishes work equally well and last just as long on all types of surfaces—smooth, rough-textured, or patterned.

How to Care for Nonstick Skillets

Although modern nonstick coatings are durable, follow these tips to extend the life of your skillet.
• Take care not to overheat nonstick pans, especially when they're empty. The coatings on these pans can be damaged by excess heat, so stay away from the high setting on your stovetop.
• Use wooden or nylon utensils, and hand-wash the pans so the coating performs better and lasts longer.
• Follow the manufacturer's instructions because various coatings have different compositions and require different care.

Heavy Stainless-Steel Skillets

You don't have to have nonstick skillets for light cooking—heavy stainless-steel skillets also work well, especially for searing meats, fish, and poultry, as well as for deglazing. If you use cooking spray or a small amount of oil in these skillets, the food won't stick.

Because stainless steel isn't a good heat conductor, most of these skillets have another metal, such as copper or aluminum, in the core or on the bottom so that foods will cook quickly and evenly.

Most of these skillets are oven safe, but check the manufacturer's information to to be sure. Some stainless-steel pans are dishwasher safe, but for others, washing by hand is recommended; always check the manufacturer's instructions for care and cleaning.

Cast-Iron Skillets

The ability of cast-iron cookware to withstand and maintain very high cooking temperatures makes it ideal for searing or frying, and its excellent heat diffusion and retention makes it a good option for long-cooking stews or braised dishes. Because cast-iron skillets develop a nonstick surface, they're also a good choice for egg dishes, particularly scrambled eggs.

How to Care for Cast-Iron Skillets

Cast iron can rust if neglected. By following some basic rules, your skillet should last for generations.

• Never put a cast-iron skillet in the dishwasher—it's not good for cast iron to be left in a moist environment.

• Cast iron can corrode when acidic foods are added, so remove acidic food, such as tomatoes, from the skillet as soon as the dish has finished cooking. If the skillet is well seasoned, corrosion is unlikely.

• As soon as food is removed, scrub the pan under hot water (soap is not recommended because it can damage the pan's seasoning), and then place it on a warm burner for a few minutes to dry. After drying, dribble some vegetable oil in it to help maintain the seasoning. Rub the oil all over the inside of the skillet with a paper towel so the skillet shines. Cool.

• If your pan rusts, scour the rust away with fine steel wool. Scrub with hot soapy water, and then scour with fine steel wool again before drying and reseasoning.

kitchen how-to: reseason a cast-iron skillet

Seasoning is the process of oiling and heating cast iron to protect its porous surface from moisture. When the pan is heated, the oil is absorbed, creating a nonstick surface. The more you use it, the more nonstick the surface becomes. However, if your pan rusts, you'll need to scour the pan to remove the rust, which will also remove or damage the seasoning; then reseason it to restore the nonstick surface.

1. Rinse the skillet in hot sudsy water. Dry the skillet well with a towel.
2. Rub the skillet generously with vegetable oil.
3. Leave the skillet on a burner turned to low heat for about an hour, or bake it in a 350° oven for 2 hours. Let the skillet cool, and then pour out any residual oil. Repeat this process two or three times before using it to get it completely seasoned.

Nonstick and Heavy Skillet Comparisons

	Nonstick skillets	Heavy skillets (stainless steel or cast iron)
General Uses	• quick sautéing and stir-frying meats, seafood, and vegetables	• searing, sautéing, and stir-frying meats, seafood, and vegetables
Best for	• cooking with very little fat • sautéing delicate foods like fish • cooking recipes that have lots of liquid	• browning • creating "crusts" on foods
Absolutely Necessary for	• scrambled eggs, pancakes, and crêpes	• deglazing (scraping off browned bits stuck to the pan to use in flavoring)
Limitations	• doesn't brown foods or conduct heat as well as stainless steel • shouldn't be placed over high heat • many have plastic handles that can't go in the oven	• can't cook completely free of fat (some oil must be added to the pan) • delicate foods tend to stick

An 8-quart Dutch oven

A Dutch oven is neither Dutch nor an oven; rather, it's a deep pot with a tight-fitting lid that can go from stovetop to oven and is great for preparing casseroles, roasts, and stews. Dutch ovens range in size from 3 quarts on up. For a small kitchen, an 8-quart pot can handle just about anything you make.

A stainless-steel 3-quart saucepan

A high-quality saucepan with a heavy bottom ensures even heating and browning. Thin or uneven pans tend to have hot spots that can cause foods to cook unevenly. It's best to go with a light metal interior, such as stainless steel, because dark metal can make it difficult to see when some foods, like caramel, begin to brown.

Baking sheets

Baking sheets have a rim on one or two sides and come in shiny and dark finishes. Some also have nonstick surfaces. You can use a baking sheet to make an array of dishes, from scones and biscuits to pizza and calzones.

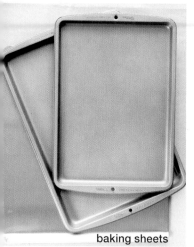

baking sheets

Baking dishes

Two glass baking dishes—an 11 x 7–inch dish and a square 8-inch dish—will give you the flexibility to prepare one-dish casseroles, bake sweets, and roast or bake meats, poultry, fish, and vegetables. Baking pans are made of metal; baking dishes are made of glass or ceramic materials. Glass conducts heat better than metal, so if you use a baking dish in a recipe that calls for a pan, you'll need to decrease the oven temperature by 25°.

baking dishes

7-cup food processor

Food processors can make speedy work of slicing and chopping fruits and vegetables and blending ingredients. They come in different sizes to accommodate different amounts of food, and most come with a set of blades for different tasks, such as shredding and slicing. Most of the food processors in our Test Kitchens are 7-cup machines, and that's adequate for most of the recipes we test. A mini food processor is handy for small food prep tasks, such as chopping onions, garlic, herbs, and nuts, and it doesn't take up much room on the countertop or in a kitchen cabinet.

We use food processors in a lot of recipes, and we always choose a processor over a blender for ingredients that are thick or dry, such as beans or flour.

food processor

If a *Cooking Light* recipe calls for a blender or a food processor, this means we've tested the recipe using both appliances and found that both give similar results.

Blender

A blender actually does a better job with liquid mixtures than a food processor and is especially great for pureeing soups, emulsifying salad dressings, and whipping up smoothies. We've also found that recipes like dips and thick sauces, normally made in a food processor, work great in a blender, too.

You can use a blender instead of a food processor as long as the ingredients are tender enough to be chopped by its blade and there is enough liquid to keep the contents from clinging to the sides of the container.

When you're blending hot liquids be careful because the steam can increase

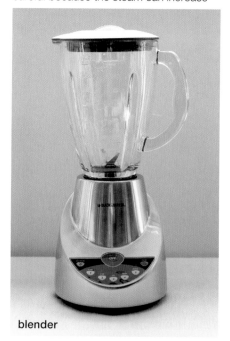

blender

the pressure inside the blender container and blow off the lid. To avoid this, make sure you fill the blender only halfway full and blend the mixture in batches if necessary. You should always hold a potholder or towel over the lid when blending.

If you don't have much space, an immersion blender is a good substitute. It doesn't take up much storage space, and you can puree soups, sauces, salad dressings, and desserts in their pot or bowl of origin.

immersion blender

Essential Tools and Utensils

Box grater

A box-style grater gives you a choice of hole sizes. Use the smaller holes for grating hard cheese or chocolate. For shredding an ingredient like Cheddar cheese or carrots, use the largest holes.

Cutting boards

We use both wood and plastic cutting boards in the Test Kitchens. Whichever you choose, wash cutting boards thoroughly to avoid food contamination and keep separate ones for animal and nonanimal foods. Use diluted bleach on wooden boards, and wash thoroughly; sanitize plastic ones in the dishwasher.

cutting boards

colander

box grater

strainer

Colander/strainer

We use both metal and plastic colanders in varying sizes, so pick one that best suits your needs. A large colander works well for draining pasta and salad greens and rinsing vegetables. A small strainer is great for separating fruit juice or pulp from seeds. Mesh strainers are the most versatile because nothing can get through those holes except liquid.

Heatproof spatula

Silicone or nylon spatulas are the best because they won't scratch nonstick cookware surfaces.

Kitchen shears/scissors

Keep kitchen shears handy to mince small amounts of herbs, chop canned tomatoes, trim fat from meat and skin from poultry, and make slits in bread dough.

Measuring cups

Accurate measuring is crucial in light cooking. Dry measuring cups, available in metal or plastic, are flat across the rim. Fill the cup to just above the rim, and scrape off the excess with a knife. We use the standard 1, ½, ⅓, and ¼ nest of cups. Use dry measuring cups for ingredients like flour, grains, cereals, nuts, and seeds. If you measure liquid ingredients in dry measuring cups, the amount may not be accurate. Liquid measuring cups are available in clear glass or plastic so you can see the level of liquid through the side of the cup. Liquid measuring cups come in various sizes from 1 cup to 4 cups.

Measuring spoons

Sometimes a "pinch of this" and a "pinch of that" results in a less-than-desired flavor. Use measuring spoons to make sure your recipes come out just right.

High-quality, sharp knives

Paring, chef's, and serrated knives are the basic knives you need. See page 62 for additional information.

Whisks

Whisks in assorted sizes are ideal for beating eggs and egg whites, blending salad dressings, and dissolving solids in liquids. We consider them essential for making creamy sauces. Whisks are available both in stainless steel and nylon; the nylon ones won't scratch nonstick surfaces.

Vegetable peeler

A peeler removes skin from vegetables and fruits. Select one with a comfortable grip and an eyer to remove potato eyes and other blemishes on vegetables and fruit.

Instant-read thermometer

Use an instant-read thermometer to check meringues, meat, and poultry to make sure they're cooked to the correct temperature. Don't leave the thermometer in the oven while the food is cooking; remove it from the food after you read the temperature.

The Next Step

If you have some extra space, here are some additional tools you may need.

Cookware
- Bundt pan
- Jelly-roll pan
- Loaf pan
- Muffin pans
- Pie plate
- Round cake pans
- Round removable-bottom tart pan
- Saucepan
- Shallow baking dish (glass or ceramic)
- Springform pan
- Square baking pan
- Tube pan

Utensils
- Handheld juicer
- Handheld grater
- Oven thermometer
- Potato masher

Other Equipment
- Food scale
- Glass mixing bowls
- Mixer: handheld and/or stand
- Pepper mill
- Slow cooker

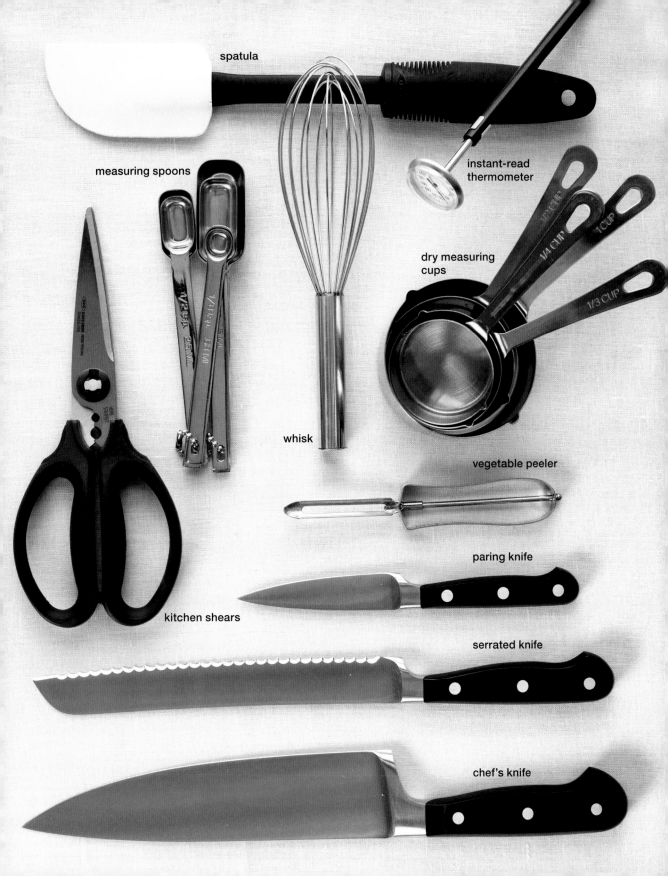

spatula

measuring spoons

instant-read
thermometer

dry measuring
cups

whisk

vegetable peeler

paring knife

kitchen shears

serrated knife

chef's knife

Essential Knives

If you want your food to look more appealing and you hate hauling out the food processor every time a recipe calls for an ingredient to be "minced" or "chopped," get a knife. There are three—a chef's knife, a paring knife, and a long serrated knife—that can cover an array of tasks. Each has functions unique to its shape and design. Learn to use them efficiently and safely.

How to Choose the Right Knife

Is there really a difference between a $100 knife and one that costs $20? Definitely. Inexpensive knives wear out more quickly and don't hold their edge as well. If you're a casual cook, these knives are probably fine for you. But if you're a more serious cook, opt for a higher-quality knife. See the photo at right for tips on what to look for when buying one.

Built Right

Most professional cooks use a high-carbon steel, forged knife with a full tang, which means that the blade metal runs from the tip of the knife through the handle to the opposite end.

The Blade: In a forged knife, the blade is formed from heated metal and is individually hammered. The best blades are made from a mixture of alloys that help a knife take and hold a sharp cutting edge and resist corrosion. Look for a high-carbon stainless-steel blade with a Rockwell rating of at least 55, which indicates the knife sharpens easily and holds its edge. The Rockwell Scale is a measure of steel hardness, and it should be listed on the knife's product description.

The Handle: Look for a handle with a precise fitting and no gaps or burrs. It should feel comfortable and secure. Materials range from wood to stainless steel. It should have enough weight to balance the blade on the knife.

kitchen how-to:
sharpen knives

It can be tedious, but regular sharpening is the most important aspect of maintaining your knives. If your knife seems dull no matter how often you sharpen it, have your sharpening steel professionally sharpened at a specialty knife store, butcher shop, or fabric store (which often sharpens scissors and knives).

1. For regular maintenance, use a sharpening steel to sharpen and straighten the edge of the blade. Frequent use of this tool will maintain a good blade edge for up to two years. Hold the knife in one hand and the steel in the other, and slide the knife's blade on the steel at a 20° angle several times, either from the top of the steel to the bottom or vice versa. Turn the knife over and repeat the process. Take your time. Sliding the knife quickly doesn't mean better sharpening, and going too fast can cause the tip to slip off the steel.

2. After two years of sharpening with a sharpening steel, you may need to resharpen your knives with

1

2

3

a whetstone. Buy a stone from your knife's manufacturer, or ask a reputable dealer what type is best for your specific type of knife. (You can't sharpen a serrated knife with a stone.) Before you sharpen, coat the stone's top surface with mineral oil or water. Wipe off the excess liquid. Make sure the stone is stable and won't slide.

3. To sharpen, hold the knife in your dominant hand, and place the edge horizontally against the stone at a 20° angle. Rest your other hand on top of the knife to helping steady and guide it. Draw the knife across the top of the stone a few times to sharpen the blade. Sharpen the edges evenly from tip to heel, and be sure to sharpen both sides of the blade. Finish with the steel, and then clean your knife and stone.

Cleaning and Storing Knives

While many manufacturer's claim their knives can go in the dishwasher, you should always wash knives by hand—washing a knife in the dishwasher can dull the blade. Use a soft sponge and warm, soapy water to maximize the life and performance of your knife. Avoid soaking knives in water; prolonged immersion can loosen the handles.

Keep your knives in a knife block, on a magnetic strip designed to hold knives that's mounted somewhere safe, or in a special drawer insert that has slots for the blades. Never store them loose in a drawer—the free movement could result in nicked or dulled blades, as well as nicked hands when you reach in to pull them out.

Making the Cut

Here are some common cuts often called for in recipes:

Minced

Diced

Chopped

Coarsely chopped

chef's knife

Chef's Knife

This is probably the largest knife you'll own, and it's the most versatile. The chef's knife is used for more tasks than any other. It works for almost all chopping: herbs, onions, garlic, fruits, and vegetables. It's also great for cutting boneless meats (even through small bones, such as those in chicken and fish), slicing and dicing, and general cutting tasks.

The curved blade and relatively heavy weight of the knife give it an advantage for chopping. Leave the tip of the knife on the chopping board, and rock the rest of the knife back and forth with a subtle movement of the wrist and forearm. The weight of the thickest part of the blade, near the handle, adds force as it slices through food. A heavy handle also does more of the work for you, reducing the amount of force with which your arm has to move the knife.

Three More Tasks for a Chef's Knife

1. Peel and crush garlic: Place a garlic clove on a cutting board, and place the flat side of the knife on top of the clove. Press down using the heel of your hand to crush the clove; separate the peel. See page 44 for a how-to of this procedure.

2. Pit olives: Follow the instructions above for crushing and peeling garlic. The olive will pop open, exposing the pit for easy removal.

3. Cut up a whole chicken: The size and weight of the knife make this job smooth and easy.

paring knife

serrated knife

Paring Knife

With a blade of 2½ to 4 inches, the paring knife looks like a miniature chef's knife, but its use is very different. The paring knife is great for peeling fruits and vegetables; slicing a single garlic clove or shallot; controlled, detailed cutting, such as cutting shapes or vents in dough; and scoring designs and patterns on surfaces of food. Use it for any job that requires precise and delicate work, like removing the ribs from a jalapeño or coring an apple.

Unlike a chef's knife, which is always used on a cutting board, you can cut with a paring knife while holding it aloft, as if it's an extension of your hand. The small handle gives you maximum control over the tip and the edge of the blade.

Three More Tasks for a Paring Knife

1. Hull strawberries: Use the tip of the knife to remove the stem and carve out the white center core from the stem end of each berry.

2. Section an orange or a lemon: Hold the fruit over a bowl to catch all the juice that drips. Peel the fruit to the flesh, and then cut between the white membranes to extract each section. Because you hold the fruit as you cut it, this job is much safer when performed with a paring knife than a chef's knife.

3. Devein shrimp: Cut a shallow slit down the outside curve of the shrimp; remove the dark vein, and rinse the shrimp under cold water. See page 31 for more information about this procedure.

Serrated Knife

Serrated knives, with their scalloped, toothlike edge, are ideal for cutting through foods with a hard exterior and softer interior, such as a loaf of crusty bread. The principle behind a serrated knife is similar to that of a saw—the teeth of the blade catch and then rip as the knife smoothly slides through the food. It cuts cleanly through the resistant skin and juicy flesh of a ripe tomato without crushing it. Crusty bread is easier and neater to cut using a serrated knife because the crust will splinter less.

Three More Tasks for a Serrated Knife

1. Slice whole citrus fruits: Because citrus skin is tough and slick, the serrated blade is best for this task.

2. Cut baked phyllo dough: The blade gently saws through the delicate pastry so it crumbles less.

3. Slice a layer cake: A serrated knife is thinner and more delicate than a chef's knife and cuts cleanly through tender, moist cakes.

way to cook healthy
stocking the kitchen

The majority of these ingredients can be found at your local grocery store. For some of the items, you may need to visit an Asian market or a specialty grocery store.

advanced pantry

Beginner's Pantry

The Foundations
- ❏ Brown rice
- ❏ Pasta: spaghetti, penne, couscous
- ❏ Canned beans: black, pinto, Great Northern
- ❏ Canned tuna
- ❏ Pita bread
- ❏ Tortillas
- ❏ All-purpose flour

The Flavor Builders
- ❏ Vinegars: red wine, balsamic
- ❏ Extra-virgin olive oil
- ❏ Dark sesame oil
- ❏ Low-sodium soy sauce
- ❏ Dijon mustard
- ❏ Salsa
- ❏ Capers
- ❏ Fresh garlic
- ❏ Dried herbs
- ❏ Peanut butter

The Assistants
- ❏ Fat-free, less-sodium chicken and/or vegetable broth
- ❏ Whole and diced canned tomatoes
- ❏ Tomato paste
- ❏ Pasta sauce
- ❏ Baking powder

Sweet Returns
- ❏ Honey
- ❏ Brown sugar
- ❏ Granulated sugar
- ❏ Cocoa

Cool Stuff
- ❏ Boneless, skinless chicken breasts
- ❏ Parmesan cheese
- ❏ Mozzarella cheese
- ❏ Frozen spinach
- ❏ Eggs, egg substitute
- ❏ Fresh parsley
- ❏ Slivered almonds
- ❏ Butter
- ❏ Jellies or preserves
- ❏ Lemons and limes

intermediate pantry

beginner's pantry

Intermediate Pantry

Add to our Beginner's Pantry:

Extra Foundations
❑ Pasta: cavatappi, fusilli, farfalle, angel hair
❑ Beans: cannellini, garbanzo
❑ Rice: Arborio, basmati, wild
❑ Canned salmon

Extra Flavor Builders
❑ Sun-dried tomatoes

Extra Assistants
❑ Canned crushed tomatoes

Sweeter Returns
❑ Molasses
❑ Powdered sugar
❑ Semisweet chocolate
❑ Maple syrup

More Cool Stuff
❑ Cheese: Romano, Asiago
❑ Fresh herbs: basil, cilantro, thyme, rosemary
❑ Pork tenderloin
❑ Fresh fish: catfish, salmon
❑ Fresh shrimp
❑ Nuts: pecans, walnuts
❑ Fresh chiles: jalapeño, Serrano
❑ Tubes of polenta
❑ Olives: kalamata, niçoise
❑ Tofu: firm, soft

Advanced Pantry

Everything contained in the Beginner's Pantry and the Intermediate Pantry, plus:

Extra Foundations
❑ Cornmeal, grits, semolina flour
❑ Beans: fava, soybeans
❑ Grains: barley, millet, quinoa, bulgur
❑ Rice: sticky, sweet, jasmine
❑ Canned clams

Extra Flavor Builders
❑ Specialty oils: walnut, truffle-scented
❑ Specialty vinegars: herbed, Champagne
❑ Mustards: spicy brown, coarse-ground
❑ Spirits: Marsala, Madeira, sake, mirin, port
❑ Espresso powder
❑ Apricot and raspberry preserves
❑ Orange marmalade
❑ Sun-dried tomato paste
❑ Curry powder

Very Cool Stuff
❑ Homemade stocks (chicken, vegetable)
❑ Fresh fish: grouper, monkfish, amberjack
❑ Broader selection of cheeses: fontina, provolone, Gorgonzola
❑ Refrigerated fresh pasta: tortellini, ravioli
❑ Nuts: pine nuts, macadamia nuts, hazelnuts

way to
freeze

Preparing double or even triple recipes and freezing portions for later means you don't have to cook every night to have a delicious and nutritious meal on the table.

Freezer-unfriendly Foods

Freezing is a great make-ahead strategy, but it doesn't work for all foods. Some things simply don't freeze well.

• Gravies and sauces thickened with cornstarch or flour will separate during the freezing process. You can freeze an unthickened sauce, and then add thickeners after thawing.

• Fruits and vegetables with a high water content, such as lettuce and watermelon, will become limp and soggy when thawed.

• Cooked potatoes develop a gritty texture when frozen.

• Fully cooked pasta may become mushy once reheated. Slightly undercook pasta before freezing it.

• Some dairy products, such as yogurt, sour cream, milk, and light cream, will separate when frozen.

moussaka
5·13·10

kitchen how-to:
properly freeze foods

1 **2** **3**

4

5

Freshness and quality of the food at the time of freezing affect the condition of frozen foods. If foods are frozen at the peak of their quality, they emerge tasting better than foods frozen near the end of their freshness. So freeze items you won't use in the near future sooner rather than later. It's important to store all foods at 0° or lower in order to retain vitamin content, color, flavor, and texture.

1. Some food is better suited to freezing and reheating than others. Casseroles, soups, stews, chili, and meat loaf all stand up to the freezer well.

2. To keep food safe, cool freshly cooked dishes quickly before freezing. Putting foods that are still warm in the freezer can raise the temperature, causing surrounding frozen items to partially thaw and refreeze, which can alter the taste and texture of some foods. Place food in a shallow, wide container and refrigerate, uncovered, until cool. To chill soup or stew even faster, pour it into a metal bowl and set in an ice bath—a larger bowl filled halfway with ice water. Stir occasionally.

For stews, braises, or other semiliquid dishes with some fat content, chill completely, and then skim the fat from the top before freezing. Fat spoils over time in the freezer and shortens a dish's frozen shelf life.

3. Avoid freezer burn by using moisture-proof zip-top plastic bags and wrap. Remove the air from bags before sealing. Store soups and stews in freezer bags, which can be placed flat and freeze quickly.

Store foods in small servings, no more than 1 quart, to help them freeze quickly. This also allows you to defrost only what you need.

Use a permanent marker to label each container with the name of the dish, volume or weight if you've measured it, and the date you put it in the freezer.

4. The quicker food freezes, the better its quality once thawed. Do not crowd the freezer—arrange containers in a single layer in the freezer to allow enough room for air to circulate around them so food will freeze rapidly. Slowly frozen food forms large ice crystals that may turn the food mushy. Most cooked dishes will keep for two to three months in the freezer. Use a freezer thermometer to ensure that your unit remains at 0° or below.

5. Defrost food in the refrigerator or in the microwave. We recommend allowing enough time for the food to defrost in the refrigerator—roughly 5 hours per pound. To avoid the risk of contamination, never defrost food at room temperature.

fresh

& fast

way to
assemble
(no cook)

Preparing a healthy meal doesn't require spending lots of time in the kitchen; sometimes it doesn't require cooking at all. The keys are using fresh produce and healthy convenience products, and then enhancing them with flavorful condiments, herbs, and spices to create quick soups, fresh salads, flavorful sandwiches, and tasty desserts.

Grocery stores offer plenty of convenient options that can help you save time but won't sacrifice flavor or your health. But not all convenience products are healthy, and it's important to read nutrition labels carefully to make sure you know exactly what you're buying. With that in mind, you can have the best of both worlds— great-tasting food with timesaving convenience.

assemble, defined

Preparing a meal doesn't have to mean turning up the heat in your kitchen. You can create something fresh and fast without a stove, oven, or heat source of any kind.

Safety Concerns

Since you won't be cooking the food, make sure produce, including organic, is thoroughly washed to remove dirt and surface bacteria. Properly cleaning produce can also help remove some of the chemical residues found on conventionally grown food. Wash all produce thoroughly under cold or warm (not hot) running water. The water pressure from running water has an abrasive effect that cleans produce better than soaking. Berries and other tender fruits as well as fresh herbs should be rinsed well, while tough-skinned produce, such as apples, need to be scrubbed with a vegetable brush.

Equipment

The best tools to have to assemble a no-cook recipe are a food processor and blender for blending dips, spreads, or beverages and quickly shredding or chopping produce. You'll also need a colander for thoroughly cleaning and rinsing your produce (see Safety Concerns above).

Quality Counts

With no-cook recipes, the quality of ingredients is more important than ever, so always start with the freshest produce available. Although many fruits,

low-sodium and lean sandwich meats. Buy shrimp from the seafood counter at your local grocery store, and have it steamed while you finish the rest of your shopping. Rotisserie chicken is also an easy way to add flavor and protein to sandwiches and salads; it can also serve as a main dish all by itself. But, some convenience products aren't the healthiest options—they can be loaded with excess fat and sodium—so be sure to read the nutrition labels carefully to make sure you know exactly what you're buying.

vegetables, and herbs are available year-round, you'll get better flavor and prices when you buy what's in season. By using the freshest produce, you don't have to do much to make it taste great. Refer to the Seasonal Produce Guide on page 481 to help you choose the season's best.

Healthy and Convenient
With the number of healthy ready-to-eat foods on the market today, assembling a meal is easier than ever. In addition to utilizing fresh seasonal produce, you can also amp up your meals by purchasing canned beans or

the bottom line
The three most important elements to remember about assembling:

1. Thoroughly wash all produce to remove dirt and surface bacteria.

2. Buy seasonal produce to ensure you're getting the best flavor and price.

3. Utilize healthy convenience products to easily add zest to your no-cook meals.

way to assemble

beverages

Cold beverages are the ultimate no-cook recipes. They're refreshing and take only minutes to make. Prepare a cool drink for your next meal or get-together for an easy, flavorful addition to the menu.

kitchen how-to:
seed a pomegranate

Unlike most fruits, the seeds of a pomegranate are the edible portion. Each fruit contains hundreds of them, and the seeds can stain. To help keep you and your kitchen clean, use a bowl of water to prevent those delicious, stain-causing seeds from doing their dirty work. In addition to following these steps, you may want to wear an apron for extra protection.

Champagne-Pomegranate Cocktail

In the tradition of sparkling libations like the Buck's Fizz and Bellini, this cocktail starts with Champagne and fruit juice.

 4 cups crushed ice
 2 cups pomegranate juice
 ½ cup ginger ale
 ¼ cup brandy
 1 (750-milliliter) bottle Champagne
    or sparkling wine
 Pomegranate seeds (optional)

1. Combine first 5 ingredients in a pitcher. Pour about 1 cup Champagne mixture into each of 8 glasses. Garnish with seeds, if desired. **Yield: 8 servings.**

CALORIES 125; FAT 0g; PROTEIN 0.3g; CARB 11.7g; FIBER 0g; CHOL 0mg; IRON 0.1mg; SODIUM 8.6mg; CALC 10mg

1. Place the pomegranate in a bowl of water large enough to fit both the fruit and your hands without spilling over. Under the water, use a medium-sized knife to carefully slice off the crown and opposite end of the pomegranate so the seeds are just visible (don't slice too deeply). Then score the pomegranate lengthwise into 1½-inch-wide wedges. With your thumbs, carefully pry the pomegranate apart beneath the water, and turn each section inside out.
2. Begin to separate the seeds from the inner white membrane, taking care not to burst the individual juice sacs. The membrane will float to the top while the seeds sink to the bottom.
3. With a large slotted spoon, skim off the floating membrane. Sort through the seeds beneath the water, discarding any stray pieces of membrane (it's unpleasantly bitter). Drain the pomegranate seeds in a fine mesh strainer. Use immediately, or refrigerate for up to one week.

Peach Mojitos

This classic Cuban cocktail refreshes from the very first sip. We kept mostly to the traditional recipe— we still muddle mint with lime and sugar, use rum, and top it off with crisp club soda. But fresh peach puree forms the base of our version. The stone fruit makes an irresistible partner for the citrus and mint. Use a wooden muddler, if available, to crush the mint mixture in the pitcher. This procedure releases the mint's essential oils, melding them with the lime juice.

  3 cups coarsely chopped peeled ripe
     peaches (about 1 pound)
  1 teaspoon grated lime rind
  1 cup fresh lime juice (about 4 large limes)
  ¾ cup sugar
  ½ cup packed fresh mint leaves
  2 cups white rum
  4 cups club soda, chilled
Crushed ice
Mint sprigs (optional)

1. Place peaches in a blender or food processor; process until smooth. Press peach puree through a fine sieve into a bowl; discard solids.
2. Combine rind and next 3 ingredients in a large pitcher; crush juice mixture with the back of a long spoon. Add peach puree and rum to pitcher, stirring until sugar dissolves. Stir in club soda. Serve over crushed ice. Garnish with mint sprigs, if desired.
Yield: 10 servings (serving size: about ⅔ cup).

CALORIES 186; FAT 0.1g (sat 0g, mono 0g, poly 0.1g); PROTEIN 0.6g; CARB 21.6g; FIBER 0.9g; CHOL 0mg; IRON 0.3mg; SODIUM 21mg; CALC 14mg

kitchen how-to:
juice a lime

To get the most juice out of a fresh lime, bring it to room temperature, and then use the palm of your hand to roll the lime on a countertop a few times, applying a bit of pressure. Cut the fruit in half, and then squeeze. Or, for easier work, use a handheld press to release the most juice while safely trapping the seeds. Place the lime half, cut side down, in the press, and lower the handle.

Blackberry Limeade

- 6 cups water, divided
- 3 cups fresh blackberries
- 1 cup sugar
- ⅔ cup fresh lime juice (about 4 limes)
- 8 thin lime slices
- Fresh blackberries (optional)

1. Place 1 cup water and 3 cups blackberries in a blender; process until smooth. Press blackberry puree through a sieve into a large pitcher; discard seeds. Add remaining 5 cups water, sugar, and juice to pitcher; stir until sugar dissolves. Place 1 lime slice and a few blackberries, if desired, into each of 8 glasses; pour about 1 cup limeade over each serving. **Yield: 8 servings.**

CALORIES 125; FAT 0.3g (sat 0g, mono 0g, poly 0.2g); PROTEIN 0.8g; CARB 31.9g; FIBER 0.7g; CHOL 0mg; IRON 0.4mg; SODIUM 5mg; CALC 22mg

way to assemble

dips & spreads

Dips and spreads are party-food staples for a reason. They're usually easy to prepare and often don't require any cooking. Most can be made a day or two in advance—their flavor only improves with time. Prepare a few different ones with different flavor profiles for your next party.

Traditional Hummus

This is a classic Middle Eastern dip. Prepare and refrigerate it a day ahead; let it stand at room temperature for 30 minutes before serving. Garnish with a lemon slice and fresh parsley sprig, if desired, and serve with baked pita chips.

  2 **(15.5-ounce) cans no-salt-added chickpeas (garbanzo beans), rinsed and drained**
  2 **garlic cloves, crushed**
  ½ **cup water**
  ¼ **cup tahini (sesame seed paste)**
  3 **tablespoons fresh lemon juice**
  2 **tablespoons extra-virgin olive oil**
  ¾ **teaspoon salt**
  ¼ **teaspoon black pepper**

1. Place beans and garlic in a food processor; pulse 5 times or until chopped. Add ½ cup water and remaining ingredients; pulse until smooth, scraping down sides as needed. **Yield: 3¼ cups (serving size: 2 tablespoons).**

CALORIES 44; FAT 2.5g (sat 0.3g, mono 1.2g, poly 0.7g); PROTEIN 1.5g; CARB 4.4g; FIBER 0.9g; CHOL 0mg; IRON 0.3mg; SODIUM 74mg; CALC 12mg

Classic Pesto

Fresh basil is at the core of pesto, the quintessential Italian sauce. You don't have to stick to the classic recipe. Throw in some roasted red bell peppers or sun-dried tomatoes and experiment with almost any kind of nut. Then use it on bruschetta as an appetizer, add it to pizza to give it a new flavor, or mix it with mayo to spread on a sandwich.

  2 **tablespoons coarsely chopped walnuts or pine nuts**
  2 **garlic cloves, peeled**
  3 **tablespoons extra-virgin olive oil**
  4 **cups fresh basil leaves (about 4 ounces)**
  ½ **cup (2 ounces) grated fresh Parmesan cheese**
  ¼ **teaspoon salt**

1. Drop nuts and garlic through food chute with food processor on; process until minced. Add oil; pulse 3 times. Add basil, cheese, and salt; process until finely minced, scraping sides of bowl once. **Yield: ¾ cup (serving size: 1 tablespoon).**

CALORIES 58; FAT 5.3g (sat 1.3g, mono 3g, poly 0.8g); PROTEIN 2.1g; CARB 0.9g; FIBER 0.6g; CHOL 3mg; IRON 0.5mg; SODIUM 125mg; CALC 72mg

kitchen how-to:
freeze pesto

Thanks to olive oil, pesto retains its bright color when frozen. Just drop a tablespoon of pesto into each section of an ice tray and freeze. Transfer the frozen cubes to a heavy-duty zip-top plastic freezer bag. Before using it, let the pesto thaw for a few hours. Pesto will keep in the freezer for up to three months and in the refrigerator for up to five days.

Mixed Olive Tapenade

This piquant specialty of Provence, France, features classic ingredients from the region—olives, capers, and anchovies. Garnish with a lemon wedge and fresh parsley sprig, if desired. Serve at room temperature with baguette slices or crackers. For a fast entrée option, stir the tapenade into hot cooked pasta.

- 1 **cup kalamata olives, pitted (about 4 ounces)**
- 1 **cup green olives, pitted (about 4 ounces)**
- 1 **tablespoon chopped fresh flat-leaf parsley**
- 1 **tablespoon capers, rinsed and drained**
- 2 **teaspoons chopped fresh thyme**
- 1 **teaspoon grated lemon rind**
- ¼ **teaspoon freshly ground black pepper**
- 10 **oil-cured olives, pitted (about 1 ounce)**
- 3 **canned anchovy fillets (about ¼ ounce)**
- 1 **garlic clove, chopped**

1. Place all ingredients in a food processor; pulse 10 times or until olives are finely chopped. **Yield: 16 servings (serving size: about 2 tablespoons).**

CALORIES 39; FAT 3.6g (sat 0.4g, mono 2.3g, poly 0.5g); PROTEIN 0.3g; CARB 2g; FIBER 0.4g; CHOL 0mg; IRON 0.1mg; SODIUM 310mg; CALC 5mg

kitchen how-to:
pit an olive

To make easy work of pitting olives (or cherries), you can use a pitter (shown at right). If you don't have a pitter, place the olives on a cutting board. Place the flat side of a chef's knife on top, and press down using the heel of your hand. The olives will pop open, exposing the pits for easy removal. To pit a large number of olives, wrap them in a dish towel, and smack them with a rolling pin or heavy skillet.

all about olive nutrition

Dishes like tapenade that include olives can be better for your heart than other dishes. Between 75 and 85 percent of the caloric content of olives is monounsaturated fat, which, when replacing saturated fat in the diet, can help lower harmful LDL cholesterol levels. It also prevents the buildup of plaque along artery walls. If you're on a low-sodium diet, be sure to check the label because some olives are high in sodium.

way to assemble
fruit desserts

Seasonal fruit is the easiest place to begin a no-cook dessert. Add ice cream or whipped topping to fresh cut fruit or stir in some sugar and a dash of your favorite liqueur or fruit juice to create a refreshingly cool, sweet treat. Choose fruits by the season so they're at their peak. In preparation for those cooler months when fresh fruit isn't widely available, stock up on your favorite fruits and freeze them.

Strawberries Romanoff

In this classic dessert recipe, the strawberries are marinated—also known as macerating—in orange-flavored liqueur, which complements their fresh taste. Macerate the strawberries for only the length of time specified so the strawberries retain their texture.

 4 cups sliced strawberries
    (about 1½ pounds)
 3 tablespoons powdered sugar
 ¼ cup Cointreau or Grand
    Marnier (orange-flavored
    liqueur)
 ⅓ cup whipping cream, chilled
 3 tablespoons powdered sugar
 ¼ teaspoon vanilla extract
 Mint sprigs (optional)

1. Combine first 3 ingredients in a bowl. Cover and chill 3½ hours.
2. Place cream, 3 tablespoons sugar, and vanilla in a small bowl; beat with a mixer at high speed until stiff peaks form. Spoon over strawberry mixture. Garnish with mint, if desired. Serve immediately.
Yield: 4 servings (serving size: about ¾ cup strawberry mixture and 3 tablespoons whipped cream mixture).

CALORIES 207; FAT 6.7g (sat 3.9g, mono 1.9g, poly 0.5g); PROTEIN 1.6g; CARB 31.2g; FIBER 3.4g; CHOL 22mg; IRON 0.7mg; SODIUM 10mg; CALC 41mg

kitchen how-to:
freeze fresh berries

Stocking up on and freezing seasonal berries, such as strawberries, blueberries, and cranberries, allows you to enjoy them year-round. In some cases, you don't need to thaw the berries before using them; for example, just add frozen berries straight to cake or bread batters.

1. Trim away any green leaves or stems, place berries in a colander, and gently rinse in cool water until clean.
2. Remove berries from colander, and spread on a dish towel; allow them to air-dry completely.
3. Distribute evenly on a jelly-roll pan, and place in the freezer for about an hour or until slightly frozen.
4. Remove from freezer, and transfer berries to a plastic zip-top bag. Store in the freezer for up to six months.

1

2

3

4

way to assemble
ice cream

Ice cream is a frozen custard (or milk mixture) with air whipped into it. The custard or mix, especially for light ice cream, is a delicate balance of dairy products, sweetener, flavorings, and sometimes eggs. For no-cook ice cream, the eggs are omitted and less sugar is used—it's replaced with liquid sweeteners, such as maple syrup, honey, sweetened condensed milk, or cream of coconut.

Banana-Coconut Ice Cream

The added creaminess of 2 percent milk makes richer ice cream with fewer ice crystals. Cream of coconut, a sweet, thick mixture made from fresh coconuts mixed with sugar, is used to make piña coladas. Look for it in cans near the drink mixes in your grocery store.

1½   cups 2% reduced-fat milk
1   cup cream of coconut
⅓   cup sugar
1½   cups mashed ripe banana (about 3 bananas)

1. Combine first 3 ingredients in a medium bowl, stirring until sugar dissolves. Stir in banana; cover and chill.
2. Pour mixture into the freezer can of an ice-cream freezer; freeze according to manufacturer's instructions. Spoon ice cream into a freezer-safe container. Cover and freeze 1 hour or until firm. **Yield: 8 servings (serving size: about ⅔ cup).**

CALORIES 203; FAT 6g (sat 4.6g, mono 0.8g, poly 0.2g); PROTEIN 2g; CARB 37.2g; FIBER 1.1g; CHOL 3mg; IRON 0.1mg; SODIUM 38mg; CALC 58mg

kitchen how-to:
make ice cream

1

2

3

4

It's easy to make ice cream at home. Prepare the ice-cream base (or mix), and then follow these steps to churn out fabulous no-cook ice cream. (Some recipes require the ice-cream base to be cooked. If so, you'll need to completely cool the cooked mixture before freezing it. You can do this quickly by placing the pan in a large ice-filled metal bowl.)

1. The most important piece of equipment is an ice-cream maker. You've got a couple of options: an old-fashioned bucket churn or a countertop freezer.
2. Traditional bucket-style freezers require rock salt and ice, but tabletop models rely strictly on a freezer bowl filled with a coolant.
3. Place the mixture in the freezer can. When using a traditional bucket-style freezer, use coarse rock salt because it won't slip easily between the ice or drain through the cracks of the bucket. Freeze according to manufacturer's instructions.
4. Ripen the ice cream by transferring it to a freezer-safe container. Let it stand in the freezer at least 1 hour or until firm.
5. Let the ice cream stand at room temperature for about 5 minutes to soften slightly after it ripens. If it's still frozen solid, heat the scoop under hot running water, pat it dry, and scoop.

5

way to assemble
salads

While the familiar pairing of salad greens and ripe tomatoes is enjoyable, a good salad can be so much more. Adding fruits, nuts, and other well-chosen ingredients offers new flavors and textures, and more importantly, helps you create a more healthful dish by adding a variety of nutritional benefits. Choose among them to suit your palate and needs.

Arugula, Grape, and Sunflower Seed Salad

   3 tablespoons red wine vinegar
   1 teaspoon honey
   1 teaspoon maple syrup
   ½ teaspoon stone-ground mustard
   2 teaspoons grapeseed oil
   7 cups loosely packed baby arugula
   2 cups red grapes, halved
   2 tablespoons toasted sunflower seed kernels
   1 teaspoon chopped fresh thyme
   ¼ teaspoon salt
   ¼ teaspoon freshly ground black pepper

1. Combine first 4 ingredients in a small bowl. Gradually add oil, stirring with a whisk.
2. Combine arugula and next 3 ingredients in a large bowl. Drizzle vinegar mixture over arugula; sprinkle with salt and pepper. Toss gently to coat. **Yield: 6 servings (serving size: about 1 cup).**

CALORIES 81; FAT 3.1g (sat 0.3g, mono 0.5g, poly 2g); PROTEIN 1.6g; CARB 13.1g; FIBER 1.2g; CHOL 0mg; IRON 0.7mg; SODIUM 124mg; CALC 47mg

Fruits
What they add: All fruit provides abundant nutrients (vitamin C and potassium, in particular) and a laundry list of disease-fighting chemicals in a package that's naturally low in fat, sodium, and calories. Blueberries and grapes contain polyphenols (a phytochemical linked to heart disease and cancer prevention) called anthocyanins and proanthocyanins that may play a role in preserving memory. The fiber in fruits can help lower blood cholesterol levels and reduce risk of heart disease.

Nuts and Seeds

What they add: One-fourth cup of nuts or seeds adds nearly 5 grams of high-quality protein, as well as generous amounts of vitamin E, fiber, minerals, and arginine, a compound that helps blood vessels function properly. Nuts are also high in the healthful unsaturated kind of fat.

Greens

What they add: Most leafy greens contribute folate, the B vitamin critical to red blood cell health and the reduction of neural tube birth defects like spina bifida. They also provide a generous amount of vitamin A and the antioxidants lutein and zeaxanthin, which may help protect against macular degeneration.

Onions

What they add: Onions are plentiful sources of disease-fighting phenols and flavonoids, both potential cancer fighters and weapons against some chronic diseases. The richer its phenolic and flavonoid content, the better an onion's protective effect.

Seafood and Other Proteins

What they add: Fatty fish, such as salmon and tuna, offer omega-3 fats, which help lower the risk for heart disease. The American Heart Association suggests eating at least two 3-ounce cooked servings of fish per week.

Vegetable Oils

What they add: Liquid vegetable oils are rich in vitamin E and unsaturated fats (monounsaturated and polyunsaturated), which don't clog arteries. Olive oil is particularly rich in phenol antioxidants.

Tomatoes

What they add: With plenty of vitamin C, some blood pressure-lowering potassium, and folate, tomatoes also impart the plant chemicals flavonoids (potential cancer fighters) and phytosterols (which may help lower cholesterol).

Crab, Corn, and Tomato Salad with Lemon Dressing

You can pick up lump crabmeat from your grocery's seafood counter. It's an easy no-cook addition to salads, sandwiches, dips, and soups. The tart dressing contrasts with the sweet corn, tomatoes, and crab. Pair this salad with cucumber soup or a grilled sandwich.

    1   tablespoon grated lemon rind
    5   tablespoons fresh lemon juice, divided
    1   tablespoon extra-virgin olive oil
    1   teaspoon honey
    ½   teaspoon Dijon mustard
    ¼   teaspoon salt
    ⅛   teaspoon freshly ground black pepper
    1   cup fresh corn kernels (about 2 ears)
    ¼   cup thinly sliced fresh basil leaves
    ¼   cup chopped red bell pepper
    2   tablespoons finely chopped red onion
    1   pound lump crabmeat, shell pieces removed
    8   (¼-inch-thick) slices ripe beefsteak tomato
    2   cups cherry tomatoes, halved
    4   lemon wedges (optional)

1. Combine rind, 3 tablespoons juice, and next 5 ingredients in a large bowl, stirring well with a whisk. Reserve 1½ tablespoons juice mixture. Add remaining 2 tablespoons juice, corn, and next 4 ingredients to remaining juice mixture; toss gently to coat.
2. Arrange 2 tomato slices and ½ cup cherry tomatoes on each of 4 plates. Drizzle about 1 teaspoon reserved juice mixture over each serving. Top each serving with 1 cup corn and crab mixture. Serve with lemon wedges, if desired. **Yield: 4 servings.**

CALORIES 242; FAT 5.6g (sat 0.6g, mono 2.7g, poly 0.7g); PROTEIN 30g; CARB 17.7g; FIBER 3.6g; CHOL 128mg; IRON 1.8mg; SODIUM 613mg; CALC 161mg

way to assemble
salad dressings

Orange-Sesame Dressing

This Asian-inspired recipe takes little time and effort to prepare. It's flavorful and versatile enough to toss on a simple green salad, drizzle over grilled salmon fillets, or use as a dipping sauce for seared tofu.

½ cup fresh
orange juice

1 tablespoon
sesame oil

¼ cup low-sodium
soy sauce

1 tablespoon
fresh lime juice

1 tablespoon black
sesame seeds

Combine all ingredients in a small bowl, stirring well with a whisk. **Yield: 15 tablespoons (serving size: 1 tablespoon).**

CALORIES 19; FAT 1.3g (sat 0.2g, mono 0.5g, poly 0.6g); PROTEIN 0.5g; CARB 1.5g; FIBER 0.1g; CHOL 0mg; IRON 0.1mg; SODIUM 173mg; CALC 7mg

way to assemble
sandwiches

Everyone loves sandwiches. They're fresh, convenient, portable, and easy to assemble. An assortment of ripe fruits and vegetables, fresh bread, flavorful spreads, and top-quality meats can make a sandwich that's greater than the sum of its parts.

Little Italy Chicken Pitas with Sun-Dried Tomato Vinaigrette

Use oil from the sun-dried tomatoes to prepare the vinaigrette for this zesty sandwich. Chilled green grapes make a cool side.

    2   tablespoons balsamic vinegar
  1½   tablespoons sun-dried tomato oil
    1   tablespoon chopped drained oil-packed
        sun-dried tomatoes
   ¼   teaspoon freshly ground black pepper
    1   garlic clove, minced
    4   cups shredded cooked chicken breast
        (about ¾ pound)
    1   cup chopped tomato (about 1 medium)
   ½   cup (2 ounces) grated Asiago cheese
   ¼   cup thinly sliced fresh basil
    6   (6-inch) pitas, cut in half
    3   cups mixed baby greens

1. Combine first 5 ingredients in a bowl. Stir in chicken and next 3 ingredients. Line each pita half with ¼ cup greens. Divide chicken mixture evenly among pita halves. **Yield: 6 servings (serving size: 2 stuffed pita halves).**

CALORIES 342; FAT 9.1g (sat 2.8g, mono 4.2g, poly 1.3g); PROTEIN 26.4g; CARB 37.3g; FIBER 2.4g; CHOL 56mg; IRON 2.7mg; SODIUM 397mg; CALC 162mg

Match the Bread to the Filling
Some breads just work better with particular fillings. Here's a guide:

• Use wraps, lavash, hollowed-out French bread, and pita bread for sandwiches with salad-type dressings since these breads will contain the spread better than sliced bread.
• Rye bread partners well with heavier meats, such as beef with a horseradish spread or smoked ham with mustard.
• Flavorful, hearty-textured sourdough, ciabatta, focaccia, and multigrain breads provide a tasty contrast to milder fillings like chicken and turkey.

Pesto Chicken Salad Sandwiches

Substitute baguettes for focaccia, if you'd like. You can make the chicken salad ahead to have on hand to prepare a quick lunch. Chop, slice, and shred rotisserie chicken from the supermarket for a short-cut sandwich topping. It's easy to slice and remove the meat from the bone. An average 2-pound rotisserie chicken yields 3 to 3½ cups of meat.

½ cup low-fat mayonnaise
⅓ cup plain fat-free yogurt
⅓ cup commercial pesto (such as Buitoni)
1½ tablespoons fresh lemon juice
½ teaspoon salt
½ teaspoon black pepper

4 cups cubed skinless, boneless rotisserie chicken breast
1 cup diced celery
⅓ cup chopped walnuts, toasted
1 (1-pound) focaccia bread, cut in half horizontally, toasted, and cut into 20 slices
1 (12-ounce) bottle roasted red bell peppers, drained and chopped
10 romaine lettuce leaves

1. Combine first 6 ingredients in a large bowl, stirring with a whisk. Stir in chicken, celery, and walnuts.
2. Spread ½ cup salad onto each of 10 bread slices. Top each serving with about 2 tablespoons bell pepper, 1 lettuce leaf, and 1 bread slice. **Yield: 10 servings (serving size: 1 sandwich).**

CALORIES 324; FAT 10g (sat 1.2g, mono 0.6g, poly 2.2g); PROTEIN 26.4g; CARB 31.6g; FIBER 1.6g; CHOL 55mg; IRON 2.3mg; SODIUM 725mg; CALC 39mg

Lobster Wraps with Lemon Mayonnaise

Flatbread replaces buttered rolls in this take on the New England classic. You can purchase cooked lobster tails at your grocery's seafood counter.

Lemon Mayonnaise:
- ¼ cup light mayonnaise
- 2 tablespoons chopped fresh chives
- 1 teaspoon fresh lemon juice
- ⅛ teaspoon freshly ground black pepper

Remaining Ingredients:
- ¾ cup chopped seeded tomato (about 1 medium)
- 4 (4-ounce) lobster tails, cooked and chopped
- 4 (2.8-ounce) whole wheat flatbreads (such as Flatout)
- 8 Bibb lettuce leaves

1. To prepare lemon mayonnaise, combine first 4 ingredients; stir well.
2. Combine lemon mayonnaise, tomato, and lobster; stir well. Divide lobster mixture evenly among flatbreads. Top each serving with 2 lettuce leaves. Roll up jelly-roll fashion.
Yield: 4 servings (serving size: 1 wrap).

CALORIES 371; FAT 8.6g (sat 1g, mono 1.5g, poly 0.6g); PROTEIN 31g; CARB 41.7g; FIBER 3.6g; CHOL 113mg; IRON 0.7mg; SODIUM 1,098mg; CALC 66mg

kitchen how-to:
make a sandwich spread

Sandwich spreads are an easy way to add a punch of flavor to any sandwich. You can quickly turn low-fat or light mayonnaise into a gourmet spread by stirring in herbs, citrus juices, and freshly ground black pepper. Vary the herbs according to your taste preferences. Fresh chives and lemon add flavor to the recipe above, while fresh tarragon and rosemary would complement a chicken sandwich and fresh dill would work nicely with fish.

way to assemble
soups

Chilled soups are some of the best no-cook recipes and make ideal hot-weather fare. It only takes tossing the ingredients together in a bowl or processing them in a blender to transform lush fruits and vegetables into flavorful and easy soups that are perfect as an appetizer or light supper.

Chunky Tomato-Fruit Gazpacho

The mangoes, melons, and nectarines give this gazpacho a sweet spin. If you like a soup with more zip, don't seed the jalapeño.

- 2 cups finely chopped tomatoes (about ¾ pound)
- 2 cups finely diced honeydew melon (about ¾ pound)
- 2 cups finely diced cantaloupe (about ¾ pound)
- 1 cup finely diced mango (about 1 medium)
- 1 cup finely diced seeded peeled cucumber (about 1 medium)
- 1 cup finely diced nectarines (about 3 medium)
- 1 cup fresh orange juice (about 4 oranges)
- ½ cup finely chopped Vidalia or other sweet onion
- ¼ cup chopped fresh basil
- 3 tablespoons chopped fresh mint
- 3 tablespoons fresh lemon juice
- 1 teaspoon sugar
- ½ teaspoon salt
- 1 jalapeño pepper, seeded and finely chopped

1. Combine all ingredients in a large bowl. Cover and chill at least 2 hours. **Yield: 7 servings (serving size: 1 cup).**

CALORIES 95; FAT 0.5g (sat 0.1g, mono 0.1g, poly 0.2g); PROTEIN 2.1g; CARB 23g; FIBER 2.8g; CHOL 0mg; IRON 0.9mg; SODIUM 189mg; CALC 33mg

kitchen how-to:
cut a mango

1

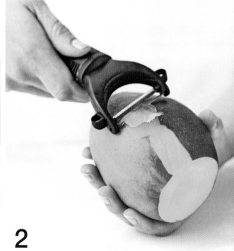

2

The taste of mango has been compared to a cross between a pineapple and a peach. Use this tropical fruit to add sublime sweetness to salsas, relishes, smoothies, soups, and salads.

1. Use a sharp knife to trim about half an inch from the top and bottom to create a sturdy surface for cutting.
2. Hold the mango in one hand, and use a vegetable peeler to slice the skin from the flesh.
3. Cut the flesh from around the pit with two curved cuts down the plumpest sides; trim remaining sides.
4. Cut the fruit's flesh according to your need—julienned for salads or diced for soups and salsas.

3

4

Avocado Soup with Citrus-Shrimp Relish

Ask the attendant at the fish counter to steam the shrimp while you shop for the rest of your groceries. Pair this lovely soup with a green salad for a complete meal.

Relish:
- 2 tablespoons chopped fresh cilantro
- 1 teaspoon grated lemon rind
- 1 teaspoon finely chopped red onion
- 1 teaspoon extra-virgin olive oil
- 8 ounces peeled and deveined medium shrimp, steamed and coarsely chopped

Soup:
- 2 cups fat-free, less-sodium chicken broth
- 1¾ cups chopped avocado (about 2)
- 1 cup water
- 1 cup rinsed and drained canned navy beans
- ½ cup fat-free plain yogurt
- 1½ tablespoons fresh lemon juice

- ¼ teaspoon salt
- ¼ teaspoon black pepper
- ¼ teaspoon hot pepper sauce (such as Tabasco)
- 1 small jalapeño pepper, seeded and chopped
- ¼ cup (1 ounce) crumbled queso fresco cheese

1. To prepare relish, combine first 5 ingredients in a small bowl, tossing gently.

2. To prepare soup, place broth and next 9 ingredients in a blender; puree until smooth, scraping sides. Ladle 1¼ cups avocado mixture into each of 4 bowls; top each serving with ¼ cup shrimp mixture and 1 tablespoon cheese. **Yield: 4 servings.**

CALORIES 292; FAT 13.2g (sat 2.2g, mono 7.8g, poly 2.6g); PROTEIN 23.9g; CARB 22.5g; FIBER 7.3g; CHOL 118mg; IRON 3.4mg; SODIUM 832mg; CALC 146mg

kitchen how-to:
prepare avocados

Avocados contain heart-healthy monounsaturated fat and are loaded with antioxidants and potassium (more per serving than bananas). Add their buttery texture and mild, nutty flavor to sandwiches, salads, and soups. To easily dice, start with an 8- to 10-inch chef's knife. Insert it into the top where the stem was (it will be a darker area), and gently press down until you reach the pit. Then follow these tips.

1. Holding the knife steady, rotate the fruit so the knife moves around the pit, cutting the entire avocado.

2. Remove the knife; then slowly and gently twist the two sides away from each other to separate.

3. Strike the pit, and pierce it with the blade. Then twist and remove the knife; the pit will come with it.

4. Use the knife's tip to cut the flesh in horizontal and vertical rows. Be careful not to cut through the skin.

5. Remove the flesh gently with a spoon. To prevent browning, squeeze lemon juice on the flesh.

way to
steam

Steaming is a staple preparation for a number of international cuisines. It's relatively quick, easy to master, and offers a healthful way to cook since steaming achieves great results with no added fat. The result is light, fresh fare with textures ranging from crisp-tender green beans to chewy Asian-style dumplings.

Once you master the basics of steaming, the possibilities are endless. Experiment with different vegetables, poultry, fish and shellfish, and dumpling fillings. And this technique isn't only for Asian dishes—try curry spices, barbecue, or Mediterranean flavors. You'll love being able to put together an entrée or healthful side with little effort and plenty of flavor.

steaming, defined

This technique involves cooking food over boiling liquid in a tightly sealed pan. The steam released from the liquid surrounds and permeates the food with moisture and heat.

What Steaming Does

Steaming cooks food more gently than almost any other method. Because the liquid never touches the food, it's less likely to jostle, overcook, or absorb too much water. This means food retains its shape, color, flavor, and texture. Steaming is a great light cooking technique because it involves no fat. And unlike boiling, which leaches water-soluble nutrients from food, steaming retains most of the nutrients.

Best Bets for Steaming

Steaming is ideal for foods that need moisture and foods that should be soft and silken rather than crunchy or caramelized. For example, steamed Asian dumplings develop a soft-chewy texture rather than a firm or crunchy one. Almost all vegetables are good candidates (excluding mushrooms, eggplant, and other spongy vegetables or tough ones, such as greens).

When selecting a protein, choose light, delicate ingredients, such as chicken breast and most fish and shellfish. Avoid bold-flavored seafood, such as bluefish, or firm-fleshed fish, such as tuna. Also, stay away from beef or pork, which fare best by browning.

Steam Safely

Three tips will ensure your safety:
1. Open the lid away from you so that the steam is released to the back of the stove away from your face.
2. Use silicone baking mitts to pick up a steaming rack. Because the rack will be damp, scalding water can soak through cloth oven mitts and cause a burn.
3. Use tongs or spatulas to remove food from the steamer. Steamed food often retains heat longer because the hot steam has permeated the food.

Equipment

Steaming requires little more than a pan with a well-fitting lid and a rack to support the food over the liquid in the pan. Creating a good seal with the lid is crucial for holding in steam. If the lid doesn't fit tightly, cover the pan with foil, and then top with the lid. Many cookware sets come with steamer inserts, as do woks. If you don't have these, there are other options.

A collapsible metal vegetable steamer works well for vegetables and certain shellfish—foods that you don't mind touching or stacking on top of one another as they cook. If you don't have a vegetable steamer, you can improvise by placing a footed metal colander in the pan (make sure the lid will close) or setting a round cooling rack on top of two ramekins in the bottom of the pan so the food will be higher than the water level.

For foods that need to lie flat or shouldn't touch (such as salmon fillets or dumplings), try a bamboo steamer. Available at most Asian markets, these steamers come with two or three tiers that can be stacked, allowing you to cook a lot of food at one time. They also come with a lid that rests atop the uppermost tier. Set this type of steamer in a wok or large skillet with an inch of water.

En Papillote

Another steaming method involves baking sealed packets in the oven, a practice known in French as *en papillote*. Meat, fish, and vegetables are sealed in parchment paper or aluminum foil with some liquid, set on a baking sheet, and placed in the oven. This method works well for individual entrées and vegetables, but dumplings, buns, and steamed puddings are better steamed on the stovetop.

Aromatics

Seasonings in the liquid can permeate the food. As it cooks, the food's various cellular layers open up in the heat and trap flavors in the steam, thereby enhancing the overall taste. Hard spices and aromatic roots, such as cinnamon sticks, lemongrass stalks, star anise pods, and ginger, are good options.

Finishing Flavors

Because steamed foods lack the rich taste of those roasted, sautéed, or seared, many benefit from a sauce: cheese sauce for broccoli or herbed butter for shellfish, for example. Sometimes, the steaming liquid itself can become the sauce, especially if aromatics and spices have been added and if the sauce is reduced to a thicker consistency, which concentrates its flavor.

Let the food guide the sauce. Spirits other than wine often become too intense when reduced, thus overpowering the fresh-steamed flavors. Steamed buns, fish, and vegetables are delicate, a bonanza of natural flavors. A too-strong sauce will mask the subtlety of these foods.

Steaming Liquid

Use translucent, thin liquids, such as water, broth, juice, wine, beer, or other spirits. These will bubble and steam to create a hot, moist environment. Forgo cloudy liquids, such as dairy milk or coconut milk, which will curdle, or thick liquids, such as tomato sauce, which might burn.

Add just enough liquid to produce a high volume of steam without intruding through the holes or slats in the steamer or rack. Do not allow the liquid to touch the food, or you'll end up boiling and, most likely, overcooking it. You'll need a ½-inch to 1-inch clearance between the steamer basket and the liquid.

No matter how firmly you cover the pan, the liquid will eventually boil away. For foods that cook longer than 15 or 20 minutes, check the liquid level occasionally. Keep extra liquid boiling on the stovetop in a separate pan or teakettle; carefully add it to the pot or wok, but not directly over the food.

the bottom line

The three most important elements to remember about steaming:

1. Keep the food positioned above the liquid.
2. Make sure the pan is covered tightly.
3. Check the liquid level after 15 minutes; add more boiling liquid, if necessary, so the pan doesn't go dry.

way to steam

dumplings

Dumplings are comforting and familiar and completely
unpretentious, which might explain their universal appeal.
In much of the world, dumplings likely evolved from peasant
food. There are various methods used to make dumplings,
but in Asian countries particularly, dumplings are often
steamed, which creates their signature soft, chewy texture.

Steamed Pork Buns
(Char Siu Bao)

Use a multitray bamboo steamer so you can cook all the buns at one time. To make them up to two months ahead, fill the dough, and freeze unsteamed buns on a tray in the freezer before placing them in a freezer-safe zip-top plastic bag. Steam the buns directly from the freezer for an additional 5 minutes.

Filling:
- ½ teaspoon five-spice powder
- 1 pound pork tenderloin, trimmed
- Cooking spray
- 1 cup thinly sliced green onions
- 3 tablespoons hoisin sauce
- 2 tablespoons rice vinegar
- 1 tablespoon low-sodium soy sauce
- 1½ teaspoons honey
- 1 teaspoon minced peeled fresh ginger
- 1 teaspoon minced garlic
- ¼ teaspoon salt

Dough:
- 1 cup warm water (100° to 110°)
- 3 tablespoons sugar
- 1 package dry yeast (about 2¼ teaspoons)
- 14.7 ounces all-purpose flour (about 3¼ cups)
- 3 tablespoons canola oil
- ¼ teaspoon salt
- 1½ teaspoons baking powder

1. To prepare filling, rub five-spice powder evenly over pork. Heat a grill pan over medium-high heat. Coat pan with cooking spray. Add pork to pan; cook 14 minutes or until a thermometer registers 145°, turning pork occasionally. Remove pork from pan; let stand 15 minutes.

2. Cut pork crosswise into thin slices; cut slices into thin strips. Place pork in a medium bowl. Add onions and next 7 ingredients; stir well to combine. Cover; refrigerate.

3. To prepare dough, combine 1 cup warm water, sugar, and yeast in a large bowl; let stand 5 minutes.

4. Weigh or lightly spoon flour into dry measuring cups; level with a knife. Add flour, oil, and ¼ teaspoon salt to yeast mixture; stir until a soft dough forms. Turn dough out onto a lightly floured surface. Knead until smooth and elastic (about 10 minutes). Place dough in a large bowl coated with cooking spray, turning to coat top. Cover and let rise in a warm place (85°), free from drafts, 1 hour or until doubled in size. (Gently press two fingers into dough. If indentation remains, dough has risen enough.)

5. Punch dough down; let rest 5 minutes. Turn dough out onto a clean surface; knead in baking powder. Let dough rest 5 minutes.

6. Divide dough into 10 equal portions, forming each into a ball. Working with 1 dough ball at a time (cover remaining dough balls to keep from drying), roll ball into a 5-inch circle. Place ¼ cup filling in center of dough circle. Bring up sides to cover filling and meet on top. Pinch and seal closed with a twist (see photo above). Repeat procedure with remaining dough balls and filling.

7. Arrange 5 buns, seam sides down, 1 inch apart, in each tier of a 2-tiered bamboo steamer. Stack tiers; cover with steamer lid.

8. Add water to a skillet to a depth of 1 inch; bring to a boil over medium-high heat. Place steamer in pan; steam 15 minutes or until puffed and set. Cool 10 minutes before serving. **Yield: 10 servings (serving size: 1 bun).**

CALORIES 259; FAT 6.1g (sat 0.9g, mono 3.2g, poly 1.5g); PROTEIN 14.3g; CARB 35.7g; FIBER 1.6g; CHOL 27mg; IRON 2.9mg; SODIUM 343mg; CALC 54mg

See page 246 for another way to prepare dumplings.

Steamed Vegetarian Dumplings

Dumplings have a prominent place in Chinese cuisine and are prepared in many different ways for holidays and festivals. They vary by region, and the ingredients depend on area availability.

½ pound firm tofu, drained and cut into ½-inch slices
½ cup dried wood ear mushrooms (about ½ ounce)
½ cup drained, sliced water chestnuts
¾ cup shredded carrot
1 tablespoon minced peeled fresh ginger
1 tablespoon minced green onions
1 teaspoon salt
2 teaspoons low-sodium soy sauce
½ teaspoon dark sesame oil
1 large egg, lightly beaten
4 teaspoons cornstarch
50 wonton wrappers or gyoza skins
1 teaspoon cornstarch
Cooking spray
½ cup low-sodium soy sauce
¼ cup water

1. Place tofu on several layers of paper towels; cover with additional paper towels. Let stand 30 minutes, pressing down occasionally. Place tofu in a large bowl, and mash with a fork until smooth. Set tofu aside.
2. Place mushrooms in a bowl; cover with boiling water. Let stand, covered, 20 minutes or until soft. Drain. Place mushrooms and water chestnuts in a food processor; pulse 5 times or until minced. Add mushroom mixture, carrot, and next 7 ingredients to tofu; stir well.
3. Working with 1 wonton wrapper at a time (cover remaining wrappers with a damp paper towel to prevent drying), spoon 1 teaspoon tofu mixture into center of each wrapper. Moisten edges of wrapper with water; bring 2 opposite corners to center, pinching points to seal. Bring remaining 2 corners to center, pinching edges together to seal. Place dumpling, seam sides up, on a large baking sheet sprinkled with 1 teaspoon cornstarch; cover loosely with a damp towel to prevent drying. Repeat procedure with remaining wrappers and tofu mixture.
4. Arrange one-third of dumplings in a single layer in a steamer coated with cooking spray. Steam, covered, 15 minutes. Remove from steamer; set aside, and keep warm. Repeat procedure with remaining dumplings.
5. Combine ½ cup soy sauce and ¼ cup water in a small bowl. Serve with dumplings. **Yield: 50 appetizers (serving size: 1 dumpling and about ¾ teaspoon sauce).**

CALORIES 35; FAT 0.6g (sat 0.1g, mono 0.1g, poly 0.2g); PROTEIN 1.5g; CARB 5.8g; FIBER 0.2g; CHOL 5mg; IRON 0.6mg; SODIUM 179mg; CALC 10mg

1

make steamed vegetarian dumplings

2

3

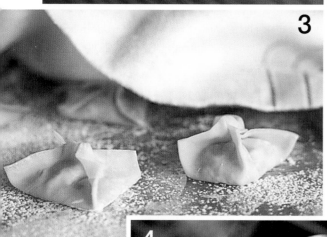

Cook dumplings soon after they're formed, and eat soon after they're cooked. Little pockets of steam trapped inside make them tender. Once the steam dissipates, the dumplings toughen and become dense.

1. Working with 1 wonton wrapper at a time, spoon 1 teaspoon tofu mixture into center of each wrapper (keep remaining wrappers covered to prevent drying).
2. Moisten edges of wrapper with water, and bring 2 opposite corners to center, pinching points to seal. Bring other 2 corners to center, pinching points together.
3. Place dumplings on a large baking sheet sprinkled with cornstarch; cover loosely with a towel to keep them from drying.
4. Arrange one-third of dumplings in single layer in a vegetable steamer coated with cooking spray. Steam dumplings, covered, for 15 minutes.

4

Shrimp and Mushroom Sui Mei

Round gyoza skins work best here. If you can't find them, cut square wonton wrappers into circles using a 3-inch biscuit cutter. To vary the texture and taste, top each dumpling with lump crabmeat or a small piece of scallop instead of shrimp, and dot with hoisin sauce instead of hot sauce.

Cooking spray
3½ cups thinly sliced cremini mushrooms (about 6 ounces)
1¾ cups thinly sliced shiitake mushroom caps (about 4 ounces)
1 cup thinly sliced green onions
2 tablespoons low-sodium soy sauce
1 tablespoon dry sherry
2½ teaspoons minced peeled ginger
2 teaspoons dark sesame oil
4 ounces peeled and deveined medium shrimp
24 gyoza skins (round wonton wrappers)
6 peeled and deveined medium shrimp, each cut crosswise into 4 pieces
4 large napa (Chinese) cabbage leaves
1 tablespoon sambal oelek (ground fresh chile paste) or Sriracha (hot chile sauce)

1. Heat a large nonstick skillet over medium-high heat. Coat pan with cooking spray. Add mushrooms to pan; sauté 8 minutes or until liquid evaporates. Spoon mushrooms into a food processor. Add onions and next 5 ingredients; process 10 seconds or until finely chopped.
2. Working with 1 gyoza skin at a time (cover remaining skins with a damp towel to prevent drying), spoon about 1 tablespoon shrimp mixture into center of each skin. Moisten edges of skin with water. Gather up and crimp edges of skin around filling (see photo at right); lightly squeeze skin to adhere to filling, leaving top of dumpling open. Place 1 shrimp piece on top of filling, pressing gently into filling. Place dumpling on a baking sheet; cover loosely with a damp towel to prevent drying. Repeat procedure with remaining skins, filling, and shrimp pieces.
3. Line each tier of a 2-tiered bamboo steamer with 2 cabbage leaves. Arrange 12 dumplings, 1 inch apart, over cabbage in each steamer basket. Stack tiers, and cover with steamer lid.
4. Add water to skillet to a depth of 1 inch, and bring to a boil. Place steamer in pan, and steam dumplings 15 minutes or until done. Remove dumplings from steamer, and spoon ⅛ teaspoon sambal oelek onto each dumpling. Discard cabbage. **Yield: 8 servings (serving size: 3 dumplings).**

CALORIES 120; FAT 1.9g (sat 0.3g, mono 0.6g, poly 0.8g); PROTEIN 7.2g; CARB 17.6g; FIBER 1.3g; CHOL 31mg; IRON 1.8mg; SODIUM 357mg; CALC 36mg

sui mei (shoe-MY)

These open-faced dumplings are a staple of Hong Kong dim sum. Lining the bamboo steamer with cabbage leaves ensures the dumplings won't stick.

fish & shellfish

Salmon en Papillote with Dill-Yogurt Sauce

Dill-Yogurt Sauce:
- ½ cup grated seeded peeled cucumber
- ¾ cup plain low-fat yogurt
- 1 tablespoon chopped fresh dill
- 1 teaspoon fresh lemon juice
- ¼ teaspoon minced garlic
- ¼ teaspoon pepper
- ⅛ teaspoon kosher salt

Remaining Ingredients:
- 2 cups thinly sliced fennel bulb (about 1 medium)
- ½ cup thinly sliced leek (about 1 small)
- 2 teaspoons extra-virgin olive oil
- 4 (6-ounce) salmon fillets, skinned
- 1 teaspoon kosher salt
- ½ teaspoon freshly ground black pepper
- ¼ cup dry vermouth
- Fresh lemon slices (optional)

1. To prepare dill-yogurt sauce, place grated cucumber on several layers of paper towels; cover with additional paper towels. Let stand 5 minutes, pressing down occasionally. Combine cucumber, yogurt, and next 3 ingredients in a bowl. Stir in ¼ teaspoon pepper and ⅛ teaspoon salt. Cover and refrigerate 1 hour.

2. Preheat oven to 425°.

3. Cut 4 (15 x 24–inch) pieces of parchment paper. Fold in half crosswise. Draw a large heart half on each piece, with the fold of the paper being the center of the heart. Cut out heart; open. Place ½ cup fennel near fold of each piece of parchment. Top each serving with 2 tablespoons leek and ½ teaspoon oil. Sprinkle salmon evenly with 1 teaspoon salt and ½ teaspoon pepper. Place 1 fillet on each serving. Drizzle 1 tablespoon vermouth over each serving. Starting at the top of the heart, fold edges of parchment, sealing edges with narrow folds. Twist the end tip to secure tightly. Place packets on a baking sheet. Bake at 425° for 15 minutes. Remove from oven; let stand 5 minutes. Place on plates; cut open. Garnish with lemon slices; if desired. Serve immediately with dill-yogurt sauce. **Yield: 4 servings (serving size: 1 packet and about ⅓ cup yogurt sauce).**

CALORIES 358; FAT 16.2g (sat 3.9g, mono 7.5g, poly 3.4g); PROTEIN 39.7g; CARB 9.9g; FIBER 2.2g; CHOL 90mg; IRON 1.4mg; SODIUM 675mg; CALC 144mg

kitchen how-to:
prepare a packet

This steaming method involves baking sealed packets in the oven, a practice known in French as *en papillote*. Fish, meat, poultry, and vegetables are baked in parchment paper or aluminum foil with some liquid, yielding flavorful, tender results.

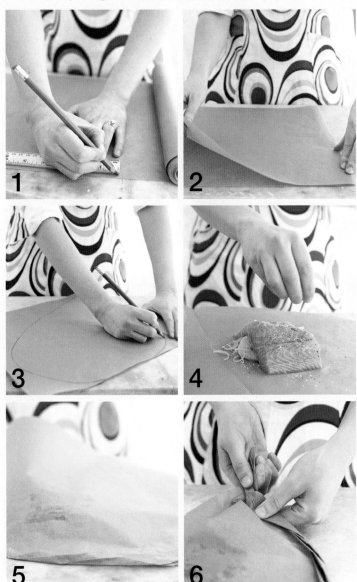

Choose your packet. Parchment paper works with all ingredients. Foil is a good substitute except with acidic foods; the foil can react with acidic ingredients and create off flavors or colors.

Prepare the packets. Aluminum sheets can simply be folded over the ingredients and sealed with a series of narrow folds. For parchment packets, we found the following method creates the tightest seal.

1. Cut 1 (15 x 24–inch) piece of parchment.

2. Fold parchment in half crosswise, making a crease down the center.

3. Draw half of a heart shape on paper. Cut out heart, and open the parchment.

4. Layer ingredients in one half of the sheet, making sure to leave at least a 1-inch border around the edges. Top with the fish, meat, or poultry, and drizzle with remaining liquids or sprinkle with seasonings or fresh herbs. Use hardy vegetables like cabbage and carrots as a bed on the bottom; add more tender ingredients like tomatoes on top to bathe the fish, meat, or poultry with moisture.

5. Starting at the top of heart, fold paper, tightly sealing edges with narrow folds.

6. Twist the end tip of the heart to seal.

Bake. Carefully place packets on an ungreased baking sheet, and bake. Don't cut open the packets to check if food is done. In some instances, we call for a standing time of about 5 minutes before opening the packet to ensure flavors meld while the fish, meat, or poultry finishes cooking in the steam without the risk of overcooking.

Serve. Carefully transfer packets to individual plates, and serve immediately. Use caution because steam will be released when the packets are opened.

Steamed Mussels and Clams with Two Sauces

A large collapsible metal vegetable steamer set inside a Dutch oven works best for this recipe since that setup can accommodate a large volume of shellfish.

Cocktail Sauce:
  ¼ cup bottled chili sauce
  1 tablespoon fresh lemon juice
  1½ teaspoons minced fresh dill
  1½ teaspoons prepared horseradish

Chive Butter:
  2 tablespoons butter, melted
  2 tablespoons minced fresh chives

Shellfish:
  2 cups white wine
  2 tablespoons Old Bay seasoning
  24 littleneck clams
  2 pounds mussels, scrubbed and debearded

1. To prepare cocktail sauce, combine first 4 ingredients in a small bowl.
2. To prepare chive butter, combine butter and chives in a small bowl; cover and keep warm.
3. To prepare shellfish, place wine and Old Bay seasoning in a large Dutch oven; set a large vegetable steamer in pan. Bring wine mixture to a boil over high heat.
4. Add clams to steamer. Steam clams, covered, 8 minutes. Add mussels to steamer. Steam mussels and clams, covered, 8 minutes or until clam and mussel shells open. Discard any unopened shells, and discard wine mixture. Serve shellfish immediately with sauces.
Yield: 6 servings (serving size: about 7 mussels, 4 clams, 2½ teaspoons cocktail sauce, and 1¼ teaspoons chive butter).

CALORIES 196; FAT 6.9g (sat 2.9g, mono 1.6g, poly 1g); PROTEIN 22.5g; CARB 9.6g; FIBER 0.1g; CHOL 65mg; IRON 14.9mg; SODIUM 699mg; CALC 66mg

See page 25 for information about how to scrub and debeard mussels.

Clams
What they add: In addition to providing a low-calorie source of protein, clams are an excellent source of iron, which is part of hemoglobin (the oxygen-carrying component of the blood), and vitamin B_{12}, which is needed for normal nerve cell activity and tissue growth.

Mussels
What they add: Mussels are an excellent source of protein that's low in calories and fat. They're also a good source of folate, a B vitamin needed for cell replication and growth that's particularly crucial for pregnant women.

Steamed Lobster

The two best methods for cooking fresh lobster are steaming and boiling. Steaming cooks lobsters slower than boiling, so it reduces the chance of overcooking.

    4   cups water
    2   tablespoons salt
    4   (1½-pound) live Maine lobsters

1. Bring 4 cups water and salt to a boil in a 5-gallon stockpot. Place a vegetable steamer or rack in bottom of pot. Add lobsters, and steam, covered, 14 minutes or until done. **Yield: 4 servings (serving size: 1 lobster).**

CALORIES 111; FAT 0.7g (sat 0.1g, mono 0.2g, poly 0.1g); PROTEIN 23.2g; CARB 1.5g; FIBER 0g; CHOL 82mg; IRON 0.4mg; SODIUM 504mg; CALC 69mg

See page 255 for information about how to boil lobster.

extract meat from a lobster

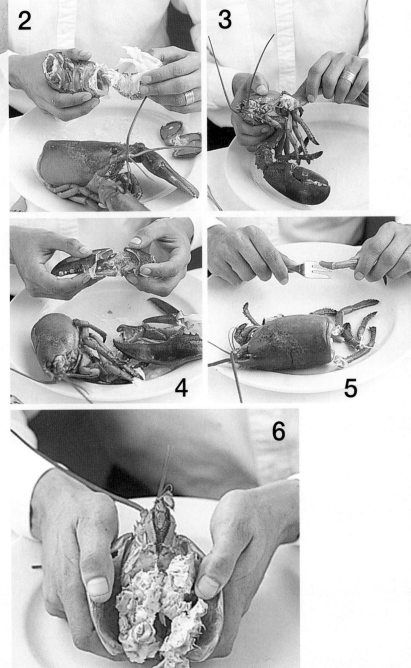

Lobster tastes delicious, but eating it can be messy. If there were a tidy way to do it, restaurants wouldn't supply their customers with a bib, but the succulent meat makes all the effort worthwhile. Although techniques can vary depending on local tradition and personal preference, here's a general guide that will help you get the most out of your next lobster dinner.

1. Separate the tail from the rest of the body by bending the lobster backward.
2. Snap off the flippers, and push the meat out of the shell using a fork at the flipper end of the tail.
3. Twist off the claws, and gently move the pincher from side to side until you feel it snap. Gently pull it away.
4. Gently crack the claws open with a nutcracker to release the meat.
5. Pluck off the legs. If you'd like, use a small fork to break the shell.
6. Crack the body of the lobster open to remove the meat.

way to steam
tamales

Tamales have been around for more than 5,000 years. Centuries ago, the Aztecs prepared these cylinders of ground corn bound with lard, stuffed with savory or sweet filling, rolled in corn husks or banana leaves, and steamed for special occasions. Today, these handmade home-cooked specialties remain holiday fare in Latino communities. Tamales aren't difficult to prepare, and the filling is limited only by your imagination and preference.

Pork and Ancho Chile Tamales with Mexican Red Sauce

The pork mixture can be made a day or two ahead to make assembly time easier. Serve with Spanish saffron-flavored rice.

24 dried corn husks
½ cup fat-free, less-sodium chicken broth
⅓ cup dried cherries
1 ancho chile, stemmed
1 cup chopped onion
2 tablespoons brown sugar
3 tablespoons fresh lime juice
1 teaspoon ground cumin
½ teaspoon salt
5 garlic cloves
1 (1-pound) pork tenderloin
Cooking spray
4½ cups Basic Masa Dough
2 cups hot water
1¼ cups Mexican hot-style tomato sauce
Lime wedges (optional)

1. Place corn husks in a large bowl; cover with water. Weigh husks down with a can; soak 30 minutes. Drain.
2. Combine broth, cherries, and ancho chile in a microwave-safe dish. Microwave at HIGH 2 minutes or until cherries and ancho are tender. Place broth mixture, onion, and next 5 ingredients in a blender; process until smooth. Reserve ½ cup broth mixture; cover and chill. Place remaining broth mixture in a large zip-top plastic bag. Add pork; seal and marinate in refrigerator 1 hour, turning bag occasionally.
3. Preheat oven to 450°.
4. Remove pork from bag; discard marinade. Place pork on a broiler pan coated with cooking spray. Bake at 450° for 25 minutes or until a thermometer registers 145°. Let pork stand 20 minutes; shred with 2 forks. Toss shredded pork with reserved ½ cup broth mixture.
5. Working with 1 husk at a time, place about 3 tablespoons Basic Masa Dough in center of husk, about ½ inch from top of husk; press dough into a 4-inch-long by 3-inch-wide rectangle. Spoon about 1 heaping tablespoon pork mixture down 1 side of dough. Using corn husk as your guide, fold husk over tamale, being sure to cover filling with dough; fold over 1 more time. Fold under bottom end of husk. Place tamale, seam side down, on rack of a broiler pan lined with a damp towel. Repeat procedure with remaining husks, Basic Masa Dough, and filling. Cover filled tamales with another damp towel. Pour 2 cups hot water in bottom of a broiler pan; top with prepared rack.
6. Steam tamales at 450° for 55 minutes, adding hot water as necessary to maintain a depth of about ½ inch. Let tamales stand 10 minutes. Serve with sauce and lime wedges, if desired. **Yield: 12 servings (serving size: 2 tamales and about 5 teaspoons sauce).**

CALORIES 283; FAT 7.6g (sat 2.3g, mono 2.8g, poly 1.8g); PROTEIN 13.3g; CARB 42g; FIBER 5.3g; CHOL 28mg; IRON 3.3mg; SODIUM 720mg; CALC 122mg

Basic Masa Dough

Prepare this dough up to three days ahead, and refrigerate it in an airtight container.

2 cups fat-free, less-sodium chicken broth
2 ancho chiles
1½ cups fresh corn kernels (about 3 ears)
3¾ cups masa harina
1½ teaspoons salt
1½ teaspoons baking powder
¼ cup chilled lard

1. Combine broth and chiles in a microwave-safe bowl. Microwave at HIGH 2 minutes or until chiles are tender; cool slightly. Place broth mixture and corn in a blender; process until smooth.
2. Lightly spoon masa harina into dry measuring cups; level with a knife. Combine masa harina, salt, and baking powder, stirring well with a whisk. Cut in lard with a pastry blender or 2 knives until mixture resembles coarse meal. Add broth mixture to masa mixture; stir until a soft dough forms. Cover and chill until ready to use. **Yield: 26 servings (serving size: about 3 tablespoons).**

CALORIES 97; FAT 3g (sat 0.9g, mono 1.1g, poly 0.8g); PROTEIN 2.2g; CARB 16.2g; FIBER 2.1g; CHOL 2mg; IRON 0.8mg; SODIUM 233mg; CALC 51mg

kitchen how-to:
make tamales

Traditionally, tamales are cooked in a *tamalera,* a metal pot with a steamer tray that can cook up to 6 dozen tamales. We found that you can achieve similar results with an oven method that doesn't require special equipment. Place up to 2 dozen tamales on a broiler rack lined with a damp towel, cover tamales with another damp towel, and place rack in a broiler pan filled with hot water to a depth of about ½ inch. (Use old towels if possible because they may discolor.)

1. Weigh corn husks down; cover with water. Soak them at least 30 minutes.
2. Shape about 3 tablespoons Basic Masa Dough into a rectangle, and spoon filling on top.
3. Fold corn husk over, covering filling with dough.
4. Fold husk over again.
5. Fold bottom end of husk up and over tamale.
6. Place tamales, seam sides down, on the rack of a broiler pan lined with a damp towel; cover.

Tamales are an ideal make-ahead treat. Cool cooked tamales to room temperature, and freeze in zip-top plastic freezer bags for up to two months. To reheat, wrap the frozen tamales in a damp towel, and microwave at HIGH for 2 minutes.

tamale ingredients

Look for specific ingredients at local supermarkets and Latin markets.

Masa harina: This flour is made from sun-dried corn kernels cooked in limewater, and then ground.

Lard: You'll find lard, made from rendered pork fat, in refrigerated cases or the frozen foods section of some specialty markets. Our recipe for Basic Masa Dough (page 121) uses just a touch of lard to bind and flavor the dough. If you can't find lard, you can use an equal amount of vegetable shortening.

Dried corn husks: Used to wrap tamales and keep them moist while cooking, corn husks are not eaten. Other traditional wrappers include banana and plantain leaves.

way to steam
vegetables

Steaming helps vegetables retain their water-soluble vitamins. Unlike boiling, which surrounds food with water causing the nutrients to leach out, more nutrients remain inside steamed vegetables because little water is used and there is minimal contact between the food and water.

Chive Green Beans

Leave green beans whole for a restaurant-caliber look. Or try this recipe with other vegetables, such as fresh carrots or asparagus.

1 pound fresh green beans, trimmed
1 tablespoon chopped fresh chives
1 tablespoon chopped fresh parsley
2 teaspoons butter
½ teaspoon stone-ground mustard
¼ teaspoon salt
⅛ teaspoon pepper

1. Steam green beans, covered, 5 minutes or until crisp-tender. Remove from steamer, and toss with remaining ingredients. **Yield: 4 servings (serving size: ¾ cup).**

CALORIES 53; FAT 1.9g (sat 1.2g, mono 0.6g, poly 0.1g); PROTEIN 1.5g; CARB 7.1g; FIBER 4.2g; CHOL 5mg; IRON 0.6mg; SODIUM 175mg; CALC 58mg

Steamed Carrots with Garlic-Ginger Butter

1 pound baby carrots with tops, peeled
1 tablespoon butter
2 garlic cloves, minced
1 teaspoon minced peeled fresh ginger
1 tablespoon chopped fresh cilantro
½ teaspoon grated lime rind
1 tablespoon fresh lime juice
¼ teaspoon salt

1. Steam carrots, covered, 10 minutes or until tender.
2. Heat butter in a large nonstick skillet over medium heat. Add garlic and ginger to pan; cook 1 minute, stirring constantly. Remove from heat; stir in carrots, cilantro, and remaining ingredients. **Yield: 4 servings.**

CALORIES 69; FAT 3g (sat 1.8g, mono 0.8g, poly 0.2g); PROTEIN 0.9g; CARB 10.3g; FIBER 3.4g; CHOL 8mg; IRON 1.1mg; SODIUM 257mg; CALC 41mg

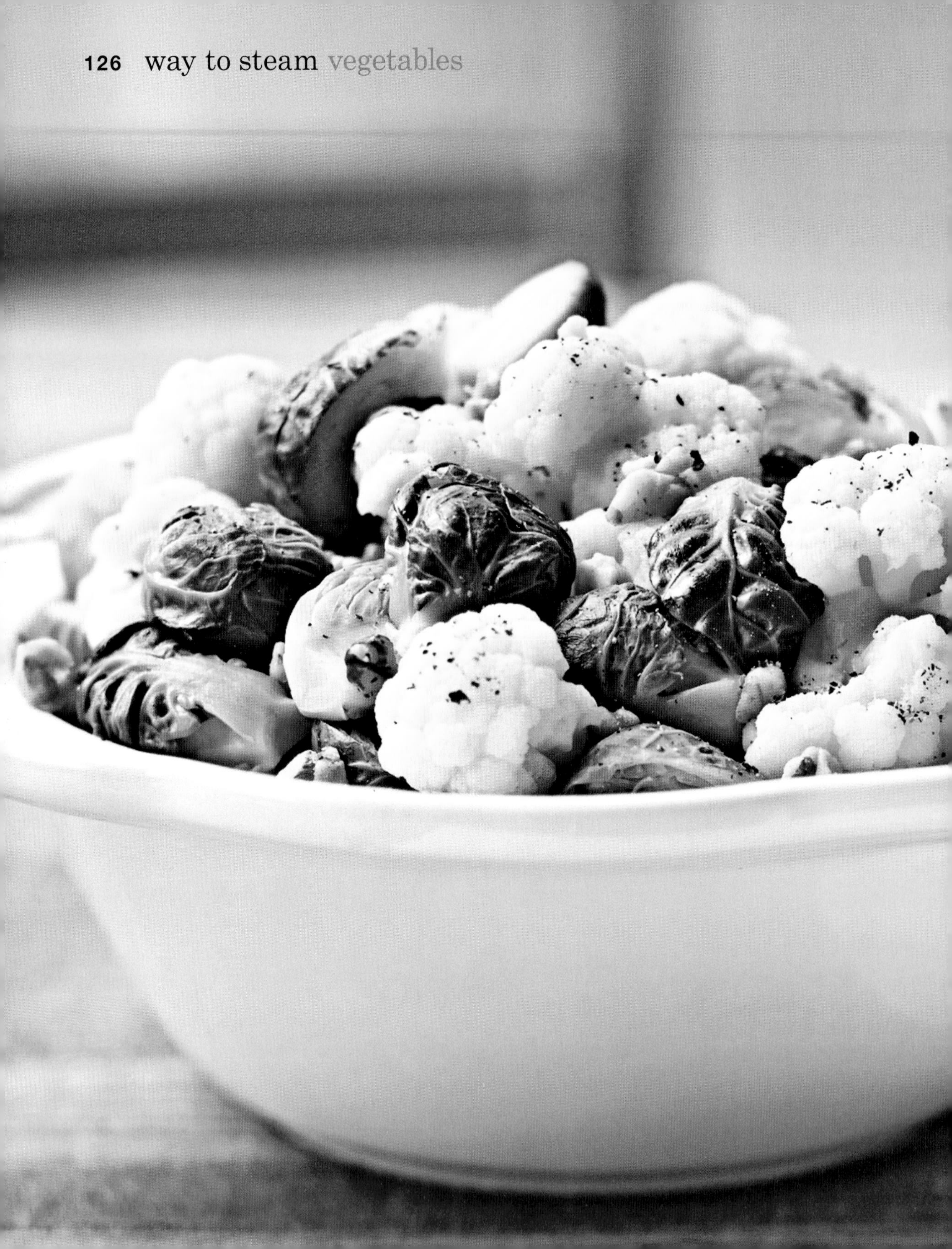

Steamed Brussels Sprouts and Cauliflower with Walnuts

This quick and versatile side dish is good with roasts or chicken. A serving boasts nearly one-fourth of daily fiber needs, while the walnuts add a dose of heart-healthy unsaturated fat.

6 tablespoons coarsely chopped walnuts
2¼ cups trimmed Brussels sprouts (about 1 pound), halved
3 cups cauliflower florets
½ teaspoon kosher salt
¼ teaspoon freshly ground black pepper
½ teaspoon fresh lemon juice

1. Place walnuts in a small skillet over medium heat; cook 3 minutes or until walnuts are lightly browned, shaking pan frequently. Remove from heat.
2. Steam Brussels sprouts, covered, 10 minutes or until tender. Add cauliflower to pan; steam, covered, 2 minutes or just until tender. Drain. Combine Brussels sprouts, cauliflower, salt, pepper, and juice in a medium bowl; toss to combine. Sprinkle evenly with walnuts.
Yield: 6 servings (serving size: about ¾ cup).

CALORIES 104; FAT 3.5g (sat 0.4g, mono 0.5g, poly 2.5g); PROTEIN 6.4g; CARB 15.2g; FIBER 6.3g; CHOL 0mg; IRON 1.8mg; SODIUM 222mg; CALC 68mg

kitchen how-to:
trim Brussels sprouts

Thoroughly wash Brussels sprouts before trimming. Pull off any limp outer leaves, and closely trim the stem end—don't cut too much off or the Brussels sprouts may fall apart.

way to
sauté

Sautéing is a method of cooking food quickly in a small amount of fat over relatively high heat. It's a great technique for tender vegetables and cuts of meat, such as mushrooms, bell peppers, onions, chicken breasts, and beef tenderloin, that will cook rapidly. Food browns as it sautés, adding another level of flavor to its exterior.

Sautéed dishes come together quickly since the ingredients are comparatively tender to begin with, making this cooking method a perfect choice for weeknight cooking when time can be in short supply. And because you use little fat—usually just enough to coat the pan and prevent food from sticking—it's also a healthful way to cook.

sautéing, defined

To sauté is to cook food quickly in a minimal amount of fat over relatively high heat. The word comes from the French verb *sauter,* which means "to jump," and it describes not only how food reacts when placed in a hot pan but also the method of tossing the food in the pan. The term also refers to cooking tender cuts of meat (such as chicken breasts or filet mignon) in a small amount of fat over moderately high heat without frequent stirring—just flip it over when one side is browned.

What Sautéing Does

The browning achieved by sautéing lends richness to meats and produce. And because the food is cooked quickly, the integrity of the flavor and texture remains intact; asparagus, for example, retains its slightly grassy punch, as well as a pleasing crisp-tender bite.

Equipment

Use either a skillet (a wide pan with sloped sides) or sauté pan (a wide pan with straight sides). Both have a large surface area so food is less likely to become overcrowded. Choose a pan with a dense bottom that evenly distributes heat. Nonstick, anodized aluminum, and stainless steel options work well.

Size Matters

Cutting food to a uniform thickness and size ensures that it will cook evenly. Vegetables should be no larger than bite-sized, and meat no larger than portion-sized. Meat that is too thick or vegetables that are too large run the risk of burning or forming a tough, overly browned outer crust in the time that it takes to completely cook them. Prep the ingredients before you heat the pan.

Best Bets for Sautéing

Whether it's meat or vegetables, time in the pan is brief so it's important that the food be naturally tender. Cuts such as beef tenderloin, fish fillets, and chicken breasts are good candidates; tougher cuts such as brisket or pork shoulder are better for long cooking over low heat. The same principle holds for produce—asparagus tips will be more successfully sautéed than beets. Many other tender vegetables, including baby artichokes, sugar snap peas, mushrooms, and bell peppers, also lend themselves to this technique. That's not to say that denser, tougher vegetables can't be sautéed—they just may need to be blanched (briefly cooked in boiling water) first to get a head start on cooking.

Heat the Pan

Be sure to warm the pan over medium-high heat for a few minutes. It needs to be quite hot in order to cook the food properly. If the heat is too low, the food will release liquid and steam rather than sauté.

Add Fat

Fats such as butter, oil, or bacon fat coat the food and prevent it from sticking to the pan, aid in browning, and add flavor. Once the pan is hot, add the fat, and swirl to coat the bottom of the pan. (Heating the fat with the pan may cause food to stick.) Heat the fat for 10 to 30 seconds—until oil shimmers or the foam on butter subsides—and then add the food.

In general, use fats that have a high smoke point—peanut oil, regular olive oil, canola oil, or rendered pork fat. Once the fat begins to smoke, the flavor changes and can affect the taste of the food. Butter adds great flavor, but it can burn, so you will either need to clarify it to remove the milk solids, which are prone to burning (see page 14 for information about how to clarify butter), or combine it with oil so there's less chance of burning. Oils that have low smoke points, including extra-virgin olive oil and many nut and infused oils, lose their characteristic taste when heated to the high temperatures reached in sautéing. It's fine to sauté with these oils—just remember that their flavor will not be as pungent. See page 10 for more information about oils.

Don't Overcrowd

It's crucial that only one layer of food cooks in the pan at a time. When sautéing cuts of meat, leave at least a half-inch between each piece (see photo A). Food releases steam when cooking. If that steam doesn't have enough room to escape, it stays in the pan, and the food won't brown because it ends up steaming rather than sautéing. If you've ever tried to sauté a large amount of cubed beef for a stew, you may have experienced this problem (see photo B). Simply sauté the food in smaller batches.

Toss and Turn

When sautéing tender vegetables and bite-sized pieces of meat, stir frequently (but not constantly) to promote even browning and cooking. Dense vegetables such as cubed potatoes, though, should be stirred once every few minutes so they don't fall apart as they become tender. Portion-sized cuts of meat (chicken breasts, steaks, or pork medaillons, for example) should only be turned once so they have enough time to form a nice crust, which will also keep the meat from sticking to the pan (see photo C).

Stir-fry vs. Sauté

Stir-frying and sautéing share some similarities. Both methods cook food quickly in a small amount of fat. But stir-frying cooks food over intensely high heat, stirring constantly. Sautéing involves only moderately high heat, and the food is not in continuous motion.

the bottom line

The three most important elements to remember about sautéing:

1. Heat the pan (then the fat) adequately before adding the food.

2. Don't overcrowd the pan.

3. Stir frequently but not constantly.

fish & shellfish

Sautéed Tuna and Green Onion Stalks on Romaine

Carrot contributes the antioxidant beta-carotene, while bok choy, a unique and hearty choice for a salad, is rich in potential cancer-fighting indoles. And tuna is a good source of heart-healthy omega-3 fats.

- 1   large carrot
- 1   tablespoon rice vinegar
- 1   tablespoon fresh orange juice
- 1   teaspoon salt, divided
- ½   teaspoon chili garlic sauce (such as Lee Kum Kee)
- ½   teaspoon Dijon mustard
- 1   tablespoon dark sesame oil, divided
- 1   tablespoon canola oil, divided
- 4   (6-ounce) yellowfin tuna steaks
- ¼   teaspoon freshly ground black pepper
- 16 green onions, cut into 5-inch pieces (about 2 bunches)
- 4   cups torn romaine lettuce
- 2   cups shredded bok choy
- 2   cups grape tomatoes, halved
- 1   tablespoon toasted sesame seeds

1. Cut carrot lengthwise into ribbons using a vegetable peeler. Curl ribbons around fingers, and place carrot curls in a bowl of ice water.
2. Combine vinegar, juice, ¾ teaspoon salt, chili garlic sauce, and mustard. Add 1½ teaspoons sesame oil and 1½ teaspoons canola oil, stirring with a whisk.
3. Heat a large nonstick skillet over medium-high heat. Add 1 teaspoon sesame oil and 1 teaspoon canola oil to pan, swirling to coat. Sprinkle fish evenly with remaining ¼ teaspoon salt and pepper. Add fish to pan; cook 5 minutes on each side or until desired degree of doneness. Remove fish from pan.
4. Add remaining ½ teaspoon sesame oil and remaining ½ teaspoon canola oil to pan, swirling to coat. Add onions to pan; sauté 5 minutes or until lightly browned, turning occasionally.
5. Combine lettuce, bok choy, and tomatoes in a large bowl. Drain carrot curls; add carrot curls to lettuce mixture. Drizzle vinegar mixture over lettuce mixture; toss gently to coat. Arrange 1½ cups lettuce mixture on each of 4 plates. Cut each tuna steak into thin slices. Arrange 1 tuna steak and 4 onions on top of each serving; sprinkle each serving with ¾ teaspoon sesame seeds. **Yield: 4 servings.**

CALORIES 314; FAT 10.1g (sat 1.4g, mono 4.2g, poly 3.6g); PROTEIN 43.3g; CARB 12.9g; FIBER 4.9g; CHOL 77mg; IRON 3.4mg; SODIUM 731mg; CALC 143mg

kitchen how-to:
sauté fish

Typically, you'll turn portion-sized cuts of fish in the pan only once. If they're cooked until done, the process is still referred to as sautéing. Heat a large nonstick skillet over medium-high heat. Add oil, swirling to coat. Add fish to pan; cook 5 minutes on each side or until desired degree of doneness.

all about bok choy

Cultivated in China for centuries, bok choy is used raw or cooked in a variety of dishes from soups and stir-fries to salads and main dishes. While bok choy is a member of the cabbage family, it bears little resemblance to the round cabbages found in supermarkets. It has thick white stalks with rounded dark green leaves and a mild, sweet flavor and crisp texture. Small heads, known as baby bok choy, are more tender than the larger ones. When purchasing, select heads with firm stalks that are pure white and dark green leaves that aren't wilted. Avoid bok choy with brown spots on the leaves.

Asparagus
What it adds: Asparagus is a good source of vitamin C and also contains flavonoids and the compound rutin, all of which help strengthen capillary walls. It also contains fiber, which helps decrease risk for heart disease.

Shrimp
What they add: Shrimp are a wonderfully nutritious alternative to meat proteins. They are high in protein and low in calories and saturated fat. Shrimp are also a good source of vitamin B12, a nutrient that can help protect against heart disease.

Sautéed Asparagus and Shrimp with Gremolata

Sauté the two main ingredients separately to avoid overcrowding the pan. A fresh lemon-herb topping rounds out the flavors of this entrée. You could also try this recipe with chicken and broccoli.

Gremolata:
- ¼ cup finely chopped fresh flat-leaf parsley
- 2 teaspoons grated lemon rind
- ⅛ teaspoon salt
- ⅛ teaspoon freshly ground black pepper
- 3 garlic cloves, minced

Shrimp:
- 4 teaspoons olive oil, divided
- 3 cups (1½-inch) slices asparagus (about ½ pound)
- 1½ pounds peeled and deveined medium shrimp
- ⅛ teaspoon salt
- ⅛ teaspoon freshly ground black pepper

1. To prepare gremolata, combine first 5 ingredients; set aside.
2. To prepare shrimp, heat a large nonstick skillet over medium-high heat. Add 2 teaspoons oil to pan, swirling to coat; heat 20 seconds. Add asparagus to pan; sauté 3 minutes, stirring frequently. Remove asparagus from pan; keep warm.
3. Add remaining 2 teaspoons oil to pan, swirling to coat; heat 20 seconds. Add shrimp to pan; sauté 3 minutes or until done, stirring occasionally. Add asparagus, ⅛ teaspoon salt, and ⅛ teaspoon pepper to pan; sauté 1 minute or until thoroughly heated. Sprinkle evenly with gremolata. **Yield: 4 servings (serving size: 1½ cups).**

CALORIES 240; FAT 7.6g (sat 1.2g, mono 3.7g, poly 1.7g); PROTEIN 36.1g; CARB 5.2g; FIBER 1.6g; CHOL 259mg; IRON 5.6mg; SODIUM 403mg; CALC 115mg

kitchen how-to:
prepare asparagus

Asparagus is at its peak from April through late June. Look for stalks with smooth skin and uniform color. All asparagus should have a dry, compact tip. Fibrous stems and shriveled stalks are signs of age. To prepare the asparagus, trim the fibrous ends from all the spears. You can cook the asparagus as is or peel the spears using a vegetable peeler to make the stalks more tender.

way to sauté
tofu

Tofu is packaged in water to keep it fresh. But you need to press some of the moisture out in order to create a crisp, browned exterior when sautéing.

Thai Noodle Salad with Sautéed Tofu

Tofu:
- ¾ pound firm water-packed tofu, drained
- 2 tablespoons fresh lime juice
- 1 tablespoon low-sodium soy sauce
- 1 tablespoon chili garlic sauce (such as Lee Kum Kee)
- 1 teaspoon sugar
- 2 teaspoons grated peeled fresh ginger
- ½ teaspoon crushed red pepper
- 2 garlic cloves, minced
- 1 tablespoon peanut oil

Noodles:
- ¾ pound uncooked rice vermicelli

Dressing:
- ¼ cup fresh lime juice
- 3 tablespoons chili garlic sauce (such as Lee Kum Kee)
- 2 tablespoons low-sodium soy sauce
- 2 tablespoons peanut oil
- 1 tablespoon Thai fish sauce (such as Three Crabs)
- 2 teaspoons sugar
- 2 teaspoons grated peeled fresh ginger
- ¼ teaspoon salt
- ¼ teaspoon crushed red pepper

Remaining Ingredients:
- 2 cups thinly sliced romaine lettuce
- 1 cup shredded carrot
- ½ cup chopped fresh cilantro
- ¼ teaspoon salt

1. To prepare tofu, cut tofu into ¾-inch-thick slices. Arrange tofu slices in a single layer on several layers of paper towels. Top with several more layers of paper towels; top with a cast-iron skillet or other heavy pan. Let stand 30 minutes. Remove tofu from paper towels; cut into ¾-inch cubes. Combine tofu, 2 tablespoons juice, and next 6 ingredients in a zip-top plastic bag. Seal; marinate at room temperature 2 hours, turning bag occasionally.

2. Heat a large nonstick skillet over medium-high heat. Add 1 table-spoon oil to pan, swirling to coat; heat 30 seconds. Remove tofu from bag; discard marinade. Add tofu to pan; sauté 5 minutes or until crisp, carefully turning to brown all sides. Remove from heat.

3. To prepare noodles, while tofu marinates, place vermicelli in a large bowl. Cover with boiling water. Let stand 20 minutes or until tender. Drain and rinse under cold water; drain well. Set noodles aside.

4. To prepare dressing, combine ¼ cup juice and next 8 ingredients, stirring with a whisk.

5. Combine vermicelli, lettuce, and remaining ingredients in a large bowl. Add dressing; toss well to combine. Top with tofu. **Yield: 6 servings (serving size: about 2 cups).**

CALORIES 336; FAT 9.8g (sat 1.5g, mono 5g, poly 2.8g); PROTEIN 10.3g; CARB 57.2g; FIBER 2.4g; CHOL 0mg; IRON 2.5mg; SODIUM 794mg; CALC 132mg

kitchen how-to:
press tofu

Tofu is the Japanese word for soybean curd. It's made from soymilk (similar to the way Cheddar cheese is made from cow's milk) and then shaped into spongelike blocks. Tofu comes in five varieties—silken, soft, medium, firm, and extra-firm— and most tofu is packaged in water to keep the product fresh. It's best to remove some of that water from the medium to extra-firm varieties before sautéing or stir-frying so the tofu will brown more easily and won't release excess water into the pan. Before marinating and cooking, follow these tips for pressing.

1. Remove tofu from the package, and cut it into slices for easier draining.
2. Lay each slice flat on a few absorbent heavy-duty paper towels.
3. Top with another layer of paper towels; place a heavy pan on top.
4. Let stand for 30 minutes, pressing occasionally to release excess water.

way to sauté
meats

When sautéing portion-sized cuts of meat, turn them only once so they have enough time to form a nice browned crust. Heat a large nonstick skillet over medium-high heat. Coat the pan with cooking spray. Add the steaks, and sauté for 3 minutes on each side until desired degree of doneness.

Beef Tenderloin Steaks with Shiitake Mushroom Sauce

The steaks sauté in cooking spray to create a crust, while the mushrooms sauté in butter for flavor. Since the mushrooms release liquid as they cook, the butter is less likely to burn. Shiitake mushrooms create a sublime sauce with deep, earthy flavor, but you can substitute any other mushroom variety. Serve with mashed potatoes and Broccolini.

    4   (4-ounce) beef tenderloin steaks, trimmed
        (1 inch thick)
    ½   teaspoon salt, divided
    ¼   teaspoon freshly ground black pepper, divided
    Cooking spray
    2   teaspoons butter
    2   garlic cloves, minced
    4   cups thinly sliced shiitake mushroom caps
        (about 8 ounces)
    ½   teaspoon chopped fresh thyme
    2   tablespoons balsamic vinegar
    1   tablespoon water
    1   teaspoon low-sodium soy sauce
    1   tablespoon fresh thyme leaves

1. Sprinkle steaks with ¼ teaspoon salt and ⅛ teaspoon pepper. Heat a large nonstick skillet over medium-high heat. Coat pan with cooking spray. Add steaks to pan; sauté 3 minutes on each side or until desired degree of doneness. Transfer steaks to a serving platter.

2. Heat pan over medium-high heat. Add butter to pan, swirling to coat; cook 15 seconds or until foam subsides. Add garlic to pan; sauté 30 seconds, stirring constantly. Add mushrooms, ½ teaspoon chopped thyme, remaining ¼ teaspoon salt, and remaining ⅛ teaspoon pepper to pan; sauté 3 minutes or until mushrooms are tender, stirring frequently. Stir in vinegar, 1 tablespoon water, and soy sauce; cook 1 minute or until liquid almost evaporates. Spoon mushroom mixture over steaks. Sprinkle with thyme leaves. **Yield: 4 servings (serving size: 1 steak, ¼ cup mushroom mixture, and ¾ teaspoon thyme leaves).**

CALORIES 326; FAT 11.2g (sat 4.7g, mono 4.2g, poly 0.5g); PROTEIN 34.9g; CARB 22.9g; FIBER 3.2g; CHOL 95mg; IRON 2.9mg; SODIUM 428mg; CALC 34mg

Lamb with Dates, Apricots, and Saffron over Couscous

Middle Eastern–style stews, like this recipe, often combine meat, spices, and fruit. When sautéing the lamb, make sure you leave at least a half-inch between each piece so there's room for steam to escape. Otherwise, the meat won't brown.

- 1 teaspoon olive oil
- 1 (1-pound) boneless leg of lamb, trimmed and cubed
- ½ teaspoon salt, divided
- ¼ teaspoon freshly ground black pepper, divided
- 1 cup chopped onion
- ¼ cup fresh orange juice (about 1 large orange)
- 6 garlic cloves, minced
- ½ teaspoon ground cumin
- ½ teaspoon ground coriander
- ¼ teaspoon saffron threads, crushed
- 1½ cups fat-free, less-sodium beef broth
- 1½ cups (¼-inch-thick) slices carrot
- ½ cup dried apricots, cut into ¼-inch-thick strips
- ½ cup halved pitted dates
- 2 tablespoons chopped fresh mint
- 2 cups hot cooked couscous

1. Heat a medium saucepan over medium-high heat. Add oil, swirling to coat. Add lamb, ¼ teaspoon salt, and ⅛ teaspoon pepper to pan; sauté 8 minutes or until browned. Remove from pan.
2. Add onion, juice, and garlic to pan; cook until liquid evaporates, scraping pan to loosen browned bits. Stir in cumin, coriander, and saffron; cook 15 seconds. Return lamb to pan. Stir in broth; bring to a boil.
Cover, reduce heat, and simmer 30 minutes. Stir in carrot, apricots, and dates. Cover and cook 18 minutes or until carrot is tender. Remove from heat; stir in remaining ¼ teaspoon salt, remaining ⅛ teaspoon pepper, and mint. Serve over couscous.
Yield: 4 servings (serving size: 1 cup lamb mixture and ½ cup couscous).

CALORIES 416; FAT 7.5g (sat 2.6g, mono 3.4g, poly 0.5g); PROTEIN 29.4g; CARB 57.7g; FIBER 5.5g; CHOL 73mg; IRON 3.6mg; SODIUM 584mg; CALC 70mg

all about saffron

Saffron enchants with its luminous red-orange color, delicate bittersweet flavor, and honeylike fragrance. Saffron threads are the bright red stigma of a crocus plant, *Crocus sativus,* grown primarily in Iran, Spain, and India. One crocus flower has three stigmas, and it takes 13,000 stigmas—about 4,330 flowers—to produce one ounce of saffron. The threads are gathered by hand and dried over a low fire. This labor-intensive process makes saffron the world's most expensive spice— high-quality, 100 percent pure red saffron threads cost about $12 for approximately two teaspoons. It's a delicious investment, and most recipes require a half-teaspoon or less.

Sriracha

What it adds: Named after a seaside town in Thailand, Sriracha is a hot chile sauce that includes red Thai chiles, sugar, vinegar, salt, and garlic. The flavor is a combination of sweet and sour and hot and spicy. It's enjoyed as a table condiment in Thai and Vietnamese restaurants, but it's also great with non-Asian dishes. It can be used in place of ketchup on almost anything—French fries, omelets or scrambled eggs, pizza, hot dogs, and hamburgers.

Garlic Pork with Tomato and Basil

Serve with fiery chile sauce on the side.

12 ounces pork tenderloin, thinly sliced
 2 teaspoons cornstarch, divided
 ¼ teaspoon salt
 ⅛ teaspoon freshly ground white pepper
 3 tablespoons cold water
 2 tablespoons oyster sauce
 1 teaspoon sugar
 1 teaspoon Sriracha (hot chile sauce, such as Huy Fong)
 2 teaspoons peanut oil
 2 teaspoons minced fresh garlic
 2 cups chopped seeded plum tomatoes (about 3 tomatoes)
 ¾ cup chopped fresh basil
 2 green onions, cut into 1-inch pieces (about ¼ cup)
 2 cups hot cooked brown rice

1. Combine pork, 1 teaspoon cornstarch, salt, and pepper in a small bowl, tossing to coat.
2. Combine water, oyster sauce, sugar, Sriracha, and remaining 1 teaspoon cornstarch in a small bowl.
3. Heat a large nonstick skillet over medium-high heat. Add oil, swirling to coat. Add minced garlic and pork mixture; sauté 3 minutes or until pork is done. Add chopped tomatoes; sauté 1 minute. Add cornstarch mixture; cook 1 minute or until thickened. Add basil; stir to combine. Remove from heat, and sprinkle with onions. Serve with brown rice. **Yield: 4 servings (serving size: 1 cup pork mixture and ½ cup rice).**

CALORIES 257; FAT 6.2g (sat 1.6g, mono 2.7g, poly 1.4g); PROTEIN 21.2g; CARB 28.5g; FIBER 2.9g; CHOL 55mg; IRON 2mg; SODIUM 294mg; CALC 39mg

kitchen how-to:
seed a tomato

Seeding tomatoes gets rid of excess liquid and the bitter seeds that can sometimes alter a dish's flavor. Cut the tomato in half horizontally. Using a spoon, scoop the seeds and pulp away from the flesh, and discard. Or, cup the tomato half in the palm of your hand, and gently squeeze out the seeds. Either way, you're left with two clean tomato halves.

way to sauté
poultry

Chicken breasts are a staple of healthful cooking because they're lean and cook in a flash. Cook chicken breasts, deglaze the caramelized juice and browned bits in the pan with liquid, add a few other seasonings, and you're ready for supper in less than 30 minutes.

Chicken with Cider and Bacon Sauce

Serve with broccoli and a combination of white and wild rice.

4 (6-ounce) skinless, boneless chicken breast halves
¼ teaspoon salt
¼ teaspoon freshly ground black pepper
2 bacon slices, chopped
¼ cup minced fresh onion
¾ cup unsweetened apple cider
½ cup fat-free, less-sodium chicken broth

1. Place each chicken breast half between 2 sheets of heavy-duty plastic wrap; pound to ½-inch thickness using a meat mallet or rolling pin. Sprinkle chicken evenly with salt and pepper.

2. Cook bacon in a large nonstick skillet over medium heat until crisp. Remove bacon from pan. Add chicken to drippings in pan; cook 6 minutes on each side or until done. Remove chicken from pan; keep warm.

3. Add onion to pan; sauté 2 minutes or until tender, stirring constantly. Add cider and broth; bring to a boil, scraping pan to loosen browned bits. Cook until broth mixture is reduced to ½ cup (about 5 minutes). Stir in cooked bacon; serve sauce over chicken.

Yield: 4 servings (serving size: 1 chicken breast half and about 2 tablespoons sauce).

CALORIES 269; FAT 7.2g (sat 2.3g, mono 2.8g, poly 1g); PROTEIN 41.1g; CARB 6.9g; FIBER 0.2g; CHOL 106mg; IRON 1.3mg; SODIUM 412mg; CALC 22mg

kitchen how-to:
sauté chicken

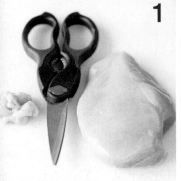

For the best results, use a nonstick skillet, and scrape up the sauce thoroughly from the bottom of the pan to get the concentrated flavor left behind by sautéing.

1. Trim the fat and any small pieces of meat attached to the breast.

2. Place the breast between plastic wrap. Pound to a ½-inch thickness so it cooks quickly and evenly.

3. To tell if the chicken is done, pierce it with a fork. If the juices run clear, it's done.

4. After adding liquid to the pan, scrape the bottom to loosen the browned bits. This will add flavor to the sauce.

5. Pour the sauce into a measuring cup to be sure that it has reduced enough.

Thai Fish Sauce and Lime Chicken

Sweetened chili sauce, found in Asian markets, is often served alongside egg rolls. A similar condiment available in most grocery stores is called Thai sweet red chile dipping sauce. Serve this chicken with white rice.

- 4 (6-ounce) skinless, boneless chicken breast halves
- ¼ teaspoon salt
- 1 tablespoon canola oil
- 1 cup fat-free, less-sodium chicken broth
- 3 tablespoons sweetened chili sauce
- 2 teaspoons fish sauce
- ¼ cup fresh lime juice
- 1 teaspoon creamy peanut butter
- 2 tablespoons chopped roasted peanuts
- Lime wedges (optional)

1. Place each chicken breast half between 2 sheets of heavy-duty plastic wrap; pound to ½-inch thickness using a meat mallet or rolling pin. Sprinkle chicken evenly with ¼ teaspoon salt.

2. Heat a large nonstick skillet over medium heat. Add oil, swirling to coat. Add chicken, and cook 6 minutes on each side or until done. Remove chicken from pan; keep warm.

3. Add broth, chili sauce, and fish sauce to pan; bring to a boil, scraping pan to loosen browned bits. Cook until broth mixture is reduced to ⅔ cup (about 4 minutes). Remove from heat; add lime juice and peanut butter, stirring until smooth. Serve sauce over chicken; sprinkle with peanuts. Garnish with lime wedges, if desired. **Yield: 4 servings (serving size: 1 chicken breast half, about 3 tablespoons sauce, and 1½ teaspoons peanuts).**

CALORIES 296; FAT 8.5g (sat 1.7g, mono 3.6g, poly 2.4g); PROTEIN 41.8g; CARB 12.1g; FIBER 0.6g; CHOL 99mg; IRON 1.4mg; SODIUM 649mg; CALC 25mg

way to sauté
vegetables

Sautéed Baby Squash with Basil and Feta

This simple preparation yields delicious results in a versatile side dish. If baby pattypan squash are not available, substitute four cups of thinly sliced zucchini or yellow squash.

1 tablespoon olive oil
4 cups baby pattypan squash, halved (about 18 ounces)
2 cups sliced leek (about 2 leeks)
½ teaspoon salt
⅛ teaspoon freshly ground black pepper
3 tablespoons crumbled reduced-fat feta cheese
2 tablespoons finely chopped fresh basil

1. Heat a large nonstick skillet over medium-high heat. Add oil to pan, swirling to coat; heat 20 seconds. Add squash and leek to pan; sauté 5 minutes or until tender, stirring frequently. Stir in salt and pepper. Transfer squash mixture to a serving platter. Sprinkle with cheese and basil. **Yield: 6 servings (serving size: ⅔ cup).**

CALORIES 61; FAT 2.9g (sat 0.6g, mono 1.6g, poly 0.3g); PROTEIN 2.3g; CARB 7.5g; FIBER 1.7g; CHOL 1mg; IRON 0.7mg; SODIUM 253mg; CALC 30mg

1

cut & clean leeks

2

3

4

5

Although they resemble large, sturdy green onions, leeks have a mild, slightly sweet onion flavor. Accessing it just requires a little prep work. You'll need to thoroughly clean a leek because dirt can become trapped in its many layers. Follow these directions, and you'll be cooking in no time.

1. Trim the root portion right above the base. (Cutting too far up the stalk will remove the part that holds the layers together.)

2. Slice off the fibrous green tops, leaving only the white-to-light-green stalk. Discard greens.

3. Cut the leek in half lengthwise, and then cut it according to your recipe—slice, chop, or dice.

4. Place the cut leek in a colander, and submerge it in a bowl of water. Agitate the pieces of leek so any dirt falls to the bottom.

5. Remove the pieces from the colander, and drain them on paper towels to remove excess moisture.

Brussels Sprouts with Currants and Pine Nuts

1½ pounds Brussels sprouts, trimmed
1 tablespoon pine nuts
1 tablespoon butter
¼ cup finely chopped shallots
2 tablespoons dried currants
1 teaspoon chopped fresh thyme
¼ teaspoon salt
¼ teaspoon freshly ground black pepper
½ cup fat-free, less-sodium chicken broth

1. Separate Brussels sprouts into leaves, leaving just the center intact. Set aside.
2. Heat a large nonstick skillet over medium-high heat. Add nuts to pan; cook 2 minutes or until toasted, stirring constantly. Coarsely chop nuts.
3. Melt butter in pan over medium-high heat. Add shallots to pan; sauté 1 minute or until golden, stirring frequently. Stir in Brussels sprouts centers and leaves, currants, thyme, salt, and pepper; toss to combine. Add broth. Cover, reduce heat, and cook 7 minutes. Increase heat to medium-high. Uncover; cook 4 minutes or until liquid evaporates and sprouts centers are tender, stirring frequently. Remove from heat; sprinkle with nuts. **Yield: 6 servings (serving size: about ½ cup).**

CALORIES 90; FAT 3.2g (sat 1.4g, mono 0.8g, poly 0.7g); PROTEIN 4.5g; CARB 13.9g; FIBER 4.7g; CHOL 5mg; IRON 1.9mg; SODIUM 173mg; CALC 56mg

all about Brussels sprouts

Members of the cabbage family, Brussels sprouts range from 1 to 1½ inches in diameter. Look for small, firm sprouts with compact, bright-green heads—the smaller the head, the sweeter the taste. Avoid soft, wilted, puffy, or dull-colored heads, as well as those with loose or yellowish leaves. Choose sprouts of similar size so they'll cook evenly.

Remove any loose leaves, seal unwashed sprouts in an airtight plastic bag, and place them in the refrigerator. Use them as quickly as possible since their flavor will start to become unpleasantly strong after three or four days. They're available year-round, but the peak growing season is from September to mid-February.

bruschetta (broo-SKEH-tah)

Bruschetta comes from the Italian word *bruscare*, which means "to roast over coals." In this case, the treatment applies to thin slices of bread, which are traditionally toasted, and then rubbed with garlic, drizzled with olive oil, and served warm. While toppings may vary, bruschetta is simple to prepare and can be enjoyed as a savory appetizer or snack.

Goat Cheese Bruschetta

Chopping the vegetables into small pieces allows them to cook quickly. We used a sliced baguette and a base layer of goat cheese, which adds a tangy flavor background that pairs well with our mixture of sautéed vegetables.

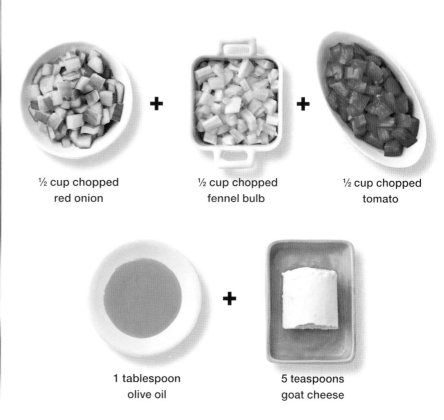

½ cup chopped red onion

+

½ cup chopped fennel bulb

+

½ cup chopped tomato

1 tablespoon olive oil

+

5 teaspoons goat cheese

Slice a baguette into 10 (½-inch-thick) slices, and set aside. Heat a nonstick skillet over medium-high heat. Coat pan with cooking spray. Add onion and fennel, and sauté 10 minutes. Add tomato, and sauté 5 minutes. Remove from heat, and stir in olive oil. Grill baguette slices, about 20 to 30 seconds per side, and then spread ½ teaspoon goat cheese on each round. Divide vegetable mixture over toasts. Top with fresh parsley or basil, if desired. **Yield: 10 servings (serving size: 1 bruschetta).**

CALORIES 76; FAT 2.1g (sat 0.7g, mono 1.2g, poly 0.2g); PROTEIN 2.4g; CARB 12.8g; FIBER 0.7g; CHOL 2mg; IRON 0.7mg; SODIUM 138mg; CALC 12mg

way to
stir-fry

Stir-frying is one of the fastest and healthiest cooking methods. It's also easy, so even a novice in the kitchen will feel confident using this technique.

The secret is to have all your ingredients cut, measured, and next to the stovetop. Once the oil is heated in the wok or pan, add the bite-sized pieces of food, and simply toss and turn them over high heat. In five minutes or less, the work is done. Vegetables emerge crisp and bright, while meats cook up flavorful, tender, and well seared.

stir-frying, defined

Stir-frying requires cooking over a high temperature, which sears food quickly and preserves the natural juices. It takes only minutes (two to five, usually), so vegetables stay bright and crisp, and meat browned and succulent.

Origin

Stir-frying was first developed in China as an efficient cooking method that used a small, hot fire in a simple brick stove. The typical stovetop had a hole over the fire chamber. A round-bottomed wok fit over the lipped hole and captured the heat of the fire. After the wok became hot, oil and chopped ingredients were stirred and tossed in the pan, cooking the food in minutes.

What Stir-frying Does

When the heat is high and the cooking quick, the Cantonese describe the result as *wok hay*—loosely translated "the breath of a wok." It's a difficult quality to define, but you can experience it in the first few moments after food is removed from the wok. Not only does the food taste vibrant and fresh, but it also has concentrated, harmonious flavors with a hint of smokiness. To appreciate wok hay, serve the food immediately.

Best Bets for Stir-frying

It's ideal for most vegetables to be cut into thin, bite-sized pieces, especially those with high moisture content, such as summer squash and bell peppers. Denser vegetables like broccoli work well, too, but they may need to either be blanched first or allowed to steam briefly with a little liquid after the initial stir-frying to become tender. Leafy greens such as spinach cook in seconds once they hit the hot oil.

Tender cuts of meat—such as chicken breasts, flank steak, or pork tenderloin—stir-fry beautifully when cut into thin, bite-sized strips. Avoid large or tough chunks of pork shoulder, beef stew meat, or other cuts that require long, slow cooking to become tender. Shrimp, scallops, and firm-fleshed fish such as halibut work well, but delicate, flaky fish such as flounder or tilapia can fall apart.

Mise en Place

Stir-frying proceeds at a fast pace and requires close attention. The total cooking time may be only 5 or so minutes, which doesn't allow time to prepare ingredients midstream. Read the recipe through. Cut, measure, and mix the ingredients, and set them near the wok. Get out the serving dish. *Then* turn on the heat.

Equipment

All you need for stir-frying are a wok and a broad, curved spatula. A wok, which is shaped like a big, wide bowl with high sloping sides, is designed for stir-frying. The curve of the pan makes it easy for a spatula to scrape down the sides and toss the food without accidentally turning it out of the pan.

The best choice for the typical home cooktop is a rolled carbon steel or enamel-clad cast-iron wok, 14 inches across, with a flat bottom. Over time and with frequent use, carbon steel and cast-iron woks darken and develop a patina that effects a natural nonstick finish. Avoid pans that come with a nonstick finish because they can't be used over high heat and the finish deters browning.

If you don't have a wok, you can use a 12-inch nonstick skillet or a stainless-steel sauté pan with sloped sides. If using a stainless-steel pan, choose one that conducts heat well. Since these pans don't develop a nonstick patina, they often require more oil for cooking, and food may stick more readily. With the flatter shape and shallow sides of the pan, it's also a bit harder to move the food. You'll also need a wide spatula. Wok spatulas, shaped like wide shovels, are slightly curved so they can easily slide down the sides of the pan. Use a lid when stir-frying dense vegetables that may need to be briefly steamed at the end of cooking.

Caring for Your Wok

Properly caring for your wok will extend its lifetime. Treat a carbon steel or cast-iron wok much like a cast-iron pan. Coat it with oil and heat before the first use, and keep it dry to avoid rust. You'll need to follow the manufacturer's specific instructions. To remove any residual metallic taste before cooking in a new wok, stir-fry onions in the seasoned pan until charred. Discard the onions, wash the pan, and it's ready to use.

Clean carbon steel or cast-iron woks with soapy water and a gentle scrub, if needed. Don't scrub aggressively, or you may remove the patina. If food is stuck, cool the wok, soak it in water until food is loose, and then scrub gently. Rinse well and then heat the wok over high heat until completely dry. Coat the pan lightly with oil before storing if it's new or used infrequently.

Fats

Choose oil that can take high heat. An all-purpose, neutral-flavored oil such as canola oil works well. Don't waste expensive extra-virgin olive oil for stir-frying. The high heat will diminish the distinctive taste. Use them only at the end or in a marinade to add flavor. Also, avoid butter, which burns easily at high temperatures.

Temperature

Preheat the wok over high heat until it is very hot, at least two minutes. The wok is hot enough to cook in if you see a little smoke rise, or if you flick a drop of water into the pan and it sizzles rapidly and instantly evaporates. Add the oil and rotate the wok so the oil coats the surface. The oil will become hot immediately and ripple across the surface.

Keep It Moving

Once you put the food in the pan, you need to constantly toss and flip it to prevent burning. Use your spatula to efficiently scoop the food.

Size Wise

When stir-frying, foods must be cut into thin, bite-sized pieces so they'll cook quickly. Generally, they should be of similar shape and size. If the sizes vary widely, foods will cook unevenly.

Make Room

Stir-fry thinly sliced meat in small batches of 6 ounces or less to avoid overcrowding—otherwise, you risk a soggy result. With less juicy foods, cornstarch-coated pieces, or thicker pieces such as shrimp, you can sometimes cook up to 1 pound at a time. Limit vegetables to about 4 to 6 cups at a time (or 8 to 10 cups for leafy greens). If you use more than one vegetable, add the thickest, densest pieces first, followed by smaller, thinner pieces so everything finishes cooking at the same time.

the bottom line

The three most important elements to remember about stir-frying:

1. Heat the wok over high heat for at least two minutes before adding the oil.

2. Place a workable amount of food in the wok.

3. Keep moving the food with a wide spatula while it's in the pan.

way to stir-fry
fish & shellfish

When stir-frying, it's important to cut fish and shellfish into bite-sized pieces. The small size of shrimp and scallops make them ideal for stir-frying. Firm-fleshed fish such as halibut work well, but delicate, flaky fish such as flounder and tilapia can fall apart.

Sizzling Shrimp with Corn Relish

Serve over rice for a hearty dinner or over a bed of baby spinach for a lighter meal.

1½   tablespoons fresh lime juice
1   tablespoon fish sauce
½   teaspoon sugar
2   tablespoons canola oil
½   cup chopped shallots
1   tablespoon minced garlic
1   tablespoon minced jalapeño pepper (about 1 small)
1½   pounds peeled and deveined medium shrimp
1½   cups fresh corn kernels (about 3 ears)
⅓   cup chopped fresh cilantro

1. Combine first 3 ingredients; set aside.
2. Heat a 14-inch wok over high heat. Add oil to wok, swirling to coat. Add shallots, garlic, and jalapeño to wok; stir-fry 30 seconds or just until shallots begin to brown. Add shrimp; stir-fry 3 minutes or until shrimp are done. Add corn; stir-fry 1 minute or just until corn is heated. Stir in juice mixture; sprinkle with cilantro.
Yield: 4 servings (serving size: 1 cup).

CALORIES 332; FAT 11.2g (sat 1.2g, mono 4.8g, poly 3.6g); PROTEIN 37.6g; CARB 19.9g; FIBER 2.1g; CHOL 259mg; IRON 4.8mg; SODIUM 612mg; CALC 101mg

See page 401 for information about how to shuck fresh corn.

kitchen how-to:
de-kernel corn

The fresher the corn, the better it tastes. That's because as soon as corn is picked, its sugar starts converting to starch, which lessens the natural sweetness. So it's important to buy corn and cook it as soon as possible after its picked.

1. Cut about ½ inch from the tip of each ear to create a flat base on which to stand the cob while removing the kernels.
2. Stand the cob upright in a pie plate or bowl to catch the kernels, and use a sharp knife to slice away the kernels in a slow, sawing motion.

Shrimp and Broccoli Fried Rice with Toasted Almonds

Cooling rice in the freezer helps ensure that the grains stay separate once they're stir-fried. You can use other protein sources, such as chicken or tofu, in this recipe and substitute any vegetables you prefer.

1¾ cups water, divided
1½ cups instant white rice (such as Minute Rice)
4 cups broccoli florets
1 large red bell pepper, chopped (about 1⅓ cups)
2 tablespoons roasted peanut oil, divided
1 teaspoon grated peeled fresh ginger
3 garlic cloves, minced
1¼ pounds large shrimp, peeled and deveined
½ cup fat-free, less-sodium chicken broth
3 tablespoons low-sodium soy sauce
1 teaspoon cornstarch
¼ cup sliced almonds, toasted
¼ cup chopped green onions

1. Place 1½ cups water in a medium saucepan; bring to a boil. Add rice to pan; cover, reduce heat, and simmer 5 minutes. Remove pan from heat; let stand 5 minutes. Spoon rice into a 13 x 9–inch baking dish; place dish in freezer.
2. Combine broccoli, bell pepper, and remaining ¼ cup water in a microwave-safe dish. Microwave at HIGH 5 minutes or until crisp-tender. Set aside.
3. Heat a large nonstick skillet over medium heat. Add 1½ teaspoons oil to pan, swirling to coat. Add ginger and garlic to pan; cook 1 minute, stirring frequently.
4. Increase heat to medium-high. Add shrimp to pan; stir-fry 4 minutes or until shrimp are done. Remove shrimp mixture from pan. Remove rice from freezer.
5. Heat remaining 1½ tablespoons oil in pan over medium-high heat. Add rice to pan; cook 3 minutes or until thoroughly heated, stirring frequently. Combine broth, soy sauce, and cornstarch in a small bowl, stirring with a whisk. Stir broth mixture into rice. Add shrimp mixture and broccoli mixture to pan; cook 1½ minutes or until sauce thickens. Sprinkle with almonds and onions.
Yield: 4 servings (serving size: about 1¾ cups).

CALORIES 442; FAT 12.6g (sat 1.9g, mono 5.4g, poly 4g); PROTEIN 37.5g; CARB 45.8g; FIBER 4.1g; CHOL 215mg; IRON 7mg; SODIUM 693mg; CALC 141mg

kitchen how-to: toast almonds

Toasting slivered almonds gives them a richer, nuttier taste.
Spread the almonds on a baking sheet, and bake at 350° for 6 to 8 minutes. Or place the almonds in a dry skillet, and cook over medium heat, stirring frequently, for 1 to 2 minutes or until they're toasted. Be sure to watch them carefully—they can go from toasted to burned very quickly.

all about fried rice

The secrets of making good fried rice are high heat and minimal oil. Using leftover rice is best as it's had time to dry out slightly in the refrigerator, and the dryness facilitates frying. But you can start the rice when you begin preparing the recipe, and simply place it in the freezer before frying it. If you use freshly cooked, hot rice, it will contain too much moisture, which makes it soggy and mushy.

way to stir-fry
meats

Tender cuts of meat stir-fry beautifully when cut into thin, bite-sized strips. Avoid large or tough chunks of pork shoulder, beef stew meat, or other cuts that require long, slow cooking to become tender.

Sirloin and Vegetable Stir-fry

Either sirloin or flank steak will work—just slice it thinly and cook briefly so it stays tender. Try boil-in-bag rice; it cooks in about half the time required for traditional long-grain rice. You'll need two bags for this recipe.

- ½ teaspoon salt
- ½ teaspoon five-spice powder
- ¼ teaspoon freshly ground black pepper
- 1 (1-pound) sirloin steak, trimmed and thinly sliced
- 2 teaspoons cornstarch
- ½ teaspoon sugar
- ¼ teaspoon crushed red pepper
- ¾ cup fat-free, less-sodium beef broth
- 2 tablespoons low-sodium soy sauce
- 2 teaspoons canola oil
- 1 cup (¼-inch-thick) diagonally cut slices carrot
- 1 cup broccoli florets
- 1½ cups snow peas, trimmed
- 3 cups hot cooked rice

1. Combine first 3 ingredients in a bowl, stirring well; sprinkle evenly over steak. Combine cornstarch, sugar, and red pepper in a medium bowl, stirring well with a whisk. Stir in broth and soy sauce.
2. Heat a large nonstick skillet over medium-high heat. Add oil to pan, swirling to coat. Add carrot to pan; stir-fry 2 minutes. Add steak and broccoli; stir-fry 1 minute. Stir in broth mixture; cook 1 minute, stirring constantly. Add snow peas; cook 30 seconds or until desired degree of doneness. Serve with rice. **Yield: 4 servings (serving size: 1½ cups beef mixture and ¾ cup rice).**

CALORIES 323; FAT 10.8g (sat 3.3g, mono 4.5g, poly 1.3g); PROTEIN 24.4g; CARB 30.1g; FIBER 2.4g; CHOL 55mg; IRON 4.7mg; SODIUM 728mg; CALC 40mg

kitchen how-to:
slice beef into strips

When purchasing beef, look for a cherry red color, or—if it's vacuum-packed—a dark, purplish red color. The visible fat should be very white. The steak will be easier to slice if you partially freeze it first. Slice it diagonally across the grain into thin slices.

Bell Peppers
What they add: With their crisp texture and sweet flavor, bell peppers are usually popular with kids, which makes them a good vegetable choice for a family meal. Try any combination of red, yellow, orange, and green bell peppers in this dish.

Szechuan Pork

Fresh sliced pineapple makes a nice companion for this one-dish meal.

    6   ounces soba (buckwheat) noodles, uncooked
    2   teaspoons dark sesame oil
    1   (1-pound) pork tenderloin, trimmed and cut
        into 2-inch strips
    1   tablespoon chili garlic sauce (such as Lee
        Kum Kee)
    1   teaspoon bottled ground fresh ginger (such
        as Spice World)
    ¾   cup red bell pepper strips (about 1 small
        pepper)
    ¼   cup fat-free, less-sodium chicken broth
    1½ tablespoons low-sodium soy sauce
    1   tablespoon peanut butter
    ¾   cup (2-inch) diagonally cut green onions
        (about 4 green onions)

1. Cook noodles according to package directions. Drain and rinse with cold water; drain.
2. Heat a large nonstick skillet over medium-high heat. Add oil to pan, swirling to coat. Add pork, chili garlic sauce, and ginger to pan; stir-fry 2 minutes. Add bell pepper; stir-fry 2 minutes. Add broth, soy sauce, and peanut butter to pan. Reduce heat to low, and cook 1 minute or until sauce is slightly thick. Stir in onions. Serve over noodles. **Yield: 4 servings (serving size: 1 cup pork mixture and ½ cup noodles).**

CALORIES 338; FAT 8.6 (sat 2.2g, mono 3.5g, poly 1.9g); PROTEIN 30.4g; CARB 36.8g; FIBER 1.7g; CHOL 63mg; IRON 2.9mg; SODIUM 693mg; CALC 40mg

kitchen how-to:
slice bell peppers

If you plan to use the bell peppers within a day or two, keep them at room temperature for better flavor. You can also store them in a plastic bag in the fridge for up to a week. Be sure to wash and cut the peppers just before using them.

1. Use a knife to slice the pepper in half, and then cut it into quarters.
2. Pull the stems and seeds away, and slice each quarter into strips.

Black Bean Pork and Zucchini

Pork:
- ¾ pound pork tenderloin, trimmed
- 1 tablespoon Shaoxing (Chinese rice wine), dry sherry, or sake
- 1 tablespoon low-sodium soy sauce
- 1 teaspoon cornstarch

Sauce:
- ½ cup water
- 2 tablespoons Shaoxing (Chinese rice wine), dry sherry, or sake
- 1 tablespoon black bean and garlic sauce (such as Lee Kum Kee)
- 2 teaspoons cornstarch
- ¼ teaspoon salt

Remaining Ingredients:
- 1 pound zucchini
- 2 tablespoons canola oil, divided
- 1 tablespoon minced peeled fresh ginger
- ¼ cup thinly sliced green onions
- 3 cups hot cooked short-grain rice

1. To prepare pork, cut pork crosswise into 3-inch pieces. Cut each piece lengthwise into ¼-inch slices. Lay slices flat, and cut into ½-inch-wide strips. Combine pork, 1 tablespoon wine, soy sauce, and 1 teaspoon cornstarch; cover and refrigerate 20 minutes.

2. To prepare sauce, combine ½ cup water and next 4 ingredients; set aside.

3. Cut zucchini crosswise into 2-inch pieces. Cut each piece lengthwise into ¼-inch slices; cut slices into ½-inch-wide strips.

4. Heat a 14-inch wok over high heat. Add 2 teaspoons oil to wok, swirling to coat. Add zucchini and ginger; stir-fry 1 minute or until crisp-tender. Spoon into a bowl.

5. Add 2 teaspoons oil to wok, swirling to coat. Add half of pork mixture to wok; stir-fry 2 minutes or until browned. Add cooked pork mixture to zucchini mixture. Repeat procedure with remaining 2 teaspoons oil and remaining pork mixture. Return zucchini mixture to wok. Stir sauce; add sauce to wok. Stir-fry 1 minute or until thickened. Spoon into a serving dish. Sprinkle with onions. Serve over rice. **Yield: 4 servings (serving size: about ¾ cup pork mixture and ¾ cup rice).**

CALORIES 398; FAT 10.6g (sat 1.7g, mono 5.6g, poly 2.7g); PROTEIN 23.1g; CARB 48.1g; FIBER 3.1g; CHOL 55mg; IRON 4.1mg; SODIUM 654mg; CALC 29mg

kitchen how-to:
cut pork for black bean pork and zucchini

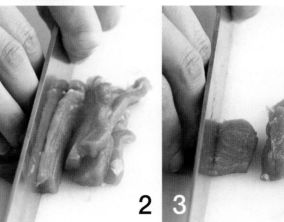

It's important to cut the pork into bite-sized pieces so that it cooks quickly and evenly.

1. Cut the pork crosswise into 3-inch pieces
2. Cut each piece lengthwise into ¼-inch slices.
3. Lay the slices flat; cut them into ½-inch-wide strips.

Cornstarch

What it adds: Cornstarch is just what the name implies: starch made from corn. It's a dense white powder ground from the endosperm at the heart of corn kernels that is used to thicken sauces in stir-fries, stews, and puddings.

Tofu

What it adds: Tofu, which is a nondairy food made with calcium sulfate, can help you meet your daily calcium needs. It's recommended that adults consume 1,000 milligrams per day (1,200mg for those 51 and older). Be sure to look at the nutrition label to verify that the tofu you buy does indeed contain calcium sulfate. Nigari (magnesium chloride) is another common coagulating agent used to make tofu, but its calcium content is lower.

Ma Po Tofu

You can customize the heat in this mix of lean ground pork, tofu, and Asian spices by using more or less chili garlic sauce. Add a side of chilled melon and a cold glass of dry riesling for a satisfying supper.

- 1 (1-pound) package reduced-fat firm tofu, cut into 6 slices
- ½ cup fat-free, less-sodium chicken broth
- 1 tablespoon cornstarch
- 2 tablespoons low-sodium soy sauce
- 1 tablespoon oyster sauce
- 1 to 2 teaspoons chili garlic sauce (such as Lee Kum Kee)
- 4 ounces lean ground pork
- 1 tablespoon grated peeled fresh ginger
- 3 garlic cloves, minced
- 2 cups hot cooked long-grain brown rice
- ⅓ cup chopped green onions

1. Arrange tofu slices in a single layer on several layers of paper towels; top with several more layers of paper towels. Top with a cast-iron skillet or other heavy pan; let stand 30 minutes. Remove pan; discard paper towels. Cut tofu slices into ½-inch cubes.
2. Combine broth and next 4 ingredients, stirring with a whisk.
3. Heat a large nonstick skillet over medium-high heat. Add pork; stir-fry 4 minutes or until done, stirring to crumble. Add ginger and garlic; cook 1 minute, stirring constantly. Add tofu; cook 4 minutes or until golden, stirring frequently. Add broth mixture to pan. Bring to a boil; cook 1 minute or until mixture thickens. Remove from heat.
4. Serve tofu mixture over rice. Sprinkle with onions.
Yield: 4 servings (serving size: ½ cup rice, about ⅔ cup tofu mixture, and about 1 tablespoon onions).

CALORIES 290; FAT 8.4g (sat 1.9g, mono 2.5g, poly 3.3g); PROTEIN 21.5g; CARB 32.5g; FIBER 4.6g; CHOL 21mg; IRON 2.8mg; SODIUM 390mg; CALC 72mg

kitchen how-to:
brown ground meat

Browning ground meat is simple, but there are some rules you should follow to ensure the best flavor. If you add cold meat to a hot pan or add warm meat to a cold pan and start cooking it, the meat can water out and lose its juiciness. Those are juices you want in your meat. Here's how to prevent that.

- Let the meat come to room temperature before cooking it for best results.
- Don't add meat to a cold pan. Heat the pan until it's hot before adding the meat.
- Don't overcrowd your pan. If you are using a small pan or are cooking more than 1 pound of meat, cook it in batches. Allow the pan to reheat between batches.

way to stir-fry
poultry

Curried Chicken and Cashews

Madras curry powder delivers more intensity than regular curry powder. For less heat, leave the chiles whole.

Sauce:
- ⅓ cup fat-free, less-sodium chicken broth
- 3 tablespoons water
- 1½ tablespoons fish sauce
- 1 teaspoon sugar
- 1 teaspoon rice vinegar

Remaining Ingredients:
- ¾ pound skinless, boneless chicken breast halves
- 2 tablespoons canola oil, divided
- 1½ cups vertically sliced onion
- 1 tablespoon minced peeled fresh ginger
- 1 tablespoon minced garlic
- 1 teaspoon Madras curry powder
- 3 small dried hot red chiles, broken in half
- ⅓ cup chopped fresh cilantro
- ¼ cup dry-roasted salted cashews, chopped
- 3 cups hot cooked short-grain rice

1. To prepare sauce, combine first 5 ingredients; set aside.

2. Cut chicken across grain into ¼-inch slices; cut slices into ½-inch-wide strips. Cut strips into 3-inch-long pieces.

3. Heat a 14-inch wok over high heat. Add 1 tablespoon oil to wok, swirling to coat. Add half of chicken to wok; stir-fry 2 minutes. Spoon cooked chicken into a bowl. Repeat procedure with 2 teaspoons oil and remaining chicken.

4. Add remaining 1 teaspoon oil to wok, swirling to coat. Add onion, ginger, and garlic; stir-fry 1 minute or until lightly browned. Add curry powder and chiles; stir-fry 30 seconds. Add sauce and chicken; stir-fry 1 minute. Spoon into a serving dish. Sprinkle with cilantro and cashews. Serve over rice.

Yield: 4 servings (serving size: 1 cup chicken mixture and ¾ cup rice).

CALORIES 439; FAT 13g (sat 1.7g, mono 6.9g, poly 3.2g); PROTEIN 26g; CARB 52.6g; FIBER 3.2g; CHOL 49mg; IRON 3.9mg; SODIUM 669mg; CALC 37mg

kitchen how-to:
vertically slice onion

When slicing onions, start at the end opposite the root. Onions contain sulfuric compounds that are released when they are peeled or sliced.

Those compounds irritate the eyes and produce tears. More of these compounds are found in the root so it's best to cut that last. Slice the top off the onion, leaving the root end intact. Remove the papery skin, and slice the onion in half vertically. Continue cutting the onion vertically into thin slices.

all about madras curry powder

Madras curry powder, named for a city in southern India, is hotter than standard curry powder. It features a wide range of ingredients, including chile pepper, curry leaves, turmeric, coriander, cumin, cinnamon, cloves, bay leaves, fenugreek, allspice, and black pepper. It's often used in soups and stews, meats, poultry, burgers, and salads and to add a punch of heat to sauces and marinades. Since curry powder quickly loses its pungency, store it in an airtight container, and use it within two months.

way to stir-fry
vegetables

Mustard Greens
What they add: Mustard greens have a spicy, peppery flavor; the smaller the leaves, the sharper and hotter the taste. These greens work well in stir-fries and sautés. You can substitute escarole, kale, Swiss chard, or spinach.

Edamame
What they add: Edamame (eh-dah-MAH-meh), or fresh soybeans, have a buttery, nutty flavor and wonderfully crisp texture. The pods look like large, fuzzy sugar snap peas. These beans are packed with potential health benefits—each ½-cup serving contains 4 grams of fiber and only 3 grams of fat, all of which is the heart-healthy mono- and polyunsaturated kind.

Vegetable Lo Mein with Edamame and Mustard Greens

The peppery bite of mustard greens contrasts with tender, fresh Asian egg noodles in this meatless main dish. If you can't find them, substitute fresh pasta such as spaghetti.

½ cup boiling water
¼ cup dried wood ear mushrooms
2 quarts water
3 cups chopped mustard greens
1 (14-ounce) package fresh Chinese egg noodles
¼ cup low-sodium soy sauce, divided
1 tablespoon dark sesame oil
2 tablespoons canola oil
1 tablespoon grated peeled fresh ginger
1¼ cups (¼-inch-thick) red bell pepper strips (about 1 medium)
¾ cup chopped green onions
1 garlic clove, minced
1½ cups frozen shelled edamame (green soybeans), thawed
3 tablespoons hoisin sauce

1. Combine ½ cup boiling water and mushrooms in a bowl; cover and let stand 15 minutes. Drain mushrooms in a sieve over a bowl, reserving soaking liquid. Remove and discard stems. Chop mushroom caps; set aside.
2. Bring 2 quarts water to a boil in a Dutch oven. Add greens, and cook 1 minute or until greens wilt. Remove greens from water with a slotted spoon. Plunge greens into ice water; drain and squeeze dry. Set aside.

3. Return water in pan to a boil. Add egg noodles, and cook 2 minutes or until done. Drain and rinse with cold water, and drain well. Place noodles in a large bowl. Add 1 tablespoon soy sauce and sesame oil, tossing to coat, and set aside.
4. Heat a wok or large nonstick skillet over medium-high heat. Add canola oil to wok, swirling to coat. Add ginger; stir-fry 5 seconds. Add mushrooms, bell pepper, onions, and garlic; stir-fry 2 minutes or until bell pepper is crisp-tender. Stir in greens and edamame; stir-fry 30 seconds. Stir in reserved mushroom soaking liquid, noodle mixture, remaining 3 tablespoons soy sauce, and hoisin sauce; cook 2 minutes or until thoroughly heated. **Yield: 6 servings (serving size: 1⅓ cups).**

CALORIES 339; FAT 9.8g (sat 1g, mono 4.1g, poly 3.2g); PROTEIN 15.8g; CARB 47g; FIBER 4.9g; CHOL 0mg; IRON 2.1mg; SODIUM 710mg; CALC 73mg

kitchen how-to: wash greens

After bringing fresh greens home from the market, wrap them, unwashed, in damp paper towels, and store them in an unsealed plastic bag in the refrigerator. They'll stay fresh for three to five days. When ready to use, follow these steps to clean them.

1. Begin by pulling apart the bunch of greens and examining each leaf. Remove and discard any yellowed or limp portions.
2. Wash greens in cool water, agitating them with your hands. Replace the water two or three times until there are no traces of dirt or grit.
3. Lay the washed greens flat to dry on a dish towel. To speed the process, use another towel to pat them dry or use a salad spinner.

Stir-fried Bok Choy and Lettuce with Mushrooms

1 cup boiling water

8 dried shiitake mushrooms (about 2 ounces)

2 tablespoons low-sodium soy sauce

1 tablespoon Shaoxing (Chinese rice wine) or dry sherry

½ teaspoon sugar

4 teaspoons canola oil, divided

1 teaspoon minced peeled fresh ginger

½ cup fat-free, less-sodium chicken broth

2 tablespoons oyster sauce

½ teaspoon cornstarch

2 medium garlic cloves, thinly sliced

8 heads baby bok choy, halved lengthwise

1 medium head romaine lettuce, cut crosswise into 1-inch pieces (about 8 cups)

1. Combine 1 cup boiling water and shiitake mushrooms in a bowl; cover and let stand 20 minutes. Drain mushrooms in a colander over a bowl, reserving liquid. Rinse mushrooms. Remove and discard stems; cut each cap into quarters. Set aside.

2. Combine soy sauce, wine, and sugar in a small bowl, stirring with a whisk.

3. Heat a small saucepan over medium-high heat. Add 1 teaspoon oil and ginger to pan; sauté 30 seconds. Add reserved mushrooms; sauté 1 minute. Add reserved mushroom liquid and broth; bring to a boil. Cover, reduce heat, and simmer 20 minutes.

4. Combine oyster sauce and cornstarch in a small bowl, stirring with a whisk; stir into mushroom mixture. Bring to a boil, stirring constantly. Cook 1 minute or until thickened. Remove from heat; keep warm.

5. Heat a wok or large skillet over high heat. Add remaining 1 tablespoon oil to pan. Add garlic; stir-fry 10 seconds. Add bok choy; stir-fry 2 minutes or until bok choy begins to soften. Add lettuce; stir-fry 2 minutes or until lettuce wilts. Stir in mushroom mixture and soy sauce mixture; cook 3 minutes or until bok choy is tender. **Yield: 8 servings (serving size: about ⅔ cup).**

CALORIES 105; FAT 3.4g (sat 0.3g, mono 1.5g, poly 1.2g); PROTEIN 7.7g; CARB 15.5g; FIBER 5.9g; CHOL 0mg; IRON 4.1mg; SODIUM 468mg; CALC 463mg

all about shaoxing (shaow-SHEEN)

Shaoxing, which is produced in northern China, is one of the most well-known varieties of traditional Chinese rice wines. It's used widely in cooking and also consumed as a beverage. Look for it in Asian grocery stores. Substitute dry sherry if you can't find it.

Stir-fried Water Spinach (Kangkung)

If your local Asian grocery store doesn't carry water spinach, use regular spinach and cook it for two minutes. The flavor of roasted peanut oil is bolder than peanut oil, but you can use the regular version.

- 1 tablespoon roasted peanut oil
- 1 large garlic clove, minced
- ½ teaspoon sugar
- 2 pounds water spinach, trimmed and cut into 2-inch pieces (about 16 cups)
- 2 tablespoons low-sodium soy sauce
- ¼ teaspoon black pepper

1. Heat a large nonstick skillet over medium-high heat. Add roasted peanut oil to pan, swirling to coat. Add minced garlic to pan; stir-fry 30 seconds or until golden. Add sugar and water spinach; stir-fry 3 minutes or until spinach wilts. Add soy sauce; stir-fry 1 minute. Remove from heat; stir in pepper. **Yield: 6 servings (serving size: about ⅓ cup).**

CALORIES 54; FAT 2.6g (sat 0.4g, mono 1.1g, poly 0.9g); PROTEIN 4.3g; CARB 5.8g; FIBER 3.3g; CHOL 0mg; IRON 2.7mg; SODIUM 349mg; CALC 119mg

all about water spinach

Common in Southeast Asia, water spinach has a pleasingly mild and delicate flavor that works well in stir-fries and sautés. All but the bottom half of the stems are used in cooking. Make sure you wash these leafy greens in several changes of cold water to remove sand or soil.

way to
pan-fry &
oven-fry

Everyone loves the flavor, crisp exterior, and moist, juicy interior of fried foods. To deliver that characteristic texture without the extra calories and fat, we turn to pan-frying and oven-frying. In both techniques, the foods are breaded, battered, or both to give them a crisp and crunchy exterior. Since pan-frying and oven-frying involve less oil than deep-frying, the results are inherently healthier, and both are easy to master once you learn a few tricks.

pan-frying & oven-frying, defined

Pan-frying entails cooking food in a moderate amount of fat in an uncovered pan. It's similar to sautéing but requires more fat and often lower temperatures. Oven-frying utilizes the oven to mimic deep-frying by breading foods and then baking using a moderate amount of oil.

Best Bets for Pan-frying and Oven-frying

Fish fillets; thin, tender cuts such as pork chops or boneless, skinless chicken breast halves; and sturdy vegetables such as potatoes, green tomato slices, and onions are good choices. Juicy foods such as ripe tomatoes will be rendered mushy, and tougher cuts such as brisket or pork shoulder won't cook long enough to become tender.

Equipment

For pan-frying, use a skillet or sauté pan—a wide pan with sloped or straight sides. Choose a heavy-bottomed pan for evenly distributed heat with no hot spots. For oven-frying, you'll need a baking sheet. We prefer nonstick skillets and baking sheets to help ensure that the coatings stay on the food, not stuck in the pan. These pans also allow you to use less oil than traditional pan-fried or oven-fried recipes.

Coatings

Many pan-fried and oven-fried dishes benefit from a coating of flour, breadcrumbs, cracker meal, or cornmeal. These coatings help create the desired crisp crust and also insulate the food to prevent it from overcooking. Panko (Japanese breadcrumbs) often works well because it doesn't absorb oil as readily as dry breadcrumbs and resists sogginess. Place each of the coating ingredients in a separate shallow dish, such as a pie plate, so there's enough room for the food to lie flat.

Most of our breaded recipes use a three-step approach: The food is first dusted in flour to help all the other coatings cling, then dipped into an egg wash to help the main coating adhere, and finally dredged in the main/heavier coating of panko or breadcrumbs. You'll find it helpful to designate one of your hands as the dry hand (for handling the food as it goes into the dry ingredients) and the other as the wet hand (for dipping food into the egg wash). If you use the same hand or both hands for every step, you'll end up with a mess of flour-egg-breadcrumbs stuck to your skin. Don't let the food sit too long after it's breaded or it may become gummy.

Breading Amounts

As you prepare these recipes, you'll notice we call for more breading ingredients than will actually stick to the food. (You'll discard whatever is left over.) Having more than you need makes it easier to coat the food. Plus, it's hard—and messy—to add additional breadcrumbs or flour once you've started the process.

Temperature

For the crunchiest texture when pan-frying, it helps to start many foods on medium-high heat to initiate browning, and then reduce the heat to allow the foods to finish cooking more slowly. Other recipes will be successful using medium-high or medium heat for the entire cook time; follow the recipe's specific instructions. For oven-frying, use high heat. Set the oven temperature between 400° and 475° to sear the food and crisp the surface.

Allow Some Breathing Room

Take care not to overcrowd the pan or the baking sheet to avoid lowering the temperature and causing the food to stick. Overcrowding can also hinder evaporation as the food cooks, creating steam in the bottom of the pan and ultimately a soggy crust.

Do Not Disturb

Be aware that the side of the food you put down in the pan or on the baking sheet first will look the best, so place the food in the pan presentation side down. For chicken breasts, this means the rounded side; for fish fillets, it's the rounded rib side (not the skin side). To make sure the coatings stay on the food, turn it only once as it cooks. Disturbing it too soon may cause the breading to fall off or stick to the pan or baking sheet.

Fats for Frying

Choose oil with a neutral flavor—such as canola oil, regular olive oil, or peanut oil—that can withstand moderately high heat on the stovetop and in the oven. Flavorful oils such as extra-virgin olive oil or dark sesame oil can burn or create harsh flavors in the food. Butter can also burn at high temperatures, but it can work over medium-high heat for shorter cook times or over medium heat for longer periods. To prevent food from sticking, heat the pan first and then add the oil or butter. For oven-frying, preheat the baking sheet, which helps the underside of the foods you're cooking stay crisp.

Serve Immediately

Pan-fried and oven-fried offerings are best just after they're cooked, when they're hot and crunchy.

the bottom line

The three most important elements to remember about pan-frying and oven-frying:

1. Don't overcrowd the pan or baking sheet.

2. Cook the food shortly after applying the coatings.

3. Turn the food only once as it cooks.

way to pan-fry
fish & shellfish

Striped Bass Meunière

Meunière refers to a classic preparation of lightly seasoned fish dredged in flour and cooked in butter. Any firm-fleshed white fish will work well in this recipe; try halibut or mahimahi. Serve with rice to soak up the piquant sauce and garnish with a lemon wedge.

- ½ cup all-purpose flour
- ½ cup 2% reduced-fat milk
- 4 (6-ounce) striped bass fillets
- ½ teaspoon salt, divided
- ½ teaspoon freshly ground black pepper, divided
- 2 tablespoons butter, divided
- ¼ cup minced shallots
- ¼ cup white balsamic vinegar
- ¼ cup fat-free, less-sodium chicken broth
- 2 tablespoons chopped fresh parsley

1. Place flour in a shallow dish. Place milk in another shallow dish. Sprinkle fish evenly with ¼ teaspoon salt and ¼ teaspoon pepper. Working with 1 fillet at a time, dredge fish in flour, shaking off excess. Dip fish in milk, allowing excess to drip off; dredge again in flour. Set aside. Repeat procedure with remaining fish, flour, and milk.

2. Heat a large nonstick skillet over medium-high heat. Add 1 tablespoon butter to pan, swirling until butter melts. Add 2 fillets to pan; reduce heat to medium, and cook 4 minutes on each side or until golden brown and fish flakes easily when tested with a fork or until desired degree of doneness. Remove fish from pan, and keep warm. Repeat procedure with remaining 1 tablespoon butter and remaining 2 fillets. Remove fish from pan; keep warm.

3. Increase heat to medium-high. Add shallots and remaining ¼ teaspoon salt to pan; sauté 1 minute or until tender. Add vinegar and broth; simmer 1 minute. Add parsley and remaining ¼ teaspoon pepper. Spoon sauce over fish. **Yield: 4 servings (serving size: 1 fillet and 2 tablespoons sauce).**

CALORIES 258; FAT 9.9g (sat 4.6g, mono 2.7g, poly 1.6g); PROTEIN 32.1g; CARB 7.7g; FIBER 0.3g; CHOL 156mg; IRON 2mg; SODIUM 493mg; CALC 48mg

kitchen how-to:
bread fish

The key when breading fish or meat is to use one hand for the wet ingredients and one hand for the dry. Dip a fillet in the milk (or wet mixture) with your wet hand, and place the fillet in the flour (or dry mixture). Then, with your dry hand, dredge the fillet in the flour. This technique prevents your hands from becoming covered in the breading mixture.

Oven-fried Catfish Sandwiches

¼ cup light mayonnaise
1 tablespoon sweet pickle relish
2 teaspoons capers, chopped
⅜ teaspoon salt, divided
¼ teaspoon hot pepper sauce (such as Tabasco)
2 tablespoons all-purpose flour
1 teaspoon paprika
¾ teaspoon garlic powder, divided
¼ teaspoon black pepper
2 large egg whites, lightly beaten
⅔ cup yellow cornmeal
4 (4-ounce) catfish fillets
Cooking spray
4 (2-ounce) hoagie rolls, toasted
1 cup shredded romaine lettuce
4 (¼-inch-thick) slices red onion
8 (¼-inch-thick) slices tomato

1. Preheat oven to 450°. Place baking sheet in oven.
2. Combine mayonnaise, relish, capers, ⅛ teaspoon salt, and pepper sauce in a small bowl, stirring well. Set aside.
3. Combine flour, paprika, ½ teaspoon garlic powder, ⅛ teaspoon salt, and pepper in a shallow dish. Place egg whites in a shallow dish. Combine cornmeal, remaining ⅛ teaspoon salt, and remaining ¼ teaspoon garlic powder in a shallow dish. Working with 1 fillet at a time, dredge in flour. Dip in egg whites; dredge in cornmeal mixture. Place fillet on a plate; repeat procedure with remaining fillets, flour, egg whites, and cornmeal mixture.
4. Transfer fillets to preheated baking sheet coated with cooking spray. Lightly coat fillets with cooking spray. Bake at 450° for 6 minutes. Turn fillets and coat with cooking spray; bake 6 minutes or until fish flakes easily when tested with a fork or until desired degree of doneness.
5. Place 1 bottom half of roll on each of 4 plates. Top each serving with ¼ cup lettuce, 1 fillet, 1 onion slice, and 2 tomato slices. Spread 4 teaspoons mayonnaise mixture on cut side of each roll top; place on top of sandwiches. Serve immediately. **Yield: 4 servings (serving size: 1 sandwich).**

CALORIES 431; FAT 16.2g (sat 3.5g, mono 5.5g, poly 5.6g); PROTEIN 25.4g; CARB 45.2g; FIBER 4.8g; CHOL 60mg; IRON 2.9mg; SODIUM 785mg; CALC 91mg

all about capers

Capers are the unopened, immature flower buds of the *Capparis spinosa* shrub. Native to the Mediterranean—particularly Italy and France—capers are cultivated and harvested by hand. They range from the size of a pea to that of an almond. Once picked, they're sun-dried and cured in vinegar, wine, salt, or brine. (The latter two methods can make capers high in sodium. To reduce the sodium, drain the amount of capers you need in a colander and rinse under running water.)

Piquant, sharp, and tangy are just a few words that describe their flavor, which melds the pungent salinity of olives with the tartness of lemons. Use capers sparingly to infuse a savory sauce, salad, pizza, pasta, dressing, or vegetable dish with intense flavor.

way to pan-fry
crab cakes

Fresh crabmeat is the key to creating a great crab cake, but using a crunchy coating and pan-frying them is the way to make a deliciously crisp version without the extra fat and calories.

Crab Cakes with Roasted Vegetables and Tangy Butter Sauce

Panko gives these crab cakes an irresistibly crisp coating. Chilling the crab mixture helps the cakes hold their shape as they cook.

Crab Cakes:
- ¼ cup finely chopped red onion
- 2 tablespoons chopped fresh parsley
- 3 tablespoons light mayonnaise
- 2 teaspoons Dijon mustard
- ¾ teaspoon Old Bay seasoning
- ½ teaspoon Worcestershire sauce
- 2 large egg whites, lightly beaten
- 1 pound lump crabmeat, drained and shell pieces removed
- 1½ cups panko (Japanese breadcrumbs), divided
- 1 tablespoon olive oil, divided
- Cooking spray

Vegetables:
- 21 baby carrots (about 12 ounces)
- 5 small red potatoes, quartered (about 8 ounces)
- 4 medium shallots, halved lengthwise
- ⅛ teaspoon salt
- 8 ounces haricots verts, trimmed

Sauce:
- ⅔ cup fat-free, less-sodium chicken broth
- 3 tablespoons chopped shallots
- 2 tablespoons white wine vinegar
- 2½ tablespoons butter

1. To prepare crab cakes, combine first 7 ingredients in a medium bowl. Gently fold in crabmeat. Gently stir in ¾ cup panko. Cover and chill 30 minutes.

2. Divide crab mixture into 8 equal portions (about ½ cup each); shape each into a ¾-inch-thick patty. Place remaining ¾ cup panko in a shallow dish. Working with 1 patty at a time, dredge in panko. Repeat procedure with remaining patties and panko.

3. Heat a nonstick skillet over medium heat. Add 1½ teaspoons oil, swirling to coat. Coat both sides of crab cakes with cooking spray. Add 4 crab cakes to pan; cook 7 minutes. Carefully turn cakes over; cook 7 minutes or until golden. Remove crab cakes from pan; keep warm. Repeat procedure with remaining 1½ teaspoons oil, cooking spray, and remaining 4 crab cakes.

4. Preheat oven to 450°.

5. To prepare vegetables, leave root and 1-inch stem on carrots; scrub with a brush. Combine carrots, potatoes, and shallots in a small roasting pan. Coat vegetables with cooking spray; sprinkle with ⅛ teaspoon salt. Toss. Bake at 450° for 20 minutes, turning once. Coat haricots verts with cooking spray. Add haricots verts to vegetable mixture; toss. Bake an additional 10 minutes or until vegetables are tender.

6. To prepare sauce, combine broth, shallots, and vinegar in a small saucepan; bring to a boil. Cook until reduced to ¼ cup (about 4 minutes); remove from heat. Stir in butter. Serve with crab cakes and vegetables.

Yield: 4 servings (serving size: 2 crab cakes, about 1 cup vegetables, and about 1½ tablespoons sauce).

CALORIES 443; FAT 16.7g (sat 5.6g, mono 5.2g, poly 2.9g); PROTEIN 32.8g; CARB 42g; FIBER 7g; CHOL 103mg; IRON 2mg; SODIUM 969mg; CALC 163mg

way to pan-fry
soft-shell crabs

Lighter versions of soft-shell crabs are traditionally pan-fried or oven-fried to give them a crisp exterior. They shouldn't be boiled or steamed or they'll end up a soggy mess.

Soft-Shell Crab Sandwiches

Typically considered restaurant-only fare, soft-shell crabs are surprisingly easy to prepare at home.

    4 jumbo soft-shell crabs, cleaned
    3 tablespoons all-purpose flour
    1 teaspoon Old Bay seasoning
    1 tablespoon butter
    ¼ cup Lemon Tartar Sauce
    8 (1-ounce) slices French bread
   12 (¼-inch-thick) slices plum tomato
    4 Bibb lettuce leaves

1. Rinse crabs; pat dry with paper towels.
2. Combine flour and Old Bay seasoning in a shallow dish. Dredge each crab in flour mixture.
3. Melt butter in a large skillet over medium-high heat until butter begins to brown. Add crabs; cook 3 minutes, gently pressing body and legs against pan. Turn crabs; cook 3 minutes or until brown and cooked through. Drain on paper towels.

4. Spread 1 tablespoon Lemon Tartar Sauce over each of 4 bread slices. Top each with 1 crab, 3 tomato slices, and 1 lettuce leaf. Top each with 1 bread slice. **Yield: 4 servings (serving size: 1 sandwich).**

CALORIES 324; FAT 7.9g (sat 3.5g, mono 1.4g, poly 1.2g); PROTEIN 29.2g; CARB 33g; FIBER 1.5g; CHOL 112mg; IRON 2.9mg; SODIUM 981mg; CALC 211mg

See page 27 for more information about how to clean soft-shell crabs.

Lemon Tartar Sauce

    ¼ cup light mayonnaise
    ⅓ cup reduced-fat sour cream
    ⅓ cup finely chopped sweet pickles
    1 tablespoon grated lemon rind
    ¼ teaspoon salt

1. Combine all ingredients in a small bowl, stirring well.
Yield: 6 servings (serving size: 2 tablespoons).

CALORIES 65; FAT 5g (sat 1.7g, mono 1.2g, poly 2g); PROTEIN 0.7g; CARB 4.6g; FIBER 0.2g; CHOL 10mg; IRON 0.1mg; SODIUM 270mg; CALC 24mg

way to pan-fry
meats

Thin, tender cuts of meat, such as pork chops and boneless, skinless chicken breast halves, work best for pan-frying or oven-frying. Larger cuts won't cook long enough to become tender.

Parmesan and Sage–Crusted Pork Chops

High-quality Parmigiano-Reggiano cheese and fresh sage add robust flavors to lean pork chops. Serve with sautéed Swiss chard and creamy polenta for a quick weeknight dinner.

- 1 (1¼-ounce) slice white bread, torn into pieces
- ¼ cup (1 ounce) grated Parmigiano-Reggiano cheese
- 1 tablespoon chopped fresh sage
- ¼ teaspoon salt
- ¼ teaspoon freshly ground black pepper
- ¼ cup all-purpose flour
- 1 tablespoon prepared mustard
- 2 large egg whites, lightly beaten
- 4 (4-ounce) boneless thin-cut pork loin chops, trimmed
- 1½ tablespoons canola oil

1. Place bread in a food processor; pulse bread 10 times or until coarse crumbs measure about 1 cup. Combine breadcrumbs, cheese, sage, salt, and pepper in a shallow dish. Place flour in another shallow dish. Combine mustard and egg whites in another shallow dish, stirring with a whisk.

2. Working with 1 pork chop at a time, dredge pork in flour, shaking off excess. Dip pork into egg white mixture, allowing excess to drip off. Coat pork completely with breadcrumb mixture; set aside. Repeat procedure with remaining pork, flour, egg white mixture, and breadcrumb mixture.

3. Heat a large nonstick skillet over medium heat. Add oil to pan, swirling to coat. Add pork; cook 3 minutes on each side or until browned and done. **Yield: 4 servings (serving size: 1 pork chop).**

CALORIES 272; FAT 13.6g (sat 3.7g, mono 6.6g, poly 2.2g); PROTEIN 28.8g; CARB 7g; FIBER 0.4g; CHOL 69mg; IRON 1.3mg; SODIUM 409mg; CALC 102mg

kitchen how-to:
make breadcrumbs

Homemade breadcrumbs can improve the flavor of your dish. They are easy to make and more economical than purchasing commercial breadcrumbs. You can make breadcrumbs from any type of bread and combine any varieties you have on hand. To make breadcrumbs, place the bread in a food processor, and pulse until the crumbs reach the desired consistency.

way to pan-fry & oven-fry
poultry

Easy Schnitzel

Complete this meal with a tossed salad of mixed greens, cherry tomatoes, sliced cucumber, and carrot ribbons.

- 4 (6-ounce) skinless, boneless chicken breast halves
- ¼ teaspoon salt
- ¼ teaspoon freshly ground black pepper
- 2 tablespoons all-purpose flour
- 2 tablespoons Dijon mustard
- 1 large egg, lightly beaten
- ½ cup dry breadcrumbs
- 1½ tablespoons grated fresh Parmesan cheese
- 2 teaspoons finely chopped fresh parsley
- 2 teaspoons chopped fresh chives
- 1 garlic clove, minced
- 1 tablespoon olive oil

1. Preheat oven to 350°.
2. Place each chicken breast half between 2 sheets of heavy-duty plastic wrap; pound to ½-inch thickness using a meat mallet or rolling pin. Sprinkle chicken evenly with salt and pepper.
3. Place flour in a shallow bowl. Combine mustard and egg in a shallow dish. Combine breadcrumbs, cheese, parsley, chives, and garlic in a shallow dish. Dredge 1 chicken breast half in flour, turning to coat; shake off excess flour. Dip in egg mixture; dredge in breadcrumb mixture. Repeat procedure with remaining chicken, flour, egg mixture, and breadcrumb mixture.
4. Heat a large ovenproof nonstick skillet over medium-high heat. Add oil, swirling to coat. Add chicken; sauté 2½ minutes or until browned. Remove from heat. Turn chicken over; place pan in oven. Bake at 350° for 10 minutes or until chicken is done. **Yield: 4 servings (serving size: 1 chicken breast half).**

CALORIES 328; FAT 8.1g (sat 1.9g, mono 3.8g, poly 1.3g); PROTEIN 45.3g; CARB 16.7g; FIBER 0.7g; CHOL 153mg; IRON 2.6mg; SODIUM 636mg; CALC 85mg

kitchen how-to:
bread a chicken breast

1

2

3

The coating of flour and breadcrumbs helps create the desired crisp crust and also insulates the chicken breast to prevent it from overcooking.

1. Pound chicken breast between 2 sheets of heavy-duty plastic wrap.
2. Working with 1 chicken breast at a time, dredge breast in flour, turning to coat. Shake off excess flour.
3. Dip floured chicken breast in egg mixture.
4. Dredge chicken breast in breadcrumb mixture.

4

Prosciutto and Fontina–Stuffed Chicken Breasts

Finely ground saltine cracker crumbs create a golden crust. You can save the step of making the crumbs if your supermarket stocks cracker meal; if so, start with about 1½ cups. Serve chicken with a crisp green salad with apple wedges to contrast the creamy, melted cheese filling.

Cooking spray
- 1 ounce chopped prosciutto
- 1½ teaspoons minced fresh rosemary
- 2 garlic cloves, minced
- ¼ cup (1 ounce) shredded fontina cheese
- 4 (6-ounce) skinless, boneless chicken breast halves
- ¼ teaspoon freshly ground black pepper
- 42 saltine crackers (about 1 sleeve)
- ½ cup all-purpose flour
- 2 large egg whites, lightly beaten
- 1 tablespoon Dijon mustard
- 2 tablespoons canola oil

1. Heat a large nonstick skillet over medium-high heat. Coat pan with cooking spray. Add prosciutto to pan; sauté 2 minutes or until browned. Add rosemary and garlic to pan; sauté 1 minute. Spoon prosciutto mixture into a bowl; cool to room temperature. Stir in fontina cheese; set aside.

2. Cut a horizontal slit through thickest portion of each chicken breast half to form a pocket (see photo below). Stuff about 2 tablespoons prosciutto mixture into each pocket; press lightly to flatten. Sprinkle chicken evenly with pepper.

3. Place crackers in a food processor, and process 2 minutes or until finely ground. Place cracker crumbs in a shallow dish. Place flour in another shallow dish. Combine egg whites and mustard in another shallow dish, stirring mixture with a whisk.

4. Working with 1 chicken breast half at a time, dredge chicken in flour, shaking off excess. Dip chicken into egg white mixture, allowing excess to drip off. Coat chicken completely with cracker crumbs. Set aside. Repeat procedure with remaining chicken, flour, egg white mixture, and cracker crumbs.

5. Heat pan over medium-high heat. Add oil to pan, swirling to coat. Add chicken to pan; reduce heat to medium, and cook 10 minutes on each side or until browned and done. **Yield: 4 servings (serving size: 1 stuffed chicken breast half).**

CALORIES 381; FAT 14g (sat 3g, mono 6.4g, poly 2.9g); PROTEIN 46.6g; CARB 14.1g; FIBER 0.6g; CHOL 113mg; IRON 2.4mg; SODIUM 591mg; CALC 74mg

Oven-fried Crust

What it adds: Traditional fried chicken is high in fat for two main reasons: the frying oil and the skin on the chicken. By cooking the chicken in the oven using less oil and removing the skin, we were able to create a healthier version. We also dipped the chicken in buttermilk just like many traditional recipes, but we opted for the lower-fat version. To maintain the crispy exterior, we supplemented some of the flour with cracker meal to give it crunch. These changes reduced the calories by 54 percent and the fat content by 78 percent when compared to traditionally fried chicken to create a healthier but still tasty meal.

Buttermilk Oven-fried Chicken with Coleslaw

Coleslaw:
- 4 cups packaged cabbage-and-carrot coleslaw
- 3 tablespoons fat-free mayonnaise
- 1½ teaspoons sugar
- ½ teaspoon celery seeds
- 1½ teaspoons cider vinegar
- ⅛ teaspoon salt

Chicken:
- 1 cup low-fat buttermilk
- 4 (8-ounce) bone-in chicken breast halves, skinned
- ⅓ cup all-purpose flour
- ⅓ cup cracker meal
- ½ teaspoon salt
- ½ teaspoon freshly ground black pepper
- 2 tablespoons butter

1. To prepare coleslaw, combine first 6 ingredients; toss to coat. Cover and chill.

2. Preheat oven to 425°.

3. To prepare chicken, combine buttermilk and chicken in a shallow dish, turning to coat.

4. Combine flour and cracker meal in a dish. Transfer chicken from buttermilk to a work surface. Sprinkle chicken evenly with ½ teaspoon salt and pepper. Working with 1 chicken breast half at a time, dredge chicken in flour mixture, shaking off excess; set aside. Repeat procedure with remaining chicken and flour mixture.

5. Melt butter in a large ovenproof nonstick skillet over medium-high heat. Add chicken to pan, meat side down; cook 4 minutes or until golden brown. Turn chicken over; place pan in oven. Bake at 425° for 32 minutes or until a thermometer registers 165°. Serve chicken with slaw.

Yield: 4 servings (serving size: 1 chicken breast half and ¾ cup slaw).

CALORIES 342; FAT 8.8g (sat 4.5g, mono 2.2g, poly 0.8g); PROTEIN 45.1g; CARB 18.5g; FIBER 2.6g; CHOL 123mg; IRON 2.3mg; SODIUM 672mg; CALC 95mg

way to oven-fry
vegetables

Firm, sturdy vegetables, such as potatoes, green tomatoes, okra, and onions, are the best choices for pan-frying or oven-frying. They can support the hearty breading and stand up to the heat needed to create a crispy coating.

Oven-fried Okra

Fried okra is a classic Southern treat. This version produces a crisp coating without frying.

1½ cups yellow cornmeal
 ¾ teaspoon kosher salt, divided
 ½ teaspoon freshly ground black pepper
Dash of ground red pepper
 ½ cup fat-free buttermilk
 1 large egg, lightly beaten
 1 pound fresh okra pods, trimmed and cut
    into ¾-inch slices (about 3 cups)
Cooking spray

1. Preheat oven to 450°.
2. Combine cornmeal, ½ teaspoon salt, black pepper, and red pepper in a shallow dish; set aside.
3. Combine buttermilk and egg in a large bowl, stirring with a whisk. Add okra, and toss to coat. Let stand 3 minutes.

4. Dredge okra in cornmeal mixture. Place okra on a preheated jelly-roll pan coated with cooking spray. Lightly coat okra with cooking spray. Bake at 450° for 40 minutes, stirring once. Sprinkle with remaining ¼ teaspoon salt. **Yield: 8 servings (serving size: about ½ cup).**

CALORIES 144; FAT 0.7g (sat 0.2g, mono 0.3g, poly 0.1g); PROTEIN 4.5g; CARB 29.3g; FIBER 2.6g; CHOL 27mg; IRON 1.3mg; SODIUM 204mg; CALC 68mg

all about okra

Okra has a mild flavor similar to that of green beans and, once cooked, a characteristic viscous texture. Select smaller okra pods (less than 4 inches long) that are firm, brightly colored, and free of blemishes. Refrigerate for up to three days in a plastic bag.

Barbecue-Flavored Onion Rings

Regular yellow onions will work in this recipe, but sweet onions have a milder flavor.

3 tablespoons all-purpose flour
1 tablespoon sugar
1 teaspoon chili powder
1 teaspoon ground cumin
½ teaspoon salt
½ teaspoon paprika
¼ teaspoon ground allspice
2 large eggs, lightly beaten
1 pound Vidalia or other sweet onions, cut into ¼-inch-thick slices and separated into rings (about 2 large)
1½ cups dry breadcrumbs, divided
Cooking spray

1. Preheat oven to 450°. Place baking sheet in oven.

2. Combine first 8 ingredients in a large bowl. Dip onion rings in flour mixture. Place half of onion rings in a zip-top plastic bag; add ¾ cup breadcrumbs, shaking bag to coat onion rings. Repeat procedure with remaining onion rings and remaining ¾ cup breadcrumbs.

3. Arrange onion rings in a single layer on 2 preheated baking sheets coated with cooking spray. Lightly coat onion rings with cooking spray. Bake at 450° for 5 minutes. Rotate pans on racks; bake 5 minutes. Turn onion rings over; lightly coat with cooking spray and bake 5 minutes. Rotate pans and bake 5 minutes or until crisp. Serve immediately. **Yield: 6 servings.**

CALORIES 188; FAT 3.3g (sat 0.9g, mono 0.9g, poly 0.8g); PROTEIN 6.9g; CARB 32.6g; FIBER 2.6g; CHOL 71mg; IRON 2.1mg; SODIUM 431mg; CALC 79mg

kitchen how-to:
make onion rings

Coating the onion rings with breadcrumbs in batches keeps the crumbs dry for maximum crispness. Preheat the baking sheet to achieve better results—it helps the undersides stay crisp. Rotate the pans and turn the onion rings once during cooking for even browning.

1. Dip onion rings in flour mixture. Place half of onion rings in a zip-top plastic bag; add half of the breadcrumbs, shaking bag to coat onion rings. Repeat procedure with remaining onion rings and remaining half of breadcrumbs.

2. Arrange onion rings in a single layer on 2 preheated baking sheets coated with cooking spray. Leave ample space between rings on the baking sheet. If it's too crowded, the rings will steam instead of crisp. Lightly coat onion rings with cooking spray. Place in the oven, and bake according to recipe directions.

all about latkes

Latkes, or potato pancakes, are traditionally eaten during Hanukkah. They're usually fried in oil, which symbolizes the one-day supply of oil that miraculously kept the Second Temple of ancient Israel lit for eight days. They may be topped with a variety of condiments—sour cream for a savory flavor and applesauce for sweet—or served without a garnish.

Basic Potato Latkes

The reserved potato starch helps bind the potato-onion mixture and adds heft to this traditional Hanukkah treat. Use the shredding blade of a food processor for the quickest prep and fluffiest texture. Thoroughly combine the potato and onion; the onion helps prevent discoloration. Serve the latkes with applesauce and sour cream.

> 2 pounds baking potato, peeled
> 1 small onion (about 6 ounces), peeled
> ¼ cup egg substitute
> 2 tablespoons all-purpose flour
> 1 teaspoon kosher salt
> ¼ teaspoon freshly ground black pepper
> ¼ cup chopped fresh flat-leaf parsley
> 3 tablespoons canola oil, divided

1. Shred potato and onion using the shredding blade of a food processor. Combine shredded potato and onion in a colander over a large bowl, tossing well to combine. Let mixture stand 15 minutes, pressing occasionally with the back of a spoon until most of liquid drains off. Remove colander from bowl. Carefully pour off the potato liquid, reserving thick white layer of potato starch in the bottom of the bowl (see photo at right). Discard potato liquid.
2. Combine egg substitute and next 3 ingredients in a small bowl, stirring with a whisk. Add egg mixture to potato starch in large bowl, stirring well with a whisk. Add potato mixture and parsley to bowl, tossing well to combine.
3. Heat a 12-inch nonstick skillet over medium-high heat. Add 1½ tablespoons oil to pan, swirling to coat. Add potato mixture in ¼-cupfuls to pan to form 6 latkes; flatten slightly. Cook 4 minutes on each side or until golden brown. Remove latkes from pan; keep warm. Repeat procedure with remaining 1½ tablespoons oil and remaining potato mixture. **Yield: 6 servings (serving size: 2 latkes).**

CALORIES 208; FAT 7.2g (sat 0.6g, mono 4.1g, poly 2.1g); PROTEIN 4.9g; CARB 32.3g; FIBER 2.6g; CHOL 0mg; IRON 1.8mg; SODIUM 345mg; CALC 34mg

Open-Faced Bacon, Lettuce, and Fried Green Tomato Sandwiches

Double-breading the tomato slices gives them a crunchy coating. Soaking the tomatoes in hot water draws out their moisture, which helps keep them crisp when cooked. Picked before ripe, green tomatoes have a sharp, tart taste and firm flesh, which makes them excellent for frying. You don't want to eat them raw, but cooking green tomatoes softens the flesh and tempers the acidity. Serve the fried green tomatoes on their own as a side dish.

  2 medium green tomatoes, cut into
     12 (¼-inch-thick) slices (about 1 pound)
  2 tablespoons fat-free milk
  4 large egg whites, lightly beaten
1½ cups yellow cornmeal
  ¾ teaspoon salt
  ¼ teaspoon freshly ground black pepper
  2 tablespoons olive oil, divided
  5 tablespoons light mayonnaise
  1 teaspoon fresh lemon juice
  ¼ teaspoon hot sauce
  6 (1½-ounce) slices white bread, toasted
  6 Bibb lettuce leaves
  9 bacon slices, cooked and cut in half
  2 tablespoons chopped fresh chives

1. Place tomato slices in a large bowl; cover with hot water. Let stand 15 minutes. Drain and pat dry with paper towels. Combine milk and egg whites, stirring with a whisk. Combine cornmeal, salt, and pepper in a shallow dish, stirring with a whisk. Working with 1 tomato slice at a time, dip slice in milk mixture, and dredge in cornmeal mixture. Return tomato slices, 1 at a time, to milk mixture; dredge in cornmeal mixture.
2. Heat a large nonstick skillet over medium-high heat. Add 1 tablespoon oil, swirling to coat. Add half of tomato slices; cook 4 minutes on each side or until crisp and golden. Repeat procedure with remaining oil and tomato slices.

3. Combine mayonnaise, juice, and hot sauce, stirring with a whisk. Spread about 1 tablespoon mayonnaise mixture onto each bread slice; top with 1 lettuce leaf, 3 bacon pieces, and 2 tomato slices. Sprinkle each sandwich with 1 teaspoon chives. Serve immediately.
Yield: 6 servings (serving size: 1 sandwich).

CALORIES 386; FAT 12.8g (sat 2.8g, mono 4.5g, poly 2.6g); PROTEIN 12.2g; CARB 56.2g; FIBER 3.9g; CHOL 16mg; IRON 2.2mg; SODIUM 834mg; CALC 44mg

kitchen how-to:
chop fresh chives

Chives vary in shape from grass-fine to pencil-thick. The thicker the chive, the more flavor it packs. In order to chop chives safely, hold them in a bunch and place on a clean cutting board. Using a sharp knife, chop chives to desired size. Keep them in the refrigerator until they're ready to be used.

way to
broil

Broiling is a dry-heat cooking method that works nicely for a wide variety of foods and creates delicious browned edges and hearty flavors. This technique is useful for health-conscious cooks because little or no butter or oil is needed to glean superb results.

Like grilling, broiling provides an intense source of heat that cooks the food—usually thin or small pieces—from one side (in this case, from the top). The high heat cooks the food quickly and browns the surface, which mimics some of the pleasing effects of grilling.

broiling, defined

To broil is to cook foods under an intense source of heat. It's similar to grilling, except the heat comes from above instead of below. The dry, high heat creates a crisp outer layer while keeping the inside moist, and the food cooks quickly, often taking just a few minutes to prepare.

Best Bets for Broiling

Cooking time under the high heat of a broiler is quick, so it's important that foods are naturally tender, particularly meats, since there's not enough time to soften the fibers of tougher cuts. The best cuts to use are lean, tender meats such as beef tenderloin, pork chops, fish fillets, and chicken breasts. Unless you're cooking a thin cut, you may need to flip the food halfway through to ensure that it cooks evenly. The same is true for produce. Tender fruits and vegetables like asparagus, yellow squash or zucchini, or peaches brown nicely under a broiler. You can also use the broiler to melt cheese or finish cooking casseroles and other dishes to get a nice browned top.

Equipment

As in grilling, you want the grease and fat to drip away as the food broils. Use a broiler pan so meats don't sit in their juices, and be sure to spray the broiler pan and rack with cooking spray to keep foods from sticking. It's always best to preheat the broiler and the pan for 5 minutes before cooking—if they're hot, the foods will cook more uniformly.

Keep Close Watch

This high heat also has a tendency to char foods, which helps create the nice brown exterior, but it also means that foods can quickly burn and smoke. Unlike grilling, broiling is done inside your home, which means that any excess smoke isn't able to dissipate in an open space, so keep a close eye on foods as they broil. It's also helpful to avoid meats that have a high fat content and trim any excess fat from those that do.

the bottom line

The three most important elements to remember about broiling:

1. Use a broiler pan coated with cooking spray so the food won't stick and excess fat and grease can drip away.
2. Preheat the broiler and broiler pan.
3. Keep a close eye on foods as they broil to avoid overcooking.

way to broil
fish & shellfish

Pine Nuts
What they add: Pine nuts, or *pignolias,* are high in good-for-you mono- and polyunsaturated fats. Toasting the nuts enhances their flavor.

Red Snapper
What it adds: Red snapper has a firm texture, rich color, and a sweet mild flavor similar to shrimp.

Broiled Red Snapper with Sicilian Tomato Pesto

Plum tomatoes work best in this recipe; juicier tomatoes thin the pesto. No need to seed or peel the tomatoes. You can make the pesto ahead and keep it chilled. Stir in the tomatoes just before serving.

Pesto:
- 2 cups basil leaves
- 2 tablespoons pine nuts, toasted
- 2 tablespoons extra-virgin olive oil
- 2 garlic cloves, minced
- ¼ cup (1 ounce) grated Parmigiano-Reggiano cheese
- ⅛ teaspoon crushed red pepper
- 1½ cups chopped plum tomato (about 3 medium)
- ½ teaspoon salt
- ½ teaspoon freshly ground black pepper

Fish:
- 6 (6-ounce) red snapper or other firm whitefish fillets
- ¼ teaspoon salt
- Cooking spray

Remaining Ingredient:
- 3 cups hot cooked orzo

1. To prepare pesto, place first 4 ingredients in a food processor; process until smooth. Add cheese and red pepper; process until blended. Transfer mixture to a bowl. Add tomato, ½ teaspoon salt, and black pepper, stirring gently to combine.
2. Preheat broiler and broiler pan.
3. To prepare fish, sprinkle fish with ¼ teaspoon salt. Arrange fish on broiler pan coated with cooking spray, and broil 8 minutes or until fish flakes easily when tested with a fork. Place orzo on each of 6 plates, and top each serving with fish and pesto. **Yield: 6 servings (serving size: ½ cup orzo, 1 fillet, and ¼ cup pesto).**

CALORIES 437; FAT 10.8g (sat 2.4, mono 4.8, poly 2); PROTEIN 44.9g; CARB 38.9g; FIBER 3.1g; CHOL 67mg; IRON 2.9mg; SODIUM 497mg; CALC 156mg

kitchen how-to:
broil fish

Arrange fish on a preheated broiler pan coated with cooking spray to prevent it from sticking. The thickness of the fish will dictate how long it needs to broil, so follow your recipe's instructions. To test for doneness, flake the fish with a fork while it's on the broiler pan; it should flake easily, but still be firm.

way to broil
fruit

When you sprinkle fruit with a little sugar and place it under the broiler for a few minutes, the sugar caramelizes, creating an intensely flavorful dessert.

Broiled Peaches and Hazelnuts with Vanilla Ice Cream

You can also shave the chocolate with a vegetable peeler, if you'd like.

- ¼ cup hazelnuts
- 4 cups peeled sliced peaches (about 1 pound)
- ¼ cup sugar
- Cooking spray
- 2 cups vanilla fat-free ice cream (such as Breyers)
- 1 ounce bittersweet chocolate, grated

1. Preheat oven to 350°.
2. Place hazelnuts on a baking sheet. Bake at 350° for 15 minutes, stirring once. Transfer nuts to a colander or dish, and rub briskly with a towel to remove skins. Chop nuts.
3. Preheat broiler and broiler pan.
4. Combine hazelnuts, peaches, and sugar in a large bowl, tossing to coat. Arrange peach mixture in a single layer on broiler pan coated with cooking spray; broil 5 minutes or until lightly browned. Cool.
5. Spoon ⅓ cup ice cream into each of 6 bowls; top each serving with 1 cup peach mixture and 2 teaspoons grated chocolate. **Yield: 6 servings.**

CALORIES 187; FAT 5.7g (sat 1.3g, mono 2.8g, poly 0.5g); PROTEIN 3.9g; CARB 33.7g; FIBER 2.2g; CHOL 0mg; IRON 0.4mg; SODIUM 30mg; CALC 61mg

kitchen how-to:
skin hazelnuts

Toasting enhances the flavor of hazelnuts—they become smoky and the texture is crisp and crunchy. After toasting, it's important to remove the bitter brown skin for a better flavor.

1. Spread shelled hazelnuts on a baking sheet in a single layer. Bake at 350° for 15 minutes or until the skins begin to split, stirring once.
2. Transfer the warmed hazelnuts to a colander or dish, and rub briskly with a towel to remove the skins.

way to broil
meats

Cooking under the high heat of a broiler is quick. Since there's not enough time to soften the fibers of tougher cuts, use meats that are naturally tender.

Quick Barbecue Flank Steak

Round out the meal with coleslaw and Texas toast. To make the toast, combine 1 tablespoon softened butter and 1 minced garlic clove; spread on 4 (1½-ounce) slices toasted sourdough bread.

1	cup barbecue sauce
¼	cup fresh lemon juice
1	tablespoon prepared mustard
1½	teaspoons celery seeds
¼	teaspoon hot sauce
2	garlic cloves, minced
1	(1-pound) flank steak, trimmed

Cooking spray

1. Preheat broiler and broiler pan.
2. Combine first 6 ingredients in a large bowl; add steak, turning to coat. Remove steak from sauce, reserving sauce mixture. Place steak on broiler pan coated with cooking spray; broil 6 minutes on each side or until desired degree of doneness. Let stand 5 minutes. Cut steak diagonally across the grain into thin slices.
3. While steak stands, bring sauce mixture to a boil in a saucepan over high heat. Reduce heat, and cook 5 minutes. Serve with steak. **Yield: 4 servings (serving size: 3 ounces steak and ¼ cup sauce).**

CALORIES 234; FAT 10.1g (sat 3.9g, mono 4.1g, poly 0.8g); PROTEIN 24.6g; CARB 10.4g; FIBER 1.1g; CHOL 57mg; IRON 3.2mg; SODIUM 625mg; CALC 38mg

kitchen how-to:
cut flank steak

Flank steak has a distinct, visible grain, and it should be cut across this grain into ⅛- to ¼-inch-thick slices for maximum tenderness. Allow 5 minutes of stand time before slicing so the flavorful juices will reabsorb and redistribute, and they won't run out as freely when you carve. Tilt your knife diagonally and slice away from you to ensure the largest surface area possible for each piece.

Lamb Chops with Herb Vinaigrette

Serve with garlic mashed potatoes and steamed broccoli florets. If you have bottled roasted red bell peppers in your refrigerator, you can substitute them for the pimiento.

- ½ teaspoon salt, divided
- ½ teaspoon black pepper
- 8 (4-ounce) lamb loin chops
- Cooking spray
- 2 tablespoons finely chopped shallots
- 1½ tablespoons water
- 1 tablespoon red wine vinegar
- 1½ teaspoons lemon juice
- 1½ teaspoons extra-virgin olive oil
- 1 teaspoon Dijon mustard
- 1½ tablespoons finely chopped fresh flat-leaf parsley
- 1½ tablespoons finely chopped fresh tarragon
- 1 tablespoon finely chopped fresh mint
- 1 tablespoon finely chopped pimiento

1. Preheat broiler and broiler pan.
2. Sprinkle ¼ teaspoon salt and pepper over lamb. Place lamb on broiler pan coated with cooking spray; broil 5 minutes on each side or until desired degree of doneness.
3. Combine shallots, 1½ tablespoons water, and vinegar in a small microwave-safe bowl; microwave at HIGH 30 seconds. Stir in remaining ¼ teaspoon salt, juice, oil, and mustard, stirring with a whisk. Add parsley and remaining ingredients, stirring well. Serve vinaigrette over lamb. **Yield: 4 servings (serving size: 2 chops and 1 tablespoon vinaigrette).**

CALORIES 349; FAT 15.2g (sat 5.1g, mono 6.7g, poly 1.4g); PROTEIN 47.7g; CARB 1.9g; FIBER 0.2g; CHOL 150mg; IRON 4.6mg; SODIUM 482mg; CALC 37mg

buying and storing mint
When buying fresh mint, look for bright green, crisp leaves with no sign of wilting.

Place the stems in a glass containing a couple inches of water, and cover the leaves loosely with plastic wrap or a zip-top plastic bag (do not seal the bag). Refrigerate for up to one week, changing the water every other day. Fresh mint can also be frozen; just rinse the leaves, pat dry, and freeze in a zip-top plastic freezer bag. The leaves will darken once they're frozen, but that doesn't affect the flavor. Take out what you need, and return the rest to the freezer.

Pork Chops Stuffed with Feta and Spinach

Lemon juice in the glaze mixture and rind in the filling add a citrusy tang to the Greek-inspired filling.

Cooking spray
4 garlic cloves, minced and divided
½ teaspoon salt, divided
¼ teaspoon freshly ground black pepper, divided
5 sun-dried tomatoes, packed without oil, diced
1 (10-ounce) package frozen chopped spinach, thawed, drained, and squeezed dry
¼ cup (1 ounce) crumbled reduced-fat feta cheese
3 tablespoons (1½-ounces) block-style fat-free cream cheese
½ teaspoon grated lemon rind
4 (4-ounce) boneless center-cut loin pork chops, trimmed
2 tablespoons fresh lemon juice
2 teaspoons Dijon mustard
¼ teaspoon dried oregano

1. Preheat broiler and broiler pan.
2. Heat a large nonstick skillet over medium-high heat. Coat pan with cooking spray. Add 2 garlic cloves; sauté 1 minute. Add ¼ teaspoon salt, ⅛ teaspoon pepper, tomatoes, and spinach; sauté until moisture evaporates. Remove from heat; stir in cheeses and rind.

3. Cut a horizontal slit through thickest portion of each pork chop to form a pocket (see photo below). Stuff ¼ cup spinach mixture into each pocket. Sprinkle remaining ¼ teaspoon salt and remaining ⅛ teaspoon pepper over pork. Arrange pork on broiler pan coated with cooking spray. Combine remaining 2 garlic cloves, juice, mustard, and oregano in a small bowl; stir well. Brush half of mustard mixture over pork. Broil 6 minutes; turn pork. Brush remaining mixture over pork; broil 2 minutes or until done. **Yield: 4 servings (serving size: 1 pork chop).**

CALORIES 232; FAT 8.6g (sat 3.4g, mono 3.1g, poly 0.7g); PROTEIN 32.1g; CARB 7.2g; FIBER 2.8g; CHOL 73mg; IRON 2.5mg; SODIUM 640mg; CALC 186mg

kitchen how-to:
grate fresh citrus rind

A Microplane® food grater is the ideal tool to use when a recipe calls for grated lemon rind or lemon zest. It's fast and efficient, and it removes only the intensely flavored yellow lemon rind without any of the bitter white pith. But be careful—one slip can result in a scraped knuckle. You can also use a zester, handheld grater, or the fine face of a box grater. Don't use too much rind—it can add bitterness rather than tartness to a recipe. One medium lemon will yield about 1 teaspoon grated rind.

way to broil
poultry

Honey
What it adds: The honey's natural sugars caramelize under the high heat of the broiler, creating a crusty, flavorful exterior.

Chicken Thighs
What they add: Skinless, boneless thighs are more flavorful than white meat. Without the skin, thighs are only marginally higher in fat and calories, and you can lower the fat content even more by trimming any visible fat from the meat.

Spicy Honey-Brushed Chicken Thighs

Serve with garlic-roasted potato wedges and tossed salad.

- 2 teaspoons garlic powder
- 2 teaspoons chili powder
- 1 teaspoon salt
- 1 teaspoon ground cumin
- 1 teaspoon paprika
- ½ teaspoon ground red pepper
- 8 skinless, boneless chicken thighs
  Cooking spray
- 6 tablespoons honey
- 2 teaspoons cider vinegar

1. Preheat broiler and broiler pan.
2. Combine first 6 ingredients in a large bowl. Add chicken to bowl, and toss to coat. Place chicken on broiler pan coated with cooking spray. Broil chicken 5 minutes on each side.
3. Combine honey and vinegar in a small bowl, stirring well. Remove chicken from oven; brush ¼ cup honey mixture on chicken. Broil 1 minute. Remove chicken from oven and turn over. Brush chicken with remaining honey mixture. Broil 1 additional minute or until chicken is done. **Yield: 4 servings (serving size: 2 chicken thighs).**

CALORIES 321; FAT 11g (sat 3g, mono 4.1g, poly 2.5g); PROTEIN 28g; CARB 27.9g; FIBER 0.6g; CHOL 99mg; IRON 2.1mg; SODIUM 676mg; CALC 21mg

all about honey

This wonderful, rich, golden liquid is a natural sweetener that can enhance a variety of dishes. The color and flavor of the honey depends on the type of flowers the bees collect the nectar from, but in general lighter-colored honeys have a milder flavor than darker ones.

Honey is available throughout the year, but it's an extraordinary treat if you can find a jar of local honey in the summer and fall when it's just been harvested.

way to broil

enchiladas

Speedy Chicken and Cheese Enchiladas

Rotisserie chicken and prechopped vegetables make this a quick casserole.

Cooking spray
- 1 cup prechopped white onion
- 1 cup prechopped green or red bell pepper
- 1 (10-ounce) can enchilada sauce (such as Old El Paso)
- 2 cups chopped skinless, boneless rotisserie chicken breast (about 8 ounces)
- 1 cup (4 ounces) preshredded reduced-fat Mexican blend cheese, divided
- ½ teaspoon ground cumin
- 8 (6-inch) corn tortillas
- ¼ cup fat-free sour cream
- ¼ cup chopped fresh cilantro

1. Preheat broiler.
2. Heat a large nonstick skillet over medium-high heat. Coat pan with cooking spray. Add onion and pepper; sauté 2 minutes or until crisp-tender. Add enchilada sauce; bring to a boil. Cover, reduce heat, and simmer 5 minutes.
3. Combine chicken, ¾ cup cheese, and cumin, tossing well.
4. Wrap tortillas in damp paper towels; microwave at HIGH 30 seconds or until warm. Spoon ¼ cup chicken mixture in center of each tortilla; roll up. Place tortillas, seam sides down, in an 11 x 7–inch baking dish coated with cooking spray. Pour sauce mixture over enchiladas; broil 3 minutes or until thoroughly heated. Sprinkle remaining ¼ cup cheese evenly over enchiladas, and broil 1 minute or until cheese melts. Serve with sour cream and cilantro. **Yield: 4 servings (serving size: 2 enchiladas, 1 tablespoon sour cream, and 1 tablespoon cilantro).**

CALORIES 364; FAT 10.9g (sat 4.9g, mono 2.9g, poly 1.4g); PROTEIN 29.7g; CARB 37.2g; FIBER 4.1g; CHOL 70mg; IRON 1.7mg; SODIUM 701mg; CALC 339mg

kitchen how-to:
heat tortillas

To heat the tortillas, wrap them, 4 at a time, in a damp paper towel and microwave at HIGH 30 seconds. Or warm them on a grill pan on the stovetop. To keep the tortillas from splitting, lightly coat them with cooking spray before heating them.

way to broil
quesadillas

Black Bean Quesadillas with Corn Salsa

A superquick corn salsa completes this tasty vegetarian meal. You might want to make a little extra salsa to have on hand later to serve with chips.

Quesadillas:
- 1 tablespoon olive oil
- 1½ teaspoons bottled minced garlic
- 2 cups chopped plum tomatoes
- ½ cup chopped fresh cilantro
- 1 (15-ounce) can black beans, rinsed and drained
- 4 (8-inch) flour tortillas
- Cooking spray
- ¾ cup (3 ounces) preshredded 4-cheese Mexican blend cheese

Salsa:
- 1 cup frozen whole-kernel corn
- ½ cup chopped fresh cilantro
- 2 tablespoons fresh lime juice
- ½ teaspoon bottled minced garlic
- 1 red bell pepper, chopped

1. To prepare quesadillas, preheat broiler and baking sheet.
2. Heat olive oil in a large skillet over medium-high heat. Add 1½ teaspoons garlic; sauté 30 seconds. Add tomatoes, ½ cup cilantro, and beans; cook 5 minutes or until liquid evaporates, stirring occasionally. Place tortillas on baking sheet coated with cooking spray. Top each tortilla with ½ cup bean mixture and 3 tablespoons cheese; fold in half. Lightly coat tops with cooking spray. Broil 3 minutes or until cheese melts and tortillas begin to brown. Cut each tortilla into 3 wedges.

3. To prepare salsa, combine corn and next 4 ingredients in a small saucepan. Bring to a boil over high heat, and cook 2 minutes, stirring frequently. Serve with quesadillas.
Yield: 4 servings (serving size: 3 quesadilla wedges and about ⅓ cup salsa).

CALORIES 420; FAT 14.4g (sat 5.5g, mono 6.4g, poly 1.3g); PROTEIN 17.8g; CARB 60g; FIBER 10.3g; CHOL 19mg; IRON 4.2mg; SODIUM 590mg; CALC 272mg

kitchen how-to:
broil quesadillas

Broiling the quesadillas in the oven saves you time in two ways: You can cook all the quesadillas together instead of one at a time in a skillet. And you don't have to flip them (or struggle to keep the filling from falling out), so your hands will be free for other last-minute meal preparations. Place the tortillas on a baking sheet coated with cooking spray. Top each tortilla with fillings and cheese; fold in half. Lightly coat the tops with cooking spray. Broil 3 minutes or until the cheese melts and the tortillas begin to brown.

way to broil
vegetables

Broiling is a quick and easy way to prepare tender vegetables, such as asparagus, zucchini, yellow squash, and bell peppers. Simply season them, arrange them on a broiler pan in a single layer, and broil until tender and slightly charred.

Orange-Herbed Asparagus

- 1 tablespoon butter, softened
- 1 teaspoon grated orange rind
- 1 garlic clove, minced
- 1 teaspoon chopped fresh thyme
- ⅛ teaspoon salt
- ⅛ teaspoon freshly ground black pepper
- ¾ pound asparagus

Cooking spray

1. Preheat broiler and broiler pan.
2. Combine first 6 ingredients. Set aside.
3. Place asparagus on broiler pan coated with cooking spray. Coat asparagus with cooking spray. Broil 7 minutes or until lightly browned. Toss asparagus with butter mixture. **Yield: 2 servings.**

CALORIES 77; FAT 5.8g (sat 3.6g, mono 1.5g, poly 0.3g); PROTEIN 2.2g; CARB 4.4g; FIBER 2.1g; CHOL 15mg; IRON 2mg; SODIUM 188mg; CALC 30mg

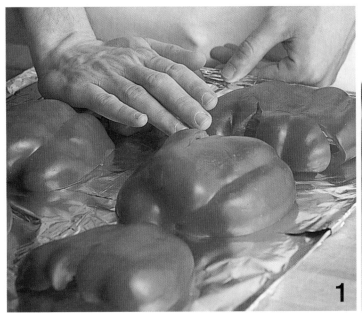

Broiling transforms crisp, plump bell peppers into a smoky and sweet version of themselves with a velvety texture. Use them on sandwiches and pizza, or stir them into hummus for a flavorful dip. All bell peppers—green, yellow, and red—can be broiled. Cutting the peppers in half before broiling them simplifies the process. Plus, lining the baking sheet with foil makes cleanup a snap. Follow these steps for broiling and peeling bell peppers with ease.

1. Cut the bell peppers in half lengthwise; discard the seeds and membranes. Place the pepper halves, skin sides up, on a foil-lined baking sheet; flatten the peppers with your hand.

2. Broil the peppers three inches from the heat for 10 to 12 minutes or until blackened.

3. Place the peppers in a heavy-duty zip-top plastic bag; seal and let stand 10 to 15 minutes. (This will loosen the skins and make peeling them much easier.)

4. Peel and discard the skins. Store peppers in an airtight container in the refrigerator.

flavorful

& slow

way to
boil &
simmer

We use both boiling and simmering to prepare everything from pasta and green vegetables to stewed meats. These essential techniques are variations of the same process—both are virtually fat-free cooking methods that require little more than a heavy-bottomed pot or saucepan to distribute the heat. Each technique, however, has a profoundly different effect on food and distinguishing characteristics that work best in certain applications. Heating water in a pan sounds elementary and a procedure an average cook can master without special skills, but learning the specifics of boiling and simmering will help you become a better cook.

boiling & simmering, defined

Boiling cooks food at a relatively high temperature—212° is the boiling point for water at sea level. When liquids boil, bubbles break through and pop on the surface while the whole batch of liquid churns vigorously.

boiling

Simmering refers to cooking food in liquid (or cooking just the liquid itself) at a temperature slightly below the boiling point—around 180° to 190°. It's gentler but trickier than boiling because it requires careful temperature regulation so that the surface of the liquid shimmers with a bubble coming up every few seconds.

simmering

What Boiling Does

In the case of pasta, churning, boiling water keeps the food in motion, prevents sticking, and cooks quickly so the pasta doesn't get soggy. Green vegetables tossed into boiling water cook as quickly as possible so they retain their flavor and bright color in a process called blanching; if they simmered gently in a covered pot, their color would dull, and they would lose much of their texture. Boiling causes speedy evaporation, a useful process for reducing sauces, where the volume of the liquid decreases and flavors are concentrated.

Boiling Liquid

When ingredients are boiled, they're done so in water, sometimes containing salt and oil or butter for flavor and texture. The food is usually added to the liquid once it reaches a boil.

Best Bets for Boiling

This intense cooking method is well suited for pasta, some grains, and green vegetables. Boiling is also useful for reducing sauces.

What Simmering Does

Simmering cooks food gently and slowly. Delicate foods such as fish are poached at or below a simmer to prevent them from breaking apart. Meats that are simmered remain moist and fork-tender, while boiled meats are often dry and tough because the heat of boiling liquid can cause the proteins in meat to toughen. Stocks are simmered so the fat and proteins released by the meat or bones float to the top where they can be skimmed off. If heated too intensely, the fat and proteins will emulsify into the liquid, making the stock cloudy.

Best Bets for Simmering

Simmering, which is more versatile than boiling, lends itself to a variety of foods. We use it to cook proteins (fish, poultry, and meats), often in the form of poaching (cooking in enough liquid to cover the food) and braising (cooking in a small amount of liquid). It's also essential when making broth or stock. Boiling works well for tender green vegetables, but tough, fibrous root vegetables (such as potatoes, turnips, and beets) are best when simmered so they cook evenly throughout.

Simmering Liquid

Food is usually simmered in a flavored liquid, such as broth/stock or wine, but sometimes we use water. As a general rule, add meat to cold liquid, and bring it to a simmer.

If you add uncooked meat to already-simmering broth, the meat immediately releases proteins that cloud the broth. When you start the meat in cold liquid, these proteins are released more gradually and become entangled with one another in a frothy mass that's easy to skim off the surface. Simmering fish is an exception; if you start poaching small pieces of fish in cold liquid, by the time the liquid comes to a simmer, the fish will be overcooked.

Maintaining a Simmer

A constant simmer isn't always easy to regulate, especially on a gas stovetop. Even at the lowest setting, the heat can be too intense and cause the liquid to boil. Turning the flame too low can cause it to extinguish, or the self-lighting mechanism can click incessantly. To avoid this, put the pot to one side of the flame, or use a device called a flame tamer or heat diffuser (or sometimes called a simmer ring) to absorb some of the stove's heat.

the bottom line

The three most important elements to remember about boiling and simmering:

1. When simmering, a small bubble or two should break through the surface of the liquid every second or two. If more bubbles rise to the surface, lower the heat, or move the pot to one side of the burner.

2. When simmering meat or large pieces of fish, place the food in cold water, and then bring it to a simmer.

3. When boiling vegetables or pasta, add the uncooked food to water that's fully churning.

way to boil & simmer
cider

Basic Spiced Apple Cider

- 2 quarts (64 ounces) apple cider
- ¼ cup packed brown sugar
- 15 whole cloves
- 10 whole allspice
- 2 (3-inch) cinnamon sticks

1. Combine cider and sugar in a large saucepan, stirring until sugar dissolves. Add remaining ingredients, and bring to a boil. Reduce heat to medium, and simmer 15 minutes. Strain through a sieve, discard solids, and serve warm. **Yield: 8 servings (serving size: 1 cup).**

CALORIES 166; FAT 0g (sat 0g, mono 0g, poly 0g); PROTEIN 1g; CARB 41.7g; FIBER 0g; CHOL 0mg; IRON 0.1mg; SODIUM 3mg; CALC 6mg

Cranberry-Apple: After cider mixture reaches a boil, reduce heat, and stir in 2 cups unsweetened cranberry juice; simmer 20 minutes. Optional: Add ½ cup whole fresh cranberries to the pan as the cider simmers; strain before serving.

Pomegranate-Vanilla: Just before the cider mixture reaches a boil, add ½ vanilla bean, split lengthwise. Reduce heat, and stir in 2 cups pomegranate juice. Simmer 20 minutes; strain before serving.

Citrusy Spiced: Use a vegetable peeler to shave two to three (2-inch) sections of lemon or orange rind (leave the white pith), and add them to the cider while it simmers; strain before serving.

Apple Cider Nog: After pouring cider into individual cups, top each with 1 tablespoon low-fat vanilla ice cream. Serve immediately.

Rosemary: Stir in three (4- to 5-inch) sprigs of fresh rosemary before the cider mixture reaches a boil. Reduce the heat, and simmer 20 minutes; strain before serving.

way to boil & simmer
pudding

Although "pudding" encompasses a variety of both savory and sweet foods, we focus here on custard-style desserts. Custards contain milk (or cream) bound by eggs, and they can be cooked gently on the stovetop or baked slowly in the oven (see pages 317 and 456) to achieve a silky consistency.

Mocha Pudding

1¾ cups fat-free milk
½ cup packed brown sugar
1 tablespoon cornstarch
1 tablespoon instant coffee granules
¼ teaspoon salt
¼ cup half-and-half
2 large egg yolks
1 tablespoon butter
1 tablespoon Kahlúa (coffee-flavored liqueur)
2 tablespoons dark chocolate shavings

1. Place milk in a medium, heavy saucepan; bring to a boil. Combine sugar, cornstarch, coffee, and salt in a large bowl, stirring well. Combine half-and-half and egg yolks. Stir egg yolk mixture into sugar mixture. Gradually add half of hot milk to sugar mixture, stirring constantly with a whisk. Return hot milk mixture to pan; bring to a boil. Reduce heat, and simmer 1 minute or until thick, stirring constantly. Remove from heat. Stir in butter and liqueur.
2. Spoon pudding into a bowl. Place bowl in a large ice-filled bowl for 15 minutes or until pudding is cool, stirring occasionally.
3. Cover the surface of the pudding with plastic wrap; chill. Sprinkle each serving with 1 teaspoon dark chocolate shavings. **Yield: 6 servings (serving size: ½ cup pudding and 1 teaspoon shavings).**

CALORIES 173; FAT 5.6g (sat 3g, mono 1.5g, poly 0.4g); PROTEIN 3.8g; CARB 26.9g; FIBER 0.2g; CHOL 78mg; IRON 0.6mg; SODIUM 155mg; CALC 124mg

kitchen how-to:
make stovetop pudding

Most puddings contain starchy ingredients, such as cornstarch or flour, while others include rice, pasta, or bread as thickeners.

1. To prepare stovetop pudding, you'll need little more than a heavy saucepan, a whisk, a rubber spatula, and a little plastic wrap.

2. Most stovetop custard recipes combine dry ingredients, such as sugar and starch. This prevents the starch from clumping when it's added to the hot milk. Separately combine the eggs with a bit of milk or cream.

3. Tempering combines a hot liquid with a cool one and protects the delicate eggs from coagulating too quickly.

4. The pudding is thick enough if it coats the back of a spoon.

5. Butter enriches the flavor and texture of pudding. Add it and other ingredients, such as flavor extracts, that can suffer from exposure to heat after the custard cooks.

6. Place plastic wrap directly on the surface of the pudding to prevent a rubbery skin from forming on the top.

way to boil & simmer
dumplings

Dumplings are easy and economical ways to fatten a stew or soup. They often simmer right along in the cooking liquid, but sometimes they're boiled separately.

Chicken with Rosemary Dumplings

Spoonfuls of seasoned buttermilk biscuit dough form light, fluffy dumplings in this classic American dish. Use two spoons to drop the sticky dumplings into the soup.

Soup:
- 4 cups fat-free, less-sodium chicken broth
- 3 cups water
- 1 pound chicken drumsticks, skinned
- 1 pound skinless, boneless chicken breast halves
- 2 fresh thyme sprigs
- 2 teaspoons olive oil
- 1½ cups diced carrots
- 1½ cups chopped celery
- 1 cup diced onion
- 2 garlic cloves, minced
- ½ teaspoon salt

Dumplings:
- 1¼ cups all-purpose flour
- 1 tablespoon chopped fresh or ½ teaspoon dried rosemary
- 2 teaspoons baking powder
- ¼ teaspoon salt
- 2 tablespoons butter, softened
- ½ cup low-fat buttermilk
- 1 large egg
- ¼ cup all-purpose flour
- ¼ cup water

Remaining Ingredient:
  Freshly ground black pepper

1. To prepare soup, combine first 5 ingredients in a large Dutch oven over medium-high heat; bring to a boil. Reduce heat, and simmer, uncovered, 15 minutes or until chicken is done. Remove pan from heat. Remove chicken pieces from broth; cool slightly. Strain broth through a sieve into a large bowl; discard solids. Remove chicken from bones. Discard bones; chop chicken into bite-sized pieces. Set chicken aside.

2. Heat oil in pan over medium-high heat. Add carrots, celery, onion, and garlic; sauté 6 minutes or until onion is tender. Add reserved broth mixture and ½ teaspoon salt; simmer 10 minutes. Discard thyme sprigs. Keep broth mixture warm.

3. To prepare dumplings, lightly spoon flour into dry measuring cups; level with a knife. Combine 1¼ cups flour, rosemary, baking powder, and ¼ teaspoon salt in a large bowl. Cut in butter with a pastry blender or 2 knives until mixture resembles coarse meal. Combine buttermilk and egg, stirring with a whisk. Add buttermilk mixture to flour mixture, stirring just until combined.

4. Return chopped chicken to broth mixture; bring to a simmer over medium-high heat. Combine ¼ cup flour and ¼ cup water, stirring with a whisk until well blended to form a slurry. Add flour mixture to pan, and simmer 3 minutes. Drop dumpling dough, 1 tablespoon per dumpling, onto chicken mixture to form 12 dumplings (see photo above). Cover and cook 7 minutes (do not let broth boil). Sprinkle with black pepper. **Yield: 6 servings (serving size: 2 dumplings and 1⅓ cups soup).**

CALORIES 366; FAT 9.7g (sat 3.8g, mono 3.5g, poly 1.3g); PROTEIN 32.5g; CARB 35.1g; FIBER 2.9g; CHOL 115mg; IRON 3.3mg; SODIUM 936mg; CALC 169mg

See page 108 for another method used to prepare dumplings.

Poached Eggs with White Corn Polenta

If you can find imported Italian white polenta, use it; the grain is very fine, resulting in a soft texture.

Salsa:
- ⅓ cup chopped bottled roasted red bell peppers
- 1 tablespoon chopped fresh basil
- ½ teaspoon extra-virgin olive oil
- ⅛ teaspoon salt
- 1 large plum tomato, seeded and diced

Polenta:
- 4 cups water
- 1½ cups frozen white corn kernels, thawed
- 1 cup white cornmeal or dry polenta
- ½ teaspoon salt, divided
- 3 tablespoons grated fresh Parmesan cheese
- 1 teaspoon butter
- ¼ teaspoon freshly ground black pepper

Eggs:
- 4 large eggs
- Cooking spray

Remaining Ingredient:
- 2 bacon slices, cooked and crumbled

1. To prepare salsa, combine first 5 ingredients; set aside.
2. To prepare polenta, bring water to a boil in a medium saucepan. Add corn, cornmeal, and ¼ teaspoon salt. Cook 2 minutes or until cornmeal mixture returns to a boil, stirring constantly. Reduce heat to low; cook 20 minutes or until thick, stirring frequently. Stir in remaining ¼ teaspoon salt, Parmesan cheese, butter, and black pepper. Cover and keep warm.
3. To prepare eggs, while polenta cooks, add water to a large skillet, filling two-thirds full; bring to a boil. Reduce heat; simmer. Break eggs into each of 4 (6-ounce) custard cups coated with cooking spray. Place custard cups in simmering water in pan. Cover pan; cook 6 minutes. Remove custard cups from water; carefully remove eggs from custard cups.

4. Spoon about 1 cup polenta onto each of 4 plates; top each serving with about 3 tablespoons salsa and 1 poached egg. Sprinkle evenly with bacon. **Yield: 4 servings.**

CALORIES 307; FAT 10.3g (sat 3.4g, mono 4g, poly 1.6g); PROTEIN 14.2g; CARB 40.5g; FIBER 4.6g; CHOL 221mg; IRON 1.9mg; SODIUM 664mg; CALC 78mg

kitchen how-to: poach eggs

Use fresh eggs for the best results. The whites of fresh eggs stay compact around the yolk when poached, making a neater, rounder shape.

1. Add water to a large skillet, filling two-thirds full; bring to a boil. Reduce heat; simmer. Break eggs into each of 4 (6-ounce) custard cups coated with cooking spray.
2. Place custard cups in simmering water in pan. Cover pan; cook 6 minutes.
3. Remove custard cups from water with tongs.
4. Carefully remove eggs from custard cups.

Egg Salad BLTs

To lighten this egg salad, we removed the yolks from two of the eight eggs. A touch of lemon rind and sour cream add a piquant edge.

¼ cup fat-free mayonnaise
3 tablespoons thinly sliced green onions
3 tablespoons reduced-fat sour cream
2 teaspoons whole-grain Dijon mustard
½ teaspoon freshly ground black pepper
¼ teaspoon grated lemon rind
8 hard-boiled large eggs
8 (1½-ounce) slices peasant bread or firm sandwich bread, toasted
4 center-cut bacon slices, cooked and cut in half crosswise
8 (¼-inch-thick) slices tomato
4 large Boston lettuce leaves

1. Combine first 6 ingredients in a medium bowl, stirring well.

2. Cut 2 eggs in half lengthwise; reserve 2 yolks for another use. Coarsely chop remaining egg whites and whole eggs. Add eggs to mayonnaise mixture; stir gently to combine.

3. Arrange 4 bread slices on a cutting board or work surface. Top each bread slice with ½ cup egg mixture, 2 bacon pieces, 2 tomato slices, 1 lettuce leaf, and 1 bread slice. Serve sandwiches immediately. **Yield: 4 servings (serving size: 1 sandwich).**

CALORIES 371; FAT 11.7g (sat 4.1g, mono 4.4g, poly 1.4g); PROTEIN 21.9g; CARB 44g; FIBER 2.4g; CHOL 329mg; IRON 4mg; SODIUM 892mg; CALC 70mg

kitchen how-to: boil eggs

Follow these steps to get the best results when boiling eggs. First, place the eggs in a large saucepan. Cover with water to 1 inch above the eggs; bring to a full boil. Immediately cover the pan and remove it from heat; let stand according to how you'd like the eggs prepared (see below for times). After the eggs have cooked, drain and rinse them with cold running water until they're cool enough to handle.

1. Soft-boiled eggs: Let stand 2 minutes. The white is solid, but the yolk is still runny. Use the side of a small spoon to crack and remove the smaller, more pointed end of the shell, making a hole large enough for a spoon to fit. Serve in an egg cup for breakfast.

2. Medium-boiled eggs: Let stand 4½ minutes. The yolk is solid, but it's still dark orange-yellow, moist, and dense in the middle. Serve on top of a salad.

3. Hard-boiled eggs: Let stand 12 minutes. The yolk will be solid, light yellow, and crumbly, with no green ring around the yolk, which is a sign of overcooking. Use for deviled eggs or in egg salad.

fish & shellfish

Cajun Crawfish Boil

¼ cup mustard seeds
3 tablespoons coriander seeds
2 tablespoons whole allspice
2 teaspoons crushed red pepper
2 teaspoons whole cloves
¼ teaspoon black peppercorns
6 bay leaves, crumbled
2 gallons water
¾ cup salt
¼ cup salt-free Cajun seasoning
3 tablespoons paprika
2 tablespoons ground red pepper

12 small red potatoes (about 12 ounces)
4 onions, halved
4 lemons, halved
4 whole garlic heads
4 ears shucked corn, halved crosswise
6 pounds live crawfish

1. Place first 7 ingredients on a double layer of cheesecloth. Gather edges of cheesecloth together; tie securely.

2. Combine cheesecloth bag, 2 gallons water, salt, and next 3 ingredients in an extra-large stockpot, and bring to a boil. Cover, reduce heat, and simmer 15 minutes.

3. Add potatoes and next 3 ingredients. Cover and return to a boil; cook 10 minutes. Add corn and crawfish. Cover and return to a boil; cook 15 minutes or until done. Let stand 30 minutes. Drain; discard cheesecloth bag. **Yield: 4 servings (serving size: 1½ pounds crawfish, 3 potatoes, and 2 corn halves).**

CALORIES 346; FAT 3.2g (sat 0.5g, mono 0.7g, poly 1.2g); PROTEIN 35.3g; CARB 46.7g; FIBER 6.9g; CHOL 226mg; IRON 3mg; SODIUM 777mg; CALC 151mg

kitchen how-to:
peel crawfish

Crawfish season peaks in April or May, when the crawfish are the fattest.

1. Before you peel the shell, separate the tail from the head. Begin by holding the head in one hand and the tail in the other.
2. Gently twist your hands in opposite directions until the crawfish splits in half.
3. Gently squeeze the sides of the tail until you hear the shell crack. Beginning at the top, peel away a few segments of the shell until enough meat is exposed for you to grasp it securely.
4. Holding the fan of the tail in one hand, pull the meat away from the shell. Tip: If the meat breaks apart, peel away the remaining shell segments.
5. Now, you're ready to eat. For a more authentic Cajun experience: Suck the seasoned cooking liquid after you remove the head before you discard it. You can use your teeth rather than your fingers to remove the crawfish meat from the cracked shell.

Cambodian Summer Rolls

Rolls:
- 6 cups water
- 36 unpeeled medium shrimp (about 1 pound)
- 4 ounces uncooked rice noodles
- 12 (8-inch) round sheets rice paper
- ¼ cup hoisin sauce
- 3 cups shredded red leaf lettuce
- ¼ cup thinly sliced fresh basil
- ¼ cup thinly sliced fresh mint

Dipping Sauce:
- ⅓ cup low-sodium soy sauce
- ¼ cup water
- 2 tablespoons sugar
- 2 tablespoons chopped fresh cilantro
- 2 tablespoons fresh lime juice
- 1 teaspoon minced peeled fresh ginger
- 1 teaspoon chile paste with garlic (such as sambal oelek)
- 1 garlic clove, minced

1. To prepare rolls, bring 6 cups water to a boil in a large saucepan. Add shrimp; cook 3 minutes or until done. Drain and rinse with cold water; drain. Peel shrimp; chill.
2. Place noodles in a large bowl; cover with boiling water. Let stand 8 minutes; drain.
3. Add cold water to a large, shallow dish to a depth of 1 inch. Working with 1 rice paper sheet at a time, place sheet in water. Let stand 2 minutes or until soft. Place on a flat surface.

4. Spread 1 teaspoon hoisin sauce in the center of sheet; top with 3 shrimp, ¼ cup lettuce, about 2½ tablespoons noodles, 1 teaspoon basil, and 1 teaspoon mint. Fold sides of sheet over filling, roll up jelly-roll fashion, and gently press seam to seal. Place roll, seam side down, on a serving platter; cover to keep from drying. Repeat procedure with remaining rice paper, hoisin sauce, shrimp, shredded lettuce, noodles, basil, and mint.

5. To prepare dipping sauce, combine soy sauce and remaining ingredients in a small bowl; stir with a whisk. **Yield: 12 servings (serving size: 1 roll and about 1½ tablespoons sauce).**

CALORIES 131; FAT 0.9g (sat 0.1g, mono 0.1g, poly 0.2g); PROTEIN 6.7g; CARB 24.1g; FIBER 0.8g; CHOL 36mg; IRON 1mg; SODIUM 379mg; CALC 37mg

kitchen how-to:
cook shrimp

To prevent overcooking shrimp, which makes them tough, leave the shell on while you cook them; the shell protects the meat and helps keep it tender. Shrimp cook quickly, so watch them closely. After the shrimp have cooked for a couple of minutes, cut one open to make sure the meat is no longer translucent, or taste it to see if it's fully cooked. Once done, remove shrimp from the heat immediately to prevent overcooking. Then peel them, and if they're medium to large-sized, devein them. Use a deveiner or a sharp paring knife to make a shallow cut along the back curve of the shrimp and scrape away any impurities.

undercooked   just right

Boiled Lobster

Use a 5-gallon pot for this recipe. If you use a smaller one, you may need to cook the lobsters in batches. Boiling is probably the most familiar way to cook lobster (and it's our preferred method), but it presents the risk of overcooking, so you'll need to pay attention to time. Boiling makes removing the meat easier since the intense, immediate heat causes it to shrink from the shell as the boiling water cooks the lobster from the outside in.

 3 gallons water
 3 tablespoons salt
 4 (1½-pound) live Maine lobsters

1. Bring water and salt to a boil in a 5-gallon stockpot. Add lobsters. Cover and cook 12 minutes or until shells are bright orange-red and tails are curled. **Yield: 4 servings (serving size: 1 lobster).**
Note: Four 1½-pound lobsters yield about 4 cups of cooked lobster meat. Most of the lobsters we used were between 1¼ pounds and 1½ pounds. If you can't get or don't want to use live lobsters, use frozen tails. Six (6-ounce) tails, which you should steam for 8 minutes, yield about 2 cups of cooked meat.

CALORIES 142; FAT 0.9g (sat 0.2g, mono 0.2g, poly 0.1g); PROTEIN 29.7g; CARB 1.9g; FIBER 0g; CHOL 104mg; IRON 0.6mg; SODIUM 708mg; CALC 89mg

See page 119 for information about how to extract meat from lobster.

way to boil & simmer
fruit

Simple Poached Pears

Many recipes for this delicate dessert are made with aggressive spices that can overwhelm the delicate taste of the fruit. This approach calls for simmering the pears in an unspiced syrup that is reduced to concentrate the fruity flavor. It's worth the effort to seek out Poire Williams (a pear-flavored eau-de-vie) to finish the dish, but you can also use another pear-flavored liqueur or brandy.

- 6 cups water
- 1 cup sugar
- 6 firm Anjou pears, peeled, cored, and halved
- 1 (2-inch) lemon rind strip
- 3 tablespoons Poire Williams or other pear-flavored liqueur
- 6 (2-inch) lemon rind strips (optional)

1. Combine first 3 ingredients in a large saucepan; bring to a simmer. Add 1 rind strip. Reduce heat, and simmer 25 minutes or until tender. Remove pears from pan with a slotted spoon; cover and chill.

2. Bring cooking liquid to a boil over high heat; cook until syrupy and reduced to 1 cup (about 20 minutes). Strain through a sieve into a bowl; cover and chill. Stir in liqueur. Arrange 2 pear halves in each of 6 shallow bowls; top each serving with about 3 tablespoons sauce and 1 rind strip, if desired. **Yield: 6 servings.**

CALORIES 277; FAT 0.3g (sat 0g, mono 0.1g, poly 0.1g); PROTEIN 0.8g; CARB 68.1g; FIBER 2.1g; CHOL 0mg; IRON 0.4mg; SODIUM 2mg; CALC 19mg

kitchen how-to: poach fruit

Poaching fruit—simmering it gently in liquid—can help you bring a simple, elegant dessert to the table quickly. As it poaches, fruit becomes tender because it absorbs some of the cooking liquid. For this reason, the flavor of the liquid is key. Create a simple poaching liquid by mixing two parts liquid (such as wine, water, or fruit juice) with one part sugar. Then try your hand at this technique with the following tips.

1. Core or pit the fruit, and peel if appropriate. Firm fruits, such as pears and apples, work best when peeled, but keep the skin on delicate stone fruits, such as peaches and plums.
2. Submerge fruit in the poaching liquid in a stainless steel pan.
3. Cover with a plate to weigh the fruit down and ensure even cooking.
4. Simmer for 10 minutes, and then check for doneness by piercing the fruit with a knife. The fruit should give without being mushy. Continue simmering to suit your taste.
5. Remove the fruit with a slotted spoon, and allow it to cool. Serve or store the fruit with the poaching liquid in the refrigerator until you're ready to serve.

grains

Tabbouleh with Chicken and Red Pepper

Use rotisserie or leftover chicken for this dish, if you'd like. If you're making the mixture a few hours or more in advance, store the cucumber and tomato separately and add them close to serving time to keep the salad at its best. Serve with hummus and whole wheat pita chips for a flavorful, Middle East–themed light lunch.

½ cup uncooked bulgur
½ cup boiling water
1½ cups diced plum tomato
¾ cup shredded cooked chicken breast
¾ cup minced fresh flat-leaf parsley
½ cup finely chopped red bell pepper
½ cup diced English cucumber
¼ cup minced fresh mint
1½ tablespoons fresh lemon juice
1 tablespoon extra-virgin olive oil
½ teaspoon salt
¼ teaspoon freshly ground black pepper

1. Combine bulgur and ½ cup boiling water in a large bowl. Cover and let stand 15 minutes or until bulgur is tender. Drain well; return bulgur to bowl. Cool.
2. Add tomato and remaining ingredients; toss well.
Yield: 4 servings (serving size: 1¼ cups).

CALORIES 150; FAT 4.7g (sat 0.8g, mono 2.9g, poly 0.7g); PROTEIN 11.2g; CARB 16.9g; FIBER 4.5g; CHOL 22mg; IRON 1.6mg; SODIUM 326mg; CALC 33mg

Whole Grain Glossary

Substituting a little whole wheat flour for some all-purpose white flour is now a familiar practice for many cooks. Enhance the nutrients and flavor of your cooking by trying other whole grains.

- **Rye, amaranth,** and **spelt** work well in homemade breads as a supplement to wheat flour. Toast a tablespoonful or two in a hot, dry skillet to add to breakfast cereal.
- Look for **pearled barley** kernels or berries to add a new starchy side to your recipe repertoire. The cereal's chewy texture enhances soups, pilafs, and salads. Its hearty flavor pairs well with mushrooms, beef, herbs, and tomatoes.
- Even though buckwheat isn't technically wheat, or even a grain at all, its nutrition profile is similar. **Soba noodles** are made from buckwheat, and you can also try roasted buckwheat grains, or kasha, for a hot cereal, a filling side dish, or as the base for vegetable stuffing.
- With its nutty flavor and chewy texture, **bulgur wheat** is especially tasty as a salad with fresh herbs and vegetables or as a binder for burgers.
- Versatility is the virtue of **millet**. You can use it toasted in cookies, or simmer and serve it with Parmesan and herbs as a side dish similar to couscous.

pastas

Spaghetti with Tomato Sauce

- 1½ pounds plum tomatoes, peeled and halved lengthwise
- 3 tablespoons extra-virgin olive oil, divided
- 2 garlic cloves, minced
- 2 tablespoons plus ½ teaspoon fine sea salt, divided
- ¼ teaspoon crushed red pepper
- 6 quarts water
- 12 ounces uncooked spaghetti
- ¼ cup minced fresh basil
- 6 tablespoons grated fresh Parmigiano-Reggiano cheese

1. Squeeze juice and seeds from tomato halves into a fine-mesh sieve over a bowl, reserving juices; discard seeds. Finely chop tomatoes.

2. Heat 2 tablespoons oil in a large nonstick skillet over medium heat. Add garlic to pan; cook 30 seconds or just until garlic begins to brown, stirring constantly. Add tomatoes, reserved juices, ½ teaspoon salt, and pepper. Increase heat to medium-high; cook 15 minutes or until liquid almost evaporates, stirring occasionally.

3. Bring 6 quarts water and remaining 2 tablespoons salt to a boil in an 8-quart pot. Add pasta to pot; stir. Cover; return water to a boil. Uncover and cook 8 minutes or until pasta is almost al dente. Drain pasta in a colander over a bowl, reserving ½ cup cooking water.

4. Add hot pasta and reserved cooking water to tomato mixture. Cook 5 minutes or until sauce is thick and pasta is al dente, tossing to combine. Remove from heat. Sprinkle with basil; toss. Place 1 cup pasta mixture on each of 6 plates. Drizzle each serving with ½ teaspoon remaining oil; sprinkle each with 1 tablespoon cheese. **Yield: 6 servings.**

CALORIES 313; FAT 9.5g (sat 2.1g, mono 5.6g, poly 1.5g); PROTEIN 10.3g; CARB 47g; FIBER 3.2g; CHOL 4mg; IRON 2.3mg; SODIUM 576mg; CALC 83mg

kitchen how-to: cook pasta

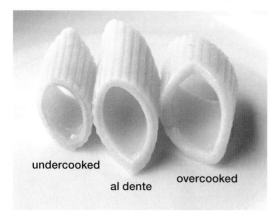

undercooked

al dente

overcooked

To make great pasta, cook it al dente, or "to the tooth." Pasta cooked al dente results in a sensation of slight resistance when chewed and adds to the overall enjoyment of pasta (and rice, too). Properly cooked pasta will be tender and not raw tasting, and it will have a firm texture and even a little "snap" at the center. With long pasta, like spaghetti and linguine, you can tell that it has been cooked al dente if there is a dot of white at the center; in round pasta, like ziti or penne, there will be a faint but clear ring of white that runs around the center of the pasta. If you're going to simmer cooked pasta together with a sauce, cook the pasta slightly less than al dente—it will finish cooking in the sauce.

kitchen how-to: make fresh tomato sauce

Fresh tomato sauce is a staple in Italy, where it's usually served with spaghetti. Although the sauce tastes rich and delicious, it only takes about 30 minutes to prepare.

1. Bring a pot of water to a boil. While you're waiting for the water to boil, cut a 1-inch X in the bottom of the tomatoes. Place the tomatoes into the boiling water for 30 seconds to a minute.
2. Quickly remove each tomato with a slotted spoon, and drop it into a bowl of ice water for 1 minute to stop the cooking process.
3. Remove the tomatoes from the water, and peel back the flaps from the X; the skin will be easy to remove. Finely chop the tomatoes.
4. Heat extra-virgin olive oil in a large skillet over medium heat. Add garlic, and cook just until it begins to brown lightly, taking care not to burn it.
5. Add the tomatoes and reserved juices, and cook until almost all the liquid evaporates. Finish cooking the pasta with the sauce in a skillet large enough to combine the two and allow for tossing. Add enough of the pasta cooking water to the sauce to give the dish a creamy texture and marry the sauce to the pasta.

1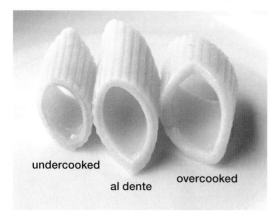

2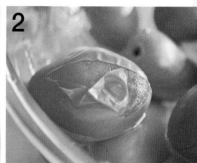

3

4

5

Lasagna Rolls with Roasted Red Pepper Sauce

These rolls require some assembly time but are a nice change of pace from layered pasta. Use baby spinach to eliminate the task of trimming stems.

Lasagna:

- 8 uncooked lasagna noodles
- 4 teaspoons olive oil
- ½ cup finely chopped onion
- 1 (8-ounce) package sliced mushrooms
- 1 (6-ounce) package fresh baby spinach
- 3 garlic cloves, minced
- ½ cup (2 ounces) shredded mozzarella cheese
- ½ cup part-skim ricotta cheese
- ¼ cup minced fresh basil, divided
- ½ teaspoon salt
- ¼ teaspoon crushed red pepper

Roasted Red Pepper Sauce:

- 1 tablespoon red wine vinegar
- ¼ teaspoon salt
- ¼ teaspoon freshly ground black pepper
- 2 garlic cloves, minced
- 1 (14.5-ounce) can diced tomatoes, undrained
- 1 (7-ounce) bottle roasted red bell peppers, undrained
- ⅛ teaspoon crushed red pepper

1. To prepare lasagna, cook noodles according to package directions, omitting salt and fat. Drain and rinse with cold water. Drain.

2. Heat oil in a large nonstick skillet over medium-high heat. Add onion, mushrooms, spinach, and 3 garlic cloves; sauté 5 minutes or until onion and mushrooms are tender. Remove from heat, and stir in cheeses, 2 tablespoons basil, ½ teaspoon salt, and ¼ teaspoon crushed red pepper.

3. To prepare sauce, place vinegar and remaining ingredients in a blender; process until smooth.

4. Place cooked noodles on a flat surface; spread ¼ cup cheese mixture over each noodle. Roll up noodles, jelly-roll fashion, starting with short side. Place rolls, seam sides down, in a shallow 2-quart microwave-safe dish. Pour ¼ cup sauce over each roll, and cover with heavy-duty plastic wrap. Microwave at HIGH 5 minutes or until thoroughly heated. Sprinkle with remaining 2 tablespoons basil. **Yield: 4 servings (serving size: 2 rolls).**

CALORIES 393; FAT 11.7g (sat 4.3g, mono 3.6g, poly 1.5g); PROTEIN 19.3g; CARB 58.3g; FIBER 5.9g; CHOL 20mg; IRON 3.8mg; SODIUM 924mg; CALC 253mg

kitchen how-to:
fill a lasagna roll

Spoon ¼ cup cheese mixture down the center of each noodle.

Black Lentil and Couscous Salad

Technically not a "bean," lentils are legumes. Unlike beans, lentils require no soaking,
so this salad is quick and easy to prepare. Serve chilled or at room temperature.

½ cup dried black lentils
5   cups water, divided
¾ cup uncooked couscous
¾ teaspoon salt, divided
1   cup cherry tomatoes, quartered
⅓ cup golden raisins
⅓ cup finely chopped red onion
⅓ cup finely chopped cucumber
¼ cup chopped fresh parsley
3   tablespoons chopped fresh mint
1   teaspoon grated lemon rind
3   tablespoons fresh lemon juice
2   tablespoons extra-virgin olive oil

1. Rinse lentils with cold water; drain. Place lentils
and 4 cups water in a large saucepan; bring to a boil.
Reduce heat, and simmer 20 minutes or until tender.
Drain and rinse with cold water; drain.
2. Bring remaining 1 cup water to a boil in a medium
saucepan; gradually stir in couscous and ¼ teaspoon
salt. Remove from heat; cover and let stand 5 minutes.
Fluff with a fork. Combine lentils, couscous, remaining
½ teaspoon salt, tomatoes, and remaining ingredients
in a large bowl. **Yield: 6 servings (serving size: 1 cup).**

CALORIES 175; FAT 4.8g (sat 0.7g, mono 3.3g, poly 0.6g); PROTEIN 4.5g; CARB 28.8g;
FIBER 2.8g; CHOL 0mg; IRON 1mg; SODIUM 322mg; CALC 31mg

way to boil & simmer
rice

Herbed Basmati Rice

Add a little chopped rotisserie chicken or cooked shrimp, and you can promote this side dish to an entrée.

- 1 teaspoon olive oil
- Cooking spray
- 1 cup uncooked basmati rice
- 1 garlic clove, minced
- 1 cup water
- 1 cup fat-free, less-sodium chicken broth
- ¼ teaspoon salt
- ¼ cup chopped green onions
- ¼ cup pine nuts, toasted
- 3 tablespoons grated fresh Parmesan cheese
- 1 tablespoon chopped fresh basil
- 1 teaspoon chopped fresh thyme
- ½ teaspoon freshly ground black pepper

1. Heat olive oil in a medium skillet coated with cooking spray over medium-high heat. Add rice and garlic to pan; sauté 2 minutes or until rice is lightly toasted. Add 1 cup water, broth, and salt; bring to a boil. Cover, reduce heat, and simmer 15 minutes or until liquid is absorbed and rice is tender. Remove from heat; let stand 5 minutes. Stir in onions, nuts, Parmesan cheese, basil, thyme, and pepper. **Yield: 6 servings (serving size: ⅔ cup).**

CALORIES 182; FAT 5.4g (sat 0.8g, mono 1.8g, poly 2.1g); PROTEIN 4g; CARB 31.9g; FIBER 1.5g; CHOL 2mg; IRON 1.5mg; SODIUM 203mg; CALC 37mg

Rice Glossary

There are many varieties of rice available. Here's a short guide to help you understand the differences.

1. Brown: This is rice that has been hulled with the bran intact. The bran lends chewy texture and nutty flavor and contains vitamins, minerals, and fiber. It requires a longer cooking time because the bran is a barrier to water.

2. Arborio: This popular Italian rice is used to make risotto. Each medium-length grain has a white "eye" that remains firm to the bite, while the rest of the grain softens and lends creaminess. Once grown exclusively in Italy, Arborio is now also grown in California and Texas. Other Italian rices used to make risotto are carnaroli and vialone nano.

3. Wild: This is the only grain native to North America, though it's actually not a rice at all but the seed from an aquatic grass. After cooking, wild rice still has a distinct crunch that makes it an excellent mix-in with more traditional whole grains, such as brown rice. It's often sold mixed with long-grain white rice.

4. Basmati: Sometimes called "popcorn rice," this long-grain variety is highly regarded for its fragrance, taste, and slender shape. True basmati is grown in India and Pakistan, although many hybrids are grown elsewhere, including the United States. Texmati, for example, is grown in Texas.

5. Parboiled: Steam-pressure treatment before milling produces this tan grain that is firm and stays separate when cooked. Don't confuse it with instant rice—parboiled rice takes longer to cook.

6. Rice Blends: Rice blends offer an easy way to get a variety of flavors and textures. Depending on the way the rice is milled, some rice blends cook quickly, while others need to simmer for longer. Check the package for specific cooking directions.

7. Instant: Also called precooked, this rice has been partially or completely cooked and dried; it takes only a few minutes to prepare.

8. Black: Both medium- and short-grain, this rice is grown mostly in Southeast Asia and in a limited quantity in California. It gets its dark color from the black bran that surrounds the endosperm, or kernel. When cooked, the rice might turn purple or lavender—the bran dyes the white kernel inside. Look for Black Japonica or Forbidden Rice.

9. Jasmine: Thailand's favorite, this aromatic rice has more amylopectin, or sticky starch, than other long-grain rice, so it's moist and tender. It's grown in Asia and the United States.

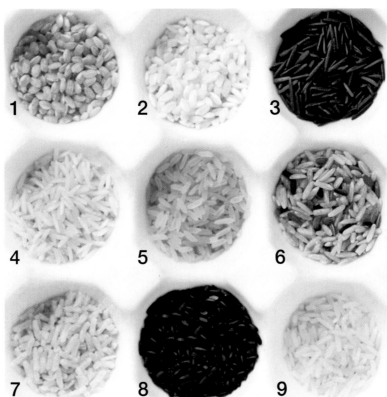

risotto

Making the creamy, grain-based dish called risotto involves the slow addition of liquid and frequent stirring to coax the starch from the rice. This creates a luscious sauce that envelops the grain and carries the flavor.

Sage Risotto with Fresh Mozzarella and Prosciutto

- 2 (14-ounce) cans fat-free, less-sodium chicken broth
- 1 tablespoon butter
- 1 cup finely chopped leek
- 2 garlic cloves, minced
- 1¼ cups Arborio rice
- ¼ teaspoon salt
- ½ cup dry white wine
- 1½ to 2 tablespoons finely chopped fresh sage
- 1 cup (4 ounces) finely chopped fresh mozzarella cheese
- 2 ounces prosciutto, chopped (about ⅓ cup)
- ¼ teaspoon freshly ground black pepper

Fresh sage sprigs (optional)

1. Bring broth to a simmer in a medium saucepan (do not boil). Keep warm over low heat.

2. Melt butter in a medium sauté pan over medium heat. Add leek and garlic; cook 3 minutes, stirring frequently. Add rice and ¼ teaspoon salt; cook 1 minute, stirring constantly. Stir in wine; cook 2 minutes or until liquid is nearly absorbed, stirring constantly. Add broth, ½ cup at a time, stirring frequently until each portion of broth is absorbed before adding the next (about 20 minutes total). Stir in chopped sage, and cook 2 minutes. Remove from heat; stir in mozzarella. Spoon 1 cup risotto into each of 4 bowls; top each serving with about 1½ tablespoons prosciutto. Sprinkle with black pepper. Garnish with sage sprigs, if desired. **Yield: 4 servings.**

CALORIES 443; FAT 12.3g (sat 7g, mono 3g, poly 1g); PROTEIN 18.8g; CARB 59.6g; FIBER 1.4g; CHOL 43mg; IRON 1.3mg; SODIUM 863mg; CALC 193mg

kitchen how-to: make risotto

Risottos are classically made with medium-grain Arborio rice, but many other grains yield terrific results. Barley, steel-cut oats, quinoa, and bulgur benefit greatly from this cooking method. Like Arborio rice, these grains contain lots of easily released starch that provides characteristic creaminess. No amount of stirring, however, will bring creaminess to grains that lack starch, such as basmati rice.

1. Bring the cooking liquid to a simmer. Whether you're using broth or water, keep the liquid hot so the risotto stays at a simmer with each addition—cold ingredients slow the release of starch. Sauté aromatic vegetables like onion, garlic, and shallots in oil or butter to provide a taste foundation on which to build the risotto.

2. Add grain. Sautéing the grain infuses it with flavors from the vegetables and allows the risotto to boil quickly when the first liquid is added.

3. Add wine before any other cooking liquid to allow the alcohol to cook out. Begin stirring as you add the wine, and continue stirring frequently until the wine is absorbed—this jostles the starch out of the grain. Slowly add hot cooking liquid. Allow only a veil of liquid to cover the grain and ensure the stirring properly agitates the grain (causing it to release its starch). This also will keep the cooking time down.

4. Add the remaining ingredients, such as meat, fish, vegetables, or cheese during the last few minutes of cooking time to keep them intact.

poultry

Julienne Vegetable–Stuffed Chicken with Ginger-Hoisin Sauce

Slow, gentle poaching keeps the meat tender and juicy, and this method doesn't require any added fat. Serve this dish with sesame noodles, if desired.

Chicken:

1½ teaspoons dark sesame oil
1 tablespoon minced peeled fresh ginger
3 garlic cloves, minced
2 cups matchstick-cut carrot
2 cups matchstick-cut zucchini
1 cup red bell pepper, cut into ¼-inch strips
1 tablespoon low-sodium soy sauce
2 teaspoons hoisin sauce
¼ cup panko (Japanese breadcrumbs)
4 (6-ounce) skinless, boneless chicken breast halves
3 quarts water

Sauce:

1 tablespoon finely chopped green onions
1 tablespoon seasoned rice vinegar
1 tablespoon low-sodium soy sauce
2 teaspoons minced peeled fresh ginger
2 teaspoons honey
5 teaspoons hoisin sauce

1. To prepare chicken, heat oil in a large nonstick skillet over medium-high heat. Add ginger and garlic; sauté 15 seconds. Add carrot, zucchini, and bell pepper; sauté 3 minutes or until crisp-tender. Add soy sauce and hoisin sauce; sauté 30 seconds. Place carrot mixture in a bowl; cool 5 minutes. Stir in panko.
2. Slice each breast half lengthwise, cutting to, but not through, other side. Open halves, laying breast flat. Place each breast half between 2 sheets of heavy-duty plastic wrap; pound to ¼-inch thickness using a meat mallet or small heavy skillet.
3. Divide carrot mixture into 4 equal portions; spoon each portion down center of each breast half, leaving a ½-inch border at each end. Fold breast sides over filling.
4. Place a 2-foot-long sheet of heavy-duty plastic wrap on a work surface with 1 long side hanging over the counter's edge 2 inches. Working with 1 stuffed breast half at a time, place breast half, seam side down, on the end farthest from you; tightly roll the chicken toward you, jelly-roll fashion. Twist the ends in opposite directions to form a cylinder. Tie plastic wrap in tight knots against the chicken on each end; trim off excess wrap close to the knot. Place a second 2-foot-long sheet of heavy-duty plastic wrap on the work surface; place rolled chicken on wrap, and repeat procedure. Repeat with remaining chicken breast halves.
5. Bring 3 quarts water to a boil in a large stockpot; add chicken. Simmer 15 minutes (do not boil), turning occasionally. Remove from water, and let stand 10 minutes before unwrapping and cutting into ½-inch-thick slices.
6. To prepare sauce, combine onions and remaining ingredients in a small bowl. Serve with chicken. **Yield: 4 servings (serving size: 1 stuffed breast half and about 1½ tablespoons sauce).**

CALORIES 289; FAT 4.5g (sat 0.9g, mono 1.3g, poly 1.4g); PROTEIN 42g; CARB 18.7g; FIBER 2.4g; CHOL 99mg; IRON 1.8mg; SODIUM 638mg; CALC 46mg

kitchen how-to: roll & wrap poultry for poaching

Begin by butterflying and pounding breast halves to an even ¼-inch thickness; even pounding promotes even cooking. Spoon the filling down the center of each breast half, leaving room at the ends.

1. Fold the sides over the filling. Breast halves vary in size; if you can't fit the filling neatly inside the chicken, remove the filling a teaspoon at a time until the breast can envelop it.

2. Place a 2-foot-long sheet of heavy-duty plastic wrap on a work surface with a long side hanging over the counter's edge by 1 or 2 inches, which allows the plastic to grip the counter as you roll the chicken. Place a stuffed breast half, seam side down, on the end of the plastic farthest from you, and tightly roll the breast toward you, jelly-roll fashion. Twist the ends of the plastic wrap in opposite directions to form a cylinder. Knot the plastic wrap tightly against the chicken.

3. To tie the first knot, brace one end of the twisted plastic between the edge of the work surface and your hip to keep the package from unraveling. Tie a tight knot against the chicken on the opposite end. Trim off the excess wrap close to the knots.

4. Place a second 2-foot-long sheet of heavy-duty plastic wrap on the work surface. Place the rolled breast on the wrap, and repeat procedure. (Double-wrapping ensures a tight seal.)

5. Add the chicken to boiling water in a large stockpot. Place a metal colander on top of the pot to help keep the chicken submerged. If a colander isn't available, turn the chicken occasionally with tongs so it cooks on all sides. The chicken will bring the temperature of the water down immediately, but do not return the water to a boil; a gentle simmer will keep the chicken tender.

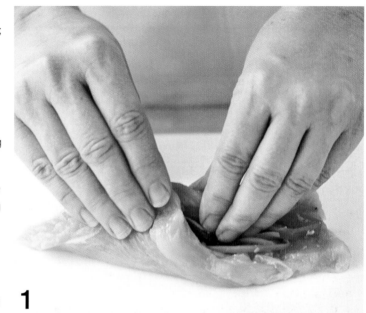

1

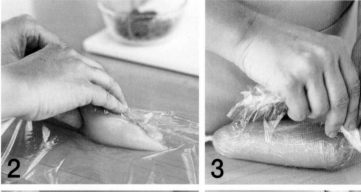

2

3

4

5

sauces

Basic Marinara

Marinara is truly a multipurpose sauce. You can base dozens of different dishes on it—sometimes as is, other times with the addition of flavors, such as lemon rind or crushed red pepper. Cook at a low simmer—just a few bubbles every few seconds will yield the richest taste. And because the cook controls the quality of the ingredients that go into the sauce, we think the flavor of our Basic Marinara is superior to that of many commercial brands. It is much lower in sodium as well. Store the sauce in the refrigerator for up to five days, or freeze it in small batches for several months.

3 tablespoons olive oil
3 cups chopped yellow onion (about 3 medium)
1 tablespoon sugar
3 tablespoons minced garlic (about 6 cloves)
2 teaspoons salt
2 teaspoons dried basil
1½ teaspoons dried oregano
1 teaspoon dried thyme
1 teaspoon freshly ground black pepper
½ teaspoon fennel seeds, crushed
2 tablespoons balsamic vinegar
2 cups fat-free, less-sodium chicken broth
3 (28-ounce) cans no-salt-added crushed tomatoes

1. Heat oil in a large Dutch oven over medium heat. Add onion to pan; cook 4 minutes, stirring frequently. Add sugar and next 7 ingredients; cook 1 minute, stirring constantly. Stir in vinegar; cook 30 seconds. Add broth and tomatoes; bring to a simmer. Cook over low heat 55 minutes or until sauce thickens, stirring occasionally. **Yield: about 12 cups (serving size: ½ cup).**

CALORIES 50; FAT 1.8g (sat 0.2g, mono 1.3g, poly 0.2g); PROTEIN 1.3g; CARB 8g; FIBER 2.1g; CHOL 0mg; IRON 0.5mg; SODIUM 270mg; CALC 28mg

Basic Cranberry Sauce

Make this tangy-sweet sauce up to two days ahead, and refrigerate it. Serve it with turkey, chicken, quail, duck, or ham.

- ½ cup packed dark brown sugar
- ½ cup fresh orange juice (about 2 oranges)
- ¼ cup water
- 1½ tablespoons honey
- ⅛ teaspoon ground allspice
- 1 (12-ounce) package fresh cranberries
- 1 (3-inch) cinnamon stick

1. Combine all ingredients in a medium saucepan over medium-high heat; bring to a boil. Reduce heat, and simmer 12 minutes or until mixture is slightly thickened, stirring occasionally. Discard cinnamon stick; cool completely. **Yield: 14 servings (serving size: 2 tablespoons).**

CALORIES 54; FAT 0g (sat 0g, mono 0g, poly 0g); PROTEIN 0.1g; CARB 13.6g; FIBER 0.9g; CHOL 0mg; IRON 0.2mg; SODIUM 3mg; CALC 8mg

all about cranberries

The tartness of cranberries makes them a good match for sweet fruits, such as apples. Their strong flavor also complements the light taste of white meats. When buying fresh berries, look for round, plump cranberries with smooth skin; don't wash them until just before using to keep them at their best. You can find them canned and frozen year-round, but stock up on fresh ones during their peak season, October through December. Store them in a zip-top plastic bag in the freezer. Once frozen, they're recipe-ready for another year. You don't even have to thaw them before using them in recipes.

way to boil & simmer
soups

Many homemade soups are simple to prepare. Actually, most soup recipes from around the world follow a surprisingly universal technique. Once you master the technique, it's easy to customize recipes to suit your personal tastes.

four steps to great soup

Homemade soups are based on a flavorful liquid, such as broth or stock. Any additional ingredients contribute specific flavors or textures, or lend visual appeal to the soup.

1. Choose a foundation. A flavorful liquid is the basis for all soups. Stock or broth is most common, but some rich, hearty soups have a milk or cream base or a combination of dairy and broth. (Stock imparts more intensity and richness than broth because it's typically made with bone-in cuts of meat or meat scraps and bones that have been roasted to bring out more flavor. Broth tastes milder since it is typically made from meat off the bone.) Homemade stock or broth is ideal, but making either can be time-consuming. Store-bought broth certainly works. Choose meat stock or broth for meat-based soups, and shrimp stock or clam juice for seafood soups.

2. Add dimension. Vegetables, herbs, spices, or meats provide a second dimension of flavor in soups. If you sauté aromatic vegetables, such as carrots, onion, and celery, in butter or oil before adding liquid, they will release more flavor into the final dish.

3. Round out the flavor. Some soups need an acidic background note, so the recipe may call to deglaze the pan (adding liquid after sautéing meat or vegetables and scraping the tasty browned bits from the bottom of the pan). Acidic ingredients, such as wine or vinegar, are often used for deglazing, and most of that liquid evaporates as it cooks, concentrating the tart flavor.

The stock or broth is added next, and it becomes infused with the flavor of the aromatic vegetables as the soup simmers.

4. Finish it. Some soups are pureed for special occasions for a refined, smooth texture. Others may be only partially pureed to give the soup body and thicken the broth. For an everyday meal, it may not be necessary to puree—chunks in the dish offer a more casual, rustic feel. Choose garnishes depending on the soup's flavor. A creamy garnish, such as cheese or sour cream, soothes a spicy or tart soup and smoothes out the acidic or spicy notes. Chopped fresh herbs or fresh citrus juice brighten other flavors in the dish. When entertaining, put out an assortment of options and allow guests to customize their bowls.

way to boil & simmer
stocks

Chicken Noodle Soup

This is the classic soup at its most basic, yet the flavorful stock makes it satisfying and surprisingly memorable. Add leftover roast chicken for a heartier version.

　5　cups Brown Chicken Stock (at right)
　¼　pound uncooked vermicelli, broken into
　　　1-inch pieces
　¾　teaspoon salt
　¼　teaspoon freshly ground black pepper

1. Bring Brown Chicken Stock to a simmer in a medium saucepan. Add pasta; cook 8 minutes or until al dente. Stir in salt and pepper. **Yield: 4 servings (serving size: about 1¼ cups).**

CALORIES 131; FAT 1.2g (sat 0.3g, mono 0.3g, poly 0.2g); PROTEIN 8.1g; CARB 21.8g; FIBER 1.1g; CHOL 14mg; IRON 1.2mg; SODIUM 460mg; CALC 10mg

Brown Chicken Stock

This recipe employs both boiling and simmering. Boiling water helps release the fond, or browned bits that stick to the bottom of the roasting pan; this process, called deglazing, enriches the stock.

　5　pounds chicken drumsticks, skinned
　2　large carrots, halved lengthwise and cut
　　　into 2-inch pieces
　1　large onion, quartered
　　　Cooking spray
　16　cups cold water, divided
　7　fresh thyme sprigs
　1　bunch fresh parsley stems
　1　bay leaf

1. Preheat oven to 450°.
2. Arrange chicken, carrots, and onion in a single layer in the bottom of 2 broiler pans or roasting pans coated with cooking spray. Bake at 450° for 30 minutes. Turn chicken over, and rotate pans on oven racks. Bake an additional 30 minutes or until browned.
3. Transfer chicken and vegetables to a 6-quart stockpot. Carefully discard drippings from broiler pans, leaving browned bits. Place 1 broiler pan on stovetop; add 2 cups water to pan. Bring to a boil over medium-high heat. Reduce heat; simmer 2 minutes, scraping pan to loosen browned bits. Carefully pour contents of broiler pan into stockpot. Repeat procedure with remaining broiler pan and 2 cups water.
4. Add remaining 12 cups water, thyme, parsley, and bay leaf to stockpot; bring to a simmer over medium-high heat. Reduce heat to low, and simmer gently 2 hours, skimming foam and fat from the surface occasionally. Strain stock through a fine sieve into a large bowl; discard solids. Cover and chill stock for 8 hours or overnight. Skim solidified fat from surface of stock; discard fat. **Yield: 8 cups (serving size: 1 cup).**

CALORIES 22; FAT 0.7g (sat 0.2g, mono 0.2g, poly 0.2g); PROTEIN 3.4g; CARB 0.4g; FIBER 0.1g; CHOL 11mg; IRON 0.2mg; SODIUM 13mg; CALC 3mg

kitchen how-to:
make brown chicken stock

1

2

The secret to keeping the stock clear is to simmer very gently so that none of the fat or insoluble specks of protein emulsify into the liquid but instead float to the top where they're easily skimmed off. The long cooking time depletes the chicken of most of its flavor and texture, so the meat is best discarded or offered to pets (discard bones). Refrigerate the stock up to one week, or freeze in 1-cup increments for up to three months.

1. Roasting the chicken and vegetables until browned creates a deep, rich caramelized flavor.

2. The browned bits from the pan add even more flavor. Deglaze the pan by adding water and scraping up the bits.

4

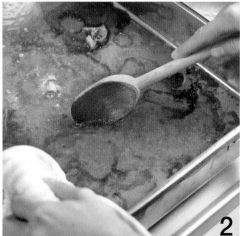

3

3. Simmer the stock ingredients for 2 hours. Then strain the stock through a fine sieve.

4. Skim the fat from the stock after it has chilled for 8 hours or overnight.

chowders

New England Clam Chowder

Serve this hearty, simple soup in a bread bowl for a fun presentation. Pair it with a tossed green salad.

  4 (6½-ounce) cans chopped clams, undrained
  2 (8-ounce) bottles clam juice
  4 bacon slices
  1 cup chopped onion
  1 cup chopped celery
  1 garlic clove, minced
  3 cups cubed red potato
1½ teaspoons chopped fresh thyme
  ¼ teaspoon black pepper
  3 fresh parsley sprigs
  1 bay leaf
  2 cups 2% reduced-fat milk
  ¼ cup all-purpose flour
  ½ cup half-and-half
     Fresh thyme sprigs (optional)

1. Drain clams through a colander into a bowl, reserving liquid and clams. Combine clam liquid and clam juice.
2. Cook bacon in a Dutch oven over medium-high heat until crisp. Remove bacon from pan, reserving 2 teaspoons drippings in pan. Crumble bacon; set aside. Add onion, celery, and garlic to pan; sauté 8 minutes or until tender. Add clam juice mixture, potato, and next 4 ingredients; bring to a boil. Cover, reduce heat, and simmer 15 minutes or until potato is tender.
3. Combine milk and flour, stirring with a whisk until smooth; add to pan. Stir in clams and half-and-half. Cook 5 minutes. Discard parsley sprigs and bay leaf. Sprinkle with bacon. Garnish with thyme sprigs, if desired. **Yield: 8 servings (serving size: 1¼ cups chowder and 1½ teaspoons bacon).**

CALORIES 194; FAT 5.4g (sat 2.7g, mono 1.9g, poly 0.4g); PROTEIN 12.3g; CARB 23.7g; FIBER 1.4g; CHOL 32mg; IRON 2.2mg; SODIUM 639mg; CALC 111mg

kitchen how-to: make a bread bowl

1

2

Bread bowls are a handy way to serve soups or dips. Start by selecting a crusty round bread—like sourdough, pumpernickel, or French bread—that will complement what you're serving. Follow these tips for prepping your bowl; use leftover bread for dipping in soup, or turn it into homemade croutons. Spray 1-inch cubes of bread with cooking spray, mix with your favorite seasonings, and bake in a preheated 350° oven until toasted.

1. Use a sharp, serrated kitchen knife to slice off about an inch from the crown of the bread.
2. Gently cut around the interior, leaving a 1-inch border of bread along bottom and sides to prevent leaks.
3. Remove chunks of bread with your hands, being careful not to take too much. Ladle in soup or dip before serving.

3

stews

Basic Beef Stew with Carrots and Mushrooms

- 1   tablespoon olive oil, divided
- 1   pound small cremini mushrooms
- Cooking spray
- 2   cups chopped onion
- 3   garlic cloves, minced
- ⅓   cup all-purpose flour (about 1½ ounces)
- 2   pounds lean beef stew meat, cut into bite-sized pieces
- ¾   teaspoon salt, divided
- 1   cup dry red wine
- 1   tablespoon chopped fresh thyme
- 2   (14-ounce) cans less-sodium beef broth
- 1   bay leaf
- 2   cups (¾-inch) cubed peeled white potato (about 1 pound)
- 1½ cups (1-inch) slices carrot (about 12 ounces)
- ½   teaspoon freshly ground black pepper
- Fresh thyme sprigs (optional)

1. Heat 1 teaspoon oil in a large Dutch oven over medium-high heat. Add mushrooms; sauté 5 minutes or until mushrooms begin to brown. Spoon mushrooms into bowl. Coat pan with cooking spray. Add onion; sauté 10 minutes or until tender and brown. Add garlic; sauté 1 minute. Add onion mixture to mushroom mixture.

2. Place flour in a shallow bowl. Dredge beef in flour, shaking off excess. Heat remaining 2 teaspoons oil in pan over medium-high heat. Add half of beef mixture; sprinkle with ⅛ teaspoon salt. Cook 6 minutes, browning on all sides; add to mushroom mixture. Repeat procedure with remaining beef mixture and ⅛ teaspoon salt.

3. Add wine to pan, scraping pan to loosen browned bits. Add thyme, broth, and bay leaf; bring to a boil. Stir in beef mixture. Cover, reduce heat to medium-low, and simmer 1 hour or until beef is just tender.

4. Stir in potato and carrot. Simmer, uncovered, 1 hour and 15 minutes or until beef and vegetables are very tender and sauce is thick, stirring occasionally. Stir in remaining ½ teaspoon salt and pepper. Discard bay leaf. Garnish with thyme sprigs, if desired. **Yield: 8 servings (serving size: about 1 cup).**

CALORIES 303; FAT 9.8g (sat 3.2g, mono 4.7g, poly 0.6g); PROTEIN 26.4g; CARB 26.8g; FIBER 2.3g; CHOL 71mg; IRON 3.9mg; SODIUM 494mg; CALC 54mg

kitchen how-to:
make stew

A stew consists of small pieces of meat that are seared and then cooked while immersed in liquid. The process creates a rich gravy and tender meat.

1. Gather the right equipment. Use a Dutch oven, a large pan with a tight-fitting lid, for the best results. A flat wooden spatula works well to deglaze the pan (step 6).

2. Use the right cuts of meat for the recipe. If the cuts are too lean, the meat might end up tough.

3. Sauté the aromatics (onions, garlic, etc.) until golden brown to deepen their flavor, and then remove them from the pan.

4. Dredge the meat in flour, and shake off the excess.

5. Brown the meat to create a delicious crust that locks in juices and establishes flavorful browned bits that stick to the bottom of the pan.

6. Deglaze the pan, scraping the bottom of the pan as you add the liquid. The browned bits that are scraped up give the stew lots of flavor.

7. Simmer over low heat to ensure the meat becomes tender.

8. Add the vegetables after the meat has cooked a while so they won't become overdone and will retain their shape and texture.

beans

Beans are the centerpiece of many wonderful dishes. Although canned beans are convenient, cooking dried beans offers clear benefits, including superior taste and texture. Perhaps most importantly, you're able to control the sodium—canned beans can contain up to 630 milligrams per half cup, as opposed to about 5 milligrams in the same amount of dried beans cooked without salt.

Hoppin' John with Mustard Greens

2	cups water
2	tablespoons whole-grain Dijon mustard
1	teaspoon salt
¼	teaspoon dried thyme
2	tablespoons olive oil
3½	cups chopped onion
1	cup uncooked long-grain white rice
⅔	cup finely chopped ham
4	garlic cloves, minced
4	cups cooked black-eyed peas
4	cups chopped trimmed mustard greens

1. Combine first 4 ingredients, stirring with a whisk; set aside.

2. Heat oil in a Dutch oven over medium-high heat. Add onion to pan; sauté 6 minutes. Add rice, ham, and garlic; sauté 2 minutes. Stir in water mixture; bring to a boil. Cover, reduce heat, and simmer 15 minutes. Add peas and greens; cover and cook 5 minutes. Stir rice mixture; cover and cook an additional 5 minutes or until greens and rice are tender. **Yield: 6 servings (serving size: about 1⅓ cups).**

CALORIES 389; FAT 7g (sat 1.4g, mono 4.1g, poly 1g); PROTEIN 18.2g; CARB 63.6g; FIBER 11g; CHOL 14mg; IRON 5.1mg; SODIUM 502mg; CALC 109mg

kitchen how-to: prepare dried beans

Follow these basic steps to easily cook a pot of beans from start to finish.

1. Since beans are not washed during processing (the key to processing beans is to dehydrate, not hydrate), it's important to rinse beans before soaking. Remove and discard any small rocks, shriveled beans, and dirt. Soak beans using either the overnight soak or the quick soak methods. For an overnight soak, place the beans in a large bowl. Cover with cool water to 2 inches above beans; cover and let stand 8 hours or overnight, and then drain. To quick soak beans, place them in a large Dutch oven. Cover with water to 2 inches above the beans; bring the water to a boil, and cook 2 minutes. Remove from the heat; cover and let stand 1 hour, and then drain. Soaking dried beans shortens the cooking time and promotes even cooking. In fact, beans can be cooked after only a quick rinse—they'll just take a good bit longer to cook until they're tender (at least 2 to 3 hours, depending on the variety).

2. Place the drained, soaked beans in a large Dutch oven.

3. Cover with water to 2 inches above the beans, and bring to a boil.

4. Partially cover, reduce heat, and simmer until tender (skim the foam from the surface of the cooking liquid as needed). It's important to cook beans at a simmer, not at a boil— boiling may cook beans too rapidly and cause their skins to split.

5. It's important to taste the beans to make sure they're tender; don't just

go by the estimated cooking times because older beans and those cooked in hard water will take longer to cook.

Note: Do not add salt or acidic ingredients (such as tomatoes, vinegar, or citrus) to beans until they are tender; cooking in salted water may lengthen the cooking time, and acid can prevent beans from becoming tender.

vegetables

With its small green florets, broccoli rabe (also raab or rapini) resembles a miniature head of broccoli, but the two vegetables are quite different. Broccoli rabe has a stronger bitter flavor and sturdier texture. Like broccoli, though, it is rich in nutritional value: One cup of the raw vegetable contains almost 100 percent of the daily vitamin C recommendation.

Broccoli Rabe with Garlic, Tomatoes, and Red Pepper

Start with 1 pound broccoli rabe, trimmed and cut into 3-inch pieces, and then add our suggested ingredients to boost the flavor and make a quick, simple, and colorful side dish.

1 pound broccoli rabe, trimmed and cut + **1 tablespoon olive oil** + **2 garlic cloves, sliced**

½ cup grape tomatoes, halved + **¼ teaspoon crushed red pepper**

Bring 2 quarts of water to a boil. Place broccoli rabe in boiling water, and cook for about 2 minutes. Drain; place in ice water to cool. Squeeze liquid from broccoli rabe; set aside. Heat oil in a skillet over medium heat; add garlic, and sauté 1 minute or until lightly browned. Add broccoli rabe, tomatoes, and pepper, and cook 3 minutes or until tender. **Yield: 4 servings (serving size: ½ cup).**

CALORIES 69; FAT 3.4g (sat 0.5g, mono 2.5g, poly 0.4g); PROTEIN 4.3g; CARB 6.6g; FIBER 0.3g; CHOL 0mg; IRON 1.1mg; SODIUM 35mg; CALC 58mg

Smashed Potatoes with Goat Cheese and Chives

If you want to make the potatoes ahead, chill them and reheat just before serving, adding extra liquid to desired consistency. Stir in the chives just before serving. For a nice presentation, sprinkle additional chives over the top.

- 3 pounds peeled baking potatoes, cut into 1-inch pieces
- 1¼ teaspoons salt, divided
- 2 tablespoons butter
- ¾ cup (6 ounces) goat cheese
- ¼ teaspoon freshly ground black pepper
- 1 cup 2% reduced-fat milk
- 3 tablespoons finely chopped fresh chives

1. Place potatoes in a saucepan, and cover with cold water to 2 inches above potatoes. Add ¼ teaspoon salt; bring to a boil. Reduce heat, and simmer 15 minutes or until tender; drain. Return potatoes to pan over low heat; add remaining 1 teaspoon salt and butter. Mash potatoes with a potato masher to desired consistency. **2.** Add cheese and pepper to potato mixture; stir until cheese melts. Stir in milk; cook 1 minute or until thoroughly heated, stirring frequently. Remove from heat; stir in chives. **Yield: 12 servings (serving size: about ⅔ cup).**

CALORIES 155; FAT 5.4g (sat 3.5g, mono 1.3g, poly 0.2g); PROTEIN 5.8g; CARB 21.7g; FIBER 1.5g; CHOL 13mg; IRON 1.3mg; SODIUM 283mg; CALC 61mg

make smashed potatoes

Cut the potatoes into uniform pieces to ensure even cooking.

1. Cook potatoes in boiling water until tender. Drain and return them to the pan over low heat.

2. Add butter to the warm spuds, and smooth them with a potato masher to your desired consistency.

3. Add cheese, stirring until cheese melts. Finally stir in milk, and cook 1 minute or until thoroughly heated.

way to braise

Braising uses low, moist heat to transform food—usually meat—into meltingly tender and flavorful dishes. It's an ideal technique for cooking cold-weather comfort foods like pot roasts and daubes.

Since much of the cooking time is hands-off as the dish simmers, braising is a boon to the busy cook. The results are always satisfying, partly because the process involves layers of flavors—browned bits from the seared meat enrich the cooking liquid, and the sauce becomes a heady, intense blend of meat juices, sweet vegetables, and fragrant herbs that infuse the dish. And you can remove a substantial amount of fat from the dish by skimming the cooking liquid before reducing it or serving the meal.

braising, defined

This method involves slowly simmering food, usually meat, over low heat in a moderate amount of liquid in a covered pot. The dish finishes cooking either in the oven or on the stovetop. Braising works wonders with inexpensive, tough cuts, such as bottom round, pork shoulder, and short ribs—as the meat bathes in the aromatic hot liquid, its connective tissue breaks down, turning it fork-tender.

Best Bets for Braising

Typically, braising is best employed with tough cuts of meat—meat with lots of collagen, which slowly melts into the broth and infuses it with flavor. (Small, tender steaks and pork chops fare poorly in a braise; lacking the necessary connective tissue, they simply dry out.) Hard, fibrous vegetables are also good in braises, which is why you'll often see hearty root vegetables in the cooking liquid.

Equipment

A braise should be cooked in a tightly closed pot—a Dutch oven is ideal. The pot should be deep enough to hold ample liquid to partially submerge the meat and vegetables so they cook in the broth, as well as steam in the aromatic flavors. The pan should also be wide enough to contain a large mix of ingredients—a whole roast and lots of vegetables, for example. Be sure to choose a heavy pan because it needs to maintain an even temperature. We use a variety of pans—aluminum, stainless steel, enamel-coated cast iron, and nonstick—and as long as the pans have a heavy bottom, they perform well.

The only other necessary component is a tight-fitting lid to seal in flavor, create internal condensation so the broth doesn't evaporate and reduce too far, and

keep the food evenly heated. If the lid doesn't fit snugly (or if you don't have a lid), place a sheet of aluminum foil over the pan (as a liner), and cover with the lid, a large skillet, or a baking sheet.

Slow Cookers

Rich pot roast, warming stews, and other hearty fare can also be prepared in an electric slow cooker. It's a convenient option because it cooks dinner while you're away, and by the day's end, you have a home-cooked meal ready and waiting. Just assemble the ingredients in the morning, and turn on the slow cooker.

Use the slow-cooker size specified by the recipe to ensure proper levels of food, thorough cooking, and safe temperatures. If you use a different-sized cooker than specified, make sure it's still between half and two-thirds full for food safety. Be aware though that changes in slow-cooker size can lead to changes in cooking time. If using a larger slow cooker than called for, the cook time may be less; if using a smaller cooker, your dish may need more cook time.

Our Test Kitchens professionals have also found that some slow cookers—particularly some newer models—cook hotter than others. In one instance, liquid imperceptibly evaporated from the cooker, leaving less sauce than when the same dish was prepared in a different model. Because not all slow cookers are created equal, don't rely on the stated cook time for a recipe until you know how your cooker performs.

Browning

Browning caramelizes the natural protein, sugars, and fat on the outside of the meat. As the meat browns, some of those proteins, fats, and sugars also stick to the bottom of the pot. The cooking liquid dissolves those browned bits, enriching the broth, coloring it deeply, and contributing a great deal of flavor.

Cooking Liquid

Braising is about layering flavors, starting with the caramelized meat and building up to a last touch of vinegar, honey, or fresh herbs. To further enhance the taste, braise in a broth enriched with another liquid: wine, fortified wine such as dry sherry or vermouth, fruit juice, liqueur such as brandy, or vinegar. Braising in broth alone may result in a finished dish without much depth. But enhanced broth provides a rich base with notes of sweet or sour, herb or floral, which will balance the flavor and texture of the meat and vegetables.

Flavorings

Dried herbs shine in braising. When they're added at the beginning and simmer for the duration, they have plenty of time to soften and release their woodsy essence; crush dried herbs to release more flavor and aroma before adding them to the pot. Fresh herbs, on the other hand, should be added at the end to brighten the taste and offer color.

Most of our recipes also include flavorings such as onions and carrots, which cook with the meat the entire time and enrich both the meat and the broth. For a more refined presentation, these ingredients would be strained out to give way to a smooth sauce. For our homey, more casual recipes, we keep these vegetables. Onions actually soften over time, and carrots provide sweet tidbits of color.

Simmering

Brown the meat on medium to medium-high, but braise on low, just so a few bubbles surface every few seconds. Be careful not to let the liquid boil—boiling will cook the meat too quickly and make it tough. Once the broth comes to a simmer, cover the pot, and turn the heat down. The meat's collagen melts when it reaches a temperature of about 160°. The trick is to bring the temperature up slowly so the sauce thickens as the meat cooks—and then hold the meat at about that temperature for the juiciest results.

Side Dish Braises

Braising is most often used with meats, but sturdy vegetables—such as sliced or quartered fennel bulbs, halved leeks, chopped kale, and cubed winter squash—can also be braised with flavorful results.

You can brown the vegetables first, or skip that step; it's not as crucial as it is for meat braises. The vegetables shouldn't be submerged; rather, some pieces should sit above and some below the liquid line. Give them a gentle stir occasionally so those in the liquid don't become too soft. Most braised vegetables are enhanced by a little acid at the end of cooking. Try a squeeze of lemon juice or a splash of vinegar. Then transfer the vegetables to a plate, and reduce the broth to a tasty glaze that can be spooned over the top.

Braising vs. Stewing

Braising is sometimes confused with stewing. The two are similar, but in stewing, the ingredients are submerged—as in soup. In braising, the meat and vegetables are partially submerged so they're cooked both in steam and liquid, a combination yielding richer results and more profound layering of the flavors.

the bottom line

The three most important elements to remember about braising:

1. Brown the meat for more flavor.

2. Don't completely submerge the meat in liquid.

3. Cover the pan, and simmer over low heat.

meats

Pot roasting is a great technique for less-expensive, tough cuts of meat, such as those from the shoulder and neck, arm, or hip and leg. These sections are typically fattier and therefore more flavorful, but they're also tough because they contain more connective tissue than more expensive cuts.

Classic Beef Pot Roast

- 1 teaspoon olive oil
- 1 (3-pound) boneless chuck roast, trimmed
- 1 teaspoon kosher salt
- ¼ teaspoon freshly ground black pepper
- 2 cups coarsely chopped onion
- 1 cup dry red wine
- 4 thyme sprigs
- 3 garlic cloves, chopped
- 1 (14-ounce) can fat-free, less-sodium beef broth
- 1 bay leaf
- 4 large carrots, peeled and cut diagonally into 1-inch pieces
- 2 pounds Yukon gold potatoes, peeled and cut into 2-inch pieces

Fresh thyme leaves (optional)

1. Preheat oven to 350°.

2. Heat oil in a large Dutch oven over medium-high heat. Sprinkle chuck roast with salt and pepper. Add roast to pan; cook 5 minutes, turning to brown on all sides. Remove roast from pan. Add onion to pan; sauté 8 minutes or until tender.

3. Return browned roast to pan. Add wine and next 4 ingredients; bring to a simmer. Cover pan and bake at 350° for 1½ hours or until roast is almost tender.

4. Add carrots and potatoes to pan. Cover and bake an additional 1 hour or until vegetables are tender. Remove thyme sprigs and bay leaf; discard. Shred meat with 2 forks. Serve roast with vegetable mixture and cooking liquid. Garnish with thyme leaves, if desired. **Yield: 10 servings (serving size: 3 ounces roast, about ¾ cup vegetables, and about 3 tablespoons cooking liquid).**

CALORIES 307; FAT 10.4g (sat 3.5g, mono 4.8g, poly 0.5g); PROTEIN 28.6g; CARB 23.7g; FIBER 2.8g; CHOL 85mg; IRON 3.9mg; SODIUM 340mg; CALC 34mg

kitchen how-to:
make pot roast

Whichever meat or cut you choose, look for a roast that's well marbled. The smaller marbling creates smaller pockets of fat, contributing to a moist and compact roast. Avoid roasts with large ribbons of fat because they will yield a greasy, misshapen, fatty pot roast.

1. Gather the right equipment. All you need to prepare pot roast are a heavy, nonreactive pot, such as a Dutch oven with a tight-fitting lid; at least one pair of sturdy tongs; and a wooden spoon.

2. Select the proper cut of meat to ensure success. Pot roasting works well to tenderize tougher cuts of meat from the shoulder, arm, or leg sections.

3. Season the meat before you cook it. Salt and pepper are essential, and some recipes include spice blends or chopped fresh herbs.

4. Brown the meat before you braise it. This builds flavor and gives the cooked roast an appealing golden-brown appearance.

5. A flavorful broth mixture yields tasty results. The cooking liquid usually consists of broth, wine, and seasonings, such as garlic, fresh herbs, bay leaves, or other aromatic ingredients.

6. Most vegetables cook more quickly than the large cuts of meat used for pot roast. To cook both to perfection, add the vegetables to the pan partway through cooking.

7. Use two forks to shred the tender meat before serving.

Beef Daube Provençal

This classic French braised beef, red wine, and vegetable stew is simple and delicious. It stands above all our other beef recipes because it offers the homey comfort and convenience of pot roast, yet it's versatile and sophisticated enough for entertaining.

2 teaspoons olive oil
12 garlic cloves, crushed
1 (2-pound) boneless chuck roast, trimmed and cut into 2-inch cubes
1½ teaspoons salt, divided
½ teaspoon freshly ground black pepper, divided
1 cup red wine
2 cups chopped carrot
1½ cups chopped onion
½ cup fat-free, less-sodium beef broth
1 tablespoon tomato paste
1 teaspoon chopped fresh rosemary
1 teaspoon chopped fresh thyme
Dash of ground cloves
1 (14.5-ounce) can diced tomatoes, undrained
1 bay leaf

3 cups hot cooked medium egg noodles (about 4 cups uncooked noodles)
Chopped fresh thyme (optional)

1. Preheat oven to 300°.
2. Heat oil in a small ovenproof Dutch oven over low heat. Add garlic to pan; cook 5 minutes or until garlic is fragrant, stirring occasionally. Remove garlic with a slotted spoon; set aside. Increase heat to medium-high. Add beef to pan. Sprinkle beef with ½ teaspoon salt and ¼ teaspoon black pepper. Cook 5 minutes, browning on all sides. Remove beef from pan. Add wine to pan, and bring to a boil, scraping pan to loosen browned bits. Add garlic, beef, remaining 1 teaspoon salt, remaining ¼ teaspoon pepper, carrot, and next 8 ingredients to pan; bring to a boil.
3. Cover and bake at 300° for 2½ hours or until beef is tender. Discard bay leaf. Serve over noodles. Garnish with chopped fresh thyme, if desired. **Yield: 6 servings (serving size: about ¾ cup stew and ½ cup noodles).**

CALORIES 367; FAT 12.8g (sat 4.3g, mono 5.8g, poly 0.9g); PROTEIN 29.1g; CARB 33.4g; FIBER 3.9g; CHOL 105mg; IRON 4.3mg; SODIUM 776mg; CALC 76mg

kitchen how-to:
chop an onion

1

2

3

Onions are about as omnipresent in cooking as salt. Our Test Kitchens staff uses this technique to quickly and safely chop onions. To avoid watery eyes while chopping an onion, peel it first, and chill it in the refrigerator before slicing.

1. Trim the stem and root ends; discard. Remove the papery outer skins.
2. Stand the onion upright on a cutting board; cut a thin slice off one side. Make vertical slices through the onion to within ¼ inch of bottom.
3. Rotate onion 90° on cutting board. Repeat step 2.
4. Turn onion so cut side is flat on board. Cut vertically through onion.

4

Lamb Shanks with Lemon and White Beans

This is an excellent example of the way braising benefits tough cuts—lamb shanks are slowly simmered in a flavorful liquid until the meat starts to fall off the bones. Mashed beans thicken the sauce, while lemon juice brightens it.

Cooking spray
4 (12-ounce) lamb shanks, trimmed
2 cups chopped yellow onion
2 cups (1-inch) cubed carrot
1 cup dry white wine
1 tablespoon grated lemon rind
1 teaspoon dried sage
¾ teaspoon salt
½ teaspoon celery seeds
½ teaspoon freshly ground black pepper
1 cup fat-free, less-sodium chicken broth
2 tablespoons fresh lemon juice
1 (16-ounce) can cannellini beans or other
   white beans, rinsed, drained, and divided
Chopped fresh parsley (optional)

1. Heat a large Dutch oven over medium heat. Coat pan with cooking spray. Add half of lamb to pan, and cook 9 minutes, browning on all sides. Remove lamb from pan. Repeat procedure with cooking spray and remaining lamb.
2. Add onion and carrot to pan; cook 4 minutes, stirring frequently. Increase heat to medium-high. Stir in wine, scraping pan to loosen browned bits. Add rind and next 4 ingredients; cook 5 minutes. Add lamb and broth; bring to a simmer. Cover, reduce heat, and simmer 2½ hours or until lamb is very tender.
3. Remove lamb and vegetables from pan with a slotted spoon; place in a large bowl. Place a large zip-top plastic bag inside an 8-cup glass measure or bowl. Pour broth mixture into bag; let stand 10 minutes (fat will rise to the top). Seal bag, and carefully snip off 1 bottom corner of bag. Drain drippings into pan, stopping before fat layer reaches opening; discard fat.

4. Combine juice and 1 cup beans in a small bowl; mash with a fork until pastelike. Add juice mixture and remaining beans to pan; stir well to combine. Add lamb mixture; cook 5 minutes or until thoroughly heated. Garnish with parsley, if desired. **Yield: 4 servings (serving size: 1 shank and about 1½ cups vegetable mixture).**

CALORIES 399; FAT 15.6g (sat 6.4g, mono 6.5g, poly 1.4g); PROTEIN 37g; CARB 25.7g; FIBER 6g; CHOL 119mg; IRON 4.1mg; SODIUM 757mg; CALC 95mg

kitchen how-to:
reduce the sodium in canned beans

Canned beans are a convenient option when you don't have time to prepare dried beans—the drawback is the sodium content. Canned beans are generally high in sodium, and the amount varies among different brands and varieties. More and more brands are offering no-salt-added varieties. You can reduce the sodium content of any variety of canned beans by 40 percent simply by draining and rinsing them.

all about cannellini beans

Quite popular in Italy, cannellini beans, also called white kidney beans, are prized for their smooth texture and mellow nutty flavor. Because of their popularity, they're available year-round, both dried and canned.

Pork Loin Braised with Cabbage

At the German table, pork is typically served with cabbage. Use red cabbage, if you'd like, for a slightly sweeter flavor. You can prepare the dish a day ahead, and chill it overnight. Cut the roast into ¼-inch slices. Gently reheat the meat in the cabbage mixture in a Dutch oven over medium-low heat. Garnish with fresh thyme, if you'd like.

   4 teaspoons Hungarian sweet paprika, divided
   2 teaspoons chopped fresh thyme, divided
1½ teaspoons kosher salt, divided
1½ teaspoons freshly ground black pepper, divided
   1 teaspoon chopped fresh sage
   1 (2-pound) boneless pork loin, trimmed
Cooking spray
   ¾ cup diced Canadian bacon (about 4 ounces)
 14 cups thinly sliced cabbage (about 2 pounds)
2½ cups thinly sliced onion (about 2 medium)
   ¾ cup thinly sliced carrot (about 1)
   1 tablespoon tomato paste
   ½ teaspoon caraway seeds
   1 (12-ounce) bottle dark lager

1. Preheat oven to 350°.
2. Combine 2 teaspoons paprika, 1 teaspoon thyme, 1 teaspoon salt, 1 teaspoon pepper, and sage; rub over pork. Heat a large ovenproof Dutch oven over medium-high heat. Coat pan with cooking spray. Add pork to pan; cook 5 minutes, browning on all sides. Remove pork from pan.
3. Add bacon to pan; cook 3 minutes. Add cabbage, onion, and carrot. Cover, reduce heat to medium, and cook 15 minutes or until cabbage begins to wilt, stirring occasionally. Stir in tomato paste, remaining 2 teaspoons paprika, remaining 1 teaspoon thyme, remaining ½ teaspoon pepper, caraway seeds, and lager. Return pork to pan. Cover and bake at 350° for 2 hours or until tender. Sprinkle with remaining ½ teaspoon salt. **Yield: 8 servings (serving size: 3 ounces pork and ¾ cup cabbage mixture).**

CALORIES 255; FAT 9g (sat 3.3g, mono 4g, poly 0.8g); PROTEIN 28.7g; CARB 11.9g; FIBER 3.7g; CHOL 76mg; IRON 1.7mg; SODIUM 596mg; CALC 84mg

kitchen how-to:
prepare cabbage

Start by removing and discarding the tough outer leaves from the head of cabbage. Unlike its loose-leafed cousins mustard and kale, cabbage is tightly wound, so it doesn't pick up grit from the garden. Rinse under running water to clean it sufficiently, and then slice or chop it depending on the needs of the recipe.

Veal Osso Buco with Gremolata

Gremolata, a combination of parsley, lemon rind, and garlic, is a traditional finishing touch for osso buco. Serve this dish with polenta or mashed potatoes.

 6 (8-ounce) veal shanks, trimmed
 ¾ teaspoon salt, divided
 ¼ teaspoon freshly ground black pepper
 ¼ cup all-purpose flour (about 1 ounce)
 1 tablespoon butter, divided
 1 cup finely chopped yellow onion (about 1 medium)
 ½ cup finely chopped carrot (about 1 medium)
 ½ cup finely chopped celery (about 1 stalk)
 2 bacon slices, diced (uncooked)
 1 cup dry white wine
 1 cup fat-free, less-sodium beef broth
 1 (14.5-ounce) can no-salt-added whole tomatoes, drained and chopped
 1 cup chopped fresh flat-leaf parsley
 1 teaspoon grated lemon rind
 1 garlic clove, minced

1. Sprinkle veal with ¼ teaspoon salt and pepper; dredge in flour (see photo at right).
2. Melt 1½ teaspoons butter in a large Dutch oven over medium-high heat. Add 3 veal shanks, and cook 8 minutes, browning on all sides. Remove to a plate. Repeat procedure with remaining 1½ teaspoons butter and veal.
3. Add onion, carrot, celery, and bacon to pan; sauté 5 minutes or until vegetables are tender. Add wine; cook 5 minutes or until liquid almost evaporates. Add remaining ½ teaspoon salt, broth, and tomatoes. Return veal to pan; bring to a boil. Cover, reduce heat, and simmer 2 hours or until veal is tender.
4. Combine parsley, rind, and garlic in a small bowl. Stir into veal and vegetable mixture; cook 10 minutes.
Yield: 6 servings (serving size: 1 veal shank).

CALORIES 358; FAT 12.5g (sat 4.2g, mono 4.5g, poly 1.3g); PROTEIN 49.2g; CARB 9.8g; FIBER 1.6g; CHOL 186mg; IRON 3.1mg; SODIUM 818mg; CALC 89mg

all about osso buco
This Milanese dish of braised veal shanks, whose name means "bone with a hole," cooks with the bone and marrow intact. The result is a rich, succulent flavor and tender meat. It's usually sprinkled with gremolata.

way to braise
poultry

Braised Root Vegetables and Chicken Thighs

Winter is the peak season for parsnips, rutabagas, and turnips. Their strong flavors, along with that of the chicken thighs, mellow while cooking and make this a quintessential hearty cold-weather meal. Garnish with a fresh sage leaf for a simple, elegant presentation.

- ¼ cup all-purpose flour
- 8 bone-in chicken thighs (about 2¼ pounds), skinned
- 5 teaspoons olive oil, divided
- 2 cups chopped onion
- 2 cups (¾-inch) cubed peeled rutabaga
- 2 cups (¾-inch) cubed peeled turnip (about 1 pound)
- 2 cups (¾-inch) cubed peeled butternut squash
- 1 cup (¼-inch-thick) slices parsnip
- 1 garlic clove, minced
- ½ cup fat-free, less-sodium chicken broth
- 1 teaspoon chopped fresh or ¼ teaspoon dried thyme
- 1 teaspoon chopped fresh or ¼ teaspoon dried rubbed sage
- ½ teaspoon salt
- ¼ teaspoon black pepper
- 1 bay leaf

1. Place flour in a shallow dish; dredge chicken in flour.
2. Heat 1 tablespoon oil in a large nonstick skillet over medium-high heat. Add chicken; sauté 5 minutes, turning once. Remove chicken from pan, and keep warm.
3. Heat remaining 2 teaspoons oil in pan. Add onion; sauté 3 minutes. Add rutabaga, turnip, squash, parsnip, and garlic; sauté 3 minutes. Stir in broth and next 5 ingredients, and nestle chicken into vegetable mixture. Bring to a boil; cover, reduce heat, and simmer 20 minutes or until chicken is done. Uncover and simmer 3 minutes or until thick. Remove bay leaf. **Yield: 4 servings (serving size: 2 thighs and 1¼ cups vegetable mixture).**

CALORIES 477; FAT 18.6g (sat 4.3g, mono 8.9g, poly 3.6g); PROTEIN 34.7g; CARB 44g; FIBER 5.2g; CHOL 109mg; IRON 3.7mg; SODIUM 531mg; CALC 158mg

kitchen how-to:
slice parsnips

Parsnips are similar in shape to carrots, but they taper more and are creamy white rather than orange in color. Parsnips have a flavor that's described as nutty, spicy, or peppery. They are suited to prolonged cooking, so they're great for braises. Select firm, unshriveled parsnips of moderate size (large ones can be woody). The outside should be relatively clean and free of surface blemishes. Parsnips will store well for several weeks in plastic packaging in your refrigerator's vegetable crisper. Before using parsnips, rinse them well, trim the crown, peel the outer skin, and then cut or slice them to the size you need.

Chicken with Dark Beer
(Coq à la Bière)

 3   tablespoons all-purpose flour
 ½   teaspoon salt
 ¼   teaspoon freshly ground black pepper
 2   bone-in chicken breast halves, skinned
 2   bone-in chicken thighs, skinned
 2   chicken drumsticks, skinned
 2   tablespoons butter
 1   tablespoon canola oil
 3   tablespoons dry gin
 ¾   cup chopped celery
 ¾   cup chopped peeled carrot
 ½   cup chopped shallots (about 3 medium)
 3   juniper berries, crushed
 1   (8-ounce) package mushrooms, halved
 3   sprigs fresh thyme
 3   sprigs fresh flat-leaf parsley
 1   bay leaf
 1   cup dark beer
 ¼   cup whole-milk Greek-style yogurt
 2   teaspoons white wine vinegar
 1   tablespoon chopped fresh flat-leaf parsley

1. Combine first 3 ingredients; sprinkle evenly over both sides of chicken. Heat butter and oil in a large deep skillet over medium-high heat. Add chicken to pan; sauté 5 minutes on each side or until browned. Remove pan from heat. Pour gin into one side of pan; return pan to heat. Ignite gin with a long match; let flames die down. Remove chicken from pan; keep warm.

2. Add celery and next 3 ingredients to pan; sauté 5 minutes or until vegetables are tender, stirring occasionally. Add mushrooms. Place thyme, parsley, and bay leaf on a double layer of cheesecloth. Gather edges of cheesecloth together; tie securely. Add cheesecloth bag to pan. Return chicken to pan, nestling into vegetable mixture. Stir in beer; bring to a simmer. Cover; reduce heat. Simmer 45 minutes or until a thermometer inserted in meaty parts of chicken registers 160°. (Breasts may cook quicker. Check them after 35 minutes; remove them when they're done. Keep warm.)

3. Discard cheesecloth bag. Remove chicken from pan; keep warm. Place pan over medium heat; stir in yogurt. Cook 1 minute or until thoroughly heated (do not boil or yogurt may curdle). Remove from heat; stir in vinegar. Place 1 chicken breast half or 1 drumstick and 1 thigh on each of 4 plates; top each serving with about ¾ cup sauce and vegetable mixture. Sprinkle with chopped parsley. **Yield: 4 servings.**

CALORIES 370; FAT 16g (sat 6.6g, mono 5g, poly 3g); PROTEIN 30.8g; CARB 15.1g; FIBER 1.4g; CHOL 103mg; IRON 2mg; SODIUM 465mg; CALC 55mg

kitchen how-to: make braised casseroles

Essential to success with this type of recipe is long, slow cooking. This marries the flavors, and the moist heat penetrates and tenderizes inexpensive cuts of meat that would otherwise remain tough.

1. Use a large deep skillet so the heat is diffused and food cooks evenly. The diameter of the base should be about three times the height of the sides. If it's too shallow, moisture will evaporate easily, and the food can dry out as it cooks. Check periodically, and if the liquid dips too far down, top it off. Start with large pieces of meat. Here we're using bone-in chicken pieces because they take longer to cook than boneless. Brown the meat in the skillet.

2. Begin to build flavor in the dish by adding vegetables, spices, and herbs. Add hearty ingredients like tough root vegetables, spices, and dried herbs to the skillet early, and allow them to cook and flavor the dish. It's best to garnish with delicate chopped fresh herbs just before serving.

3. Create a bouquet garni by wrapping ingredients such as sprigs of fresh herbs, peppercorns, or bay leaves in cheese-cloth. Place the bundle in the skillet to infuse the cooking liquid and meat as the dish simmers.

4. To achieve the best results, partially submerge the meat in a flavorful liquid as it cooks. Broth, milk, cream, cider, beer, wine, or spirits are all good options. Plain water is also useful in casseroles.

Red Potatoes

What they add: Sometimes called new potatoes, small, young red potatoes haven't had time to become starchy. Because of this, they have a waxy texture that makes them good for braising.

Plum Tomatoes

What they add: These tomatoes have fewer seeds than most other tomato varieties and a lower water content, which gives them a more concentrated flavor. Store them at room temperature because cold temperatures can cause them to lose their flavor.

Oven-Braised Cornish Hens with Cider Vinegar and Warm Vegetable Sauce

Warm crusty bread is all you need to complete this meal. Use it to soak up the last drops of the tart broth.

    2 (1¼-pound) Cornish hens
    3 tablespoons all-purpose flour
    ½ teaspoon salt
    ¼ teaspoon freshly ground black pepper
 1½ teaspoons butter
    1 teaspoon olive oil
    2 cups (1-inch) slices leek (about 2 large)
    ½ pound cremini mushrooms, halved
    2 garlic cloves, minced
    3 cups fat-free, less-sodium chicken broth
    1 cup cider vinegar
    3 plum tomatoes, quartered
    1 Granny Smith apple, peeled and cut into ½-inch slices
    ½ pound small red potatoes, quartered
    2 tablespoons chopped fresh parsley

1. Preheat oven to 350°.

2. Rinse hens with cold water; pat dry. Remove skin; trim excess fat. Split hens in half lengthwise. Combine flour, salt, and pepper in a shallow dish; dredge hens in flour mixture. Heat butter and oil in a large ovenproof Dutch oven over medium-high heat. Add hens, and cook 4 minutes or each side or until browned. Remove from pan.

3. Add leek, mushrooms, and garlic to pan; sauté 5 minutes. Add broth and vinegar, stirring to loosen browned bits. Return hens to pan; add tomatoes, apple, and potatoes. Bring to a simmer. Cover and bake at 350° for 30 minutes or until hens are done. Place hens on a serving platter; keep warm. Remove vegetable mixture from pan with a slotted spoon; place in a serving bowl. Reserve 2 cups cooking liquid in pan; discard remaining liquid. Bring reserved cooking liquid to a boil; cook 8 minutes or until reduced by half, stirring occasionally. Pour over vegetable mixture. Sprinkle with parsley. Serve with hens. **Yield: 4 servings (serving size: 1 hen half and 1 cup vegetable mixture).**

CALORIES 487; FAT 14.4g (sat 5g, mono 4.7g, poly 2.6g); PROTEIN 56.5g; CARB 31.5g; FIBER 3.9g; CHOL 237mg; IRON 4.7mg; SODIUM 842mg; CALC 78mg

way to braise
vegetables

Braising is most often used with meats. But sturdy vegetables—such as sliced or quartered fennel bulbs, halved leeks, chopped kale, and cubed winter squash—can also be braised with flavorful results.

Braised Leeks with Warm Pancetta Dressing

Pancetta is Italian cured pork. If you can't find it, substitute your favorite cured bacon.

Leeks:
- 4 leeks, trimmed and halved lengthwise
- ¼ teaspoon kosher salt
- ¼ teaspoon freshly ground black pepper
- 1½ cups fat-free, less-sodium chicken broth
- 1 large carrot, cut into (3-inch) pieces
- 1 garlic clove, crushed
- 1 fresh thyme sprig
- Cooking spray

Dressing:
- 1 teaspoon olive oil
- ⅓ cup finely chopped pancetta (about 1 ounce)
- 2 tablespoons finely chopped leek
- 2 tablespoons light brown sugar
- ¼ cup red wine vinegar
- ⅛ teaspoon freshly ground black pepper
- Dash of kosher salt

Remaining Ingredient:
- Fresh thyme sprigs (optional)

1. Preheat oven to 325°.

2. To prepare leeks, arrange leek halves in an 8-inch baking dish (leeks will slightly overlap); sprinkle evenly with ¼ teaspoon salt and ¼ teaspoon pepper. Add broth and next 3 ingredients. Cut 1 (8-inch) square of parchment paper; lightly coat with cooking spray. Place parchment over leek mixture, coated side down. Bake at 325° for 50 minutes or until leeks are tender.

Let stand 5 minutes; drain cooking liquid through a sieve over a bowl, reserving solids.

3. Place cooking liquid in a small, heavy saucepan; bring to a boil. Cook until reduced to ¼ cup (about 8 minutes). Chop cooked carrot; set aside. Coarsely chop cooked garlic; set aside.

4. To prepare dressing, heat oil in a small skillet over medium-high heat. Add pancetta to pan; sauté 5 minutes or until crisp. Stir in cooked garlic and chopped leek; sauté 2 minutes. Sprinkle with sugar; sauté 1 minute or until sugar dissolves. Stir in vinegar; simmer 2 minutes. Add reduced braising liquid, ⅛ teaspoon pepper, and dash of salt; simmer 2 minutes or until slightly thick. Remove from heat. Arrange leek halves in a serving dish; sprinkle with carrot. Drizzle pancetta mixture over leek halves. Garnish with thyme sprigs, if desired. **Yield: 4 servings (serving size: 2 leek halves and 2 tablespoons dressing).**

CALORIES 133; FAT 3.8g (sat 1.2g, mono 2g, poly 0.6g); PROTEIN 3.6g; CARB 22.2g; FIBER 2.6g; CHOL 5mg; IRON 2.3mg; SODIUM 391mg; CALC 74mg

See page 151 for information on how to cut and clean leeks.

all about leeks

Although increasingly available year-round, leeks are abundant in fall through early spring. Because they're a cool-weather crop, late-winter and spring leeks offer a milder flavor and delicate texture.

Choose slender, straight-sided, dry leeks that are free of blemishes and cracks; bulbous leeks or those that are thicker than 1 inch may be old and tough. Look for a bright white bulb and dark green, fresh-looking tops (trimmed leaves are often a sign of age). The longer the white and light green part, the better—that's the edible section.

Store leeks wrapped in damp paper towels in a plastic bag in the refrigerator's crisper drawer for up to six days. Wash, trim, and chop leeks just before use.

way to
caramelize

Caramelizing not only makes food rich and dark in color, but it also enhances and concentrates the taste. Consisting simply of sugar that's melted and cooked until it browns, true caramel serves as the base of many desserts and even some savory dishes.

"Caramelizing" also refers more loosely to the process of cooking foods other than sugar to a rich brown and intensifying their sweetness. Caramelized onions are perhaps the most common example, but other vegetables such as butternut squash, carrots, and even Brussels sprouts develop sweetness when caramelized. It's a healthful technique that coaxes the most out of food with little added fat or salt.

caramelizing, defined

Caramelizing is the process of cooking sugar until it browns. When granulated sugar is heated to high temperatures (about 340°), it melts and darkens. As it turns from clear to dark amber, the sugar undergoes chemical changes. The sugars break apart and form new compounds—as many as 128 different compounds have been identified during the caramel-making process—adding buttery, nutty, acidic, and bitter notes. Cooking can also "caramelize" the natural sugars in fruits and vegetables (see "Other 'Caramelized' Foods," page 315).

Equipment

High-quality heavy saucepans ensure even browning. Thin or uneven pans tend to have hot spots that can burn rather than brown the sugar. It also helps to use pans with light metal interiors, such as stainless steel. Dark metal makes it difficult to see if the caramel is browning properly.

Two Methods

The most common techniques for caramelizing sugar are the dry method and the wet method. The former involves melting and browning sugar (by itself) in a pan. This is a tricky strategy often used by candy makers.

We prefer the wet method, which involves dissolving sugar in water and then cooking the mixture until the water evaporates and the melted sugar browns. This technique works best for home cooks because it helps prevent the sugar from burning. The addition of water also lengthens the time required for the sugar to caramelize so more chemical reactions occur and produce a more complex flavor.

No Stirring

Using the wet technique, add specified amounts of sugar and water to a heavy saucepan over medium-high heat, and stir only until the sugar dissolves. Once it does, cook—without stirring—until the caramel reaches the desired color. As the water evaporates, the mixture will begin to darken (see photo at right). This darkening will occur unevenly, but do not stir the caramel because stirring incorporates air, lowers the temperature, and inhibits proper browning. If you stir before the water evaporates, the syrup may crystallize. Plus, the caramel will adhere to the spoon, creating a mess.

Keep an Eye on Color

As the caramel darkens, the flavor intensifies (see photo at left). Pale golden caramel is mild, while deep amber caramel tastes rich with a hint of bitterness. As the mixture begins to darken, it's important to watch it carefully—it takes only seconds to go from perfect dark amber to overdone. If it cooks too long, it will appear almost black and have a bitter, burned smell and flavor. If that happens, you'll need to start over.

Work Quickly

When caramel deepens to the desired shade of brown, remove it from the heat immediately and quickly continue with the specific recipe instructions. If the caramel is left in the pan too long, it can cool and begin to harden. If the caramel becomes too thick to pour, simply reheat it over low heat, swirling the pan occasionally until the mixture becomes liquid again.

Caramelizing vs. Maillard Reactions

Although baked goods and meat develop a nutty, slightly sweet richness when browned, technically they're not caramelized but rather undergo what's called "Maillard reactions." Named after the French chemist who identified the process in the early 1900s, Maillard reactions refer to the process of caramel-like flavor developing in foods as they brown. These reactions are similar to classic sugar caramelizing except they involve a series of complex reactions between proteins and sugars (rather than just sugar). Also, Maillard reactions occur at much lower heat than true sugar caramelization.

Hot Stuff

When your caramel reaches the perfect golden amber hue with a wisp of nutty aroma, you may be tempted to taste it. Don't. The molten caramel, which has been heated to about 340°, is too hot to touch or taste.

Other "Caramelized" Foods

Caramelizing is about more than just sugar; it's also a catchall culinary term for cooking foods other than sugar—most notably onions, but other vegetables and fruits, too—to a rich brown color and an intensified sweetness. Caramelized onions can be cooked to a sweet, caramel-brown, jamlike mixture. As onions sauté, their strong sulfur compounds dissolve and new compounds develop that are as sweet as sugar. Brussels sprouts also become sweeter as they brown because cooking breaks down the cell structure and makes existing sugars more pronounced. In general, most vegetables that are naturally rich in sugars and low in acid—such as carrots, onions, and members of the cabbage family—lend themselves best to caramelizing.

the bottom line

The three most important elements to remember about caramelizing:

1. Use a heavy, preferably light-colored pan.
2. Once the sugar dissolves into the water, do not stir.
3. Remove the pan from the heat immediately after the caramel reaches the desired color.

way to caramelize
desserts

Cinnamon-Orange Crème Brûlée

Bake and refrigerate this dessert the night before so all you need to do is add and caramelize the sugar topping before serving dinner. Serve the crème brûlée within an hour of melting the sugar, or the hard sugar shells will become soft as they start to dissolve into the custards.

> 1 cup 2% reduced-fat milk
> 6 tablespoons nonfat dry milk
> Dash of salt
> 1 (1-inch) orange rind strip
> 1 (1-inch) piece cinnamon stick
> ¼ teaspoon vanilla extract
> ¼ cup granulated sugar, divided
> 2 large egg yolks

1. Preheat oven to 300°.
2. Combine first 3 ingredients in a small saucepan over medium heat. Heat to 180° or until tiny bubbles form around edge (do not boil), stirring occasionally. Remove from heat; stir in orange rind and cinnamon stick. Cover and let steep 10 minutes. Strain milk mixture through a sieve into a bowl; discard solids. Stir in vanilla extract.
3. Combine 2 tablespoons sugar and egg yolks in a medium bowl; stir well with a whisk.
4. Gradually add milk mixture to egg mixture, stirring constantly with a whisk. Divide milk mixture evenly between 2 shallow (6-ounce) dishes. Place dishes in a 13 x 9–inch baking pan; add hot water to pan to a depth of 1 inch. Bake at 300° for 40 minutes or until center barely moves when dish is touched. Remove dishes from pan; cool completely on a wire rack. Cover and chill at least 4 hours or overnight.
5. Sift remaining 2 tablespoons sugar evenly over top of custards. Holding a kitchen blowtorch about 2 inches from the top of each custard, heat the sugar, moving the torch back and forth, until sugar is completely melted and caramelized (about 1 minute). Serve within 1 hour.
Yield: 2 servings (serving size: 1 brûlée).

CALORIES 301; FAT 7g (sat 3.2g, mono 2.7g, poly 0.8g); PROTEIN 15.6g; CARB 44.1g; FIBER 0g; CHOL 219mg; IRON 0.6mg; SODIUM 273mg; CALC 479mg

kitchen how-to:
brûlée two ways

You can make the custards in almost any small ovenproof dishes. Just make sure that they're shallow to provide ample surface area for the sugar shell.

Using a Torch
1. Carefully sift the sugar, using a small sieve, over each custard. This disperses the sugar evenly.
2. Torch the sugar immediately after it is sifted onto the custards or it will start to dissolve into the custards. Hold the torch about 2 inches away, and work from side to side until all the sugar is melted and caramelized.
On the Stovetop
1. In a small saucepan or skillet, cook the sugar over medium heat until golden (about 5 to 8 minutes).
2. Working quickly, evenly drizzle sugar topping over cold custards. Using a rubber spatula coated with cooking spray, spread caramel evenly to form a thin layer. Work quickly because the caramel will set.

Classic Crème Caramel

Nutty caramel coats delicate baked custard in this rich dessert, also referred to as "flan" in Spain. Although we specify cooking the caramel until golden, you can cook it longer for a deep amber color; the bitter notes of the darker caramel add a nice contrast to the sweet custard. The custards chill overnight, so they're a great make-ahead option. Baking at a low temperature means there's no need for a water bath. Since the seeds are not scraped from the vanilla bean, allow it to dry after steeping in the milk and reserve it for another use.

4 cups 2% reduced-fat milk
1 vanilla bean, split lengthwise
Cooking spray
1⅔ cups sugar, divided
¼ cup water
¼ teaspoon kosher salt
6 large eggs
3 tablespoons heavy whipping cream

1. Preheat oven to 225°.
2. Heat milk and vanilla bean over medium-high heat in a medium, heavy saucepan to 180° or until tiny bubbles form around edge (do not boil); remove pan from heat. Cover and set aside.
3. Coat 10 (6-ounce) custard cups with cooking spray; arrange cups on a jelly-roll pan.
4. Combine 1 cup sugar and ¼ cup water in a small, heavy saucepan; cook over medium-high heat until sugar dissolves, stirring frequently. Continue cooking 7 minutes or until golden (do not stir). Immediately pour into prepared custard cups, tipping quickly until caramelized sugar coats bottom of cups.
5. Combine remaining ⅔ cup sugar, salt, and eggs in a large bowl, stirring with a whisk. Remove vanilla bean from milk mixture; reserve bean for another use. Gradually pour warm milk mixture into egg mixture, stirring constantly with a whisk; stir in cream. Strain egg mixture through a sieve into a large bowl; pour about ½ cup egg mixture over caramelized sugar in each custard cup. Bake at 225° for 2 hours or until custards are just set. Remove from oven; cool to room temperature. Place plastic wrap on surface of custards; chill overnight.
6. Loosen edges of custards with a knife or rubber spatula. Place a dessert plate, upside down, on top of each cup; invert onto plate. Drizzle any remaining caramelized syrup over custards.
Yield: 10 servings (serving size: 1 custard).

CALORIES 236; FAT 6.5g (sat 3.1g, mono 2.2g, poly 0.5g); PROTEIN 7.1g; CARB 38.4g; FIBER 0g; CHOL 140mg; IRON 0.6mg; SODIUM 139mg; CALC 138mg

kitchen how-to:
make crème caramel

The custard in a crème caramel can be flavored many ways, but the process to make the dessert doesn't change. To master this dessert, follow these steps.

1. Combine the sugar and water in a heavy saucepan; cook over medium-high heat until the sugar dissolves, stirring frequently.

2. Continue to cook without stirring. The mixture will start to caramelize and turn light brown. Continue to cook until it's a deep golden brown.

3. Immediately pour just enough caramel into a ramekin or custard cup coated with cooking spray to cover the bottom of the cup.

4. Tilt the cup so the bottom is completely covered with caramel. Repeat with the remaining cups.

5. Pour the custard mixture (eggs, milk, and flavorings) evenly over the caramelized sugar in each custard cup.

6. Place the cups on a jelly-roll pan and bake until custards are just set. (Some recipes require placing the cups in a water bath to cook. See page 457 for more information about that technique.) Remove from the oven; cool to room temperature. Place plastic wrap on surface of custards; chill overnight. After the custards have chilled, run a thin knife along the edge of each to loosen it from its cup.

7. Place a dessert plate, upside down, on top of each cup. Invert the cup and plate. Lift the cup; the custard should slip out easily with the caramel syrup on top. Scrape out any remaining syrup with a rubber spatula, and drizzle over custards.

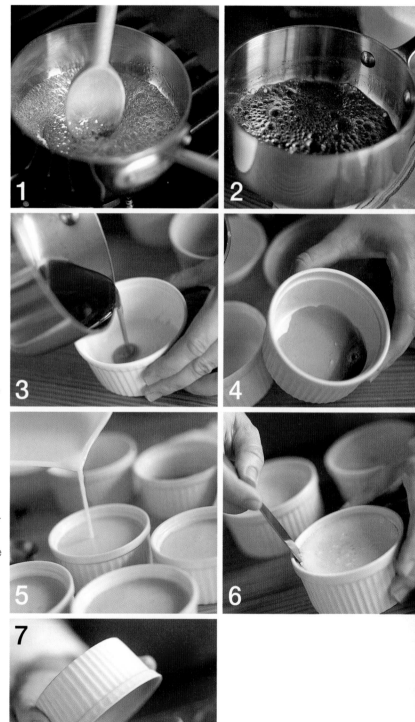

Gala Apples
What they add: Galas are aromatic, juicy apples with a firm, crisp texture and a very sweet flavor.

Tarte Tatin

Crust:
4.5 ounces all-purpose flour (about 1 cup)
1 tablespoon sugar
½ teaspoon salt
6 tablespoons unsalted butter, chilled and cut into small pieces
2 tablespoons ice water

Filling:
3½ pounds small Gala apples (about 9), peeled, cored, and each cut into 8 wedges
1 tablespoon fresh lemon juice
¼ teaspoon salt
2 tablespoons unsalted butter
¾ cup sugar

1. To prepare crust, weigh or lightly spoon flour into a dry measuring cup; level with a knife. Place flour, 1 tablespoon sugar, and ½ teaspoon salt in a food processor; pulse until combined. Add 6 tablespoons chilled butter; pulse until mixture resembles coarse meal. Add 2 tablespoons ice water, and pulse until mixture forms clumps. Gently press dough into a 6-inch circle on heavy-duty plastic wrap; cover and freeze 30 minutes.

2. To prepare filling, combine apples, juice, and ¼ teaspoon salt in a large bowl, tossing to coat. Melt 2 tablespoons butter in a 9½-inch cast-iron skillet over medium-high heat. Add ¾ cup sugar to pan; cook 4 minutes or until golden brown, stirring constantly. Remove pan from heat. Arrange half of apples, rounded side down, in a circular pattern over sugar mixture in pan. Top with remaining apples, rounded side up. Cook over medium heat 15 minutes. Remove from heat; let stand 15 minutes.

3. Preheat oven to 400°.

4. Working quickly, roll dough into an 11-inch circle on a heavily floured surface. Place dough over apples; fold edges under. Cut 4 (1-inch) slits into top of pastry using a sharp knife. Bake at 400° for 40 minutes or until crust is lightly browned. Remove from oven; let stand 5 minutes. Place a plate upside down on top of pan. Carefully invert tart onto plate. Serve warm. **Yield: 8 servings (serving size: 1 wedge).**

CALORIES 318; FAT 11.7g (sat 7.3g, mono 3g, poly 0.6g); PROTEIN 2.2g; CARB 54.2g; FIBER 2.6g; CHOL 30mg; IRON 0.9mg; SODIUM 223mg; CALC 15mg

way to caramelize
fruit

Asian Caramelized Pineapple

You can serve this side dish warm or at room temperature. Pair it with grilled fish or pork chops.

1½ teaspoons canola oil
1½ tablespoons minced red onion
1 large garlic clove, minced
2 cups diced fresh pineapple
1 tablespoon low-sodium soy sauce
1½ teaspoons chopped seeded jalapeño pepper
1½ teaspoons fresh lime juice
1 teaspoon chopped peeled fresh ginger
1½ teaspoons chopped fresh cilantro

1. Heat oil in a large nonstick skillet over medium heat. Add onion and garlic to pan; cook 2 minutes. Add pineapple; cook 5 minutes or until lightly browned. Add soy sauce, pepper, juice, and ginger; cook 2 minutes. Remove from heat; stir in cilantro. **Yield: 4 servings (serving size: about ½ cup).**

CALORIES 61; FAT 1.9g (sat 0.1g, mono 1.1g, poly 0.6g); PROTEIN 0.9g; CARB 11.6g; FIBER 1.3g; CHOL 0mg; IRON 0.4mg; SODIUM 135mg; CALC 15mg

cut a fresh pineapple

1

2

Freshly cut pineapple is a treat, but the fruit's prickly exterior may tempt you to reach for the precut varieties. Use this quick-and-easy guide to enjoy the fruit fresh in next to no time.

1. Lay the pineapple horizontally on a cutting board, and cut off the leafy top (the plume) and the base.
2. Stand the pineapple upright, and cut down the sides to remove the rind. Try to remove as little of the flesh as possible.
3. While the pineapple is upright, cut it into thirds by carefully slicing downward as shown to remove the fibrous core. You can then slice it into cubes.

3

way to caramelize
meats

Many Asian dishes balance contrasting tastes of sweet, sour, salty, and bitter. Granulated sugar in the dressing harmonizes with the savory fish sauce, acidic vinegar and lime juice, and slightly bitter fresh herbs. Brown sugar patted onto the pork caramelizes on the grill, creating crunchy blackened bits.

Vietnamese Caramelized Pork and Rice Noodle Salad

Dressing:
- ¾ cup water
- 4½ tablespoons granulated sugar
- 3 tablespoons rice vinegar
- 2 tablespoons fresh lime juice
- 1½ tablespoons fish sauce
- 2 teaspoons minced peeled fresh ginger
- ¾ teaspoon Sriracha (hot chile sauce, such as Huy Fong)
- 3 garlic cloves, minced

Salad:
- 1 (6-ounce) package rice vermicelli
- 1 pound pork tenderloin, trimmed
- 2 teaspoons fish sauce
- 1 teaspoon Sriracha (hot chile sauce, such as Huy Fong)
- ¼ teaspoon garlic powder
- ¼ teaspoon salt
- ¼ teaspoon freshly ground black pepper
- 3 tablespoons brown sugar
- Cooking spray
- 2 cups thinly sliced red leaf lettuce
- 1 cup matchstick-cut peeled English cucumber
- 1 cup matchstick-cut carrot
- 1 cup bean sprouts
- ¼ cup chopped fresh basil
- ¼ cup chopped fresh cilantro
- 3 tablespoons chopped fresh mint
- ½ cup chopped dry-roasted peanuts
- Lime wedges (optional)

1. To prepare dressing, combine first 8 ingredients in a small saucepan; cook over medium heat 5 minutes or just until sugar dissolves. Remove from heat; cool.

2. To prepare salad, place vermicelli in a large bowl. Cover with boiling water. Let stand 20 minutes or until tender. Drain and rinse under cold water; drain.

3. Prepare grill.

4. Cut tenderloin in half lengthwise. Cut each piece in half crosswise. Place each pork piece between 2 sheets of plastic wrap; pound to an even thickness using a meat mallet or small heavy skillet. Combine 2 teaspoons fish sauce and 1 teaspoon Sriracha; drizzle over pork. Sprinkle evenly with garlic powder, salt, and pepper. Pat brown sugar onto pork.

5. Place pork on a grill rack coated with cooking spray. Grill 12 minutes or until slightly pink in center, turning pieces occasionally to prevent burning. Place pork on a cutting board; let stand 5 minutes. Cut across grain into very thin slices.

6. Combine vermicelli, lettuce, and next 6 ingredients in a large bowl. Pour dressing over salad; toss well. Top with pork and nuts. Serve with lime wedges, if desired.

Yield: 6 servings (serving size: 1⅔ cups salad, about 2 ounces pork, and 4 teaspoons peanuts).

CALORIES 342; FAT 8.3g (sat 1.9g, mono 3.7g, poly 1.9g); PROTEIN 19.9g; CARB 47.6g; FIBER 2.7g; CHOL 43mg; IRON 1.9mg; SODIUM 821mg; CALC 48mg

kitchen how-to:
cut pork for Vietnamese caramelized pork and rice noodle salad

Cutting the pork into four smaller pieces allows it to cook more quickly on the grill.

1. Cut tenderloin in half lengthwise.
2. Cut each piece in half crosswise.

way to caramelize
poultry

Duck Breasts with Pinot Noir and Cherry Sauce

- 3 tablespoons sugar
- 2 tablespoons water
- ½ cup dried tart cherries
- 3 tablespoons red wine vinegar
- 1 tablespoon olive oil, divided
- ¼ teaspoon salt, divided
- ⅛ teaspoon freshly ground black pepper
- 4 (6-ounce) boneless duck breast halves, skinned
- ¼ cup chopped shallots
- 1 garlic clove, minced
- 1½ cups pinot noir or other spicy dry red wine
- ½ cup fat-free, less-sodium chicken broth
- ¼ cup whipping cream

1. Combine sugar and 2 tablespoons water in a small, heavy saucepan over medium-high heat, and cook until sugar dissolves, stirring gently as needed to dissolve sugar evenly (about 1 minute). Continue cooking 5 minutes or until golden (do not stir). Remove from heat, and carefully stir in cherries and vinegar (caramelized sugar will harden and stick to spoon). Place pan over low heat until caramelized sugar melts.
2. Heat 2 teaspoons oil in a large nonstick skillet over medium-high heat. Sprinkle ⅛ teaspoon salt and pepper over duck. Add duck to pan; cook 5 minutes. Turn duck over; cook 4 minutes or until desired degree of doneness. Remove from pan; let stand 5 minutes. Cut duck across the grain into thin slices.
3. Return skillet to medium heat. Add remaining 1 teaspoon oil, shallots, and garlic to pan; cook 1 minute or until tender, stirring frequently. Add wine to pan; increase heat to medium-high. Bring mixture to a boil; cook until reduced to ¾ cup (about 6 minutes). Add broth; bring to a boil. Cook until reduced to ½ cup (about 6 minutes). Pour wine mixture through a fine sieve into cherry mixture; discard solids. Bring cherry mixture to a simmer over medium heat. Stir in cream; simmer 3 minutes. Remove from heat; stir in remaining ⅛ teaspoon salt. Serve sauce over duck. **Yield: 4 servings (serving size: 1 duck breast half and ¼ cup sauce).**

CALORIES 416; FAT 13.2g (sat 4.9g, mono 5.6g, poly 1.2g); PROTEIN 48.1g; CARB 23.7g; FIBER 4.3g; CHOL 264mg; IRON 8.5mg; SODIUM 387mg; CALC 42mg

kitchen how-to: make a *gastrique*

Gastrique **is the French term** for a thick, syrupy reduction sauce made from caramelized sugar, vinegar, and often fruit.

1. Combine the sugar and 2 tablespoons water in a small, heavy saucepan over medium-high heat.

2. Cook until the sugar dissolves, stirring gently as needed to dissolve the sugar evenly (about 1 minute). Continue cooking 5 minutes or until golden (do not stir). Remove from heat.

3. Carefully stir in the cherries and vinegar. The caramelized sugar will harden and stick to the spoon.

4. Place the pan over low heat until the caramelized sugar melts.

way to caramelize
vegetables

Caramelized Shallots and Brussels Sprouts with Pancetta

A touch of brown sugar helps the vegetables caramelize in the oven.

1½ pounds Brussels sprouts, halved
Cooking spray
 1 tablespoon olive oil
⅔ cup thinly sliced shallots
½ teaspoon freshly ground black pepper
¼ teaspoon salt
 1 ounce finely chopped pancetta
 4 teaspoons brown sugar
 2 teaspoons vermouth

1. Preheat oven to 400°.
2. Arrange Brussels sprouts on a jelly-roll pan coated with cooking spray. Drizzle with oil; toss to coat. Bake at 400° for 15 minutes. Add shallots and next 3 ingredients to pan; toss well. Bake at 400° for 10 minutes. Add sugar and vermouth; toss to coat. Bake an additional 10 minutes or until caramelized. **Yield: 6 servings (serving size: about ⅔ cup).**

CALORIES 117; FAT 4.2g (sat 1.1g, mono 2.3g, poly 0.5g); PROTEIN 5.3g; CARB 16.9g; FIBER 4.9g; CHOL 3mg; IRON 2mg; SODIUM 209mg; CALC 61mg

all about vermouth

Vermouth is an aromatized wine, which means that herbs and spices are added to the mix; typically dozens of botanicals such as allspice, anise, clove, ginger, marjoram, thyme, rosemary, and vanilla are used. The faint spice, herbal, and floral notes of dry vermouth make it a particularly appealing substitute for white wine. These extra flavors won't overpower a dish, but they lend a welcome complexity to the overall flavor. Sweet vermouth, however, is a different story. As the name implies, it's much sweeter, and you probably won't want to substitute it for white wine. Vermouth is also lightly fortified with unaged brandy, giving it a slightly higher alcohol content than white wine, so it may need to cook longer to burn off most of the alcohol.

kitchen how-to:
caramelize onions

1

When caramelizing a smaller quantity of onions (less than 4 cups), you can use a nonstick skillet coated with oil or cooking spray. For larger quantities, a large Dutch oven works best.

1. Slice the onion in half from root to stem. Turn the cut side down, and cut into strips.
2. Sauté the onions over medium-high heat until almost tender, stirring frequently. The onions will soften and become slightly browned.
3. Reduce the heat to medium-low, and cook until the onions are a deep golden brown, stirring occasionally.

2

3

Caramelized Onion and Shiitake Soup with Gruyère–Blue Cheese Toasts

Earthy shiitake mushrooms and pungent cheese toasts give this soup more heartiness than classic French onion soup. For a light main-course option, pair it with a salad that's lightly dressed so it doesn't overpower the soup.

Soup:
- 1 tablespoon olive oil
- 8 cups vertically sliced yellow onion (about 2 pounds)
- 5 cups sliced shiitake mushroom caps (about 10 ounces whole mushrooms)
- 4 garlic cloves, minced
- 2 fresh thyme sprigs
- ½ cup dry white wine
- 1 (14-ounce) can fat-free, less-sodium chicken broth
- 1 (14-ounce) can fat-free, less-sodium beef broth
- ½ teaspoon salt
- ½ teaspoon freshly ground black pepper

Toasts:
- 12 (½-inch-thick) slices French bread baguette, toasted (about 6 ounces)
- ¼ cup (1 ounce) grated Gruyère cheese
- ¼ cup (1 ounce) crumbled Gorgonzola
- ½ teaspoon finely chopped fresh thyme

1. To prepare soup, heat oil in a large Dutch oven over medium-high heat. Add onion to pan; sauté 15 minutes or until almost tender, stirring frequently. Reduce heat to medium-low; cook until deep golden brown (about 40 minutes), stirring occasionally.

2. Increase heat to medium. Add mushrooms to pan; cook 10 minutes or until mushrooms are tender, stirring frequently. Stir in garlic and thyme sprigs; cook 2 minutes, stirring frequently. Increase heat to medium-high. Add wine to pan; cook 2 minutes or until most of the liquid evaporates. Add broths to pan; bring to a simmer. Reduce heat, and simmer 45 minutes. Stir in salt and pepper. Discard thyme sprigs.

3. To prepare toasts, preheat broiler.

4. Arrange bread in a single layer on a baking sheet. Top each bread slice with 1 teaspoon Gruyère and 1 teaspoon Gorgonzola. Broil 2 minutes or until cheese melts. Sprinkle chopped thyme over cheese. Ladle about 1 cup soup into each of 6 bowls; top each serving with 2 toasts. **Yield: 6 servings.**

CALORIES 208; FAT 5.4g (sat 2.3g, mono 2.2g, poly 0.4g); PROTEIN 8.9g; CARB 33.4g; FIBER 3.9g; CHOL 9mg; IRON 2.1mg; SODIUM 694mg; CALC 115mg

way to
roast

Roasting may be one of the easiest cooking techniques because your oven does most of the work. The food cooks in an uncovered heavy pan where dry, hot air surrounds it, browning it, and intensifying the flavors with a minimal amount of added fat. Foods can be simply prepared—meats rubbed with seasonings, vegetables cut up—and then they cook, virtually hands free, making roasting an especially handy technique for busy weeknight meals or hectic holidays.

roasting, defined

Roasting involves cooking food in an uncovered pan in the oven. It's a dry cooking technique, as opposed to wet techniques like braising, stewing, or steaming. Hot air surrounds the food, cooking it evenly on all sides. Depending on the food you're preparing, you can roast at low, moderate, or high temperatures.

Equipment

A roasting pan with a rack is a good investment for your kitchen. It has low sides, allowing more of the oven's heat to make contact with the food. Choose a heavy pan because it will distribute heat evenly and isn't as likely to burn pan drippings. A rack is helpful to suspend food that produces a lot of drippings (whole poultry or fatty roasts, for example) out of the liquid. If you don't have a rack, place a wire cooling rack in the pan. You can also use a broiler pan for roasting, but these pans are shallow, so be careful not to spill hot drippings out of the pan.

You'll need kitchen twine to truss (tie) chickens, turkeys, and some roasts so they hold their shape as they cook. Look for food-safe kitchen twine at cookware stores, some hardware stores, and many large supermarkets. Or ask your butcher to include some twine with your purchase.

A meat thermometer is essential since the key to perfectly roasted meats is to not overcook them. Choose an instant-read or a remote digital model.

Best Bets for Roasting

Large cuts of meat work well: ham, whole turkeys and chickens, and tenderloins. Smaller cuts like boneless chicken breasts or fish fillets may dry out in the oven if they're not watched closely. Roasting is also ideal for dense fruits and vegetables, such as apples, nectarines, potatoes, beets, and winter squash, because it concentrates their natural sugars and intensifies their flavor.

Oven Temperature

Choose the oven temperature according to the type of food you're roasting. Vegetables usually need a moderate temperature near 375° so that internal water evaporates quickly to concentrate the flavor without the food browning too deeply or becoming too soft.

In general, use low (250°) to moderate (375°) heat for large roasts so they'll cook evenly and slowly (high heat would burn the outside of the roast before it's done on the inside). High-heat (above 400°) roasting works well for small, tender cuts such as tenderloins because it quickly produces a browned crust and the meat cooks adequately in a short time.

Basting

Whether you should baste meat or leave it alone as it cooks depends on various factors. A standing rib roast, for example, shouldn't be basted because one of its best features is the salty crust that forms over the meat as it roasts; you wouldn't want to wash that away. And whole chickens and turkeys have enough fat under the skin (which we discard after cooking) that they self-baste as the fat slowly melts and coats the meat. Frequent basting also means you're opening the oven door and letting the heat escape, which could lengthen the cook time or prevent the meat from properly browning. Basting isn't necessary to keep food moist, but if you want to add more flavor in the form of a glaze—as in our Ham with Bourbon-Peach Glaze (page 347)—basting is a worthwhile endeavor.

About Doneness

We follow the U.S. Department of Agriculture guidelines for cooking poultry to an internal temperature of 165° and for reheating fully cooked ham to 140°. For some beef, lamb, pork, and game cuts, however, we prefer cooking to lower temperatures than the USDA recommends because it produces juicier results. If you're pregnant, older, have a compromised immune system, or are serving to children, follow the USDA recommendation to cook beef or lamb to a minimum of 145° and pork and game to 160°.

Let It Rest

All meat should rest for 10 to 20 minutes after it's removed from the oven. Larger cuts—a standing rib roast, for example—retain enough internal heat so that they continue to cook after they're taken out of the oven, up to an added 10° or so. Smaller cuts like pork tenderloins don't have enough mass to continue cooking by more than a couple of degrees.

The main reason meat should rest is to allow the juices to redistribute. If you slice into a roast chicken or beef roast immediately after you pull it out of the oven, all the juices would pour out onto the platter, and the resulting meat would be dry.

the bottom line

The three most important elements to remember about roasting:

1. Generally, choose lower oven temperatures for larger cuts of meat and higher oven temperatures for smaller cuts.

2. Use a heavy roasting pan.

3. Allow the cooked meat to rest for 10 to 20 minutes before slicing.

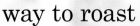

way to roast
fish & shellfish

The key to roasting thin, delicate fish fillets and shellfish is to watch them closely since the high heat of the oven can quickly dry them out.

Roasted Tilapia with Orange-Parsley Salsa

You can substitute brown, basmati, or jasmine for the white rice, if you prefer.

  3 **oranges (about 1 pound)**
  ¼ **cup chopped fresh parsley, divided**
  2 **tablespoons extra-virgin olive oil, divided**
  ¾ **teaspoon salt, divided**
  4 **(6-ounce) tilapia fillets**
  ½ **teaspoon freshly ground black pepper, divided**
  2 **cups hot cooked instant white rice**

1. Grate 2 teaspoons orange rind. Peel and section oranges over a bowl, reserving 2 tablespoons juice.

Chop sections. Combine rind, chopped orange, 2 tablespoons parsley, 5 teaspoons oil, and ¼ teaspoon salt in a bowl; toss well.
2. Preheat oven to 400°.
3. Sprinkle fish evenly with ¼ teaspoon salt and ¼ teaspoon pepper. Place fish in an ovenproof skillet coated with remaining 1 teaspoon oil. Bake at 400° for 14 minutes or until fish flakes easily when tested with a fork or until desired degree of doneness.
4. Combine 2 tablespoons reserved juice, remaining 2 tablespoons parsley, remaining ¼ teaspoon salt, remaining ¼ teaspoon pepper, and rice. Spoon ½ cup rice onto each of 4 plates; top each with 1 fillet and ¼ cup salsa. **Yield: 4 servings.**

CALORIES 423; FAT 12.1g (sat 2.6g, mono 6.7g, poly 2.1g); PROTEIN 47.4g; CARB 32.7g; FIBER 3g; CHOL 97mg; IRON 3mg; SODIUM 543mg; CALC 76mg

kitchen how-to: section citrus fruits

The acidic juices in fresh citrus fruits help heighten and balance the flavors of a variety of dishes. Be sure to wash citrus thoroughly under warm water to remove dirt and wax before you begin.

1. First, cut the top and bottom portions from the fruit to create a stable cutting surface. Next, stand the fruit upright, and use a small paring knife to slice downward in a long, slow curve to remove the rind and the white pith.
2. Hold the fruit in your palm, and gently follow the natural sections of the fruit with the knife to cut out wedges.

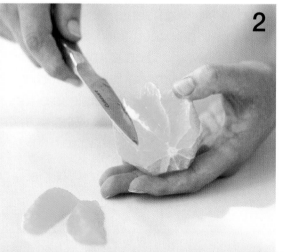

Roasted Oysters with Lemon-Anise Stuffing

1 (1½-ounce) slice white bread
2 teaspoons butter
1½ cups finely chopped fennel
1 garlic clove, minced
¼ cup fat-free, less-sodium chicken broth
¼ teaspoon kosher salt
2 tablespoons anise liqueur (such as ouzo)
⅓ cup (1½ ounces) shredded fresh
    Parmigiano-Reggiano cheese
1 tablespoon chopped fennel fronds
½ teaspoon grated lemon rind
2 teaspoons fresh lemon juice
Dash of ground red pepper
12 shucked oysters

1. Preheat oven to 350°.
2. Place bread in a food processor; pulse 7 times or until coarse crumbs measure about 1 cup. Place on a baking sheet. Bake at 350° for 8 minutes or until toasted. Transfer to a plate; cool.
3. Position oven rack to the top one-third of oven. Increase oven temperature to 425°.
4. Melt butter in a large nonstick skillet over medium heat. Add finely chopped fennel and garlic to pan; cook 2 minutes, stirring often. Add broth and salt; cover and cook 5 minutes or until fennel is tender. Uncover and cook 2 minutes or until liquid evaporates. Stir in liqueur, and cook 1 minute or until liqueur evaporates. Transfer fennel mixture to a bowl; add breadcrumbs, cheese, fennel fronds, rind, juice, and red pepper. Toss to combine.
5. Arrange oysters in a single layer on a large baking pan. Top each oyster with about 1 tablespoon fennel mixture. Bake at 425° for 10 minutes or until edges of oysters begin to curl and stuffing is lightly browned. Serve immediately. **Yield: 4 servings (serving size: 3 oysters).**

CALORIES 125; FAT 5g (sat 2.8g, mono 1.2g, poly 0.3g); PROTEIN 6.2g; CARB 12.4g; FIBER 1.4g; CHOL 21mg; IRON 2.9mg; SODIUM 395mg; CALC 143mg

all about anise liqueur

Anise liqueurs are flavored with anise, star anise, or licorice. Different countries have their own versions—*anisette* and *pastis* from France, *anesone* and *sambuca* from Italy, *anis* and *ojen* from Spain, *kasra* from Libya, and *ouzo* from Greece. When used in small amounts, this liqueur adds an intriguing licorice flavor to dishes. Ouzo is a little sweeter and smoother when compared to other anise-flavored liqueurs. It can be drunk by itself or, less often, mixed with water; when you mix ouzo with water, it will turn whitish and opaque.

Oysters

What they add: Oysters are a good source of zinc, a mineral identified with healthy immune systems, proper wound healing, and normal growth and development. It's also required to maintain a proper sense of taste and smell. A serving of this tasty appetizer offers all the zinc you need in a day, about 13 milligrams.

way to roast

fruit

Firm, dense fruits, like pears, figs, peaches, plums, nectarines, and apples, are excellent choices for roasting. It concentrates their natural sugar, creating a delicious and unforgettable dessert.

Roasted Nectarines with Buttermilk Custard

Sauce:
- ⅛ teaspoon salt
- 4 large egg yolks
- ⅓ cup sugar
- 1 cup 1% low-fat milk
- 2 tablespoons low-fat buttermilk
- ¼ teaspoon vanilla extract

Nectarines:
- 6 medium nectarines, halved and pitted
- Cooking spray
- 1 tablespoon sugar
- Fresh verbena sprigs (optional)

1. To prepare sauce, combine salt and egg yolks in a medium bowl. Gradually add ⅓ cup sugar, beating 2 minutes with a mixer at medium-high speed.
2. Heat 1% low-fat milk over medium heat in a small, heavy saucepan to 180° or until tiny bubbles form around edge (do not boil). Gradually add hot milk to sugar mixture, stirring constantly. Return milk mixture to pan; cook over medium-low heat 5 minutes or until slightly thick and mixture coats the back of a spoon, stirring constantly (do not boil). Remove from heat. Stir in buttermilk and vanilla. Place pan in a large ice-filled bowl until mixture cools completely, stirring occasionally. Spoon mixture into a bowl; cover and chill.
3. Preheat oven to 400°.
4. To prepare nectarines, place nectarines, cut sides up, in a 9 x 13–inch baking dish coated with cooking spray.

Sprinkle nectarines evenly with 1 tablespoon sugar. Bake at 400° for 25 minutes or until nectarines are soft and lightly browned. Serve with chilled sauce. Garnish with verbena sprigs, if desired. **Yield: 6 servings (serving size: 2 nectarine halves and ¼ cup sauce).**

CALORIES 176; FAT 3.4g (sat 1.4g, mono 1.4g, poly 0.5g); PROTEIN 4.3g; CARB 32.8g; FIBER 1g; CHOL 138mg; IRON 0.7mg; SODIUM 80mg; CALC 70mg

Stone fruits, such as plums, apricots, nectarines, and peaches, are delicious, but some people don't like their skins. You can remove the skin using a vegetable peeler or a paring knife if the fruit is still firm. If the fruit is soft or your peeling skills aren't up to par, the easiest way to remove the skin is by blanching. Just follow these steps to get skin-free fruit.

1. Cut an X in the bottom of each fruit, carefully cutting just through the skin.
2. Heat a large pot of water to boiling, and drop in the fruit. Cook for 20 seconds to 1 minute—the riper they are, the less time they need.
3. Remove the fruit from the water with a slotted spoon, and place them in a sink or bowl filled with ice water.
4. Use a paring knife or your fingers to remove the skin, which should slip right off.

all about nectarines

Nectarines are part of the plum family; technically, they're a type of peach but with smooth skin and a tangier taste. When buying nectarines, particularly at farmers' markets, you don't have to choose the prettiest ones. Like heirloom tomatoes, some of the ugliest ones can taste the best. Choose aromatic nectarines that yield slightly when touched. Their peak season is July through August, although you can find them in September in some areas. Store in a shady place on your counter; the cooler temperature of the refrigerator can ruin their flavor.

Classic Meat Loaf

Combining three types of ground meat lends more depth to the overall flavor. Serve with roasted carrots and onions.

- 1 (1½-ounce) slice white bread
- 2 tablespoons fat-free milk
- ½ cup ketchup, divided
- ⅔ pound extra lean ground beef
- ½ pound lean ground veal
- 6 ounces lean ground pork
- ½ cup chopped onion
- ⅓ cup chopped fresh parsley
- 1 tablespoon Dijon mustard
- 1 teaspoon dried basil
- ¾ teaspoon salt
- ¼ teaspoon black pepper
- 2 large egg whites
  Cooking spray

1. Preheat oven to 350°.
2. Place bread in a food processor; pulse 10 times or until coarse breadcrumbs measure 1½ cups.
3. Combine breadcrumbs and milk in a large bowl; let stand 5 minutes.
Add 2 tablespoons ketchup and remaining ingredients except cooking spray.
4. Shape meat mixture into a 9 x 5–inch loaf on a broiler pan coated with cooking spray. Spread remaining 6 tablespoons ketchup over top of meat loaf. Bake at 350° for 1 hour or until a thermometer registers 160°. Let stand 10 minutes. Cut loaf into 12 slices.
Yield: 6 servings (serving size: 2 slices).

CALORIES 231; FAT 7.9g (sat 3.1g, mono 3.2g, poly 0.8g); PROTEIN 26.7g; CARB 13.2g; FIBER 0.9g; CHOL 79mg; IRON 2.3mg; SODIUM 764mg; CALC 49mg

kitchen how-to:
make meat loaf

All you need to prepare a meat loaf is ground meat (beef, pork, chicken or turkey, veal, or lamb), a few seasonings, maybe a vegetable or two, and some kind of binder (usually breadcrumbs and/or eggs) to hold it all together. It's an equation that leaves a lot of room for variety, including healthier versions.

1. If you'd like, sauté the aromatics (like onions, garlic, and carrot) to intensify their flavor in the final dish.

2. Use your hands to combine the ingredients in a large bowl.

3. Shape a free-form meat loaf on a broiler pan coated with cooking spray.

4. Spread ketchup or other liquid across the top of the loaf.

5. Use a meat thermometer to test the loaf's internal temperature for doneness (160° for ground beef, pork, or veal; 165° for ground poultry).

6. Let the loaf stand for 10 minutes before slicing. Slice and serve.

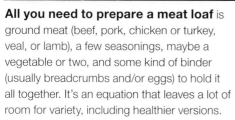

1 (6½-pound) rib roast, French-cut and trimmed
1 tablespoon kosher salt
1½ teaspoons freshly ground black pepper

Classic "Prime" Rib

This holiday classic is all about technique—roast at a low temperature to ensure gently cooked meat with a medium-rare center. We kept the seasonings simple to allow the meat to shine. Although called "prime" rib, there are only a few prime-grade beef rib roasts sold to consumers; most go to restaurants. The two grades just below prime, choice and select, are leaner than prime and still quite tasty. Ask your butcher to French the roast (to trim the meat to expose the bones).

1. Preheat oven to 325°.

2. Rub roast on all sides with salt and pepper. Place roast, bone side down, in a roasting pan. Loop and tie kitchen twine between each of the bones to help the roast hold its shape as it cooks (see image above at left). Bake at 325° for 2 hours or until a thermometer inserted into thickest portion of roast registers 130° or until desired degree of doneness. Remove from oven. Place roast on a cutting board. Let stand 10 minutes before serving. **Yield: 17 servings (serving size: about 3 ounces meat).**

CALORIES 186; FAT 10.7g (sat 4.3g, mono 4.5g, poly 0.3g); PROTEIN 20.9g; CARB 0.1g; FIBER 0.1g; CHOL 61mg; IRON 2.2mg; SODIUM 394mg; CALC 8mg

Ham with Bourbon-Peach Glaze

For a pretty presentation, garnish the platter with orange slices, cranberries, bay leaves, and parsley.

⅔ cup peach preserves
¼ cup bourbon
1 teaspoon ground cumin
½ teaspoon ground ginger
½ teaspoon ground coriander
½ teaspoon freshly ground black pepper
1 (7½-pound) 33%-less-sodium smoked, fully cooked ham half
20 whole cloves
Cooking spray
1 cup water

1. Preheat oven to 325°.
2. Combine preserves and bourbon in a small saucepan. Bring to a boil; remove from heat. Stir in cumin, ginger, coriander, and pepper. Cool slightly.
3. Trim fat and rind from ham. Score outside of ham in a diamond pattern (see image below at left); stud with cloves. Place ham on the rack of a broiler pan or roasting pan coated with cooking spray. Pour 1 cup water into pan; place rack in pan. Brush ham with ¼ cup preserves mixture. Bake at 325° for 2 hours or until a thermometer registers 140°, basting ham with remaining preserves mixture every 30 minutes. Transfer ham to a platter; let stand 15 minutes. Discard cloves before serving. **Yield: 28 servings (serving size: about 3 ounces meat).**

CALORIES 143; FAT 6.1g (sat 2g, mono 2.9g, poly 0.7g); PROTEIN 14.2g; CARB 7.1g; FIBER 0g; CHOL 51mg; IRON 0.8mg; SODIUM 871mg; CALC 1mg

Fruit and Walnut–Stuffed Pork Loin

½ cup dry red wine
¼ cup dried sour cherries
¼ cup chopped dried apricots
¼ cup chopped dried plums
2 tablespoons Triple Sec (orange-flavored liqueur)
⅓ cup finely chopped walnuts
2 tablespoons chopped shallots
1¼ teaspoons salt, divided
½ teaspoon grated lemon rind
2 (1-ounce) slices French bread
1 teaspoon chopped fresh thyme
¼ teaspoon freshly ground black pepper
2 garlic cloves, minced
1 (2½-pound) boneless center-cut pork
  loin roast, trimmed
2 tablespoons Dijon mustard
Cooking spray
Fresh parsley sprigs (optional)

1. Preheat oven to 400°.
2. Combine first 5 ingredients in a medium microwave-safe bowl; microwave at HIGH 2 minutes. Let stand 10 minutes or until fruit is plump. Drain mixture

through a sieve, reserving fruit mixture. Combine fruit mixture, walnuts, shallots, ¼ teaspoon salt, and rind.
3. Place ¾ teaspoon salt, bread, and next 3 ingredients in a food processor; pulse until fine crumbs form.
4. Cut pork in half lengthwise, cutting to, but not through, other side; open halves, laying pork flat. Starting from center, cut each half lengthwise, cutting to, but not through, other side; open halves, laying pork flat. Cover with plastic wrap; pound to an even thickness. Discard plastic wrap. Spread fruit mixture over pork, leaving a ½-inch border. Roll up pork, jelly-roll fashion, starting with one long side. Secure with kitchen twine. Sprinkle pork evenly with remaining ¼ teaspoon salt; brush evenly with mustard. Sprinkle breadcrumb mixture over pork; press gently to adhere. Place pork on a broiler pan coated with cooking spray. Bake at 400° for 50 minutes or until a meat thermometer inserted in thickest part registers 145°. Let pork stand 10 minutes. Remove twine. Cut into 16 (½-inch-thick) slices. Garnish with parsley sprigs, if desired.
Yield: 8 servings (serving size: 2 slices).

CALORIES 323; FAT 12.4g (sat 3.7g, mono 4.5g, poly 3.1g); PROTEIN 29.7g; CARB 18.9g;
FIBER 1.1g; CHOL 79mg; IRON 1.9mg; SODIUM 573mg; CALC 41mg

kitchen how-to: stuff pork tenderloin or loin roast

A stuffed pork tenderloin or boneless pork loin roast is handsome at the table, and the fillings make it versatile. Add cranberries and chèvre, apricots and brie—experiment to suit your palate. Whatever your choice, following these steps will help you prepare a crowd-pleasing meal. If you don't have kitchen twine, you can secure the meat with wooden picks.

1. Cut the pork in half lengthwise, cutting to, but not all the way through, the other side. Open the halves, laying the meat flat. Starting from the center, cut each half lengthwise, cutting to, but not through the other side. Open the halves, laying the meat flat.
2. Place the meat between two sheets of plastic wrap, and pound it with a mallet to an even ½-inch thickness.
3. Remove it from the plastic wrap; discard plastic. Slide segments of kitchen twine beneath the meat in 1- to 2-inch intervals.
4. Sprinkle or spread filling evenly on the meat, leaving a ½-inch border along edges.
5. Start at a long side of the meat, and roll it up jelly-roll style, tucking the filling in as you go.
6. Secure with twine, and bake at the recipe's specified temperature until a meat thermometer inserted into the center registers 145°. Let pork stand 10 minutes (the internal temperature will rise upon standing).

chicken

Few entrées are as familiar and welcoming as a succulent roast chicken. It can be the star of both homey weeknight suppers and company-worthy dinners. Roast chicken's broad appeal is well deserved because its neutral-tasting meat harmonizes with many flavors.

kitchen how-to:
roast chicken & make gravy

Picking up a rotisserie chicken at the supermarket provides a convenient option, but there are a number of advantages to roasting your own bird at home. Taste is the best reason because you can use almost any combination of spices that suit your preference.

Roasting the chicken yourself also helps you control the sodium and the quality of the ingredients used. Plus, you can use the browned bits and drippings from the chicken to prepare a delicious pan gravy. Best of all, it's a simple, mostly hands-free process if you follow these steps.

1. Separate the skin from the meat, and rub the seasoning mixture directly on the meat.
2. Tie the legs of the chicken together with kitchen twine for a professional presentation.

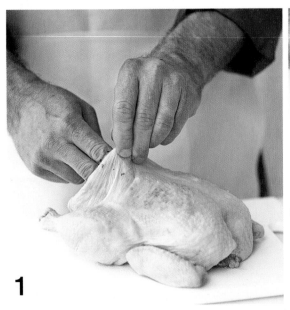

1

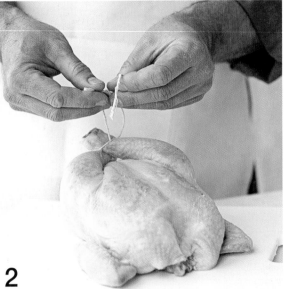

2

3

4

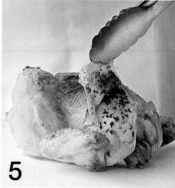

5

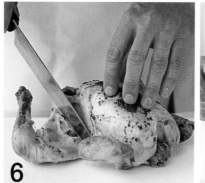

6

7

3. The bird cooks more evenly when it's elevated off the pan atop vegetables or a rack.

4. Insert the thermometer into the meaty part of the thigh to get an accurate temperature reading. This is the slowest-cooking part of the bird.

5. For a substantial fat savings, remove and discard the skin before serving.

6. Use a sharp knife to remove the legs first.

7. Combine the pan drippings with a liquid, such as broth or wine, and drain off the fat.

8. Hold the knife parallel to the chicken breast, and slice thinly.

9. Place the roasting pan over medium-high heat, and pour the liquid (along with the remaining drippings) back into the pan, scraping to loosen all the delicious browned bits. Add a bit of flour and a little more liquid, and cook until thick.

9

8

the skinny on chicken

The skin from a whole bird accounts for about half its fat, but roasting it with the skin adds moisture and protects lean meat from drying out. We routinely call to cook the chicken with the skin on and remove it before serving, which substantially reduces the fat (some of the fat from the skin absorbs into the meat during roasting). Roasting a whole chicken this way yields a bird with about 36 percent of its calories from fat—most of it unsaturated.

Classic Roast Chicken with Gravy

Be sure to soften the butter so it combines thoroughly with the herbs.

Chicken:

- 1 (3¾-pound) whole roasting chicken
- 1 tablespoon butter, softened
- ½ teaspoon salt
- ½ teaspoon dried thyme
- ½ teaspoon dried oregano
- ½ teaspoon dried rubbed sage
- ⅛ teaspoon freshly ground black pepper
- 2 carrots, peeled and halved
- 4 stalks celery, halved
- 1 onion, quartered

Gravy:

- ½ cup dry white wine
- 1½ cups fat-free, less-sodium chicken broth
- 2 tablespoons all-purpose flour
- 3 tablespoons water
- ¼ teaspoon salt

1. Preheat oven to 375°.

2. To prepare chicken, remove and discard giblets and neck from chicken; trim excess fat. Starting at neck cavity, loosen skin from breasts and drumsticks by inserting fingers, gently pushing between skin and meat to separate.

3. Combine butter and next 5 ingredients in a small bowl. Rub seasoning mixture under loosened skin and over breasts and drumsticks. Tie ends of legs together with kitchen twine. Lift wing tips up and over back; tuck under chicken. Place carrots, celery, and onion in a single layer in a roasting pan. Place chicken, breast side up, on top of vegetables.

4. Bake at 375° for 40 minutes.

5. Increase oven temperature to 450°, and bake an additional 20 minutes or until a thermometer inserted in the meaty part of thigh registers 165°. Using tongs or insulated rubber gloves, remove chicken from pan, tilting slightly to drain juices. Let stand 15 minutes. Remove vegetables from pan with a slotted spoon; reserve.

6. To prepare gravy, place a zip-top plastic bag in a 2-cup glass measure. Pour wine into bag; add drippings from pan. Let stand 2 minutes (fat will rise to the top). Seal bag; carefully snip off bottom corner of bag. Drain drippings into measuring cup, stopping before fat layer reaches opening; discard fat.

7. Return vegetables to pan. Add wine mixture and broth; cook 10 minutes over medium heat, scraping pan to loosen browned bits. Remove vegetables from pan using a slotted spoon; discard. Combine flour and water in a small bowl, stirring with a whisk to form a slurry; add slurry and ¼ teaspoon salt to pan, stirring constantly. Simmer 1 minute or until slightly thick.

8. Remove skin from chicken; discard. Carve chicken, and serve with gravy. **Yield: 4 servings (serving size: 5 ounces meat and about ¼ cup gravy).**

CALORIES 287; FAT 12.4g (sat 4.4g, mono 4.3g, poly 2.3g); PROTEIN 37g; CARB 4.4g; FIBER 0.9g; CHOL 114mg; IRON 2.4mg; SODIUM 721mg; CALC 35mg

way to roast
turkey

Turkey, the main dish of most traditional Thanksgiving dinners, is something many of us cook only once a year. Although it often causes stress for novice cooks, roasting a turkey is essentially the same process as roasting a chicken, only on a larger scale. Just follow these guidelines to cook a standout turkey.

kitchen how-to:
roast turkey

When preparing a turkey for roasting, you'll first need to remove and discard the giblets and neck. Rinse the turkey with cold water, and pat dry.

1. To cook the turkey, you'll need a roasting pan, roasting rack (or you can use a layer of vegetables in place of a roasting rack—as in Parmesan-Sage Roast Turkey with Sage Gravy on page 356), remote-read digital thermometer, bulb baster, oven thermometer, kitchen twine, kitchen shears, and foil.

2. Trim excess fat with kitchen shears.

3. Tie the legs together with kitchen twine for an attractive presentation. Lift the wing tips up and over the back, and tuck them under the turkey.

4. Cover the breast with foil to keep the white meat from cooking too fast.

5. Insert the thermometer into meaty part of the thigh, making sure not to touch the bone. The turkey is ready when the thermometer registers 165°.

6. Once you've presented the finished turkey, remove and discard the skin to dramatically reduce fat intake.

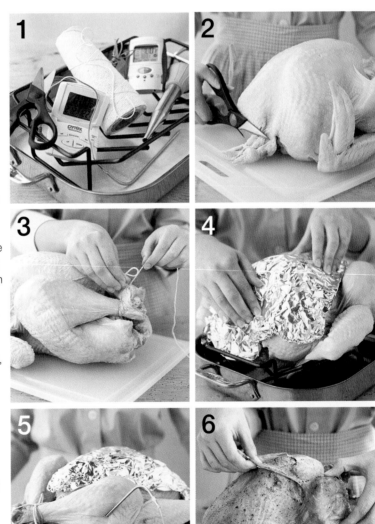

buying the right bird
You can choose from at least three types of turkey.

Frozen turkeys are the most popular option, available in any supermarket for around $1.50 per pound. But you'll need to allow time for the bird to thaw in the refrigerator (the safest method)—24 hours for every 5 pounds, or nearly three days for a 12-pound turkey. See page 37 for more information about thawing a turkey.

A **fresh** bird boasts hearty flavor and excellent texture, and it doesn't require thawing. But you will need to order your turkey a couple weeks in advance, and expect to pay nearly $2 per pound.

For a memorably vivid flavor, purchase a **heritage** turkey, which is one of the original old-breed birds (such as the Narragansett or White Holland). Heritage turkeys are free-range, antibiotic-free birds with a higher proportion of dark to light meat than the mass-market variety. Their flavor can be strong and

gamey, which some diners like more than others. They also can be expensive (as much as $150 for a 22-pound turkey) and difficult to find. Some specialty markets carry them around Thanksgiving, but your best bet is mail order.

Plan on a serving size of 4 to 6 ounces of cooked meat per person. For two to four guests, that translates to a 1 to 2-pound boneless turkey breast or a 1½ to 3-pound bone-in breast. For six to eight guests, you could use a 3 to 4-pound boneless turkey breast, a 6 to 8-pound bone-in breast, or a 6 to 8-pound whole bird. For a larger crowd—10 or more guests—you'll want at least a 12-pound whole turkey.

Whichever type you choose, the USDA recommends cooking turkey to an internal temperature of 165°. Let it stand for 30 minutes before carving to allow the juices to redistribute.

Parmesan-Sage Roast Turkey with Sage Gravy

For a handsome garnish, roast lemon halves and peeled shallots at 425° for 20 minutes; arrange them with sage sprigs on the turkey platter.

- 3 cups chopped onion
- 1 cup chopped celery
- 1 cup chopped carrot
- 10 garlic cloves
- Cooking spray
- 1 (13-pound) fresh or frozen turkey, thawed
- ⅓ cup (1½ ounces) grated fresh Parmigiano-Reggiano cheese
- 5 tablespoons chopped fresh sage, divided
- 2 tablespoons butter, softened
- 1 tablespoon minced garlic
- 1 teaspoon salt, divided
- ½ teaspoon freshly ground black pepper, divided
- 1 lemon, halved
- 2½ cups fat-free, less-sodium chicken broth, divided
- ⅓ cup chopped shallots
- 1 cup sherry
- 1 ounce all-purpose flour (about ¼ cup)
- ¼ cup water

1. Preheat oven to 425°.

2. Combine first 4 ingredients in bottom of a shallow roasting pan coated with cooking spray. Remove and discard giblets and neck from turkey. Rinse turkey with cold water; pat dry. Trim excess fat. Starting at neck cavity, loosen skin from breast and drumsticks by inserting fingers, gently pushing between skin and meat. Lift wing tips up and over back; tuck under turkey.

3. Combine cheese, ¼ cup sage, butter, minced garlic, ¾ teaspoon salt, and ¼ teaspoon pepper; rub mixture under the loosened skin and over breast and drumsticks. Rub turkey skin with cut sides of lemon halves; squeeze juice into turkey cavity. Place lemon halves in turkey cavity; tie legs together with kitchen twine.

4. Place turkey, breast side up, on vegetable mixture in pan. Bake at 425° for 30 minutes, and pour 2 cups broth over turkey. Tent turkey breast loosely with foil. Bake an additional 30 minutes.

5. Reduce oven temperature to 325° (do not remove turkey from oven). Bake at 325° for 1½ hours or until a thermometer inserted into

meaty part of thigh registers 165°, basting every 30 minutes. Remove turkey from pan. Cover and let stand 30 minutes; discard skin.

6. Place a large zip-top plastic bag inside a 4-cup glass measure. Pour drippings through a sieve into bag; discard solids. Let drippings stand 10 minutes (fat will rise to the top). Seal bag; carefully snip off 1 bottom corner of bag. Drain drippings into a medium bowl, stopping before fat layer reaches opening; discard fat. Add enough of remaining chicken broth to drippings to equal 3 cups.

7. Heat a medium saucepan over medium-high heat. Coat pan with cooking spray. Add shallots; sauté 1 minute. Add sherry; bring to a boil. Cook until reduced to ½ cup (about 5 minutes). Stir in remaining 1 tablespoon sage, and cook 30 seconds. Add reserved drippings; bring to a boil.

8. Weigh or lightly spoon flour into a dry measuring cup; level with a knife. Combine flour and ¼ cup water, stirring well with a whisk. Stir flour mixture into drippings mixture; bring to a boil. Cook 2 minutes or until thickened, stirring constantly. Stir in remaining ¼ teaspoon salt and remaining ¼ teaspoon pepper. Serve gravy with turkey. **Yield: 16 servings (serving size: about 5 ounces meat and about 3 tablespoons gravy).**

CALORIES 285; FAT 9.6g (sat 3.5g, mono 2.5g, poly 2.2g); PROTEIN 40.9g; CARB 3.5g; FIBER 0.3g; CHOL 108mg; IRON 2.7mg; SODIUM 339mg; CALC 64mg

kitchen how-to: make gravy

Thanksgiving wouldn't be complete without a side of gravy. Using our recipe for Parmesan-Sage Roast Turkey with Sage Gravy, at left, as a guide, you can also follow this basic method for your own recipe.

1. After turkey cools, remove it from roasting pan, and pour the drippings through a sieve into a heavy-duty plastic bag. Place bag standing up in a measuring cup for about 10 minutes to allow the fat to separate and rise.

2. Snip a ¼-inch hole from one bottom corner of the bag. Drain the drippings into a 4-cup glass measure. Lightly pinch the bag near the hole to keep the fat inside. Discard the bag and fat. Add enough broth to the drippings to equal 3 cups.

3. Cook the shallots; add the sherry, and bring mixture to a boil, reducing the liquid to ½ cup (use a ruler to record measurements, as shown).

Add the sage, and cook another 30 seconds. Add the reserved liquid, and bring to a boil.

4. In a separate bowl, combine the flour and water; whisk until blended. Add to the drippings mixture, and bring to a boil. Stir 2 minutes or until thickened. Add the remaining seasonings, and serve.

To freeze these meatballs, follow the cooking directions, and then allow them to cool to room temperature. Place them on a baking sheet, making sure they don't touch one another, and place the baking sheet in the freezer for an hour. Next, transfer the hardened meatballs to an airtight container, and store them in the freezer. To serve, thaw the meatballs in the refrigerator; bake them at 375° for 20 minutes or until heated.

Turkey-Ricotta Meatballs

These simple meatballs can supplement spaghetti, substitute for beef in Stroganoff, or serve as an appetizer with warmed marinara dip. Ricotta cheese helps keep the lean ground turkey breast moist. Prepare the meatballs in advance, and store in the freezer for up to three months.

½ cup part-skim
ricotta cheese

1 large egg

½ cup dry
breadcrumbs

¼ cup chopped
fresh basil

¼ teaspoon pepper
and ¼ teaspoon salt

Preheat oven to 375°. Combine 1 pound ground turkey breast with above ingredients in a bowl; shape mixture into about 18 meatballs. Heat a large nonstick skillet over medium-high heat. Coat pan with cooking spray. Add meatballs, and brown on all sides. Remove from skillet; transfer to broiler pan coated with cooking spray. Bake at 375° for 15 minutes or until done. **Yield: 18 servings (serving size: 1 meatball).**

CALORIES 63; FAT 3.1g (sat 1g, mono 1.1g, poly 0.6g); PROTEIN 6g; CARB 2.6g; FIBER 0.2g; CHOL 34mg; IRON 0.6mg; SODIUM 90mg; CALC 30mg

way to roast
vegetables

Roasting vegetables concentrates their natural sugars, creating a slightly sweet flavor. The high direct heat of this simple method also gives them a beautiful, tasty browned exterior.

Honey and Herb–Roasted Root Vegetables

Serve this versatile side dish with roast pork loin, chicken, beef, ham, or duck. Garnish with a fresh thyme sprig, if desired.

- 1½ cups sliced fennel bulb (about 1 small bulb)
- 1½ cups (½-inch) cubed peeled butternut squash
- 1¼ cups (½-inch) cubed red potato
- 1 cup (½-inch) cubed peeled turnip
- 1 cup (½-inch-thick) slices parsnip
- 1 tablespoon olive oil
- ¾ teaspoon salt
- ½ teaspoon chopped fresh thyme
- ¼ teaspoon freshly ground black pepper
- 6 garlic cloves, peeled
- 3 large shallots, peeled and halved
- Cooking spray
- 1 tablespoon honey
- 1½ teaspoons cider vinegar

1. Preheat oven to 450°.
2. Combine first 11 ingredients in a large bowl; toss well. Arrange vegetable mixture in a single layer on a jelly-roll pan coated with cooking spray. Bake at 450° for 25 minutes or until vegetables are browned and tender. Place vegetable mixture in a large bowl. Add honey and cider vinegar, and toss well. **Yield: 4 servings (serving size: about ⅔ cup).**

CALORIES 181; FAT 3.8g (sat 0.5g, mono 2.5g, poly 0.5g); PROTEIN 3.6g; CARB 36.2g; FIBER 6.4g; CHOL 0mg; IRON 1.8mg; SODIUM 496mg; CALC 104mg

kitchen how-to:
peel & cut butternut squash

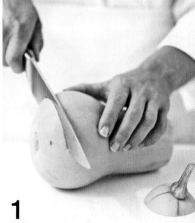

1

2

Shaped like a bowling pin—long, cylindrical, and bulbous at the base—butternut squash is a cold-weather staple. Its bright orange flesh has a slightly sweet nuttiness that's similar to a sweet potato and a texture that is even silkier. But to reach the flesh, you must first remove the squash's thick, shiny skin. A sturdy serrated peeler works better than a paring knife. To peel and cut this squash with confidence, follow these steps.

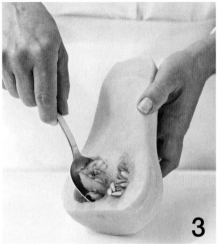

3

1. For stability, use a sharp kitchen knife to cut 1 inch from the top and bottom of the squash, and discard.
2. Using a serrated peeler, peel away the thick skin until you reach the deeper orange flesh of the squash.
3. With a spoon or melon baller, scoop away the seeds and membranes; discard. Then cut the flesh according to your recipe directions.

Indian-Inspired Butternut Squash

The sweet, slightly nutty flavor of this dish goes well with holiday turkey or ham. Prepare it in place of sweet potatoes. For make-ahead ease, peel and cube the squash a day ahead, and store it in a zip-top plastic bag in the refrigerator until ready to use.

1 tablespoon olive oil   +   **¼ cup golden raisins**   +   **1 tablespoon honey**

½ teaspoon Madras curry powder   +   **2 tablespoons minced fresh cilantro**

Preheat oven to 500°. Peel and cube 6 cups butternut squash (about 2 medium squash). Toss squash in oil, and season with salt and pepper, if desired. Place squash in a single layer on a jelly-roll pan. Bake at 500° for 10 minutes or until tender. Remove from oven; toss squash with raisins and remaining ingredients. Serve immediately. **Yield: 6 servings (serving size: about ¾ cup).**

CALORIES 97; FAT 2.4g (sat 0.4g, mono 1.7g, poly 0.3g); PROTEIN 1.3g; CARB 20.3g; FIBER 3.7g; CHOL 0mg; IRON 0.9mg; SODIUM 6mg; CALC 53mg

fire &

smoke

way to
grill

Grilling is a fun, casual, versatile cooking technique that creates charred edges, telltale grill marks, and smoky, robust tastes with minimal effort—the heat of the fire does all the work. And all these delicious qualities come with little or no added fat, making this one of the easiest and most healthful cooking methods.

It works wonders with all types of meat, poultry, and seafood, as well as vegetables, fruits, and some desserts. Grilling is a go-to option for busy cooks because small, thin cuts such as skinless, boneless chicken breasts or fish fillets grill up in a flash. Larger cuts such as bone-in pork shoulder or whole chickens also fare nicely over longer periods of time on the grill.

grilling, defined

Grilling involves cooking food on a rack over a heat source, usually a charcoal fire or ceramic briquettes heated by gas flames. Direct heat quickly sears the outside of food, producing distinctive robust, roasted—and sometimes pleasantly charred—flavors and a nice crust. If food is cooked over moderate heat, it gains a crust as well as a smokier taste.

Direct vs. Indirect Heat

Direct grilling (see photo A) involves cooking food squarely over the heat source, usually with the lid off. Similar to broiling, this method cooks food quickly with intense heat, and it works best for thin cuts of meat (burgers and several kinds of steaks and chops, for example) and most vegetables. It is not ideal for larger cuts of meat because the high heat will overcook the outside before the inside is done.

For food that needs to cook longer (pork shoulder or whole chickens, for example), use **indirect** grilling (see photo B), in which a fire is built on one or both sides of the food and the hot air circulates around it. Indirect grilling requires a covered grill, which creates convected heat. It's a gentler cooking method than direct grilling, and it allows larger cuts to cook completely through without overbrowning.

Follow this rule of thumb: If it takes less than 20 to 25 minutes to cook, use direct heat; otherwise, use indirect heat. The exception is large fish fillets, which yield better results over indirect heat even though they can typically be cooked in 15 minutes or less over direct heat. Some fish is so delicate that direct grilling can cook it too quickly and render it dry; it can also burn the oils in the skin, resulting in a fishy odor that many people dislike. If you use indirect heat, fish will cook perfectly and remain moist.

Equipment

Choosing between a gas or charcoal grill is a lifestyle choice; they perform comparably, if not equally. For the most versatility, choose a grill with a large cooking surface and a lid. Most Americans choose gas grills for their convenience and the consistent heat provided by gas flames; others enjoy the hands-on approach to lighting a charcoal fire.

Here are a few other useful tools: a chimney starter for charcoal, long-handled tongs, a basting brush, a spatula, oven mitts, a wire brush for cleaning, disposable aluminum foil pans, and a meat thermometer.

For indoor grilling, a grill pan is a must. The best are nonstick or cast-iron grills, although some cast-iron pans require seasoning or food will stick. See page 56 for information about how to season cast iron.

Keep It Clean

Each time you grill, preheat the rack with all burners on high for 10 to 15 minutes (whether you're using direct or indirect heat) to incinerate any remaining residue from the last cookout, making it easy to clean off. Then brush the cooking grates with a brass-bristle grill brush; steel bristles can damage the enamel finish of some grates. (In a pinch, if you don't have a brass-bristle cleaning brush, use a ball of crumpled heavy-duty aluminum foil between a pair of tongs to clean the grates.) Clean the grates vigorously so they're smooth and free from food that may have adhered from previous grilling.

At the beginning of grilling season, preheat your grill with all the burners on high or with an even layer of preheated charcoal for an hour before brushing the cooking grates. You should only need to do this one time to bring your grates into shape for the season; it's the grill version of the principle behind a self-cleaning oven—burning everything off.

Light Up

If you have a gas grill, simply ignite the burners and place them on high to preheat. If you're using indirect heat, turn off one side of the grill once it's preheated.

If you have a charcoal grill, the easiest way to light charcoal, briquettes, or lump hardwood, is to use a chimney starter (see photo C). It's best to choose a high-capacity chimney starter, or you'll probably discover that you need two starters to light enough charcoal for your grill (a traditional kettle grill works most efficiently with 50 briquettes). Use an odorless, tasteless fuel starter or crumpled newspaper to initiate the fire. Let the charcoal burn until it's covered with white-gray ash, which indicates it's at the perfect cooking temperature.

If you use the direct heat method, scatter the briquettes evenly across the charcoal grate. If you are using the indirect cooking method, equally divide the briquettes on either side of the grate, and place an inexpensive disposable aluminum foil pan in the empty spot (see photo D). Place the food over the drip pan, which catches drips and reflects some heat back to the food. Many cooks place charcoal on one side of the grill and leave the other empty, but distributing the briquettes to each side of the food (if space allows) creates consistent heat that envelops the food as it cooks.

C

D

Control the Heat

Maintaining a specific temperature on a gas grill is simply a matter of turning a dial to the appropriate setting. On a charcoal grill, air vents control the heat. To allow airflow, do not cover the bottom air vents with briquettes. Also, leave the vent on the top of the grill at least partially open. The more open the vents, the hotter your grill will cook. If you want medium heat, cover the vents about halfway.

Oil the Food

Whenever possible, coat the food and the grill rack with oil or cooking spray to promote caramelization and those telltale grill marks and also help prevent sticking. If you don't coat the food, its natural juices may evaporate as it grills, leaving the food dry and papery—this is especially true when grilling vegetable slices.

the bottom line

The three most important elements to remember about grilling:

1. Use direct heat for thin cuts of meat and other foods that cook quickly. Indirect heat is best for larger cuts.

2. Keep the grill rack clean.

3. Place oiled food on a hot grill rack coated with cooking spray.

way to grill
burgers

Burgers are the quintessential foods for cookouts. But you can go beyond the basic burger and create your own masterpiece with flavorful meats, robust seasonings, and unique ingredients.

kitchen how-to:
make the best burger

To create great burgers, follow these tips:

• Cook on a grill for the best charred flavor. A grill pan will work nicely, too, but it produces a more subtle char.

• Heat the grill with the rack off. Clean and coat the rack with cooking spray away from the fire so the spray doesn't cause a flare-up. Carefully place the rack on the grill shortly before adding the burgers.

• Use your hands to make the burgers, working the ingredients evenly and lightly into the meat. Be careful not to compact the meat when shaping the patties; over-working creates tough burgers.

• Avoid moving the burgers on the grill before turning them so the outside develops a good char.

• Do not press the patties with the spatula as they cook; doing so squeezes out flavorful juices.

• Use a meat thermometer to test for doneness (and wash it between tests). We follow the U.S. Department of Agriculture temperature recommendations: 160° for ground beef, veal, lamb, and pork, and 165° for ground poultry.

• Burgers, like steaks, should rest 5 minutes after they come off the heat to allow the juices to redistribute throughout the meat.

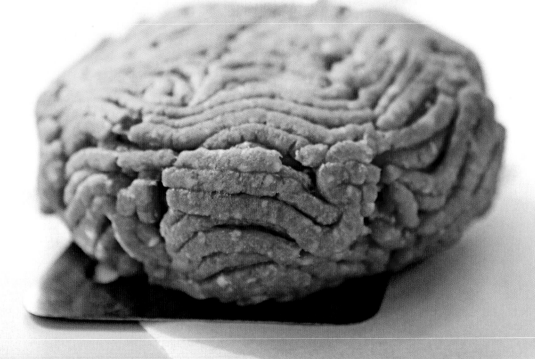

Italian Meatball Burgers

You can also serve these saucy, family-friendly meatball burgers over spaghetti with extra sauce. We enjoyed them with a side of macaroni salad.

- 8 ounces sweet turkey Italian sausage
- 1 teaspoon dried oregano
- 1 teaspoon dried basil
- ½ teaspoon salt
- ½ teaspoon fennel seeds, crushed
- ⅛ teaspoon garlic powder
- 1 pound ground sirloin
  Cooking spray
- 2 ounces fresh mozzarella cheese, thinly sliced
- 6 (2-ounce) Italian bread rolls, split
- ¾ cup fat-free tomato-basil pasta sauce (such as Muir Glen)

1. Prepare grill.

2. Remove casings from sausage. Combine sausage and next 6 ingredients. Divide beef mixture into 6 equal portions, shaping each into a ½-inch-thick patty.

3. Place patties on a grill rack coated with cooking spray; grill 5 minutes. Turn patties over; grill 2 minutes. Divide fresh mozzarella cheese evenly over patties, and grill an additional 5 minutes or until a thermometer registers 165°. Remove from grill; let stand 5 minutes.

4. Place rolls, cut sides down, on grill rack; grill 1 minute or until toasted. Place 1 patty on bottom half of each roll; top each serving with 2 tablespoons sauce and top half of roll. **Yield: 6 servings (serving size: 1 burger).**

CALORIES 375; FAT 13.9g (sat 5.3g, mono 4.4g, poly 1.7g); PROTEIN 28.1g; CARB 32.7g; FIBER 1.8g; CHOL 80mg; IRON 4.5mg; SODIUM 894mg; CALC 130mg

Ground Turkey

What it adds: Ground turkey is a leaner, healthier meat, but because it's lower in fat, turkey burgers can dry out over the high heat of the grill. Add ingredients that lend moisture, such as chopped onions in this recipe or even mashed plantains, chopped chickpeas, or dried fruit.

Wheat Germ

What it adds: Though small, wheat germ is the main nutrient source of the wheat kernel. It's rich in vitamins and minerals and high in protein. It adds a nuttiness to these burgers that complements the turkey and spices.

Southwestern Turkey-Cheddar Burgers with Grilled Onions

For more spicy heat, use Monterey Jack cheese with jalapeño peppers.

- ¾ cup finely chopped Maui or other sweet onion
- ⅓ cup wheat germ
- 1½ teaspoons ancho chile powder
- ¾ teaspoon ground cumin
- ½ teaspoon salt
- ¼ teaspoon ground red pepper
- 1½ pounds ground turkey breast
- Cooking spray
- 4 ounces extrasharp Cheddar cheese, thinly sliced
- 6 (½-inch-thick) slices Maui or other sweet onion
- 6 (2-ounce) Kaiser rolls, split
- 6 tablespoons Chipotle-Poblano Ketchup (at right)

1. Prepare grill.

2. Combine first 7 ingredients in a large bowl. Divide mixture into 6 equal portions, shaping each into a ½-inch-thick patty.

3. Place patties on a grill rack coated with cooking spray; grill 5 minutes. Turn patties over; grill 2 minutes. Divide cheese evenly over patties; grill an additional 5 minutes or until a thermometer registers 165°. Remove from grill; let stand 5 minutes.

4. Place onion slices on grill rack coated with cooking spray; grill 4 minutes on each side or until browned and tender.

5. Place rolls, cut sides down, on grill rack; grill 1 minute or until toasted. Place 1 patty on bottom half of each roll; top each serving with 1 onion slice, 1 tablespoon Chipotle-Poblano Ketchup, and top half of roll. **Yield: 6 servings (serving size: 1 burger).**

CALORIES 395; FAT 10.7g (sat 4.8g, mono 2.5g, poly 1.6g); PROTEIN 32.8g; CARB 42.6g; FIBER 3.3g; CHOL 54mg; IRON 3.4mg; SODIUM 853mg; CALC 211mg

Chipotle-Poblano Ketchup

Use this sauce with any type of meat or poultry burger. It's also great with oven fries or chicken fingers.

- 1 poblano chile (about 5 ounces)
- 1 cup ketchup
- 2 tablespoons minced seeded chipotle chiles, canned in adobo sauce (about 2 chiles)
- ½ teaspoon ground cumin

1. Preheat broiler.

2. Pierce poblano two times with the tip of a knife. Place poblano on a foil-lined baking sheet; broil 10 minutes or until blackened, turning occasionally. Place in a zip-top plastic bag; seal. Let stand 15 minutes. Peel and discard skins. Cut a lengthwise slit in poblano; discard seeds and stem. Finely chop poblano.

3. Combine poblano and remaining ingredients. Refrigerate in an airtight container for up to 2 weeks. **Yield: 1¼ cups (serving size: 1 tablespoon).**

CALORIES 15; FAT 0.2g (sat 0g, mono 0g, poly 0.1g); PROTEIN 0.3g; CARB 3.6g; FIBER 0.4g; CHOL 0mg; IRON 0.2mg; SODIUM 150mg; CALC 3mg

all about ketchup

Ketchup is a typical burger condiment, but it brings more to the table than just flavor. It also has a variety of nutritional benefits. Ketchup contains lycopene, a phytochemical found in tomatoes that may help prevent heart disease and some cancers. It also contains carotenoids, such as beta-carotene, that may help ward off cancer.

way to grill
fish & shellfish

The most important thing to know when grilling seafood is what kind to use. You want fish and shellfish that have a thick, firm, meaty texture, such as grouper, halibut, salmon, swordfish, tuna, scallops, and shrimp, so it won't fall apart while it's cooking.

Halibut with Persimmon Tomato and Dill Relish

2 cups diced Persimmon tomato (about 3 medium)
3 tablespoons finely chopped red onion
1 tablespoon finely chopped seeded jalapeño pepper
1 teaspoon chopped fresh dill
2 teaspoons fresh lemon juice
½ teaspoon salt, divided
½ teaspoon freshly ground black pepper, divided
6 (6-ounce) halibut fillets
1 tablespoon extra-virgin olive oil
Cooking spray

1. Prepare grill.
2. Combine first 5 ingredients in a medium bowl; stir in ¼ teaspoon salt and ¼ teaspoon black pepper. Toss gently to coat.
3. Brush fish with oil; sprinkle evenly with remaining ¼ teaspoon salt and ¼ teaspoon black pepper. Place fish on grill rack coated with cooking spray, and grill 2 minutes on each side or until fish flakes easily when tested with a fork or until desired degree of doneness. Serve with tomato mixture. **Yield: 6 servings (serving size: 1 fillet and ⅓ cup tomato mixture).**

CALORIES 211; FAT 6.2g (sat 0.9g, mono 2.9g, poly 1.6g); PROTEIN 34.8g; CARB 2.6g; FIBER 0.7g; CHOL 52mg; IRON 1.7mg; SODIUM 308mg; CALC 81mg

seed a chile pepper

Hot chiles like serranos or jalapeños
can add depth to a recipe, but they can also set
your taste buds on fire. To modify their scorch,
follow these tips for removing the seeds and
veins—the source of capsaicin, the chemical that
gives peppers their kick. You can control the heat
by removing as many or as few of the seeds as
you'd like. Since capsaicin can stick to your hands,
be sure to wear gloves.

1. Use a paring knife to cut off the stem and slice
the chile in half lengthwise.
2. Next, cut each half lengthwise to create four
separate strips.

3. Lay the strips skin sides down, and slide
the knife against the pepper to cut away the
vein and seeds.

all about rubs and finishing sauces

To add variety to your grilled meats, fish, and vegetables, use rubs and sauces. These concentrated blends season food quickly, and they're ideal for busy weeknights. Massage dry and wet rubs onto food just before grilling. This layer of wet or dry herbs and spices helps insulate the food from heat, which means the outer layers of the grilled food end up moist and less overcooked.

Grilled Salmon with Korean Barbecue Glaze

The sweet-salty rub is also great on steaks, pork tenderloin, dark-meat chicken, or any game bird, such as duck or quail. Garnish with a lemon wedge, if desired.

¼ cup packed brown sugar
1 teaspoon salt
2 teaspoons low-sodium soy sauce
2 teaspoons dark sesame oil
4 garlic cloves, minced
6 (6-ounce) salmon fillets
Cooking spray

1. Prepare grill.
2. Combine first 5 ingredients. Rub or brush brown sugar mixture evenly on fillets.
3. Place fish on a grill rack coated with cooking spray; grill 4 minutes on each side or until fish flakes easily when tested with a fork or until desired degree of doneness. **Yield: 6 servings (serving size: 1 fillet).**

CALORIES 328; FAT 13.9g (sat 2.1g, mono 4.1g, poly 4.9g); PROTEIN 38.8g; CARB 9.7g; FIBER 0g; CHOL 107mg; IRON 1.8mg; SODIUM 544mg; CALC 34mg

Grilled Shrimp with Dijon-Garlic Glaze

Add a bit of zing to your grilled shrimp with this quick and tasty brush-on sauce. The tangy mixture adds just enough flavor to liven up plain shrimp, while still letting its natural sweetness shine.

**3 tablespoons
Dijon mustard**

+

**2 tablespoons
honey**

**¼ cup fresh
lemon juice**

+

**2 garlic cloves,
minced**

Thread 1½ pounds of large shrimp, peeled and deveined, onto skewers. Combine above ingredients, and stir with a whisk. Brush one side of shrimp with mixture. Grill for 1 to 2 minutes. Turn shrimp, brush with glaze, and cook 2 minutes or until shrimp are done. **Yield: 4 servings.**

CALORIES 177; FAT 1.4g (sat 0.4g, mono 0.3g, poly 0.6g); PROTEIN 27.2g; CARB 12.8g; FIBER 0.1g; CHOL 252mg; IRON 4.1mg; SODIUM 560mg; CALC 55mg

way to grill
fruit

Fruit is perfect for grilling because it's so simple to prepare. With most fruits, you just need to halve them and place them on the grill. Firm fruits hold up best, while softer fruits may require a little more attention. Be careful though—soft fruits can become mushy if overcooked.

Grilled Peaches over Arugula with Goat Cheese and Prosciutto

For a bit of crunch, sauté the prosciutto in a nonstick skillet over medium-high heat for 2 minutes or until crisp.

¼ cup balsamic vinegar
2 tablespoons honey
3 peaches, pitted and each cut into 6 wedges
Cooking spray
1 tablespoon extra-virgin olive oil
⅛ teaspoon freshly ground black pepper
Dash of kosher salt
10 cups trimmed arugula (about 10 ounces)
2 ounces thinly sliced prosciutto, cut into ¼-inch strips
2 tablespoons crumbled goat cheese

1. Bring vinegar to a boil in a small saucepan over medium-high heat. Reduce heat, and simmer until vinegar is reduced to 2 tablespoons (about 2 minutes). Remove from heat, and stir in honey. Cool to room temperature.
2. Prepare grill.
3. Place peach wedges on a grill rack coated with cooking spray; grill 30 seconds on each side or until grill marks appear but peaches are still firm. Remove from grill; set aside.
4. Combine oil, pepper, and salt in a large bowl, stirring with a whisk. Add arugula, tossing gently to coat. Arrange arugula mixture on a platter. Top with peach wedges and prosciutto. Drizzle with balsamic syrup; sprinkle with cheese. **Yield: 6 servings (serving size: about 1⅓ cups arugula mixture, 3 peach wedges, about ⅓ ounce prosciutto, 1½ teaspoons balsamic syrup, and 1 teaspoon cheese).**

CALORIES 100; FAT 4g (sat 1g, mono 2.4g, poly 0.5g); PROTEIN 3.9g; CARB 13.1g; FIBER 1.3g; CHOL 7mg; IRON 0.8mg; SODIUM 183mg; CALC 61mg

kitchen how-to:
prepare the grill for fruit

A clean grill is particularly important when grilling fruit. We recommend cleaning your grill twice: once after preheating and again when you've finished grilling. Use both a metal spatula and a wire brush to scrape the grates clean. Before grilling, coat the grill rack with cooking spray to keep the food from sticking.

way to grill
meats

A sizzling steak right off the grill is something few can resist, and a variety of cuts work well. Ribeye is a tender, flavorful cut that needs little adornment. Tenderloins, true to their name, offer exceptionally supple meat, but because of the lack of fat, they benefit from added flavorings. Lean flank steak can be tough, but it lends itself nicely to salads when sliced very thin.

Basic Grilled Steak

4 (8-ounce) ribeye steaks, trimmed (about
   ¾ inch thick)
1 teaspoon salt
¾ teaspoon freshly ground black pepper
Cooking spray

1. Sprinkle both sides of steaks with salt and pepper. Let steaks stand at room temperature 20 minutes.

2. Prepare grill.

3. Pat steaks dry with a paper towel. Place steaks on grill rack coated with cooking spray; grill 2 minutes on each side or until desired degree of doneness. Remove from grill. Cover steaks loosely with foil; let stand 5 minutes. **Yield: 4 servings (serving size: 1 steak).**

CALORIES 350; FAT 15.3g (sat 6.1g, mono 6.6g, poly 0.6g); PROTEIN 49.2g; CARB 0.3g; FIBER 0.1g; CHOL 155mg; IRON 3.4mg; SODIUM 683mg; CALC 29mg

kitchen how-to:
determine degrees of doneness

While doneness standards can vary somewhat (one person's rare may be another's medium rare), we follow the U.S. Department of Agriculture guidelines for steak temperatures. The USDA does not recommend serving rare steak. A thermometer (preferably one that's an instant-read) is the only way to truly know how done meat is; you can also use the "nick and peek" method: nick the meat with a sharp knife, and take a peek inside to check its doneness. Don't worry about juices escaping when you cut into the meat; the small amount you'll lose is preferable to under- or overcooking your steak.

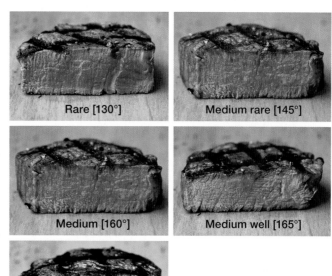

Rare [130°]

Medium rare [145°]

Medium [160°]

Medium well [165°]

Well done [170°]

kitchen how-to: create grill marks

For an attractive presentation, grill crosshatches on the steak.

1. Set the steak on the grill.
2. After about a minute—or halfway through the cooking time for the first side of the steak—rotate the meat a quarter-turn (45° for diamond-shaped crosshatches, 90° for square-shaped marks).
3. Flip the steak over, and complete cooking. Only one side of the steak will show on the plate, so both sides don't require crosshatches. Do not flip the steak back onto the marked side while grilling.

Flank Steak with Soy, Ketchup, and Sesame Marinade

Steep the flank steak in this salty, savory sauce for tenderness filled with flavor. When marinating, a few hours will transfer flavor without making the surface of the meat mushy. Low-acid mixtures like teriyaki sauce can remain on the meat for up to 48 hours, but don't let beef sit in a high-acid liquid, like lime juice, for more than an hour or two.

¾ cup low-sodium soy sauce

+

¼ cup ketchup

¼ cup chopped green onions

+

1½ tablespoons dark sesame oil

Combine all ingredients in a large zip-top plastic bag; add a 1-pound flank steak, trimmed of excess fat. Seal bag, and refrigerate 4 hours or overnight. When ready to cook, remove steak from bag, and discard marinade. Grill steak 6 minutes on each side or until desired degree of doneness. Remove from grill, and cut diagonally across grain into ¼- to ½-inch-thick slices. **Yield: 4 servings.**

CALORIES 198; FAT 9.1g (sat 3.1g, mono 2.7g, poly 0.3g); PROTEIN 24g; CARB 3.2g; FIBER 0.1g; CHOL 45mg; IRON 1.6mg; SODIUM 919mg; CALC 16mg

Greek Lamb and Red Onion Kebabs

Also try this aromatic wet rub on lamb chops, white-fleshed fish, shrimp, or any poultry. To ensure even cooking, cut the vegetables and meat the same size.

- ¼ cup fresh oregano leaves
- 2 tablespoons chopped fresh rosemary
- 3 tablespoons olive oil
- 1 tablespoon fresh lemon juice
- 2 teaspoons salt
- 2 teaspoons grated lemon rind
- 4 garlic cloves, minced
- 2½ pounds boneless leg of lamb, trimmed and cut into 1-inch cubes
- 2 medium red onions, cut into 1-inch pieces

Cooking spray

1. Prepare grill.

2. Place first 7 ingredients in a mini food processor; process until finely chopped.

3. Thread lamb and onion alternately on 16 (8-inch) skewers. Rub or brush oregano mixture over both sides of skewers. Place skewers on a grill rack coated with cooking spray; grill 9 minutes or until desired degree of doneness, turning occasionally. **Yield: 8 servings (serving size: 2 skewers).**

Note: If you use wooden skewers, soak them in water for 30 minutes before grilling.

CALORIES 239; FAT 14g (sat 4.5g, mono 7.1g, poly 1g); PROTEIN 23.2g; CARB 4.4g; FIBER 1.3g; CHOL 86mg; IRON 2.6mg; SODIUM 651mg; CALC 46mg

kitchen how-to: use wet rubs

Wet rubs create thicker crusts and are denser and a little messier than dry rubs. Prepare a wet rub just before cooking—the flavors in wet rubs tend to dull quickly, so they're not good make-ahead candidates. Fire up the grill before you coat the food, and pat the wet rub into place right before the food goes on the grill. Set the rubbed food on the grill, and leave it undisturbed for 2 to 3 minutes so the crust begins to form. Use wide, thin utensils when turning foods with wet rubs to keep the delicate crust intact. If possible, turn the food only once (or not at all) since turning can chip or break the delicate crust.

Spiced Pork Chops with Apple Chutney

Slender haricots verts provide a pretty and quick-cooking complement to this meal. Heat 2 teaspoons olive oil in a large nonstick skillet over medium-high heat. Add 12 ounces haricots verts to pan; cook 3 minutes, stirring occasionally. Stir in ¼ teaspoon salt, ⅛ teaspoon black pepper, and 2 thinly sliced garlic cloves; cook 5 minutes or until garlic is lightly browned.

Chutney:

- 1 tablespoon butter
- 5 cups (¼-inch) cubed peeled apple (about 3 apples)
- ¼ cup dried cranberries
- 3 tablespoons brown sugar
- 3 tablespoons cider vinegar
- 2 teaspoons minced peeled fresh ginger
- ¼ teaspoon salt
- ¼ teaspoon dry mustard
- ⅛ teaspoon ground allspice

Pork:

- ¾ teaspoon ground chipotle chile pepper
- ½ teaspoon salt
- ½ teaspoon garlic powder
- ½ teaspoon ground coriander
- ¼ teaspoon freshly ground black pepper
- 4 (4-ounce) boneless center-cut pork loin chops, trimmed

Cooking spray

1. To prepare chutney, melt butter in a nonstick skillet over medium-high heat. Add apple; sauté 4 minutes or until lightly browned. Add cranberries and next 6 ingredients; bring to a boil. Reduce heat, and simmer 8 minutes or until apples are tender; stir occasionally.

2. To prepare pork, while chutney simmers, heat a grill pan over medium-high heat. Combine chipotle and next 4 ingredients; sprinkle over pork. Coat grill pan with cooking spray. Add pork to pan; cook 4 minutes on each side or until done. Serve with chutney. **Yield: 4 servings (serving size: 1 chop and about ⅓ cup chutney).**

CALORIES 321; FAT 9.6g (sat 4.2g, mono 3.6g, poly 0.7g); PROTEIN 24.4g; CARB 34.6g; FIBER 2.4g; CHOL 72mg; IRON 1.1mg; SODIUM 520mg; CALC 45mg

kitchen how-to: core & chop an apple

Look for vibrantly colored apples that are firm to the touch and free of bruises. The skins should be tight and smooth. Store apples in a plastic bag in the refrigerator crisper. After slicing an apple, sprinkle the flesh with lemon juice to prevent it from browning.

1. Pierce the center of the fruit with an apple corer, and rotate the apple to remove the core. Use a paring knife to slice the apple in half vertically.
2. Place the apple halves, cut sides down, on a cutting board. Cut through the skin to create wedges or thinner slices.
3. Chop the wedges into pieces with a paring knife.

1

2

3

way to grill
poultry

Seoul-ful Chicken with Minted Cucumbers

Cucumbers:
- 1 English cucumber, peeled, halved lengthwise, and thinly sliced (about 2½ cups)
- ¼ teaspoon salt
- ¼ cup minced shallots
- 2 tablespoons chopped fresh mint
- 1 tablespoon seasoned rice vinegar
- 1 tablespoon honey
- 1 teaspoon dark sesame oil
- ¼ teaspoon ground red pepper
- 1 serrano chile, seeded and minced

Chicken:
- 8 skinless, boneless chicken thighs (about 1¼ pounds)
- ¼ cup soy sauce
- 2 tablespoons dark sesame oil
- 1 tablespoon minced peeled fresh ginger
- 1 tablespoon honey
- ½ teaspoon freshly ground black pepper
- 3 garlic cloves, thinly sliced

Cooking spray
- ¼ cup thinly sliced green onions
- 4 teaspoons sesame seeds, toasted

1. To prepare cucumbers, place cucumber slices in a colander; sprinkle with salt, tossing well. Drain 1 hour. Place cucumber slices on several layers of paper towels; cover with additional paper towels. Let stand 5 minutes, pressing down occasionally. Combine cucumber, shallots, and next 6 ingredients in a large bowl; toss gently. Cover; set aside.

2. To prepare chicken, place each chicken thigh between 2 sheets of heavy-duty plastic wrap; pound to ½-inch thickness using a meat mallet or small heavy skillet. Combine soy sauce and next 5 ingredients in a large zip-top plastic bag. Add chicken to soy sauce mixture in bag; seal. Marinate in refrigerator 30 minutes, turning occasionally.

3. Heat a grill pan over medium-high heat. Coat pan with cooking spray. Remove chicken from bag; discard marinade. Place 4 thighs in pan; cook 6 minutes on each side or until done. Repeat procedure with remaining 4 thighs. Place 2 thighs and ½ cup cucumbers on each of 4 plates; sprinkle each serving with 1 tablespoon green onions and 1 teaspoon sesame seeds. **Yield: 4 servings.**

CALORIES 262; FAT 8.9g (sat 1.9g, mono 3g, poly 2.8g); PROTEIN 29.9g; CARB 14.9g; FIBER 1.5g; CHOL 115mg; IRON 2.7mg; SODIUM 502mg; CALC 40mg

Cucumbers add a cool, refreshing crispness and flavor to soups, salads, and entrées. When shopping, look for blemish-free cucumbers with a dark green exterior. Softening first occurs at the ends, so feel the fruit to make sure it's fresh and firm. If you're buying from a supermarket, be sure to wash the cucumber with a vegetable brush before cutting since most have a waxy coating. If you prefer to leave the skin on to add some extra crunch, skip to step 2.

1. Remove the skin with a vegetable peeler.
2. Cut about ½ inch from each end.
3. Slice the cucumber in half lengthwise.

1

2

3

Grilled Chicken with Sriracha Glaze

Dense, bone-in chicken leg quarters benefit from long, slow cooking over indirect heat. The less intense heat also prevents the sweet glaze from burning. Customize the glaze according to what you have on hand; try pineapple preserves or apple jelly in place of mango jam, for example, or hot pepper sauce instead of Sriracha. Serve with a simple slaw of cabbage, carrots, lime juice, and sugar.

⅔ cup mango jam
2 tablespoons finely chopped fresh chives
2 tablespoons rice vinegar
2 tablespoons Sriracha (hot chile sauce, such as Huy Fong)
1 tablespoon olive oil
4 (12-ounce) bone-in chicken leg-thigh quarters, skinned
½ teaspoon kosher salt
¼ teaspoon freshly ground black pepper
Cooking spray

1. Prepare grill for indirect grilling. If using a gas grill, heat one side to medium-high, and leave one side with no heat. If using a charcoal grill, arrange hot coals on either side of charcoal grate, leaving an empty space in the middle.

2. Combine first 4 ingredients, stirring until smooth. Reserve ¼ cup mango mixture; set aside.

3. Brush oil evenly over chicken. Sprinkle chicken with salt and pepper.

4. Carefully remove grill rack. Place a disposable aluminum foil pan on unheated part of grill. Coat grill rack with cooking spray. Carefully return grill rack to grill. Place chicken on grill rack over unheated part. Brush chicken with about 2 tablespoons remaining mango mixture. Close lid; grill 90 minutes or until a thermometer inserted into meaty part of thigh registers 165°, turning chicken and brushing with about 2 tablespoons mango mixture every 20 minutes. Transfer chicken to a platter. Drizzle chicken with reserved ¼ cup mango mixture. **Yield: 4 servings (serving size: 1 leg-thigh quarter and 1 tablespoon mango mixture).**

CALORIES 326; FAT 10.4g (sat 2.3g, mono 4.7g, poly 2.1g); PROTEIN 38.7g; CARB 18.2g; FIBER 2.7g; CHOL 154mg; IRON 4.5mg; SODIUM 515mg; CALC 102mg

kitchen how-to: baste

Basting—brushing, spooning, or pouring liquids, sauces, and marinades over food—is one way to add additional flavor to grilled meats, poultry, and fish and shellfish and help keep them moist. The meat is left to cook and then periodically coated with a sauce or marinade using a basting brush.

The classic basting brush is made from boar or plastic bristles, which are potential traps for bacteria because they can't be cleaned in a dishwasher. To keep the brush clean, you'll need to dip it in bleach periodically to kill any bacteria. The newest brushes are made of dishwasher-safe silicone, but because they don't hold as much liquid as natural bristles, you may need to dip more frequently in the basting liquid.

way to grill
sandwiches

Something magical happens when you cook a sandwich. The bread becomes wonderfully crunchy, the cheese oozes, and the fillings marry in a way that makes them irresistible. Grilled and pressed sandwiches are warm and compact and offer endless opportunities to experiment with a variety of breads, cheeses, and fillings. You're limited only by your imagination.

Classic Italian Panini with Prosciutto and Fresh Mozzarella

Use this recipe as a template, and customize it to your liking. Experiment with hollowed-out focaccia or ciabatta, or try different herbs and cheeses, for example.

- 1 (12-ounce) loaf French bread, cut in half horizontally
- ¼ cup reduced-fat mayonnaise
- 2 tablespoons chopped fresh basil
- 1 cup (4 ounces) shredded fresh mozzarella cheese, divided
- 2 ounces very thin slices prosciutto
- 2 plum tomatoes, thinly sliced
- Cooking spray

1. Hollow out top and bottom halves of bread, leaving a ½-inch-thick shell; reserve torn bread for another use. Spread 2 tablespoons mayonnaise over cut side of each bread half. Sprinkle basil and ½ cup cheese on bottom half of loaf. Top evenly with prosciutto, tomato slices, and remaining ½ cup cheese. Cover with top half of loaf. Cut filled loaf crosswise into 4 equal pieces.

2. Heat a grill pan over medium heat. Coat pan with cooking spray. Add sandwiches to pan. Place a cast-iron or other heavy skillet on top; press gently to flatten sandwiches. Cook 3 minutes on each side or until bread is toasted (leave cast-iron skillet on sandwiches while they cook). **Yield: 4 servings (serving size: 1 sandwich).**

CALORIES 316; FAT 10.6g (sat 4.8g, mono 2.3g, poly 1.9g); PROTEIN 16.1g; CARB 39.9g; FIBER 2g; CHOL 31mg; IRON 2.8mg; SODIUM 799mg; CALC 196mg

Fresh Basil
What it adds: Fresh basil has a clean, bright flavor with hints of licorice and cloves.

Prosciutto
What it adds: Prosciutto is a silky, thinly sliced Italian ham. It adds a salty punch of flavor to this sandwich.

way to grill
vegetables

Grilling adds a whole new taste sensation to vegetables, especially when they take on a chargrilled flavor and look. Depending on the recipe, you can either grill the vegetables first, and then slice them, or you can slice them first. The best vegetables to grill are sturdy ones such as eggplant, yellow squash, zucchini, tomatoes, bell peppers, potatoes, and onions.

Grilled Vegetable Salad

Tailor the vegetables in this dish to what's available at the grocery store or farmers' market. Thin asparagus spears may need to cook only 4 minutes.

Vinaigrette:
- 2 tablespoons sherry vinegar
- 1 tablespoon extra-virgin olive oil
- ½ teaspoon kosher salt
- 1½ teaspoons honey
- ½ teaspoon Dijon mustard
- ¼ teaspoon freshly ground black pepper

Salad:
- 8 ounces asparagus, trimmed
- 2 (4-inch) portobello mushroom caps (about 6 ounces)
- 1 medium zucchini, cut lengthwise into ¼-inch-thick slices
- 1 yellow squash, cut lengthwise into ¼-inch-thick slices
- 1 small red onion, cut into ¼-inch-thick slices
- 1 red bell pepper, halved and seeded
- Cooking spray
- 2 tablespoons chopped fresh basil
- 1 tablespoon chopped fresh chives
- 1 tablespoon chopped fresh parsley
- 6 tablespoons crumbled queso fresco

1. Prepare grill.

2. To prepare vinaigrette, combine first 6 ingredients in a large bowl; set aside.

3. To prepare salad, coat asparagus and next 5 ingredients with cooking spray. Place vegetables on a grill rack coated with cooking spray, and grill 4 minutes on each side or until slightly blackened. Remove vegetables from grill; cool slightly. Cut vegetables into 1-inch pieces.

4. Add vegetables, basil, chives, and parsley to vinaigrette; toss gently to coat. Sprinkle with cheese.

Yield: 6 servings (serving size: about ¾ cup salad and 1 tablespoon cheese).

CALORIES 77; FAT 3.1g (sat 0.7g, mono 1.8g, poly 0.4g); PROTEIN 3.6g; CARB 9.7g; FIBER 2.6g; CHOL 2mg; IRON 1.4mg; SODIUM 184mg; CALC 48mg

all about zucchini

Zucchini are abundant and inexpensive during their peak months of June through late August. Select firm, unblemished zucchini. Smaller ones are tender and have bright flavor, while large ones tend to be watery and seedy (those are best used in baked goods, which benefit from their moisture). Store zucchini in a perforated plastic bag in the refrigerator crisper drawer for up to three days. The skin and seeds are edible, so you don't have to worry about peeling and seeding zucchini.

all about dry rubs

These spice blends have no added moisture, so they cook to a light crust—not chunky or thick, just a thin coating that enhances a food's basic flavors. Dry rubs are easy to prepare since they're made only with dried spices and herbs, so consider doubling or tripling the recipe to have extra on hand the next time you grill.

Cajun Grilled Corn

You can also try this fiery rub on white-fleshed fish fillets such as catfish or snapper, chicken breasts, or shrimp, and sprinkle it on burgers of any variety from turkey to beef. Store it in an airtight container for up to two weeks.

> 1   tablespoon plus 1 teaspoon paprika
> 1½ teaspoons kosher salt
> ¾   teaspoon ground cumin
> ¾   teaspoon dried thyme
> ½   teaspoon freshly ground black pepper
> ¼   teaspoon garlic powder
> ¼   teaspoon ground red pepper
> 8   ears shucked corn
> Cooking spray

1. Prepare grill.
2. Combine first 7 ingredients in a small bowl. Coat corn with cooking spray. Rub paprika mixture evenly over corn.
3. Place corn on a grill rack coated with cooking spray. Cook 10 minutes or until done, turning frequently. Remove from heat. **Yield: 8 servings (serving size: 1 ear).**

CALORIES 84; FAT 1.3g (sat 0.2g, mono 0.3g, poly 0.6g); PROTEIN 3.2g; CARB 18.3g; FIBER 3.1g; CHOL 0mg; IRON 0.9mg; SODIUM 375mg; CALC 13mg

kitchen how-to: shuck corn

Always buy fresh ears of corn in their husks. The husk is essential because it helps retain the corn's natural moisture, making it taste fresher. Look for green husks that don't appear dry. Then pull back an edge of the husk to check that the kernels are plump, tight, and a vivid color; they should not appear dull, wrinkled, or dry.

1

2

1. Hold the corn with the tip facing down, and pull the husk and silks up toward your body. This helps remove more silks.
2. Twist a damp paper towel back and forth over the corn to remove any remaining silks.

way to
smoke

Unlike the quick, high-heat methods of grilling, smoking requires a relatively low temperature for longer periods of time (it can take less than an hour or more than 8 hours, depending on the cut of meat), which allows the meat to tenderize and absorb that signature smoky flavor.

kitchen how-to:
smoke on a charcoal grill

Smoke food on a covered grill over indirect heat with a small amount of charcoal and wood chips.

1. Soak the wood chips for 30 minutes; drain. Using a charcoal chimney, fire up two dozen briquettes or a dozen handfuls of lump charcoal. Pour the coals in a single layer on one side of the lower grate, or pile them in a charcoal basket on one side. The charcoal is ready when it's coated with thick gray ash.
2. Place an aluminum foil pan filled with water on the other side of the lower grate, and toss a handful of soaked wood chips on the charcoal. Place the upper grate, or grill rack, coated with cooking spray on the grill. Arrange the food on the grill rack above the pan on the unheated side.
3. If the grill lid has a built-in thermometer, place the lid so the thermometer is directly over the food. If there's no thermometer, place the lid's vent directly over the food and insert a candy thermometer in the opening so the probe is near the food; close the vent to secure the thermometer. Close and/or open the grill's bottom vents as needed to maintain the proper temperature of 200° to 225°.

kitchen how-to: smoke on a gas grill

On some gas grills, it's impossible to hold the heat down to the desirable smoking range of 200° to 225°. In that case, smoke on the lowest heat level you can maintain, and reduce the cooking time. You won't get as much smokiness, but you'll still get a good sense of the scent.

1. Soak the wood chips for 30 minutes; drain. If your gas grill has a smoker box, add soaked wood chips; they will smolder from the heat of the nearest burner. If your gas grill doesn't have a built-in box, place the wood on a piece of heavy-duty foil, fold it up, and close loosely; pierce the foil about a half-dozen times with a fork to allow smoke to escape.
2. Turn on the burner at the end of the grill nearest the smoker box. If you're using a foil pouch, turn on the burner at one end of the grill, and arrange the pouch close to that burner. If your grill is longer than 36 inches, you may need to turn on two burners to get the proper heat.

3. Place an aluminum foil pan filled with water on the unheated side of the grill. Place the grill rack coated with cooking spray on the grill. Arrange the food on the grill rack directly above the pan. If your gas grill doesn't have a thermometer in the lid, place an oven thermometer on the cooking grate near the food. Adjust the grill knobs as needed to maintain the desired temperature.

Smoked Strip Steaks

Strip steaks offer a lot of surface area relative to their total size, which allows them to absorb a maximum amount of smoke. Serve thin slices of the steak over rice pilaf.

> 2 cups wood chips
> 2 teaspoons freshly ground black pepper
> 1 teaspoon garlic powder
> ½ teaspoon salt
> ¼ teaspoon dry mustard
> 2 (12-ounce) New York strip or sirloin strip steaks, trimmed
> 2 teaspoons Worcestershire sauce
> Cooking spray

1. Soak wood chips in water 30 minutes; drain.

2. Combine pepper and next 3 ingredients; rub evenly over both sides of steaks. Place coated steaks in a large zip-top plastic bag; add Worcestershire sauce. Seal and shake to coat. Marinate in refrigerator 30 minutes.

3. Prepare grill for indirect grilling, heating one side to low and leaving one side with no heat. Maintain temperature at 200° to 225°.

4. Heat a large, heavy skillet over high heat. Coat pan with cooking spray. Remove steaks from bag, and discard marinade. Add steaks to pan; cook 1½ minutes on each side or until browned. Remove from pan.

5. Place wood chips on hot coals. Place a disposable aluminum foil pan on unheated side of grill. Pour 2 cups water into pan. Coat grill rack with cooking spray, and place on grill. Place steaks on grill rack over foil pan on unheated side. Close lid; cook 1 hour and 15 minutes or until a thermometer inserted into steak registers 145° (medium-rare) or until desired degree of doneness. Remove steaks from grill; cover and let stand 5 minutes. Cut steaks across grain into thin slices. **Yield: 6 servings (serving size: about 3 ounces).**

CALORIES 186; FAT 8.8g (sat 3.4g, mono 3.6g, poly 0.3g); PROTEIN 24.1g; CARB 1.2g; FIBER 0.2g; CHOL 65mg; IRON 2.4mg; SODIUM 273mg; CALC 13mg

kitchen how-to:
decide between wood chips & chunks

Recipes often specify to use wood chips or chunks, but what's the difference? Wood chips work best for meats that smoke for a relatively short time (2 hours or less), such as chicken and steak. For heftier cuts of meat that cook on the grill for several hours—pork shoulder or beef brisket, for instance—larger dimensions of wood perform best. We suggest hickory, one of the most common woods for smoking; it produces deep smoke flavor. Both wood chips and chunks can be found at supermarkets.

way to
barbecue

True slow-smoked barbecue is all-American food that inspires pride and fierce loyalty in those who adhere to regional styles. Particularly popular in the South, barbecue has been deeply imbedded in American culture since before the Civil War. This culinary art form has unique regional interpretations that are defined by the type of meat and the rubs or sauces used.

Texas-Style Smoked Brisket

In Texas, barbecue is about the beef—if there's any sauce, it's a thin, spicy pan sauce using the meat drippings. Look for a flat-cut brisket, which will be a fairly even thickness, and leave the fat layer on for the best results.

Brisket:
- 1 tablespoon brown sugar
- 1 tablespoon smoked paprika
- 1 tablespoon freshly ground black pepper
- 1½ teaspoons kosher salt
- 1½ teaspoons onion powder
- 1 (7-ounce) can chipotle chiles in adobo sauce
- 1 cup chopped onion
- ¼ cup cider vinegar
- ¼ cup Worcestershire sauce
- 1 (12-ounce) can beer
- 1 (4½-pound) flat-cut brisket (about 3 inches thick)
- 8 hickory wood chunks (about 4 pounds)
- 2 cups water
- Cooking spray
- 2 cups (½-inch) sliced onion
- 2 tablespoons pickled jalapeño peppers

Sauce:
- 1 cup fat-free, less-sodium beef broth
- 2 tablespoons Worcestershire sauce
- 1 tablespoon cider vinegar
- 1 tablespoon ketchup
- 1 tablespoon pickled jalapeño liquid

1. To prepare brisket, combine first 5 ingredients. Place 2 tablespoons sugar mixture in a blender; set aside remaining sugar mixture.

2. Remove 2 chiles and 2 tablespoons sauce from can; add to blender. Reserve remaining chiles and sauce for another use. Add 1 cup chopped onion and next 3 ingredients to blender; process until smooth. Combine brisket and chipotle mixture in a 2-gallon zip-top plastic bag; seal. Marinate in refrigerator 24 hours, turning occasionally.

3. Soak wood chunks in water about 16 hours; drain. Remove brisket from bag, discarding marinade. Pat brisket dry, and rub with remaining sugar mixture. Let brisket stand at room temperature 30 minutes.

4. Remove grill rack; set aside. Prepare grill for indirect grilling, heating one side to medium-low and leaving one side with no heat; maintain temperature at 225°.

5. Pierce bottom of a disposable aluminum foil pan several times with the tip of a knife. Place pan on heated side of grill; add half of wood chunks to pan. Place another disposable aluminum foil pan (do not pierce pan) on unheated side of grill. Pour 2 cups water into pan. Coat grill rack with cooking spray, and place on grill.

6. Place brisket on grill rack over foil pan on unheated side. Close id; cook 3½ hours or until a meat thermometer registers 170°. Add additional wood chunks halfway through cooking time.

7. Preheat oven to 250°.

8. Remove brisket from grill. Place sliced onion and jalapeño on a large sheet of aluminum foil. Top with brisket; seal tightly. Place foil-wrapped brisket in a large baking pan. Bake at 250° for 1½ hours or until thermometer registers 190°. Remove from oven. Let stand, still wrapped, 1 hour. Unwrap brisket, reserving juices; trim and discard fat. Cut brisket across grain into thin slices.

9. To prepare sauce, finely chop sliced onion and jalapeño; set aside. Place brisket juices in a zip-top plastic bag inside a 2-cup glass measure; let stand 10 minutes (fat will rise to the top). Seal bag; carefully snip off 1 bottom corner of bag. Drain ½ cup drippings into a saucepan, stopping before fat layer reaches opening; discard fat and remaining drippings. Add onion, jalapeño, broth, and remaining ingredients to pan; cook over medium heat 5 minutes or until thoroughly heated. **Yield: 10 servings (serving size: about 3 ounces brisket and about 3½ tablespoons sauce).**

CALORIES 243; FAT 9g (sat 2.9g, mono 3.9g, poly 0.4g); PROTEIN 29.5g; CARB 8.2g; FIBER 0.7g; CHOL 86mg; IRON 3.2mg; SODIUM 530mg; CALC 27mg

Carolina Pulled Pork with Lexington Red Sauce

You'll need to start this recipe a day ahead to allow ample time for the wood chunks to soak and the flavors of the dry rub to penetrate the meat. Slow, low-heat cooking is key to tender pork that shreds easily. While the pork is still warm, shred it into uneven shards, mixing together some of the crisp, dark outer meat with the moister interior meat.

Pork:

- 8 hickory wood chunks (about 4 pounds)
- 2 tablespoons turbinado sugar
- 2 tablespoons coarsely ground black pepper
- 2 tablespoons paprika
- 1½ teaspoons salt
- ½ teaspoon ground red pepper
- 1 (5-pound) bone-in pork shoulder (Boston butt)
- 1 cup cider vinegar
- 2¼ cups water, divided
- 1 teaspoon salt
- 1 teaspoon canola oil
  Cooking spray

Sauce:

- 1 cup cider vinegar
- ⅓ cup ketchup
- ¼ cup water
- 2 teaspoons granulated sugar
- ½ teaspoon salt
- ½ teaspoon freshly ground black pepper
- ¼ teaspoon crushed red pepper

1. To prepare pork, soak wood chunks in water about 16 hours; drain.

2. Combine turbinado sugar and next 4 ingredients; reserve 2 tablespoons sugar mixture. Rub half of the remaining sugar mixture onto pork. Place in a large zip-top plastic bag; seal and refrigerate overnight.

3. Remove pork from refrigerator; let stand at room temperature 30 minutes. Rub remaining half of sugar mixture onto pork.

4. Combine reserved 2 tablespoons sugar mixture, 1 cup vinegar, ¼ cup water, 1 teaspoon salt, and oil in a small saucepan; cook over low heat 10 minutes or until sugar dissolves.

5. Remove grill rack; set aside. Prepare grill for indirect grilling, heating one side to medium-low and leaving one side with no heat; maintain temperature at 225°. Pierce bottom of a disposable aluminum foil pan several times with the tip of a knife. Place pan on heated side of grill; add half of wood chunks to pan. Place another disposable aluminum foil pan (do not pierce pan) on unheated side of grill. Pour remaining 2 cups water in pan. Coat grill rack with cooking spray; place on grill.

6. Place pork on grill rack over foil pan on the unheated side. Close lid, and cook for 4½ hours or until a thermometer registers 170°, gently brushing pork with vinegar mixture every hour (avoid brushing off sugar mixture). Add additional wood chunks halfway through cooking time. Discard any remaining vinegar mixture.

7. Preheat oven to 250°.

8. Remove pork from grill. Wrap pork in several layers of aluminum foil, and place in a baking pan. Bake at 250° for 2 hours or until a thermometer registers 195°. Remove from oven. Let stand, still wrapped, 1 hour or until pork easily pulls apart. Unwrap pork; trim and discard fat. Shred pork with 2 forks.

9. To prepare sauce, combine 1 cup vinegar and remaining ingredients in a small saucepan; bring to a boil. Cook until reduced to 1¼ cups (about 5 minutes). Serve sauce warm or at room temperature with pork.

Yield: 13 servings (serving size: 3 ounces pork and about 1½ tablespoons sauce).

CALORIES 230; FAT 12.9g (sat 4.6g, mono 5.8g, poly 1.3g); PROTEIN 21.4g; CARB 4.7g; FIBER 0.3g; CHOL 74mg; IRON 1.6mg; SODIUM 692mg; CALC 31mg

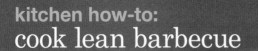

kitchen how-to:
cook lean barbecue

In an effort to keep things lean, we tried trimming the fat from pork shoulder and beef brisket prior to cooking. The results were hard, dry, and tough. As most pitmasters will tell you, the layer of fat is crucial to the success of the barbecue. It insulates the meat from the heat so it doesn't cook too quickly (which will make it dry), and it also melts into and moistens the meat. (A good bit of the fat melts into the drip pan, as well—not all of it is absorbed into the meat.)

Once the meat is fully cooked, you can trim any remaining fat before shredding or slicing. Since we discard that fat, our barbecue is leaner than most.

oven &

griddle

way to
bake

Batters and doughs have humble beginnings in the mixing bowl. They start with basic ingredients, such as flour, salt, sugar, and eggs, that are transformed into delicious treats. Of all cooking techniques, baking is one of the most complex; it's scientific and logical, based on following orderly steps and procedures. And while the nuances of baking are numerous, certain techniques and principles are always observed. Success relies not only on the right proportions of ingredients, but also on some essential skills that are easy to learn.

baking, defined

Baking is the process of cooking breads, pizza dough, and pastries, cakes, pies, and other desserts in the dry heat of an oven. The heat changes the starch in the food, creating a browned exterior or surface while sealing in moisture. Certain quick breads, such as pancakes, waffles, and crepes, are prepared on a griddle, in a waffle iron, or in a nonstick pan instead of an oven.

Batters vs. Doughs

Batters and doughs start with the same ingredients: flour, salt, sugar, and eggs. The basic difference between them is the consistency—a dough is thick, while a batter is thinner and pourable. Waffle batters can be very thick, while crepe batter is typically very thin; pancake batter is a consistency between the two. Also, dough can be made with yeast, while batter usually isn't.

Temperature Control

Preheat the oven to the specified temperature for maximum volume. Also, it's important to only check for doneness at the earliest suggested time. Opening and closing the oven too often can lower the temperature and change baking times.

The same goes for quick breads not prepared in the oven. Be sure to preheat your griddle, waffle iron, or nonstick pan for the best results. You can tell if the griddle is at the right temperature by sprinkling a few drops of water on the surface. It's just right when the drops dance on the surface of the pan and evaporate within a few seconds. The griddle is too hot if the water immediately bubbles and evaporates. If the griddle isn't hot enough, it will take the water several seconds before it appears to boil.

dough

batter

Flour Power

Be sure to use the type of flour called for in the recipe. Different types of flour contain varying levels of proteins that, when combined with liquid, form *gluten,* a stretchy substance that makes dough elastic and strong. Flours with lower protein levels, such as cake, all-purpose, and self-rising, result in light and fluffy baked goods, while higher-protein flours, such as whole wheat and bread, are best for applications that will benefit from chewiness and heft. If you don't have a particular type of flour on hand, see the Ingredient Substitution Guide on page 482 to find out if you have a suitable replacement in your pantry.

For Good Measure

Measuring flour is the single most important factor in light baking, so we list flour amounts in our ingredient lists by weight and also give an approximate cup measure if you don't have a kitchen scale. Because precision is crucial in lightened baked goods (too much flour will yield a dry product), it's preferable to measure by weight, which is more accurate and ensures the same great results we achieve in our Test Kitchens. If you use measuring cups, though, be sure to:

• Use dry measuring cups (without spouts).
• Stir the flour in the canister before spooning it out.
• (A) Lightly spoon the flour into the measuring cup without compacting it, (B) and then level off the excess flour with the flat edge of a knife.

If you measure flour in other ways (scooping it out of the canister, for example), you may end up with more flour than we intend for the recipe. Also, you should not halve, double, or otherwise multiply or divide a recipe because the ratio of wet to dry ingredients can change as the volumes of both increase or decrease, which can result in undesirable outcomes.

Fats and Sugars

Butter carries the rich flavor of other ingredients and makes baked goods tender by coating the flour proteins and preventing them from forming gluten. Butter and shortening help create fine texture and volume in cakes and quick breads and make piecrust flaky. Don't substitute whipped margarine, spreads, or low-fat margarine for butter because they have added water, which can alter the texture.

Sugar, at the simplest level, imparts sweetness. Beyond that, it helps create a light, tender crumb (texture). Sugar inhibits the development of gluten to keep cakes and quick breads tender. It helps with browning, creating crunchy, golden crusts on cookies and pound cakes. When there is more than 2 tablespoons of sugar per cup of flour in a recipe, sugar acts as a tenderizer by preventing the flour proteins from joining together to create a tough structure. Different sugars add their own unique flavors and can affect the texture—powdered sugar dissolves easily, granulated sugar creates crunch, and brown sugar contributes moisture and caramel-like flavor. Honey has its own characteristics: it makes things brown faster and darker than sugar, it attracts and holds moisture so cakes and quick breads stay fresher longer, and it makes cookies chewy, not crunchy.

Equipment

If you do much baking, you'll need a mixer to help with mixing, whipping, creaming, and kneading. All mixers come with beaters, and some come with other attachments, such as dough hooks. The two basic types are stand and handheld mixers. The type you prefer is a matter of personal choice, but we use both when testing recipes.

Stand mixers are good for mixing large amounts of batter and heavy batters. KitchenAid and other heavy-duty mixers can handle thick doughs, such as cookie or bread doughs, without burning up the motor. The bowls are generally large so they can handle large amounts of batter or dough. They usually come with multiple attachments, including whisks for beating eggs whites or whipping cream, a paddle for creaming butter and sugar, and dough hooks for kneading bread.

Handheld mixers are fine for mixing most batters. They're small, easy to store, and offer great control, but they won't be able to handle a thick cookie batter or kneading bread dough. If you don't have a stand mixer, you'll be better off kneading bread dough by hand.

There are many tools that could be useful depending on the foods you're preparing: muffin tins, a waffle iron, a springform pan for cheesecakes, a Bundt pan for pound cake—the list goes on and on. You can find specific information about the equipment you'll need in the recipes on the following pages.

the bottom line

The three most important elements to remember about baking:

1. Preheat the oven or griddle.

2. Be sure to weigh or measure flour properly to ensure delicious results.

3. Use the ingredients, particularly flour, in the amounts specified in the ingredient list.

way to bake
cakes

From birthdays to weddings and occasions in between, cakes often define life's great moments. In many ways, the cake sets the tone of the event. Cupcakes are fun and whimsical, while pound cakes often appear at family and community events. A grand cake, moist and tender with creamy frosting, marks a truly special occasion.

kitchen how-to:
make cakes

Cakes belie the simple effort required to make them, and most can be made ahead. Follow these tips for sweet success.

1. An electric mixer incorporates the most air into cake batter. You'll also need a spoon, dry measuring cups (or kitchen scale), high-quality cake pans, a rubber spatula, wax paper, and a cooling rack.

2. Coat the pans with cooking spray, and dust them lightly with flour. For layer cakes, it's often a good idea to line the bottoms of the pans with wax paper as well.

3. Be sure to weigh or measure the flour carefully. If measuring, lightly spoon flour into dry measuring cups, and level it with a knife. If you have a kitchen scale, use it for more accurate measurements.

4. Whip the butter and sugar until fluffy and well blended to incorporate air into the mixture and improve the texture of the cake; continue beating until the eggs are thoroughly incorporated.

5. Add the flour and milk (or buttermilk) alternately to the cake batter. Always begin and end with the flour mixture so the ingredients will blend evenly and thoroughly.

6. Remove the wax paper as soon as you remove the cakes from the pans, and always cool cakes completely before frosting or freezing them.

Lemon-Lime Layer Cake

To create a nutritionally sound cake that's moist and tender with luscious frosting, we use a combination of full-fat (butter), reduced-fat (⅓-less-fat cream cheese), and fat-free (egg substitute) ingredients. Garnish the cake with thin slices of fresh lemon and lime, if you'd like.

Cake:
  Cooking spray
  1½ cups granulated sugar
  ½   cup butter, softened
  ¾   cup egg substitute
  1   tablespoon grated lemon rind
  1   tablespoon grated lime rind
  1   tablespoon fresh lime juice
  10 ounces all-purpose flour (about 2¼ cups)
  1½ teaspoons baking powder
  1   teaspoon baking soda
  ½   teaspoon salt
  1⅓ cups low-fat buttermilk

Icing:
  1   teaspoon grated lemon rind
  1   teaspoon grated lime rind
  1   teaspoon fresh lime juice
  1   (8-ounce) package ⅓-less-fat cream cheese, softened
  2½ cups powdered sugar, sifted (about 10 ounces)

1. Preheat oven to 350°.
2. To prepare cake, coat 2 (9-inch) round cake pans with cooking spray; line bottoms of pans with wax paper. Coat wax paper with cooking spray.

3. Place granulated sugar and butter in a large bowl; beat with a mixer at medium speed until well blended (about 5 minutes). Add egg substitute and the next 3 ingredients; beat well. Weigh or lightly spoon flour into dry measuring cups; level with a knife. Combine flour, baking powder, baking soda, and salt, stirring well with a whisk. Add flour mixture and buttermilk alternately to sugar mixture, beginning and ending with flour mixture. Spoon batter into prepared pans; tap pans once on countertop to remove air bubbles.
4. Bake at 350° for 30 minutes or until a wooden pick inserted in center comes out clean. Cool in pans on a wire rack 10 minutes; remove from pans. Carefully peel off wax paper. Cool completely on wire racks coated with cooking spray.
5. To prepare icing, place 1 teaspoon lemon rind and next 3 ingredients in a medium bowl; beat with a mixer at medium speed until smooth (about 1 minute). Gradually add powdered sugar, beating at low speed just until blended (do not overbeat). Cover and chill 30 minutes.
6. Place 1 cake layer on a plate, and spread with ½ cup icing. Top with remaining cake layer. Spread remaining icing over top and sides of cake. Chill 1 hour. Store cake loosely covered in refrigerator. **Yield: 16 servings (serving size: 1 slice).**

CALORIES 319; FAT 10g (sat 6.1g, mono 2.7g, poly 0.6g); PROTEIN 5.6g; CARB 52.8g; FIBER 0.6g; CHOL 28mg; IRON 1.2mg; SODIUM 334mg; CALC 78mg

kitchen how-to:
frost a cake

No matter if you're making a simple sheet cake or a showier layer cake, icing is easy when you follow these tips. For the best results, use an offset spatula, which allows for even spreading and keeps your hand away from the cake. Before frosting, cool the cakes on a wire rack. Brush away loose crumbs with a pastry brush, and then cover the cakes in plastic wrap and chill in the refrigerator for 2 hours.

1. Unwrap the cakes, and place one layer on a cakestand. Slip strips of wax paper under the edges of the cake to keep the stand clean. (Place the stand on a lazy Susan to make frosting easier.)
2. To frost between the layers, place the frosting in the center of the layer, and sweep outward with the spatula. Leave a ½-inch border around the edges.
3. Place the unfrosted layer bottom-side up on the frosted layer. Apply a thin layer of frosting (known as the crumb coat) to the entire cake to seal any loose crumbs. Allow the partially frosted cake to set in the refrigerator for about 15 minutes. This is especially helpful when a light-colored frosting is used on a dark cake.
4. To frost the top of the cake, place the frosting in the center of the cake, and spread it to the edge. Cover the top with an even layer of frosting.
5. For the sides, load the spatula with frosting, and lightly push it toward the cake as you turn the stand. Continue spreading the frosting until the cake is evenly coated; let the frosted cake set before decorating.

Texas Sheet Cake

Cooking spray
  2 teaspoons all-purpose flour
  9 ounces all-purpose flour (about 2 cups)
  2 cups granulated sugar
  1 teaspoon baking soda
  1 teaspoon ground cinnamon
  ¼ teaspoon salt
  ¾ cup water
  ½ cup butter
  ½ cup unsweetened cocoa, divided
  ½ cup low-fat buttermilk
  1 tablespoon vanilla extract, divided
  2 large eggs
  6 tablespoons butter
  ⅓ cup fat-free milk
  3 cups powdered sugar
  ¼ cup chopped pecans, toasted

1. Preheat oven to 375°.

2. Coat a 13 x 9–inch pan with cooking spray; dust with 2 teaspoons flour. Set aside.

3. Weigh or lightly spoon 2 cups flour into dry measuring cups; level with a knife. Combine 2 cups flour and next 4 ingredients in a large bowl, stirring well with a whisk. Combine ¾ cup water, ½ cup butter, and ¼ cup cocoa in a small saucepan; bring to a boil, stirring frequently. Add to flour mixture. Beat with a mixer at medium speed until well blended. Add buttermilk, 1 teaspoon vanilla, and eggs; beat well. Pour batter into prepared pan. Bake at 375° for 22 minutes or until a wooden pick inserted in center comes out clean. Place on a wire rack.

4. Combine 6 tablespoons butter, fat-free milk, and remaining ¼ cup cocoa in a saucepan; bring to a boil, stirring constantly. Remove from heat. Gradually stir in powdered sugar and remaining 2 teaspoons vanilla. Spread over hot cake. Sprinkle cake with pecans. Cool completely on wire rack. **Yield: 20 servings (serving size: 1 piece).**

CALORIES 298; FAT 10g (sat 5.5g, mono 3.2g, poly 0.7g); PROTEIN 3.1g; CARB 49.8g; FIBER 0.5g; CHOL 44mg; IRON 1.1mg; SODIUM 188mg; CALC 25mg

Chocolate Cupcakes with Peppermint Frosting

Cupcakes:
- 1 cup packed brown sugar
- 6 tablespoons butter, softened
- 2 large eggs
- 5½ ounces all-purpose flour (about 1¼ cups)
- ½ cup unsweetened cocoa
- 1 teaspoon baking powder
- ½ teaspoon baking soda
- ½ teaspoon salt
- ½ cup low-fat buttermilk
- 1 teaspoon vanilla extract

Peppermint Frosting:
- 2 cups powdered sugar
- ½ cup (4 ounces) tub-style light cream cheese
- ⅛ teaspoon peppermint extract
- 16 hard peppermint candies, finely crushed (about ⅓ cup)

1. Preheat oven to 350°.

2. To prepare cupcakes, place brown sugar and butter in a large bowl; beat with a mixer at medium speed 2 minutes or until well blended. Add eggs, 1 at a time, beating well after each addition. Weigh or lightly spoon flour into dry measuring cups; level with a knife. Combine flour, cocoa, baking powder, baking soda, and salt in a bowl, stirring well with a whisk. Add flour mixture to sugar mixture alternately with buttermilk, beginning and ending with flour mixture. Stir in vanilla extract.

3. Spoon batter into 18 muffin cups lined with paper liners. Bake at 350° for 12 minutes or until cupcakes spring back when touched lightly in the center. Cool in pan 10 minutes on a wire rack; remove from pan. Cool completely on wire rack.

4. To prepare frosting, combine powdered sugar, cream cheese, and peppermint extract in a bowl, stirring until smooth. Spread about 4 teaspoons frosting on each cupcake; sprinkle evenly with candies. **Yield: 18 cupcakes (serving size: 1 cupcake).**

CALORIES 214; FAT 6.2g (sat 3.7g, mono 1.3g, poly 0.3g); PROTEIN 3g; CARB 38.2g; FIBER 1g; CHOL 38mg; IRON 1.1mg; SODIUM 205mg; CALC 45mg

way to bake
pound cakes

Sour Cream Pound Cake

We've brightened the flavor of this pound cake with a couple tablespoons of fresh lemon juice. Dusting the pan with dry breadcrumbs makes it easier to remove the cake from the pan and also creates a more attractive crust.

Cooking spray
- 3 tablespoons dry breadcrumbs
- 16 ounces sifted cake flour (about 4 cups)
- ¼ teaspoon salt
- 1½ cups light sour cream
- 1 teaspoon baking soda
- ¾ cup butter
- 2¾ cups sugar
- 2 teaspoons vanilla extract
- 3 large eggs
- 2 tablespoons fresh lemon juice

1. Preheat oven to 350°.

2. Coat a 10-inch tube pan with cooking spray; dust with breadcrumbs.

3. Weigh or lightly spoon flour into dry measuring cups; level with a knife. Combine flour and salt; stir with a whisk. Combine sour cream and baking soda; stir well. Place butter in a large bowl; beat with a mixer at medium speed until light and fluffy. Gradually add sugar and vanilla, beating until well blended. Add eggs, 1 at a time, beating well after each addition. Add juice; beat 30 seconds. Add flour mixture alternately with sour cream mixture to sugar mixture, beating at low speed, beginning and ending with flour mixture.

4. Spoon batter into prepared pan. Bake at 350° for 1 hour and 10 minutes or until a wooden pick inserted in center comes out clean. Cool in pan 10 minutes on a wire rack; remove from pan. Cool completely on wire rack. **Yield: 18 servings (serving size: 1 slice).**

CALORIES 304; FAT 10g (sat 6.1g, mono 2.3g, poly 0.5g); PROTEIN 3.7g; CARB 51g; FIBER 0.4g; CHOL 62mg; IRON 1.8mg; SODIUM 196mg; CALC 12mg

make sour cream pound cake

Using butter and eggs instead of egg whites helps give this cake a rich texture.

1. After combining the flour, salt, sour cream, and baking soda, place the butter in a large bowl; beat with a mixer at medium speed until light and fluffy.
2. Gradually add the sugar and vanilla, beating until well blended.
3. Add the eggs, 1 at a time, beating well after each addition.
4. Add the juice. Then add the flour mixture alternately with the sour cream mixture to the sugar mixture, beating at low speed, beginning and ending with the flour mixture. Spoon the batter into the prepared pan, and bake.

way to bake
angel food cakes

Classic Angel Food Cake

4 ounces sifted cake flour (about 1 cup)
1½ cups sugar, divided
12 large egg whites
1 teaspoon cream of tartar
¼ teaspoon salt
1½ teaspoons vanilla extract
1½ teaspoons fresh lemon juice
½ teaspoon almond extract

1. Preheat oven to 325°.
2. Weigh or lightly spoon flour into a dry measuring cup; level with a knife. Combine flour and ¾ cup sugar, stirring with a whisk.
3. Place egg whites in a large bowl; beat with a mixer at high speed until foamy. Add cream of tartar and salt; beat until soft peaks form. Add remaining ¾ cup sugar, 2 tablespoons at a time, beating until stiff peaks form. Beat in vanilla, juice, and almond extract.
4. Sift ¼ cup flour mixture over beaten egg white mixture; fold in. Repeat with remaining flour mixture, ¼ cup at a time.
5. Spoon batter into an ungreased 10-inch tube pan, spreading evenly. Break air pockets by cutting through batter with a knife. Bake at 325° for 55 minutes or until cake springs back when lightly touched. Invert pan; cool completely. Loosen cake from sides of pan using a narrow metal spatula. Invert cake onto a plate. **Yield: 12 servings (serving size: 1 slice).**

CALORIES 146; FAT 0.1g (sat 0g, mono 0g, poly 0.1g); PROTEIN 4.2g; CARB 31.8g; FIBER 0.1g; CHOL 0mg; IRON 0.6mg; SODIUM 104mg; CALC 4mg

endless variations

Angel food cake can be modified with just about any flavoring. Here are some ideas to use with Classic Angel Food Cake.

Chocolate: Add ¼ cup sifted unsweetened cocoa to the flour mixture.
Chocolate-glazed: Whisk together 3 tablespoons unsweetened cocoa, 1 cup powdered sugar, ½ teaspoon vanilla extract, and about 3 tablespoons water or cold coffee. Drizzle over the cooled cake.
Citrus-glazed: Whisk together 2 tablespoons lemon, lime, or orange juice and 1 cup powdered sugar until smooth. Drizzle over the cooled cake.
Ice cream: Cut the cake horizontally into 3 layers, and then spread each layer with 1 cup of softened ice cream or sorbet. Reassemble the cake, and then freeze it until ready to serve.
Nutty: Fold ½ cup finely chopped toasted nuts—such as almonds, walnuts, or hazelnuts—into the batter with the flour.
Orange: Fold 2 tablespoons grated orange peel and 1 teaspoon orange extract into the batter.

kitchen how-to: make angel food cake

Follow our how-to tips to whip up angel food cake that's perfect—or as close as mere mortals can come to perfect—every time.

1. Separate the eggs while they're still cold—the yolks and whites will be more firm and separate more easily. Don't allow any pieces of yolk to mix with the whites or the whites won't beat to maximum volume.

2. Place the egg whites in a large bowl; beat with a mixer at high speed until foamy. Make sure the beaters are clean and dry. Add cream of tartar and salt; beat until soft peaks form. The whites will look shiny, moist, and snowy, and the peaks will hold high when you lift the beaters. Don't overbeat the whites—lightly underbeaten egg whites will work, but overbeaten whites make a tough cake.

3. Sprinkle the flour over the beaten eggs whites ¼ cup at a time. Then, with a large spatula, use large sweeping motions to fold the flour into the whites. The goal is to incorporate the dry ingredients without deflating the whites.

4. Spoon the batter into an ungreased tube pan, spreading evenly. Run a knife through the batter to break any air pockets that may have formed when the batter was spooned into the pan. Place the cake in the center of the oven for even baking. Don't open the oven door until the baking time is up (or very nearly so); the fragile egg whites can begin to deflate as cool air rushes into the oven.

5. Cool the cake upside down so it doesn't deflate while it's still warm. If your pan doesn't have "feet," invert it by placing the center hole on the neck of a wine bottle.

6. To remove the cooled cake from the pan, run a narrow metal spatula or thin knife around the edges, including the center tube. If your pan has a removable bottom, push it up to dislodge the cake, and then use the same spatula method to loosen the edges.

way to bake
jelly-roll cakes

Jelly-roll cakes are thin, flat cakes that have been filled with jams, jellies, frosting, whipped cream, or any filling you prefer, and rolled into a log. While they may look complicated, they're really not. They're a relatively quick and easy dessert that offers myriad opportunities for experimentation.

kitchen how-to: roll a jelly-roll cake

To make a jelly-roll, spread jams, jellies, frosting, or whipped cream onto a thin, flat cake, and roll it into a log; use a small, rectangular dish towel when rolling to remove moisture and prevent the cake from sticking. To make the cake, you'll need a jelly-roll pan, which is a shallow rectangular pan with 1-inch-deep sides, and a dish towel. First, spray the pan with cooking spray, line it with a sheet of wax paper, and then coat the wax paper with cooking spray. Spraying both the pan and wax paper will prevent the cake from sticking. Next, pour the batter, and bake.

1. While the cake is baking, lay a dry dish towel slightly larger than the pan on a flat surface; dust the towel with a thin layer of powdered sugar to prevent the cake from sticking.
2. Remove the cake from the oven, and turn the pan over onto the towel, releasing the cake and wax paper. Slowly peel the wax paper from the cake; it's OK if a thin layer of cake remains on the paper.
3. Roll the towel and the cake together, pressing gently. Be sure to move slowly and carefully throughout the entire rolling process. The towel will end up coiled inside the cake.
4. Cool the cake on a wire rack, seam side down. After an hour, unroll and remove towel. The cake will be slightly wavy. Carefully spread the filling as directed, and reroll the cake.

Almond Jelly-Roll with Raspberry Filling

Almond paste makes the cake a bit sticky, so be sure to coat the wax paper in the pan with cooking spray and dust it with flour before spooning in the batter. Combining the almond paste and sugar in a blender or food processor helps incorporate the paste into the batter without lumps. This cake can be made a day in advance; just wrap it in plastic wrap, and store it in the fridge.

Cake:
- ¾ cup granulated sugar
- ¼ cup almond paste
- Cooking spray
- 3 ounces all-purpose flour (about ⅔ cup plus 2 teaspoons), divided
- 1 teaspoon baking powder
- ⅛ teaspoon salt
- 4 large eggs
- 1 teaspoon vanilla extract
- ¼ cup powdered sugar, divided

Remaining Ingredients:
- ⅔ cup seedless raspberry jam
- ½ cup whipping cream
- ¼ cup powdered sugar
- Fresh raspberries (optional)

1. Preheat oven to 350°.
2. To prepare cake, place granulated sugar and almond paste in a blender or food processor; process until well blended. Set aside.
3. Coat a 15 x 10–inch jelly-roll pan with cooking spray. Line bottom of pan with wax paper. Coat paper well with cooking spray. Dust with 2 teaspoons flour; set aside.
4. Weigh or lightly spoon remaining ⅔ cup flour into dry measuring cups; level with a knife. Combine flour, baking powder, and salt in a medium bowl, stirring with a whisk.
5. Place eggs in a large bowl; beat with a mixer at high speed until pale and fluffy (about 4 minutes). Gradually add granulated sugar mixture and vanilla, beating at medium speed until smooth (about 3 minutes). Sift half of flour mixture over egg mixture; fold in. Repeat procedure with remaining flour mixture. Spread batter evenly into prepared pan. Bake at 350° for 10 minutes or until cake springs back when touched lightly in center. Loosen cake from sides of pan, and turn out onto a dish towel dusted with 2 tablespoons powdered sugar; carefully peel off wax paper. Sprinkle cake with 2 tablespoons powdered sugar; cool 1 minute. Starting at narrow end, roll up cake and towel together. Place, seam side down, on a wire rack; cool completely (about 1 hour).
6. Unroll cake carefully; remove towel. Spread jam over cake, leaving a ½-inch margin around the outside edges. Reroll cake; place, seam side down, on a platter.
7. Place cream and ¼ cup powdered sugar in a medium bowl; beat with a mixer at high speed until stiff peaks form. Cut cake into 8 slices with a serrated knife. Top each slice with whipped cream and raspberries, if desired. **Yield: 8 servings (servings size: 1 slice cake and 1 tablespoon whipped cream).**

CALORIES 321; FAT 10.1g (sat 4.4g, mono 3.8g, poly 1g); PROTEIN 5.2g; CARB 53.9g; FIBER 0.6g; CHOL 126mg; IRON 1.1mg; SODIUM 139mg; CALC 71mg

way to bake
cheesecakes

All cheesecakes obviously start with cheese—usually cream cheese—and most have some type of crumb crust. Beyond that, the options for flavors, toppings, and sauces are endless.

Cheesecake with Fresh Strawberry Sauce

If you make this cake in a 9-inch springform pan, cut the baking time by about 15 minutes. The center of the cake may appear looser than you expect, but it will become firmer as the cake chills overnight.

Cheesecake:
- ½ cup sugar
- 20 reduced-calorie vanilla wafers
- ⅛ teaspoon salt, divided
- 3 large egg whites, divided
- Cooking spray
- 1½ cups sugar
- 3 tablespoons cornstarch
- 2 (8-ounce) blocks ⅓-less-fat cream cheese, softened
- ½ cup (4 ounces) block-style fat-free cream cheese, softened
- 1 teaspoon vanilla extract
- 1 teaspoon fresh lemon juice
- 4 large eggs
- Strawberries (optional)

Sauce:
- 4 cups sliced strawberries (about 1½ pounds)
- ½ cup water
- 2 tablespoons sugar
- 1 tablespoon water
- 2 teaspoons cornstarch
- 2 teaspoons fresh lemon juice

1. Preheat oven to 350°.
2. To prepare cheesecake, place ½ cup sugar, wafers, and dash salt in a food processor; process until mixture resembles sand. Place 1 egg white in a small bowl; stir with a whisk until frothy.
With the processor on, add 2 tablespoons egg white through food chute, processing until blended (discard remaining egg white). Press mixture into bottom and slightly up sides of an 8-inch springform pan coated with cooking spray. Bake at 350° for 10 minutes; cool completely on a wire rack.
3. Reduce oven to 300°.
4. Combine 1½ cups sugar, 3 tablespoons cornstarch, and remaining dash salt in a large bowl. Add cheeses; beat with a mixer at medium-high speed until smooth. Reduce mixer speed to low. Add vanilla and 1 teaspoon juice; beat just until combined. Add eggs, 1 at a time, beating after each addition just until incorporated. Add remaining 2 egg whites; beat just until incorporated.
5. Pour cheese mixture into prepared pan. Bake at 300° for 1 hour and 15 minutes or until a 3-inch circle in the center of the cheesecake barely jiggles when the side of the pan is tapped. Turn oven off. Leave cheesecake in oven with the door open for 30 minutes. Remove cheesecake from oven; run a knife around outside edge. Cool to room temperature on a wire rack. Cover and chill at least 8 hours. Garnish cake with strawberries, if desired.
6. To prepare sauce, combine sliced strawberries, ½ cup water, and 2 tablespoons sugar in a small saucepan over medium-high heat; bring to a boil. Reduce heat, and simmer 5 minutes. Remove from heat. Strain mixture through a sieve into a bowl, pressing lightly with a spatula; discard solids. Return mixture to pan. Combine 1 tablespoon water and 2 teaspoons cornstarch in a small bowl, stirring with a whisk. Add cornstarch mixture to pan. Bring to a boil; cook 1 minute, stirring constantly. Transfer mixture to a bowl; cool to room temperature. Stir in 2 teaspoons juice. **Yield: 16 servings (serving size: 1 slice cheesecake and about 2 tablespoons sauce).**

CALORIES 245; FAT 8.4g (sat 4.7g, mono 2.4g, poly 0.4g); PROTEIN 6.6g; CARB 36.8g; FIBER 0.9g; CHOL 75mg; IRON 0.6mg; SODIUM 216mg; CALC 49mg

all about springform pans

A springform pan—a round, deep pan with tall removable sides—is usually used for baking cheesecakes. If possible, use a pan with an extended edge around the base to keep the batter from leaking, or wrap the outside of the pan with aluminum foil.

way to bake
cookies

When making lower-fat cookies, there is a narrower margin for error. These cookies also may need to be handled differently than traditional cookies to achieve the same delicious results.

Equipment

Bake cookies on heavy, shiny metal baking sheets (flat pans that may have a lip on one or both ends); cookies baked on nonstick sheets tend to brown too much on the bottom. We don't advise baking on rimmed jelly-roll pans because the rims can deflect heat. Lining the pans with parchment paper prevents sticking, and you can reuse the paper for each batch. Cooling racks allow air to circulate under the cookies as they cool so they won't become soggy.

Dough preparation

As with all baked goods, measure the ingredients with precision, and use the exact ingredients specified. Many of the recipes first cream together the butter and sugar and then add the dry ingredients. For these recipes, start with softened butter—butter that yields slightly to pressure but doesn't lose its shape when touched. It's important not to overmix the dough once the dry ingredients are added because it can result in tough cookies or ones that don't rise well; mix just until the ingredients are combined.

Baking

Be sure the oven is preheated; you might want to use an oven thermometer for accuracy. Always place the dough on cool baking sheets because warm or hot pans will cause the cookies to spread or puff too much. You can quickly cool a baking sheet by placing it under cold running water, and dry it thoroughly before arranging the dough on the pan. In general, bake cookies on the second rack from the bottom. If you bake two pans at once, rotate them halfway through the cooking time.

Chocolate Chip Cookies

You can store these cookies for up to one week in an airtight container—if they last that long. We suggest keeping a dozen in the freezer for emergencies.

10 ounces all-purpose flour (about 2¼ cups)
 1 teaspoon baking soda
 ¼ teaspoon salt
 1 cup packed brown sugar
 ¾ cup granulated sugar
 ½ cup butter, softened
 1 teaspoon vanilla extract
 2 large egg whites
 ¾ cup semisweet chocolate chips
 Cooking spray

1. Preheat oven to 350°.
2. Weigh or lightly spoon flour into dry measuring cups; level with a knife. Combine flour, baking soda, and salt, stirring with a whisk.
3. Combine sugars and butter in a large bowl; beat with a mixer at medium speed until well blended. Add vanilla and egg whites; beat 1 minute. Add flour mixture and chips; beat until blended.
4. Drop dough by level tablespoons 2 inches apart onto baking sheets coated with cooking spray. Bake at 350° for 10 minutes or until lightly browned. Cool on pans 2 minutes. Remove from pans; cool completely on wire racks. **Yield: 4 dozen (serving size: 1 cookie).**

CALORIES 88; FAT 3g (sat 1.8g, mono 0.5g, poly 0.1g); PROTEIN 1g; CARB 14.6g; FIBER 0.2g; CHOL 5mg; IRON 0.4mg; SODIUM 56mg; CALC 5mg

kitchen how-to:
make drop cookies

Drop cookies are some of the simplest to make—just spoon mounds of soft dough onto baking sheets. Ensure even baking by dropping the same amount of dough for each cookie. Use a measuring spoon to scoop the dough, and then push it onto the baking sheet with your finger or another spoon. Or you can use a cookie scoop, which looks like a small ice-cream scoop; they come in a variety of sizes and are available at kitchenware stores. Coat whatever you use to scoop the dough with cooking spray first for easy release.

Classic Iced Sugar Cookies

If you want to create colorful cookies, divide the icing into portions, and use food coloring to tint it different hues. For icing that's suited for piping, decrease the milk to 2 tablespoons.

Cookies:

11.3 ounces all-purpose flour
    (about 2½ cups)
 ½ teaspoon baking powder
 ¼ teaspoon salt
 1 cup granulated sugar
 10 tablespoons butter, softened
 1½ teaspoons vanilla extract
 2 large egg whites

Icing:

 2 cups powdered sugar
 ¼ cup 2% reduced-fat milk
 ½ teaspoon vanilla extract

1. To prepare cookies, weigh or lightly spoon flour into dry measuring cups; level with a knife. Combine flour, baking powder, and salt, stirring well with a whisk. Place granulated sugar and butter in a large bowl; beat with a mixer at medium speed until light and fluffy. Beat in 1½ teaspoons vanilla and egg whites. Gradually add flour mixture to butter mixture, beating at low speed just until combined. Divide dough in half. Shape each dough half into a ball; wrap each dough half in plastic wrap. Chill 1 hour.
2. Unwrap 1 dough ball. Press dough into a 4-inch circle on heavy-duty plastic wrap. Cover with additional plastic wrap. Roll dough, still covered, to a ¼-inch thickness. Repeat procedure with remaining dough ball. Chill dough 30 minutes.
3. Preheat oven to 375°.
4. Remove one dough portion from refrigerator. Remove top sheet of plastic wrap; turn dough over. Remove remaining plastic wrap. Using a 2½-inch cutter, cut dough into 18 cookies. Place cookies 2 inches apart on baking sheets lined with parchment paper. Bake at 375° for 10 minutes or until lightly browned. Cool on pans 5 minutes. Remove cookies from pans, and cool completely on wire racks. Repeat procedure with remaining dough half.
5. To prepare icing, combine powdered sugar and remaining ingredients, stirring with a whisk until smooth. Working with 1 cookie at a time, spread about 1 teaspoon icing evenly over cookie. Let stand on a wire rack until set. **Yield: 3 dozen (serving size: 1 cookie).**

CALORIES 109; FAT 3.3g (sat 2g, mono 0.8g, poly 0.2g); PROTEIN 1.2g; CARB 19g; FIBER 0.2g; CHOL 8mg; IRON 0.4mg; SODIUM 50mg; CALC 8mg

kitchen how-to:
make rolled cookies

You make these cookies by rolling out a stiff dough into a thin layer; then you cut the dough with cookie cutters or slice it into shapes. Chill the dough thoroughly before cutting it so it holds its shape. If the dough becomes soft after rolling, place it in the refrigerator for 10 to 15 minutes or in the freezer for 5 minutes until it firms. Roll the dough between sheets of heavy-duty plastic wrap to prevent sticking or tearing. When rolling the dough, place the rolling pin in the center of the dough and roll outward using gentle strokes. After cutting the dough, gather the scraps, knead gently, and reroll. Cut out one more batch of shapes; don't reroll the scraps again because the dough will be overworked at this point, resulting in cookies that are tough.

Hello Dolly Bars

These bar cookies are also known as seven-layer bars. They can create a sticky mess in the pan, so it's crucial to line it with parchment paper. Don't pack the crumbs too tightly in the bottom of the pan because the milk needs to seep into the graham cracker crumbs.

1½ cups graham cracker crumbs (about
      9 cookie sheets)
  2 tablespoons butter, melted
  1 tablespoon water
  ⅓ cup semisweet chocolate chips
  ⅓ cup butterscotch morsels
  ⅔ cup flaked sweetened coconut
  ¼ cup chopped pecans, toasted
  1 (15-ounce) can fat-free sweetened
      condensed milk

1. Preheat oven to 350°.
2. Line the bottom and sides of a 9-inch square baking pan with parchment paper; cut off excess parchment paper around top edge of pan.
3. Place crumbs in a medium bowl. Drizzle with butter and 1 tablespoon water; toss with a fork until moist. Gently pat mixture into an even layer in pan (do not press firmly). Sprinkle chips and morsels over crumb mixture. Top evenly with coconut and pecans. Drizzle milk evenly over top. Bake at 350° for 25 minutes or until lightly browned and bubbly around edges. Cool completely in pan on a wire rack. **Yield: 24 servings (serving size: 1 bar).**

CALORIES 123; FAT 4.4g (sat 2.3g, mono 1.3g, poly 0.6g); PROTEIN 2.1g; CARB 19.1g; FIBER 0.5g; CHOL 5mg; IRON 0.3mg; SODIUM 64mg; CALC 50mg

kitchen how-to:
make bar cookies

Bake bar cookies in shiny metal pans, not glass baking dishes; glass conducts heat differently and can cook the cookies too quickly. These moist cookies are typically made by spreading the batter into a pan with sides, and cutting it into pieces after the batch is cooked. For easier removal of the cookies, line the entire pan (bottom and sides) with parchment paper. Cool the cookies completely in the pan they bake in before cutting them into portions.

Pine Nut Biscotti

13.5 ounces all-purpose flour (about 3 cups)
  1 cup sugar
  1 teaspoon baking powder
  ½ teaspoon salt
  ½ teaspoon baking soda
  ½ cup pine nuts, toasted
  ¼ cup plus 2 tablespoons water
  1 teaspoon grated lemon rind
  1 teaspoon vanilla extract
  3 large eggs

1. Preheat oven to 325°.

2. Weigh or lightly spoon flour into dry measuring cups; level with a knife. Combine flour and next 4 ingredients in a large bowl, stirring with a whisk. Stir in pine nuts. Combine ¼ cup plus 2 tablespoons water, rind, vanilla, and eggs, stirring with a whisk. Add egg mixture to flour mixture, stirring until well blended (dough will be dry and crumbly). Knead dough lightly in bowl 7 or 8 times or until a dough forms (dough will be sticky). Divide dough in half. Shape each portion into an 8-inch-long roll. Place rolls 6 inches apart on a baking sheet lined with parchment paper; flatten each roll to 1-inch thickness.

3. Bake at 325° for 30 minutes. Remove rolls from baking sheet (do not turn oven off); cool 10 minutes on a wire rack.

4. Cut each roll diagonally into 15 (½-inch-thick) slices using a serrated knife. Place slices, cut sides down, on baking sheet. Bake at 325° for 15 minutes. Turn cookies over, and bake an additional 10 minutes (cookies will be slightly soft in center but will harden as they cool). Remove from baking sheet; cool completely on wire racks. **Yield: 2½ dozen (serving size: 1 biscotto).**

CALORIES 94; FAT 2.2g (sat 0.3g, mono 0.6g, poly 0.9g); PROTEIN 2.2g; CARB 16.6g; FIBER 0.4g; CHOL 21mg; IRON 0.8mg; SODIUM 84mg; CALC 14mg

kitchen how-to:
make twice-baked cookies

Hard and crunchy twice-baked cookies are perfect for dipping into coffee or hot chocolate. Biscotti are the most common type, but mandel-brot, which means "almond bread" in German, is another kind. Once the ingredients are combined, the dough will be crumbly. Knead it in the bowl so all the flour is incorporated. The finished dough will be slightly sticky, so you may want to coat your hands with cooking spray before you shape it on the baking sheet. Leave plenty of space between the dough rolls so they don't spread and bake together. After the first cook time, the rolls will be slightly crunchy; use a serrated knife to slice them without crumbling.

way to bake
piecrust

A great pie starts with a great piecrust. Commercial piecrusts are a convenient and easy option, but when you want to make an extra-special pie, make a homemade piecrust—your tastebuds will notice the difference.

Baked Piecrust

This recipe makes a 9- or 10-inch crust that you can use for any recipe that calls for refrigerated pie dough.

6.75 ounces all-purpose flour
    (about 1½ cups)
  2 tablespoons sugar
  ¼ teaspoon salt
  3 tablespoons butter
  2 tablespoons vegetable
    shortening
  4 tablespoons ice water
Cooking spray

1. Preheat oven to 400°.
2. Weigh or lightly spoon flour into dry measuring cups; level with a knife. Combine flour, sugar, and salt in a bowl; cut in butter and vegetable shortening with a pastry blender or 2 knives until mixture resembles coarse meal. Sprinkle surface with ice water, 1 tablespoon at a time; toss with a fork until moist and crumbly (do not form a ball).
3. Press dough gently into a 4-inch circle on plastic wrap; cover. Chill 15 minutes. Slightly overlap 2 sheets of plastic wrap on a slightly damp surface. Unwrap and place chilled dough on plastic wrap. Cover dough with 2 additional sheets of overlapping plastic wrap. Roll dough, still covered, into a 13-inch circle. Place dough in freezer 5 minutes or until plastic wrap can be easily removed.
4. Remove top sheets of plastic wrap; fit dough, plastic wrap side up, into a 9- or 10-inch pie plate coated with cooking spray. Remove remaining plastic wrap. Fold edges under; flute. Pierce bottom and sides of dough with a fork; bake at 400° for 15 minutes. Cool on a wire rack.
Yield: 1 piecrust (serving size: ⅒ of crust).

CALORIES 113; FAT 6g (sat 2.7g, mono 2.1g, poly 0.8g); PROTEIN 1.8g; CARB 13g; FIBER 0.5g; CHOL 9mg; IRON 0.8mg; SODIUM 65mg; CALC 1mg

kitchen how-to:
make a piecrust

Follow these steps to make a tasty piecrust that's the perfect base for any pie.

1. Combine the flour and salt in a bowl; cut in the butter and shortening with a pastry blender or 2 knives until the mixture resembles coarse meal. Sprinkle with water, 1 tablespoon at a time; toss with a fork.

2. Press flour mixture gently into a 4-inch circle on plastic wrap; cover with additional plastic wrap. Chill 15 minutes.

3. Roll the dough, still covered, into a 13-inch circle; place the dough in the freezer 5 minutes or until the plastic wrap can be easily removed.

4. Remove the top sheet of the plastic wrap; fit the dough, plastic wrap side up, into a pie plate coated with cooking spray. Remove the plastic wrap.

5. Press the dough against the bottom and up the sides of the pie plate. Fold the edges under and flute.

6. Some recipes call for prebaking the crust using pie weights. Line the bottom of the dough with foil; arrange pie weights on the foil. Bake as directed. Remove the pie weights and foil; cool on a wire rack.

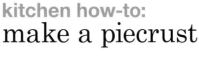

way to bake
fruit pies

Fruit pies are a delicious way to enjoy the best the season has to offer. Making these pies is a straightforward process, but there are a few tips to follow so that your pies come out looking and tasting perfect.

Fresh Cherry Pie

2 tablespoons uncooked quick-cooking tapioca
6 cups pitted sweet cherries
¾ cup granulated sugar
¼ cup cornstarch
1 tablespoon fresh lemon juice
¼ teaspoon almond extract
⅛ teaspoon salt
1 (15-ounce) package refrigerated pie dough (such as Pillsbury)
Cooking spray
2 tablespoons water
1 large egg white
2 tablespoons turbinado sugar

1. Place tapioca in a spice or coffee grinder; process until finely ground. Combine tapioca, cherries, and next 5 ingredients in a large bowl; toss well. Let cherry mixture stand 30 minutes; stir to combine.

2. Preheat oven to 400°.

3. Roll 1 (9-inch) dough portion into an 11-inch circle. Fit dough into a 9-inch pie plate coated with cooking spray, allowing dough to extend over edge of plate. Spoon cherry mixture and any remaining liquid onto dough. Roll remaining (9-inch) dough portion into a 12-inch circle. Cut dough into 12 (1-inch-wide) strips; arrange in a lattice pattern over cherry mixture. Fold edges under; crimp.

4. Combine 2 tablespoons water and egg white in a bowl. Brush egg white mixture over dough; sprinkle dough evenly with 2 tablespoons turbinado sugar. Bake at 400° for 20 minutes. Shield edges of piecrust with foil; bake an additional 40 minutes or until crust is golden brown and filling is thick and bubbly. Cool in pan 45 minutes on a wire rack. **Yield: 12 servings (serving size: 1 wedge).**

CALORIES 282; FAT 9.9g (sat 4.1g, mono 4.3g, poly 1.2g); PROTEIN 2.5g; CARB 47.3g; FIBER 1.7g; CHOL 7mg; IRON 0.3mg; SODIUM 161mg; CALC 11mg

kitchen how-to: make a decorative piecrust

There's more than one way to prepare a piecrust. Here, we flute the edge before adding the filling, and then we lay the lattice on top, pressing it gently into the side. The recipe for Fresh Cherry Pie (page 442) suggests latticing the top and then crimping. After testing each technique, we're happy to say both work, and the results will delight your eyes as much as your palate. You'll need enough dough (homemade or refrigerated pie dough) for two crusts: one for the pie plate and the other one to create the lattice.

1. Press one piecrust into the pie plate, making sure there are no air bubbles; then tuck the extra dough under the edges.

2. Pinch the dough with your thumb and index finger of one hand, while pressing inward with the thumb of your other hand.

3. Return to the reserved piecrust, and use a pastry cutter to cut 10, ½-inch-wide strips to cover the top of the pie.

4. Pour the filling into the pie. Working from the center outward, lay one strip horizontally and then one vertically.

5. Continue alternating strips, leaving about ½ inch between each as you weave them over and under.

6. Be sure each strip is long enough to reach the edge of the pie, and then push them into the side to seal them in place.

way to bake
cream pies

We love cream pies for the same reasons you do: they're simple to make, and they taste good. These delicious pies are filled with a rich custard or pudding that should hold its shape when sliced, and they're generally topped with a meringue or a whipped cream topping.

Coconut Cream Pie

This pie takes a brief turn under the broiler to brown the peaks of the Italian meringue.

Crust:
- 1 (10-inch) Baked Piecrust (page 440) or ½ (15-ounce) package refrigerated pie dough (such as Pillsbury)

Filling:
- 1.12 ounces all-purpose flour (about ¼ cup)
- ½ cup sugar
- ⅛ teaspoon salt
- 2 large eggs
- ¾ cup 2% reduced-fat milk
- ¾ cup light coconut milk
- ¼ teaspoon coconut extract
- ¼ teaspoon vanilla extract

Meringue:
- 3 large egg whites
- ⅔ cup sugar
- ¼ cup water
- 1 tablespoon flaked sweetened coconut, toasted

1. Prepare and bake crust in a 10-inch deep-dish pie plate. Cool completely on a wire rack.

2. To prepare filling, weigh or lightly spoon flour into a dry measuring cup; level with a knife. Combine flour, ½ cup sugar, salt, and eggs in a large bowl; stir well with a whisk.

3. Heat milk and coconut milk over medium-high heat in a small, heavy saucepan to 180° or until tiny bubbles form around edge (do not boil). Gradually add hot milk mixture to sugar mixture, stirring constantly with a whisk. Place mixture in pan; cook over medium heat until thick and bubbly (about 10 minutes), stirring constantly.

4. Remove from heat. Spoon custard into a bowl; place bowl in a large ice-filled bowl 10 minutes or until custard comes to room temperature, stirring occasionally. Remove bowl from ice. Stir in extracts; spoon mixture into prepared crust. Cover; chill 8 hours or until firm.

5. Preheat broiler.

6. To prepare meringue, place egg whites in a large bowl; beat with a mixer at high speed until soft peaks form. Combine ⅔ cup sugar and water in a saucepan; bring to a boil. Cook, without stirring, until candy thermometer registers 238°. Pour hot sugar syrup in a thin stream over egg whites, beating at high speed until stiff peaks form.

7. Spread meringue over chilled pie, and sprinkle with coconut. Broil 1 minute or until meringue is lightly browned; cool 5 minutes on a wire rack. Serve immediately. **Yield: 10 servings (serving size: 1 wedge).**

CALORIES 281; FAT 9.3g (sat 5.6g, mono 2.6g, poly 0.4g); PROTEIN 5.3g; CARB 45.6g; FIBER 0.6g; CHOL 63mg; IRON 1.4mg; SODIUM 208mg; CALC 28mg

kitchen how-to: make an Italian meringue

For food safety reasons, we use Italian meringue rather than the traditional (uncooked) variation. Italian meringues are made by whipping egg whites with cooked sugar, which heats the whites to 238° and makes them safe to eat. Meringues are delicate and will disintegrate over time, so add them just before serving. When beaten, egg whites increase in volume by six to eight times. To get the fluffiest whites, it's important to carefully separate the eggs; if any yolk gets into the whites, they will not beat to their maximum volume.

1. Beat the egg whites until soft peaks form.

2. Overbeating—incorporating too much air—will cause them to separate.

3. Combine sugar and water in a saucepan. Bring to a boil. Using a candy thermometer, cook until 238°. Do not stir. Slowly pour sugar syrup into egg whites, beating with a mixer at high speed until syrup is thoroughly incorporated. The meringue should look smooth and glossy.

tarts

A tart has a single layer of pastry as its base with a sweet or savory filling, such as fruit, jams, custards, flavored creams, or nuts. Tarts are baked in either a shallow tart pan that has straight, fluted sides and a removable bottom or a metal tart ring placed on a baking sheet.

Bourbon-Pecan Tart with Chocolate Drizzle

Make the tart a day ahead, and store it in the refrigerator. Instead of a tart pan, you can use a 9-inch pie plate: simply roll the dough into a 13-inch circle, fold the edges under, and flute.

    1   cup packed light brown sugar
    ¾   cup dark corn syrup
    3   tablespoons all-purpose flour
    2   tablespoons bourbon
    2   tablespoons molasses
    1   tablespoon butter, melted
    ½   teaspoon vanilla extract
    ¼   teaspoon salt
    2   large eggs
    1   large egg white
    ⅔   cup pecan halves
    ½   (15-ounce) package refrigerated pie dough
        (such as Pillsbury)
        Cooking spray
    ½   ounce bittersweet chocolate, chopped

1. Preheat oven to 350°.
2. Combine first 10 ingredients, stirring well with a whisk. Stir in pecans. Roll dough into a 13-inch circle; fit into a 9-inch removable-bottom tart pan coated with cooking spray. Trim excess crust using a sharp knife. Spoon sugar mixture into prepared crust. Bake at 350° for 45 minutes or until center is set. Cool completely on a wire rack.

3. Place chocolate in a microwave-safe bowl; microwave at HIGH 1 minute. Stir until smooth. Drizzle chocolate over tart. **Yield: 12 servings (serving size: 1 wedge).**

CALORIES 277; FAT 10g (sat 2.7g, mono 3g, poly 1.5g); PROTEIN 2.4g; CARB 45.2g; FIBER 0.7g; CHOL 39mg; IRON 0.9mg; SODIUM 156mg; CALC 32mg

kitchen how-to:
pack brown sugar

Unlike granulated sugar, which flows freely, brown sugar isn't as refined and contains more moisture. It must be packed into the measuring cup to get an accurate measurement. To pack brown sugar, spoon it into a dry measuring cup that is the size the recipe specifies. Press the sugar into the measuring cup with the back of a spoon. Continue to add and pack more sugar until it reaches the rim of the measuring cup. Level with the flat side of a knife, scraping off any excess.

way to bake
cobblers & crisps

These simple desserts have the sumptuous appeal of baked fruit pies without the work of making a pastry crust. Cobblers have a thick crust, usually made of biscuit dough. Crisps, which are also called crumbles, might even be better than pies; their toppings have a crunchier texture that juxtaposes the soft fruit filling.

Peach-Blueberry Cobbler

Filling:
- ½ cup granulated sugar
- 2 tablespoons all-purpose flour
- ½ teaspoon grated lemon rind
- ¼ teaspoon salt
- 3 cups chopped peeled peaches (about 2 pounds)
- 2 cups fresh blueberries
- 1 tablespoon fresh lemon juice
- Cooking spray

Topping:
- 6 ounces all-purpose flour (about 1⅓ cups)
- ⅓ cup granulated sugar
- ½ teaspoon baking powder
- ¼ teaspoon salt
- 3 tablespoons chilled butter, cut into small pieces
- ⅔ cup low-fat buttermilk
- 1½ tablespoons turbinado sugar

1. Preheat oven to 400°.
2. To prepare filling, combine first 4 ingredients in a large bowl. Add peaches, blueberries, and juice. Spoon mixture into an 8-inch square baking dish coated with cooking spray. Bake at 400° for 15 minutes.
3. To prepare topping, weigh or lightly spoon 1⅓ cups flour into dry measuring cups; level with a knife. Combine 1⅓ cups flour, ⅓ cup granulated sugar, baking powder, and ¼ teaspoon salt, stirring with a whisk. Cut in butter with a pastry blender or 2 knives until mixture resembles coarse meal. Add buttermilk; stir just until moist.
4. Remove dish from oven; drop dough onto peach mixture to form 8 rounds. Sprinkle dough evenly with turbinado sugar. Bake at 400° for 25 minutes or until bubbly and golden. **Yield: 8 servings (serving size: ½ cup cobbler and 1 biscuit).**

CALORIES 259; FAT 4.9g (sat 2.9g, mono 1.2g, poly 0.4g); PROTEIN 3.9g; CARB 52.1g; FIBER 2.4g; CHOL 12mg; IRON 1.3mg; SODIUM 230mg; CALC 52mg

kitchen how-to: make crisps & crumbles

Here are some basic guidelines for making a filling and a crisp and a crumble topping that will fit in a 2-quart baking dish.

The Filling:

• If you're using only firm fruit (apple, pear, plum, or peach), use 7 cups peeled and sliced or chopped fruit.

• To add berries, replace 1 or 2 cups of firm fruit with your choice of berries. If you use any more berries, your filling will have too much liquid.

• Use a light hand when sweetening the filling. Since the sweetness of fresh fruits can vary significantly, use your own flavor preference when adding sweeteners, such as sugar, brown sugar, or honey.

Basic Crisp Topping:

Place ½ cup regular oats in a food processor; pulse until coarsely ground. Weigh or lightly spoon 3.4 ounces all-purpose flour (about ¾ cup) into a dry measuring cup; level with a knife. Combine flour, ½ cup sugar, and ½ teaspoon salt in a large bowl. Cut ¼ cup chilled butter into small pieces. Add butter to flour mixture; cut in with a pastry blender or 2 knives until mixture resembles coarse meal. Stir in ground oats. Add 3 tablespoons honey; toss well.

Basic Crumble Topping:

Place ½ cup regular oats in a food processor; pulse until coarsely ground. Weigh or lightly spoon 3.4 ounces all-purpose flour (about ¾ cup) and 2.12 ounces whole wheat pastry flour (about ½ cup) into dry measuring cups; level with a knife. Combine flours, ground oats, ¼ cup chopped walnuts (or nut of your choice), ¼ cup packed brown sugar, ½ teaspoon salt, ½ teaspoon ground cinnamon, and ¼ teaspoon ground nutmeg in a large bowl. Combine 3 tablespoons honey, 2 tablespoons walnut oil (or other nut oil), and 1 egg yolk in a small bowl, stirring with a whisk. Add to flour mixture; stir just until moist.

Preparing Your Dessert:

• Preheat oven to 375°.

• Lightly coat a 2-quart baking dish with cooking spray. For crumbles, we recommend a shallow dish with a large surface area (such as an 11 x 7–inch baking dish) so the denser topping is better distributed and cooks evenly.

• Add the filling to prepared dish.

• For a crisp, sprinkle the topping evenly over the fruit.

• For a crumble, squeeze handfuls of dough to form clumps; crumble dough pieces evenly over the fruit.

• Bake at 375° for 35 minutes or until golden and bubbly.

way to bake
pastries

Handmade pastries are an impeccable marriage of
light crust and delightful fillings. Some of us are more
enamored with the buttery crust on homemade pies
than the filling. The high proportion of crust to warm
insides in fruit turnovers make them a perfect package.

Brandied Apricot-Peach Pies

Dried apricots enhance the frozen peaches in this baked version of the classic fried pie.

Pies:
- ½ cup diced dried apricots
- ¼ cup granulated sugar
- 1 tablespoon fresh lemon juice
- ½ teaspoon ground cinnamon
- ⅛ teaspoon ground nutmeg
- 1 (16-ounce) bag frozen sliced peaches, thawed, chopped, and drained
- 1½ tablespoons butter
- 1 tablespoon brandy
- 2½ teaspoons cornstarch
- 12 Sweet Cream Cheese Dough circles (page 453)

Glaze:
- 1 cup sifted powdered sugar
- 2 tablespoons 2% reduced-fat milk
- ½ teaspoon vanilla extract

1. To prepare pies, combine first 6 ingredients in a medium saucepan; cook over medium heat 8 minutes or until liquid almost evaporates. Remove from heat. Add butter, stirring until butter melts. Stir in brandy and cornstarch. Cool slightly.

2. Working with 1 Sweet Cream Cheese Dough circle at a time, remove plastic wrap from dough. Place dough on a lightly floured surface. Spoon about 2 tablespoons peach mixture into center of circle. Fold dough over filling; press edges together with a fork or fingers to seal (see photo at left). Place pie on a large baking sheet covered with parchment paper. Repeat procedure with remaining Sweet Cream Cheese Dough circles and remaining peach mixture. Freeze 30 minutes.

3. Preheat oven to 425°.

4. Remove pies from freezer. Pierce top of each pie once with a fork (see photo below). Place baking sheet on bottom rack in oven. Bake at 425° for 18 minutes or until edges are lightly browned and filling is bubbly. Cool completely on a wire rack.

5. To prepare glaze, combine powdered sugar, milk, and vanilla, stirring well. Drizzle evenly over pies. **Yield: 12 pies (serving size: 1 pie).**

CALORIES 235; FAT 6.7g (sat 3.4g, mono 2.5g, poly 0.3g); PROTEIN 3.2g; CARB 40.9g; FIBER 1g; CHOL 18mg; IRON 1.3mg; SODIUM 96mg; CALC 26mg

kitchen how-to:
work with phyllo

Working with phyllo is simple. Follow these instructions, and you'll be making delicious treats in no time. Use the filling from our Goat Cheese Tarts with Lemon-Fig Compote (page 453) to create tasty appetizers, or fill the pastries with your favorite jam or jelly. Before beginning, thaw the frozen dough in the refrigerator overnight. Wrap the unused dough in plastic wrap, and store it in the refrigerator for up to a week.

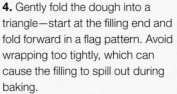

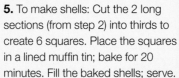

1. Carefully remove 1 dough sheet at a time. Layer 4 sheets, one atop the other, for a sturdy pastry. Coat all but top layer with cooking spray to prevent tearing.

2. Use a pizza cutter to cut the dough in half vertically, creating two long sections. Use cooking spray to bond any tearing that occurs while you're working.

3. To make triangles: Working with 1 section at a time, drop 1 tablespoon of filling onto the bottom. Leave a 1-inch border around filling to allow for folding.

4. Gently fold the dough into a triangle—start at the filling end and fold forward in a flag pattern. Avoid wrapping too tightly, which can cause the filling to spill out during baking.

5. To make shells: Cut the 2 long sections (from step 2) into thirds to create 6 squares. Place the squares in a lined muffin tin; bake for 20 minutes. Fill the baked shells; serve.

Goat Cheese Tarts with Lemon-Fig Compote

Compote:
-   2   cups finely chopped dried black Mission figs
-   1   cup water
-   ½   cup Marsala wine
-   1   tablespoon brown sugar
-   1   tablespoon grated lemon rind
-   1   tablespoon fresh lemon juice
-   ⅛   teaspoon salt

Tarts:
-   2   (2.1-ounce) packages mini phyllo shells (such as Athens)
-   ½   cup (4 ounces) fat-free cream cheese, softened
-   1   (4-ounce) package goat cheese
-   1   large egg white
-   1   tablespoon 1% low-fat milk
-   2   tablespoons powdered sugar
-   1   tablespoon all-purpose flour
-   ⅛   teaspoon salt

1. To prepare compote, combine first 7 ingredients in a medium saucepan. Bring to a boil. Cover, reduce heat, and simmer 20 minutes, stirring occasionally. Simmer, uncovered, until mixture reduces to about 1 cup (about 30 minutes). Remove from heat; cool.
2. Place fig mixture in a food processor; pulse 5 times or until finely chopped. Place in a small bowl; cover and chill.
3. To prepare tarts, preheat oven to 350°.
4. Arrange phyllo shells in a single layer on a jelly-roll pan. Combine cheeses in a medium bowl; beat with a mixer at medium speed until smooth. Add egg white; beat well. Add milk; beat well. Combine powdered sugar, flour, and salt; add to cheese mixture, beating well.
5. Spoon about 1½ teaspoons cheese mixture into each phyllo shell. Bake at 350° for 15 minutes or until lightly browned. Cool on a wire rack. Top each tart with about 1½ teaspoons compote. **Yield: 15 servings (serving size: 2 tarts).**

CALORIES 120; FAT 3.8g (sat 1.2g, mono 1.6g, poly 0.4g); PROTEIN 3.4g; CARB 17.8g; FIBER 1.6g; CHOL 4mg; IRON 1mg; SODIUM 132mg; CALC 54mg

kitchen how-to:
make sweet cream cheese dough

Packing the dough into a measuring cup helps it come together without overworking.

1. Weigh or lightly spoon 9 ounces all-purpose flour (about 2 cups) into dry measuring cups; level with a knife. Place flour, ¼ cup sugar, ¼ teaspoon baking powder, and ⅛ teaspoon salt in a food processor; pulse 3 times or until combined. Add ¼ cup chilled butter, cut into small pieces, ¼ cup (2 ounces) chilled ⅓-less-fat cream cheese, cut into small pieces, and 1 tablespoon cider vinegar; pulse 4 times. Add 4 to 5 tablespoons ice water through food chute, 1 tablespoon at a time, pulsing just until combined (do not form a ball). (Mixture may appear crumbly but will stick together when pressed between fingers.)
2. Place half of dough into a 1-cup measuring cup, pressing to compact. Remove dough from cup, and form into a ball. Divide ball into 6 equal portions. Repeat procedure with remaining dough. Cover and chill 15 minutes.
3. Place each dough portion between 2 sheets of plastic wrap. Roll each dough portion, still covered, into a 5-inch circle; chill until ready to use. **Yield: 12 servings (serving size: 1 dough circle).**

CALORIES 138; FAT 5.1g (sat 2.6g, mono 1.9g, poly 0.3g); PROTEIN 2.7g; CARB 20.3g; FIBER 0.6g; CHOL 14mg; IRON 1mg; SODIUM 81mg; CALC 14mg

way to bake
soufflés

Soufflés epitomize the art of French cooking. In fact, the French verb *souffler* means "to inflate" or "to breathe," hinting at the dish's fragile, fleeting nature. "Soufflé" is also a culinary term used in both French and English to refer to this sweet or savory dish.

kitchen how-to: make a soufflé

The basic soufflé has acquired an undeserved reputation for being difficult. Success depends on two simple techniques: first, whip the egg whites properly, and second, fold the egg whites gently into a flavored base.

1. Use soufflé dishes with tall, straight sides. Using a powerful stand mixer with a whisk attachment will incorporate the most air into egg whites; use a rubber or silicone spatula to fold the egg whites into the base.

2. Lightly coat the entire soufflé dish with cooking spray. Add breadcrumbs or sugar, and roll the dish around until it's completely covered.

3. The base gives the soufflé its characteristic flavor. After you cook and cool the base, add the egg yolks and flavorings, such as vanilla or lemon juice, to enrich the dish.

4. Whip the egg whites to stiff satiny peaks, but be careful not to overbeat them. Egg whites have reached the stiff peak stage when they stand up. Overbeaten egg whites look dry and grainy.

5. Gently fold the egg whites into the base, incorporating as much air as possible. Using a spatula, "cut" down the center and up the sides of the bowl, making an S motion and rotating the bowl as you go.

6. The soufflé is done when it's puffed and set. To make sure it is completely cooked, insert a wooden pick or skewer horizontally into the side. If it comes out clean, the soufflé is ready.

Double Chocolate Soufflés with Warm Fudge Sauce

You can prepare the ingredients ahead, spoon the batter into soufflé dishes, cover the dishes, and freeze them until you're ready to bake them. They can go straight from the freezer to the oven. Make the sauce ahead, too, and simply warm it before serving. This recipe received our Test Kitchens' highest rating.

Soufflés:
Cooking spray
½ cup plus 2 tablespoons sugar, divided
3 tablespoons all-purpose flour
3 tablespoons unsweetened cocoa
⅛ teaspoon salt
1¼ cups fat-free milk
3 ounces bittersweet chocolate, chopped
1 teaspoon vanilla extract
1 large egg yolk
6 large egg whites

Sauce:
1 tablespoon butter
⅓ cup sugar
2 tablespoons unsweetened cocoa
1 tablespoon all-purpose flour
½ cup fat-free milk
½ ounce bittersweet chocolate, chopped

1. Position oven rack to lowest setting, and remove middle rack. Preheat oven to 425°.
2. To prepare soufflés, lightly coat 6 (8-ounce) soufflé dishes with cooking spray. Sprinkle evenly with 2 tablespoons sugar. Set aside.
3. Combine remaining ½ cup sugar, 3 tablespoons flour, 3 tablespoons cocoa, and salt in a medium saucepan over medium-high heat, stirring with a whisk. Gradually add 1¼ cups milk, stirring constantly with a whisk; bring to a boil. Cook 2 minutes or until slightly thick, stirring constantly with a whisk; remove from heat. Add 3 ounces chocolate; stir until smooth. Transfer mixture to a large bowl; cool to room temperature. Stir in vanilla and egg yolk.
4. Place egg whites in a large mixing bowl; beat with a mixer at high speed until stiff peaks form (do not overbeat). Gently fold one-fourth of egg whites into chocolate mixture; gently fold in remaining egg white mixture. Gently spoon mixture into prepared dishes. Sharply tap dishes 2 or 3 times on countertop to level. Place dishes on a baking sheet; place baking sheet on the bottom rack of 425° oven. Immediately reduce oven temperature to 350° (do not remove soufflés from oven). Bake 40 minutes or until a wooden pick inserted in the side of soufflé comes out clean.
5. To prepare sauce, melt butter in a small saucepan over medium-high heat. Add ⅓ cup sugar, 2 tablespoons cocoa, and 1 tablespoon flour; stir well with a whisk. Gradually add ½ cup milk, stirring well with a whisk; bring to a boil. Cook 1 minute or until slightly thick, stirring constantly with a whisk. Remove from heat; add ½ ounce chocolate, stirring until smooth. Serve warm with soufflés. **Yield: 6 servings (serving size: 1 soufflé and about 2 tablespoons sauce).**

CALORIES 315; FAT 9g (sat 5.1g, mono 1.8g, poly 0.3g); PROTEIN 9.1g; CARB 51.8g; FIBER 2.9g; CHOL 41mg; IRON 1.4mg; SODIUM 153mg; CALC 79mg

way to bake
puddings

Baked custards and puddings contain many of the same ingredients as stovetop varieties and rely on the same principles since they, too, are basically milk bound by eggs. Delicate baked custards, such as crème brûlée, are one variety. Here we focus on the more forgiving baked puddings.

Bourbon Bread Pudding

Day-old toasted bread cubes work best in this recipe because they absorb plenty of the custard.

Pudding:
- 2 **tablespoons butter, softened**
- 4 **cups fat-free milk**
- 9 **cups (½-inch) cubed French bread**
- 2 **cups sugar**
- 2 **teaspoons vanilla extract**
- 4 **large egg whites**
- 1 **large egg**
- ½ **cup raisins**

Sauce:
- ¾ **cup sugar**
- 6 **tablespoons butter**
- 1 **large egg**
- ¼ **cup bourbon**

1. Preheat oven to 350°.

2. To prepare pudding, spread 2 tablespoons butter onto bottom and sides of a 13 x 9–inch baking dish. Set aside.

3. Heat milk in a heavy saucepan over medium-high heat to 180° or until tiny bubbles form around edge (do not boil). Place bread in a large bowl; pour hot milk over bread.

4. Combine 2 cups sugar and next 3 ingredients in a medium bowl, stirring with a whisk until well blended. Gradually add the egg mixture to milk mixture, stirring constantly with a whisk. Stir in raisins; pour into prepared dish. Place dish in a roasting pan; add hot water to pan to a depth of ½ inch. Bake at 350° for 50 minutes or until browned and set.

5. To prepare sauce, combine ¾ cup sugar, 6 tablespoons butter, and 1 egg in a small, heavy saucepan over low heat. Cook 4 minutes or until a candy thermometer registers 165° and mixture is thick, stirring constantly. Remove from heat, and stir in bourbon. Serve sauce with bread pudding. **Yield: 16 servings**

(serving size: ½ cup bread pudding and 1 tablespoon sauce).

CALORIES 294; FAT 6.9g (sat 3.8g, mono 1.7g, poly 0.3g); PROTEIN 5.6g; CARB 52g; FIBER 0.7g; CHOL 43mg; IRON 0.8mg; SODIUM 224mg; CALC 96mg

See page 244 for information about how to prepare puddings on the stovetop.

kitchen how-to: make a water bath

Most puddings bake in a water bath, which surrounds delicate custard-based dishes with gentle heat to keep the custard from breaking. Use a 13 x 9–inch metal baking pan or roasting pan for the water bath.

quick breads

Quick breads are simple to make, requiring only that you measure ingredients precisely and mix lightly. When combining dry ingredients with liquid ingredients, mix the batter with a few swift strokes, just until the dry ingredients are moistened; it's OK if there are a few lumps. If you overmix the batter, the bread's texture won't be light and springy; if you undermix the batter, the bread will have white patches of flour.

Banana-Oatmeal Loaf

6.75 ounces all-purpose flour
    (about 1½ cups)
 ⅔ cup sugar
1½ teaspoons baking powder
 ¼ teaspoon baking soda
 ¼ teaspoon salt
 ¾ cup regular oats
 1 cup mashed ripe banana
    (about 2 large)
 ⅓ cup low-fat buttermilk
 ¼ cup vegetable oil
 1 teaspoon vanilla extract
 2 large eggs, lightly beaten
Cooking spray

1. Preheat oven to 350°.
2. Weigh or lightly spoon flour into dry measuring cups; level with a knife. Combine flour and next 4 ingredients in a large bowl, stirring well with a whisk. Stir in oats.
3. Combine banana and next 4 ingredients; add to flour mixture. Stir just until moist.
4. Spoon batter into an 8 x 4–inch loaf pan coated with cooking spray. Bake at 350° for 55 minutes or until a wooden pick inserted in center comes out clean. Cool 15 minutes in pan on a wire rack; remove from pan. Cool completely on wire rack.

Yield: 12 servings (serving size: 1 slice).

CALORIES 192; FAT 6g (sat 1.1g, mono 1.5g, poly 2.9g); PROTEIN 3.8g; CARB 31.4g; FIBER 1.3g; CHOL 36mg; IRON 1.2mg; SODIUM 154mg; CALC 52mg

kitchen how-to:
make quick bread

Whether it takes the form of a muffin or a loaf, most quick breads rely on a four-step process that produces a coarse, yet tender, crumb. Pancakes and waffles also fall into the category of quick breads because they are leavened with baking powder or baking soda, as compared to yeast breads, which require long rising times before baking. Quick breads are mixed together much like muffins, but they have a higher liquid-to-dry ingredient ratio.

1. Weigh or lightly spoon the flour into dry measuring cups; level with a knife.
2. Combine the dry ingredients in a large bowl, and make a well in the center for the wet ingredients.
3. Add the wet ingredients to the flour mixture.
4. Stir the batter just until moist.

way to make
pancakes & waffles

Easy and delicious, pancakes and waffles are crowd-pleasers for guests and family. Follow these tips to make your best batch.

Buttermilk Pancakes

Serve these classic pancakes with maple syrup.

6.75 ounces all-purpose flour (about 1½ cups)
 2 tablespoons sugar
 1 teaspoon baking powder
 ½ teaspoon salt
1½ cups fat-free buttermilk
 1 tablespoon butter, melted
 1 large egg, lightly beaten

1. Weigh or lightly spoon flour into dry measuring cups; level with a knife. Combine flour, sugar, baking powder, and salt in a bowl; stir with a whisk. Combine buttermilk, butter, and egg; add to flour mixture, stirring until smooth. **2.** Pour about ¼ cup batter per pancake onto a hot nonstick skillet or griddle. Cook 2 minutes or until tops are covered with bubbles and edges look cooked. Carefully turn pancakes over; cook 2 minutes or until bottoms are lightly browned. **Yield: 4 servings (serving size: 3 pancakes).**

CALORIES 272; FAT 4.5g (sat 2.2g, mono 1.3g, poly 0.5g); PROTEIN 9.8g; CARB 47.4g; FIBER 1.3g; CHOL 61mg; IRON 2.4mg; SODIUM 583mg; CALC 126mg

kitchen how-to: make pancakes

Premix the dry ingredients the night before to save time during a busy morning. Always pour the wet ingredients into the dry ones to avoid clumps. Stir until the batter is smooth, and use it immediately; if you wait too long, it will thicken. Coat a preheated nonstick skillet or griddle with cooking spray for easy pancake flipping and removal. To test the surface's heat, sprinkle a few drops of water on it. If the drops dance on the surface and evaporate within a few seconds, the pan or griddle is ready.

1. For precision, use about ¼ cup batter for each pancake. Pour the batter into the center of the pan or griddle and let it spread—don't pour it in a circle. **2.** Once the edges turn golden and bubbles surface, slide a wide nylon spatula under the pancake—the width will help you grab more, and the nylon won't scratch. Quickly flip the pancake over, and cook it 2 more minutes.

Gingerbread Waffles

9 ounces all-purpose flour
(about 2 cups)
1½ teaspoons baking powder
½ teaspoon baking soda
¼ teaspoon salt
¼ teaspoon ground cinnamon
1½ cups fat-free buttermilk
3 tablespoons canola oil
3 tablespoons molasses
2 teaspoons finely grated
peeled fresh ginger
2 large egg yolks
1 (4-ounce) container
applesauce
3 tablespoons minced
crystallized ginger
2 large egg whites
Cooking spray

1. Weigh or lightly spoon flour into dry measuring cups; level with a knife. Combine flour and next 4 ingredients in a bowl; stir with a whisk. Combine buttermilk and next 5 ingredients in a bowl. Add milk mixture to flour mixture, stirring just until combined. Stir in crystallized ginger.
2. Beat egg whites with a mixer at high speed until soft peaks form. Gently fold egg whites into batter.

3. Coat a waffle iron with cooking spray, and preheat. Spoon about ⅓ cup batter per 4-inch waffle onto hot waffle iron, spreading batter evenly to edges. Cook 5 minutes or until steaming stops; repeat procedure with remaining batter.
Yield: 9 servings (serving size: 2 waffles).

CALORIES 208; FAT 6.1g (sat 0.7g, mono 3.2g, poly 1.7g); PROTEIN 5.8g; CARB 32.5g; FIBER 1g; CHOL 47mg; IRON 2mg; SODIUM 277mg; CALC 124mg

way to make
crepes

These superthin pancakes are delicious in both savory and sweet recipes. Once you master the basic techniques for making the batter and cooking the crepes, variations abound with the simple addition of spices or herbs, and the possibilities for fillings are almost endless.

Basic Crepes

Although you'll need only about 3 tablespoons of batter to make each crepe, we found that a ¼-cup dry measuring cup is the best tool to scoop and pour the batter into the pan so the crepes cook evenly.

- 4.5 ounces all-purpose flour (about 1 cup)
- 2 teaspoons sugar
- ¼ teaspoon salt
- 1 cup low-fat 1% milk
- ½ cup water
- 2 teaspoons butter, melted
- 2 large eggs

1. Weigh or lightly spoon flour into a dry measuring cup; level with a knife. Combine flour, sugar, and salt in a small bowl. Combine milk and remaining ingredients in a blender. Add flour mixture to milk mixture, and process until smooth. Cover batter; chill 1 hour.
2. Heat an 8-inch nonstick crepe pan or skillet over medium heat. Pour a scant ¼ cup batter into pan; quickly tilt pan in all directions so batter covers pan with a thin film. Cook about 1 minute. Carefully lift the edge of the crepe with a spatula to test for doneness. The crepe is ready to turn when it can be shaken loose from the pan and the underside is lightly browned. Turn crepe over, and cook 30 seconds or until center is set.
3. Place crepe on a towel; cool completely. Repeat procedure with the remaining batter, stirring batter between crepes. Stack crepes between single layers of wax paper to prevent sticking. **Yield: 13 crepes (serving size: 1 crepe).**

CALORIES 62; FAT 1.6g (sat 0.8g, mono 0.5g, poly 0.2g); PROTEIN 2.6g; CARB 8.9g; FIBER 0.3g; CHOL 35mg; IRON 0.6mg; SODIUM 70mg; CALC 29mg

four easy variations

Be creative with crepe batter, or use one of our favorite variations. Different flours, such as buckwheat or chickpea, vary the flavor and texture of crepes. Seasonings, such as fresh chopped herbs, citrus rind, spices, chopped nuts, grated cheese, or cocoa powder lend distinct flavor to the finished dish.

Herbed Crepes: Add 1 teaspoon chopped fresh parsley and 1 teaspoon chopped fresh chives to the Basic Crepes batter.
Espresso Crepes: Add 2 teaspoons instant espresso powder to the Basic Crepes batter.
Buckwheat Crepes: Omit ⅔ cup all-purpose flour and add ⅔ cup buckwheat flour to the Basic Crepes recipe.
Cinnamon Crepes: Add 1 teaspoon ground cinnamon to the Basic Crepes batter.

kitchen how-to:
make crepes

Making crepe batter is quick and easy. It's important to cover the batter and let it rest, chilled, for 1 hour. This allows the proteins and the starch to absorb water, which ensures that the crepes will be tender. It also allows the air incorporated into the batter to dissipate so the crepes will be paper thin.

1. An 8-inch nonstick skillet or crepe pan, ¼ cup dry measuring cup, and a rubber spatula are the only things needed to cook beautiful crepes. But a blender and whisk will help you make a smooth batter.

2. Simply combine all of the ingredients, and blend to make the batter.

3. The batter's consistency after it rests should be about that of (unwhipped) heavy whipping cream.

4. Add the batter to the center of the pan, and gently tilt the pan in a circular motion, allowing the batter to reach the sides of the pan.

5. The edges of the crepe should be crisp, the underside brown, and the center will come loose if you gently shake the pan. These visual cues alert you that the crepe is ready to flip.

6. The ultimate convenience food, crepes will keep for up to five days if you stack them between layers of wax paper and chill them. You can freeze them for up to two months.

7. Spoon the filling evenly down the center of the crepes.

8. Stack, roll, or fold the crepes for a variety of presentation options. Many of our recipes call to fold the ends and sides over to completely cover the filling.

way to bake
biscuits

Dropped and rolled biscuits are the two most common types. To make dropped biscuits, simply drop the dough by tablespoonfuls onto the baking sheet; they have a higher proportion of liquid to dry ingredients so you have a thick batter instead of a soft dough. Rolled biscuits take a little more practice because the dough must be lightly kneaded, rolled out, and cut with a biscuit cutter; be careful—it's easy to overdo it on the kneading and the rolling, and you end up with tough biscuits.

Flaky Buttermilk Biscuits

A light hand with the dough will help ensure tender biscuits, and this method of folding the dough creates irresistible flaky layers. To maximize the number of biscuits you get from the recipe, gather the dough scraps after cutting and gently pat or reroll to a ¾-inch thickness.

    9   ounces all-purpose flour (about 2 cups)
    2½ teaspoons baking powder
    ½   teaspoon salt
    5   tablespoons chilled butter, cut into small
        pieces
    ¾   cup fat-free buttermilk
    3   tablespoons honey

1. Preheat oven to 400°.
2. Weigh or lightly spoon flour into dry measuring cups; level with a knife. Combine flour, baking powder, and salt in a large bowl; cut in butter with a pastry blender or 2 knives until mixture resembles coarse meal. Chill 10 minutes.
3. Combine buttermilk and honey, stirring with a whisk until well blended. Add buttermilk mixture to flour mixture; stir just until moist.
4. Turn dough out onto a lightly floured surface; knead lightly 4 times. Roll dough into a (½-inch-thick) 9 x 5–inch rectangle; dust top of dough with flour. Fold dough crosswise into thirds as if folding a piece of paper to fit into an envelope (see photo on page 464). Reroll dough into a (½-inch-thick) 9 x 5–inch rectangle; dust top of dough with flour. Fold dough crosswise into thirds; gently roll or pat to a ¾-inch thickness. Cut dough with a 1¾-inch biscuit cutter to form 14 dough rounds. Place dough rounds, 1 inch apart, on a baking sheet lined with parchment paper. Bake at 400° for 12 minutes or until golden. Remove from pan; cool 2 minutes on wire racks. Serve warm.
Yield: 14 servings (serving size: 1 biscuit).

CALORIES 121; FAT 4.2g (sat 2.6g, mono 1.1g, poly 0.2g); PROTEIN 2.4g; CARB 18.4g; FIBER 0.5g; CHOL 11mg; IRON 0.9mg; SODIUM 198mg; CALC 63mg

kitchen how-to: cut in butter

You must cut the butter into the dry ingredients so the biscuits will be tender. The "cutting" action distributes little lumps of butter throughout the dough; the butter melts during baking and gives biscuits their trademark flakiness.

1. Cut in chilled butter with a pastry blender until the mixture resembles coarse meal.
2. If you don't have a pastry blender, use 2 knives, and pull them through the butter until the mixture resembles coarse meal.

muffins & scones

Tropical Muffins with Coconut-Macadamia Topping

Most of the monounsaturated fat in each serving comes from mild-flavored canola oil and rich macadamia nuts. Flaked sweetened coconut is high in saturated fat for a plant food (nearly 94 percent of the fat is saturated), but a little offers nutty flavor to the batter as well as texture to the topping.

Muffins:
- 6 ounces all-purpose flour (about 1⅓ cups)
- 1 cup regular oats
- 1 teaspoon baking powder
- ½ teaspoon baking soda
- ½ teaspoon salt
- 1 cup mashed ripe banana (about 2)
- 1 cup low-fat buttermilk
- ½ cup packed brown sugar
- 2 tablespoons canola oil
- 1 teaspoon vanilla extract
- 1 large egg
- ½ cup canned crushed pineapple in juice, drained
- ⅓ cup flaked sweetened coconut
- 3 tablespoons finely chopped macadamia nuts, toasted
- Cooking spray

Topping:
- 2 tablespoons flaked sweetened coconut
- 1 tablespoon finely chopped macadamia nuts
- 1 tablespoon granulated sugar
- 1 tablespoon regular oats

1. Preheat oven to 400°.
2. To prepare muffins, weigh or lightly spoon flour into dry measuring cups; level with a knife. Combine flour and next 4 ingredients in a large bowl; make a well in center of flour mixture. Combine banana and next 5 ingredients in a medium bowl; add to flour mixture, stirring just until moist. Stir in pineapple, ⅓ cup coconut, and 3 tablespoons nuts. Spoon batter into 12 muffin cups coated with cooking spray.
3. To prepare topping, combine 2 tablespoons coconut and remaining ingredients in a small bowl.
4. Sprinkle about 1 teaspoon of topping over each muffin. Bake at 400° for 18 minutes or until muffins spring back when touched lightly in center. Remove muffins from pans immediately; place on a wire rack.
Yield: 1 dozen (serving size: 1 muffin).

CALORIES 205; FAT 6.7g (sat 1.7g, mono 3.4g, poly 1g); PROTEIN 4.3g; CARB 33.3g; FIBER 2g; CHOL 19mg; IRON 1.5mg; SODIUM 215mg; CALC 69mg

Coffee-Nut Scones

⅔ cup 1% low-fat milk
2½ tablespoons instant coffee granules
1 teaspoon vanilla extract
1 large egg, lightly beaten
10.1 ounces all-purpose flour (about 2¼ cups)
⅓ cup sugar
2½ teaspoons baking powder
¾ teaspoon salt
¼ teaspoon ground cinnamon
¼ cup chilled butter, cut into small pieces
3 tablespoons finely chopped walnuts
Cooking spray
2 teaspoons 1% low-fat milk
2 teaspoons sugar

1. Combine ⅔ cup milk and coffee granules in a microwave-safe bowl. Microwave at HIGH 1 minute; stir until coffee dissolves. Cover and chill completely. Stir in vanilla and egg.
2. Preheat oven to 425°.
3. Weigh or lightly spoon flour into dry measuring cups; level with a knife. Combine flour and next 4 ingredients in a bowl; cut in butter with a pastry blender or 2 knives until mixture resembles coarse meal. Stir in walnuts. Add milk mixture, stirring just until moist (dough will be sticky).
4. Turn dough out onto a lightly floured surface; knead lightly 4 times with floured hands. Pat dough into an 8-inch circle on a baking sheet coated with cooking spray. Cut dough into 10 wedges, cutting into, but not through, dough. Brush dough with 2 teaspoons milk; sprinkle with 2 teaspoons sugar. Bake at 425° for 20 minutes or until browned. Serve warm. **Yield: 10 servings (serving size: 1 wedge).**

CALORIES 207; FAT 7g (sat 3.3g, mono 1.9g, poly 1.3g); PROTEIN 4.9g; CARB 31g; FIBER 1g; CHOL 35mg; IRON 1.7mg; SODIUM 361mg; CALC 101mg

kitchen how-to: make scones

The secret to tender scones is handling the dough as little as possible.

1. Cut the butter into the flour mixture until it resembles coarse meal. If you don't have a pastry blender, you can use 2 knives (although this takes considerably longer). Or you can pulse the flour mixture and butter in your food processor.
2. After adding the milk mixture, turn the dough out onto a lightly floured surface. With lightly floured hands, gather the dough into a ball. Knead lightly 4 to 5 times. The dough will be sticky, but resist the temptation to add more flour because it will make the scones dry.
3. Pat the dough into an 8-inch circle. Cut the circle into 10 wedges, cutting into, but not through, the dough. This allows the wedges to bake as one large scone, and they will be much moister than scones baked separately.

way to bake
yeast breads

Anyone cake make top-quality yeast bread. Really—anyone. All it takes is a little patience and instruction.

make yeast bread

Baking with yeast is different from any other form of cooking. Yeast bread is literally alive—dry yeast, which is made of living, single-cell organisms in a state of suspended animation, is brought back to life with moisture and warmth. Bread is kneaded, shaped, and baked. It's more than cooking—it's an act of creation with a delicious outcome.

1. Making sure the yeast is alive, a process known as proofing, is the most crucial step in baking yeast bread because if the yeast is dead, it can't leaven the bread. Live yeast will swell and foam (or activate) a few minutes after it's stirred into the warm liquid.

2. To make the initial bread dough, add most of the flour to the liquid ingredients all at once, and stir just until the mixture is combined. (Be sure to save some of the flour for kneading.) Then dump the dough onto a floured surface, and you're ready to knead.

3. To knead the dough, push it out with the heels of your hands, fold it over, give it a quarter-turn, and repeat. You may not use all the remaining flour—in fact, try to use as little of it as possible. After about 10 minutes of kneading, the dough should be smooth and elastic but still feel tacky.

4. For the first rising, place the dough in a large bowl because the dough will double in size. Cover the bowl with a slightly damp lightweight dish towel. To tell when the dough has risen enough, simply press two fingers into it. If an indentation remains, the dough is ready; if the dough springs back, it needs more rising time.

5. Punch the dough down to deflate it. Then turn the dough out onto a floured surface for rolling.

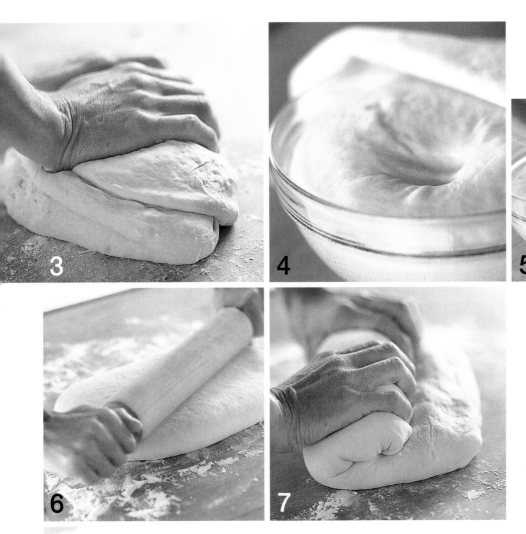

6. To shape the bread, begin by rolling it out. Lift the rolling pin up slightly as you near each end of the rectangular shape.

7. Rolling up the dough, or shaping, is just as important as rolling it out. The purpose is to eliminate air bubbles, giving a better crumb—or texture—to the bread. To accomplish this, roll the dough tightly, pressing firmly as you go.

8. Once you roll up the dough and place it in a loaf pan, let it rise a second time. Watch it carefully—if the dough rises too much and starts to fall, the bread will be dense. To avoid this, check the dough to be sure it has not begun to deflate. Once it's doubled in size, the dough is ready to bake.

Dinner Rolls, Five Ways

You can bake these rolls up to a month in advance. Cool completely, wrap in heavy-duty aluminum foil, and freeze them. Thaw the rolls completely, and reheat them (still wrapped in foil) at 350° for 12 minutes or until warm. To warm the milk, pour it into a 2-cup glass measure, and heat it in the microwave, or heat the milk in a saucepan on the stovetop. Check the temperature with an instant-read or candy thermometer.

- 2 **teaspoons sugar**
- 1 **package dry yeast (about 2¼ teaspoons)**
- 1 **(12-ounce) can evaporated fat-free milk, warmed (100° to 110°)**
- 18 **ounces all-purpose flour (about 4 cups), divided**
- 1 **large egg, lightly beaten**
- 1 **teaspoon salt**
- **Cooking spray**
- ½ **teaspoon cornmeal**
- 2 **tablespoons butter, melted and cooled**

1. Dissolve sugar and yeast in warm milk in a large bowl; let stand 5 minutes.

2. Weigh or lightly spoon flour into dry measuring cups; level with a knife. Add 3 cups flour and egg to milk mixture, stirring until smooth; cover and let stand 15 minutes.

3. Add ¾ cup flour and salt; stir until a soft dough forms. Turn dough out onto a floured surface. Knead until smooth and elastic (about 8 minutes); add enough of remaining flour, 1 tablespoon at a time, to prevent dough from sticking to hands (dough will feel tacky).

4. Place dough in a large bowl coated with cooking spray, turning to coat top. Cover and let rise in a warm place (85°), free from drafts, 30 minutes or until doubled

in size. (Press two fingers into dough. If indentation remains, dough has risen enough.) Punch dough down; cover and let rest 5 minutes.

5. Divide dough into 16 equal portions. Working with one portion at a time (cover remaining dough to prevent drying), shape each portion into desired form (see how-to at right). Place shaped dough portions on a baking sheet lightly sprinkled with cornmeal. Lightly coat shaped dough portions with cooking spray; cover with plastic wrap. Let rise in a warm place (85°), free from drafts, 20 minutes or until doubled in size.

6. Preheat oven to 400°.

7. Gently brush shaped dough portions with butter. Bake at 400° for 20 minutes or until lightly browned on top and hollow-sounding when tapped on bottom. Place on wire racks. Serve warm, or cool completely on wire racks. **Yield: 16 servings (serving size: 1 roll).**

CALORIES 151; FAT 2.1g (sat 1.1g, mono 0.5g, poly 0.2g); PROTEIN 5.4g; CARB 27g; FIBER 0.9g; CHOL 18mg; IRON 1.7mg; SODIUM 187mg; CALC 69mg

kitchen how-to: shape dough

Use one simple dough to yield five rich, tender dinner roll variations.

Roll: Divide the dough into 16 equal portions; shape each portion into a ball.

Knot: Divide the dough into 16 equal portions; shape each portion into an 8-inch rope. Tie each rope into a single knot; tuck the top end of the rope under the bottom edge of the roll.

Snail: Divide the dough into 16 equal portions; shape each portion into a 20-inch rope. Working on a flat surface, coil each rope in a spiral pattern.

Cloverleaf: Divide the dough into 16 equal portions; divide each portion into three balls. Working with three balls at a time, arrange the balls in a triangle pattern on baking sheet (be sure the balls are touching each other).

Twist: Divide the dough into 16 equal portions; shape each portion into an 18-inch rope. Fold each rope in half so that both ends meet. Working with one folded rope at a time, hold the ends of the rope in one hand and the folded end in the other hand; gently twist.

roll

knot

snail

cloverleaf

twist

kitchen how-to:
make cinnamon-date-pecan rolls with maple glaze

These frosted sweet rolls make a delectable breakfast or holiday brunch offering.

1. Roll dough into a 15 x 10–inch rectangle, and brush with 2 tablespoons butter.

2. Sprinkle the brown sugar mixture over the dough, leaving a ½-inch border. Sprinkle the dates and pecans over sugar mixture.

3. Beginning with a long side, roll up the dough jelly-roll fashion; pinch the seam to seal (do not seal ends of roll). Cut the roll into 18 (½-inch) slices. Place the slices, cut sides up, in a 13 x 9–inch baking pan coated with cooking spray. Cover and let rise in a warm place (85°), free from drafts, about 1 hour or until the rolls have doubled in size. Bake.

Cinnamon-Date-Pecan Rolls with Maple Glaze

Dough:
- 1 teaspoon granulated sugar
- 1 package dry yeast (about 2¼ teaspoons)
- ¾ cup warm water (100° to 110°)
- ⅓ cup granulated sugar
- 3 tablespoons butter, melted
- ½ teaspoon salt
- 1 large egg
- 14.5 ounces all-purpose flour (about 3¼ cups)
- Cooking spray

Filling:
- ⅔ cup packed brown sugar
- 1 teaspoon ground cinnamon
- 1 teaspoon grated orange rind
- 2 tablespoons butter, melted
- ¾ cup chopped pitted dates
- ¼ cup chopped pecans, toasted

Glaze:
- 1 cup powdered sugar
- 2 tablespoons maple syrup
- 1 tablespoon fat-free milk

1. To prepare dough, dissolve 1 teaspoon granulated sugar and yeast in ¾ cup warm water; let stand 5 minutes. Combine ⅓ cup granulated sugar, 3 tablespoons butter, salt, and egg in a large bowl. Add yeast mixture; beat with a mixer at medium speed until blended.

2. Weigh or lightly spoon flour into dry measuring cups; level with a knife. Gradually add 3 cups flour to yeast mixture, beating mixture at low speed until a soft dough forms. Turn dough out onto a lightly floured surface. Knead until smooth and elastic (about 5 minutes); add enough of remaining flour, 1 tablespoon at a time, to prevent dough from sticking to hands. Place dough in a large bowl coated with cooking spray, turning to coat top. Cover and let rise in a warm place (85°), free from drafts, 1 hour or until doubled in size. Punch dough down; turn out onto a lightly floured surface.

3. To prepare filling, combine brown sugar, cinnamon, and rind in a small bowl. Roll dough into a 15 x 10–inch rectangle; brush with 2 tablespoons butter. Sprinkle brown sugar mixture over dough, leaving a ½-inch border. Sprinkle dates and pecans over sugar mixture. Beginning with a long side, roll up jelly-roll fashion; pinch seam to seal (do not seal ends of roll). Cut roll into 18 (½-inch) slices. Place slices, cut sides up, in a 13 x 9–inch baking pan coated with cooking spray. Cover and let rise in a warm place (85°), free from drafts, about 1 hour or until rolls have doubled in size.

4. Preheat oven to 375°.

5. Uncover dough. Bake at 375° for 20 minutes or until rolls are golden brown.

6. To prepare glaze, combine powdered sugar, syrup, and milk in a small bowl; stir with a whisk until smooth. Drizzle glaze over warm rolls. Serve immediately. **Yield: 18 rolls (serving size: 1 roll).**

CALORIES 226; FAT 4.9g (sat 2.2g, mono 1.6g, poly 0.6g); PROTEIN 3.2g; CARB 43.4g; FIBER 1.5g; CHOL 20mg; IRON 1.5mg; SODIUM 96mg; CALC 21mg

way to bake
pizza

Homemade pizza is a special treat because you control the ingredients, from what goes into the dough to the cheese sprinkled on top. Your pizza will be even more delicious than store-bought or restaurant varieties but lower in fat and sodium.

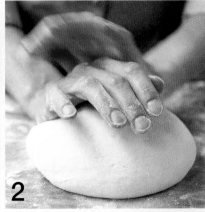

With just a little practice, you can master preparing the dough and toppings.

1. All you need are two rimless baking sheets, a rolling pin to shape the dough, a spatula to guide the dough onto the preheated baking sheet, and a pizza wheel, large knife, or kitchen shears to cut the pizza.

2. Knead the dough on a lightly floured surface until it's smooth and elastic.

3. Roll the dough into a 12-inch circle. Don't worry about making it a perfect circle as much as ensuring it's an even thickness so it will cook evenly.

4. Drape dough over the rolling pin to transfer it to a baking sheet sprinkled with cornmeal.

5. Crimp the edges of the dough to form a rim to corral the toppings on the surface of the pizza.

6. Holding the baking sheet at about a 45° angle and using a spatula to guide it, slide the dough onto the preheated sheet. Place the dough on the lowest oven rack to prebake.

7. Remove the prebaked crust from the oven. Add the toppings, and return the pizza to the middle oven rack to bake until the crust is deep golden brown and the cheese melts.

Basic Pizza Dough

Mix up a batch of this dough whenever you're in the mood for homemade pizza. Use it in the recipes here, create your own versions, or add mix-ins to customize the crust. Don't worry about rolling the dough into a perfect circle—just make it an even thickness.

> 2 teaspoons honey
> 1 package active dry yeast (about 2¼ teaspoons)
> ¾ cup warm water (100° to 110°)
> 10 ounces all-purpose flour (about 2¼ cups), divided
> ½ teaspoon salt
> Cooking spray
> 2 tablespoons stone-ground yellow cornmeal

1. Dissolve honey and yeast in ¾ cup warm water in a large bowl; let stand 5 minutes or until bubbly. Weigh or lightly spoon flour into dry measuring cups; level with a knife. Add 2 cups flour and salt to yeast mixture; stir until a soft dough forms. Turn dough out onto a lightly floured surface. Knead until smooth and elastic (about 6 minutes); add enough of remaining flour, 1 tablespoon at a time, to prevent dough from sticking to hands (dough will feel slightly sticky).
2. Place dough in a large bowl coated with cooking spray, turning to coat top. Cover and let rise in a warm place (85°), free from drafts, 30 minutes or until doubled in size. (Gently press two fingers into dough. If the indentation remains, the dough has risen enough.)
3. Roll dough into a 12-inch circle (about ¼ inch thick) on a lightly floured surface. Place dough on a rimless baking sheet sprinkled with cornmeal. Crimp edges of dough with fingers to form a rim. Lightly spray surface of dough with cooking spray, and cover with plastic wrap. Place the dough in refrigerator for up to 30 minutes. Bake according to recipe directions. **Yield: 1 (12-inch) crust.**

(Totals are for 1 [12-inch] pizza crust) CALORIES 1,155; FAT 3.4g (sat 0.6g, mono 0.5g, poly 1.3g); PROTEIN 33.8g; CARB 242.5g; FIBER 10.8g; CHOL 0mg; IRON 14.3mg; SODIUM 1,195mg; CALC 49mg

customize the crust

Our Basic Pizza Dough yields a delicious crust. And you can customize the flavor and texture by adding ingredients during the last minute or so of kneading to enhance the flavor of the crust without overwhelming the toppings.

Wheat Germ Dough: Replace ¼ cup of the all-purpose flour with ¼ cup toasted wheat germ.
Asian Dough: Add 2 teaspoons raw sesame seeds.
Herb Dough: Add 2 tablespoons chopped fresh herbs (use a mix of herbs or just one, such as basil or oregano).
Nutty Dough: Add 2 tablespoons finely chopped walnuts or pecans.
Cheese Dough: Add 2 tablespoons finely grated Parmesan, fontina, or other cheese.
Pepper Dough: Add 1 teaspoon coarsely ground black pepper.

kitchen how-to:
determine if dough has risen enough

Once you've kneaded the dough, place it in a large bowl coated with cooking spray, turning to coat the top. Cover and let rise in a warm place (85°), free from drafts, 30 minutes or until doubled in size. Gently press two fingers into the dough. If the indentation remains, the dough has risen enough.

Cheese Pizza

Basic Pizza Dough (page 476)
2 teaspoons olive oil
1 cup fat-free bottled pizza sauce
2 cups (8 ounces) shredded part-skim
   mozzarella cheese
½ cup (2 ounces) grated fresh Parmesan
   cheese

1. Position one oven rack in the middle setting and another rack in lowest setting; place a rimless baking sheet on bottom rack. Preheat oven to 500°.

2. Remove plastic wrap from Basic Pizza Dough; discard plastic. Brush olive oil over dough. Remove preheated baking sheet from oven, and close oven door. Slide dough onto preheated baking sheet, using a spatula as a guide. Bake on lowest oven rack at 500° for 8 minutes. Remove from oven.

3. Spread sauce in an even layer over crust, leaving a ¼-inch border. Top with mozzarella and Parmesan cheeses. Bake on middle rack an additional 10 minutes or until crust is golden brown and cheese melts. Cut into 12 wedges. **Yield: 6 servings (serving size: 2 wedges).**

CALORIES 356; FAT 10.8g (sat 5.8g, mono 3.7g, poly 0.7g); PROTEIN 19.1g; CARB 44.5g; FIBER 2.5g; CHOL 30mg; IRON 3mg; SODIUM 633mg; CALC 357mg

way to bake
calzones

Sometimes called a stuffed pizza or Italian turnover, calzones are traditionally made from pizza dough that is filled with your favorite toppings—like cheese, meat, and veggies—and then folded, sealed, and baked. Calzones are easy to assemble, and they can be prepared ahead and frozen until ready to bake.

Tex-Mex Calzones

Although this recipe calls for refrigerated pizza dough, you can make your own using our recipe on page 476. Brush the tops of the calzones with beaten egg yolk before baking them to give them a pleasing browned surface and shine. Serve calzones with a black bean and tomato salad.

 8 ounces ground turkey breast
 ½ cup chopped onion
 ½ cup chopped green bell pepper
 ½ cup chopped red bell pepper
 ¾ teaspoon ground cumin
 ½ teaspoon chili powder
 2 garlic cloves, minced
 ½ cup fat-free fire-roasted salsa verde
 1 (11-ounce) can refrigerated thin-crust pizza dough
 ¾ cup (3 ounces) preshredded Mexican blend cheese
   Cooking spray
 ¼ cup fat-free sour cream

1. Preheat oven to 425°.
2. Heat a large nonstick skillet over medium-high heat. Add ground turkey to pan; cook 3 minutes, stirring to crumble. Add onion and next 5 ingredients; cook 4 minutes or until vegetables are crisp-tender, stirring mixture occasionally. Remove turkey mixture from heat; stir in salsa.
3. Unroll dough; divide into 4 equal portions. Roll each portion into a 6 x 4–inch rectangle. Working with one rectangle at a time, spoon about ½ cup turkey mixture on one side of dough. Top with 3 tablespoons cheese; fold dough over turkey mixture, and press edges together with a fork to seal. Place on a baking sheet coated with cooking spray. Repeat procedure with remaining dough and turkey mixture. Bake at 425° for 12 minutes or until browned. Serve with sour cream. **Yield: 4 servings (serving size: 1 calzone and 1 tablespoon sour cream).**

CALORIES 416; FAT 14.1g (sat 6.1g, mono 4.9g, poly 1.6g); PROTEIN 25.7g; CARB 46.2g; FIBER 2.5g; CHOL 44mg; IRON 2.5mg; SODIUM 771mg; CALC 195mg

Use whatever fillings you'd like—shredded chicken, ground turkey or beef, an assortment of vegetables and cheese. The combinations are virtually limitless. Just be sure you cook the filling before placing it in the calzone. Time in the oven is short, and it's only meant to bake the dough, turning it golden brown—there won't be enough time or heat to cook the filling.

1. Place the dough on a lightly floured surface, and roll into a 7-inch circle.

2. Apply the spreadable fillings first, and then sprinkle the vegetables, meats, and cheese on half of the dough. Leave a ½-inch border around the edges, and brush border with beaten egg yolk. (The egg yolk helps the dough stick together, giving the calzone a more secure seal.)

3. Fold the unfilled side over the filling, and pinch the edges together to seal the calzone. Then transfer the calzone to a baking sheet coated with cooking spray.

4. Brush the calzone with egg yolk, and puncture it with a fork to allow the steam to escape during cooking. Bake at 425° for 12 to 15 minutes or until golden brown.

Nutritional Analysis

How to Use It and Why

To interpret the nutrition analysis in *Cooking Light,* use the figures below as a daily reference guide. One size doesn't fit all, so take lifestyle, age, and circumstances into consideration. For example, pregnant or breast-feeding women need more protein, calories, and calcium. Go to choosemyplate.gov for your own individualized plan.

In Our Nutritional Analysis, We Use These Abbreviations

sat	saturated fat	**CHOL**	cholesterol
mono	monounsaturated fat	**CALC**	calcium
poly	polyunsaturated fat	**g**	gram
CARB	carbohydrates	**mg**	milligram

Daily Nutrition Guide

	Women ages 25 to 50	Women over 50	Men ages 25 to 50	Men over 50
Calories	2,000	2,000*	2,700	2,500
Protein	50g	50g	63g	60g
Fat	65g*	65g*	88g*	83g*
Saturated Fat	20g*	20g*	27g*	25g*
Carbohydrates	304g	304g	410g	375g
Fiber	25g to 35g	25g to 35g	25g to 35g	25g to 35g
Cholesterol	300mg*	300mg*	300mg*	300mg*
Iron	18mg	8mg	8mg	8mg
Sodium	2,300mg*	1,500mg*	2,300mg*	1,500mg*
Calcium	1,000mg	1,200mg	1,000mg	1,000mg

*Or less, for optimum health.

NUTRITIONAL VALUES USED IN OUR CALCULATIONS EITHER COME FROM THE FOOD PROCESSOR, VERSION 10.4 (ESHA RESEARCH), OR ARE PROVIDED BY FOOD MANUFACTURERS.

Seasonal Produce Guide

When you use fresh fruits, vegetables, and herbs, you don't have to do much to make them taste great. Although many fruits, vegetables, and herbs are available year-round, you'll get better flavor and prices when you buy what's in season. The Seasonal Produce Guide below helps you choose the best produce so you can create sensational meals all year long.

Spring

Fruits
Bananas
Blood oranges
Coconuts
Grapefruit
Kiwifruit
Lemons
Limes
Mangoes
Navel oranges
Papayas
Passionfruit
Pineapples
Strawberries
Tangerines
Valencia oranges

Vegetables
Artichokes
Arugula
Asparagus
Avocados
Baby leeks
Beets
Belgian endive
Broccoli
Cauliflower
Dandelion
 greens
Fava beans
Green onions
Green peas
Kale
Lettuce
Mushrooms
Radishes
Red potatoes
Rhubarb
Snap beans
Snow peas
Spinach
Sugar snap peas
Sweet onions
Swiss chard

Herbs
Chives
Dill
Garlic chives
Lemongrass
Mint
Parsley
Thyme

Summer

Fruits
Blackberries
Blueberries
Boysenberries
Cantaloupes
Casaba melons
Cherries
Crenshaw melons
Grapes
Guava
Honeydew melons
Mangoes
Nectarines
Papayas
Peaches
Plums
Raspberries
Strawberries
Watermelons

Vegetables
Avocados
Beets
Bell peppers
Cabbage
Carrots
Celery
Chili peppers
Collards
Corn
Cucumbers
Eggplant
Green beans
Jicama
Lima beans
Okra
Pattypan squash
Peas
Radicchio
Radishes
Summer squash
Tomatoes

Herbs
Basil
Bay leaves
Borage
Chives
Cilantro
Dill
Lavender
Lemon balm
Marjoram
Mint
Oregano
Rosemary
Sage
Summer savory
Tarragon
Thyme

Autumn

Fruits
Apples
Cranberries
Figs
Grapes
Pears
Persimmons
Pomegranates
Quinces

Vegetables
Belgian endive
Bell peppers
Broccoli
Brussels
 sprouts
Cabbage
Cauliflower
Eggplant
Escarole
Fennel
Frisée
Leeks
Mushrooms
Parsnips
Pumpkins
Red potatoes
Rutabagas
Shallots
Sweet potatoes
Winter squash
Yukon gold
 potatoes

Herbs
Basil
Bay leaves
Parsley
Rosemary
Sage
Tarragon
Thyme

Winter

Fruits
Apples
Blood oranges
Cranberries
Grapefruit
Kiwifruit
Kumquats
Lemons
Limes
Mandarin oranges
Navel oranges
Pears
Persimmons
Pomegranates
Pomelos
Tangelos
Tangerines
Quinces

Vegetables
Baby turnips
Beets
Belgian endive
Brussels sprouts
Celery root
Chili peppers
Dried beans
Escarole
Fennel
Frisée
Jerusalem
 artichokes
Kale
Leeks
Mushrooms
Parsnips
Potatoes
Rutabagas
Sweet potatoes
Turnips
Watercress
Winter squash

Herbs
Bay leaves
Chives
Parsley
Rosemary
Sage
Thyme

Ingredient Substitution Guide

If you're right in the middle of cooking and realize you don't have
a particular ingredient, refer to the substitutions in this list.

Ingredient	Substitution
Baking Products	
Baking powder, 1 teaspoon	½ teaspoon cream of tartar and ¼ teaspoon baking soda
Chocolate	
Semisweet, 1 ounce	1 ounce unsweetened chocolate and 1 tablespoon sugar
Unsweetened, 1 ounce	3 tablespoons cocoa and 1 tablespoon butter or margarine
Cocoa, ¼ cup	1 ounce unsweetened chocolate (decrease fat in recipe by ½ tablespoon)
Coconut, fresh, grated, 1½ tablespoons	1 tablespoon flaked coconut
Cornstarch, 1 tablespoon	2 tablespoons all-purpose flour or granular tapioca
Flour	
All-purpose, 1 tablespoon	1½ teaspoons cornstarch, potato starch, or rice starch
Cake, 1 cup sifted	1 cup minus 2 tablespoons all-purpose flour
Self-rising, 1 cup	1 cup all-purpose flour, 1 teaspoon baking powder, and ½ teaspoon salt
Sugar, Powdered, 1 cup	1 cup sugar and 1 tablespoon cornstarch (processed in food processor)
Honey, ½ cup	½ cup molasses or maple syrup
Eggs	
1 large	2 egg yolks for custards and cream fillings or 2 egg yolks and 1 tablespoon water for cookies
1 large	¼ cup egg substitute
2 large	3 small eggs
1 egg white (2 tablespoons)	2 tablespoons egg substitute
1 egg yolk (1½ tablespoons)	2 tablespoons sifted dry egg yolk powder and 2 teaspoons water or 1½ tablespoons thawed frozen egg yolk
Fruits and Vegetables	
Lemon, 1 medium	2 to 3 tablespoons juice and 2 teaspoons grated rind
Juice, 1 teaspoon	½ teaspoon vinegar
Peel, dried	2 teaspoons freshly grated lemon rind
Orange, 1 medium	½ cup juice and 2 tablespoons grated rind
Tomatoes, fresh, chopped, 2 cups	1 (16-ounce) can (may need to drain)
Tomato juice, 1 cup	½ cup tomato sauce and ½ cup water
Tomato sauce, 2 cups	¾ cup tomato paste and 1 cup water

Ingredient	Substitution
Dairy Products	
Milk	
Buttermilk, low-fat or fat-free, 1 cup	1 tablespoon lemon juice or vinegar and 1 cup low-fat or fat-free milk (let stand 10 minutes)
Fat-free milk, 1 cup	4 to 5 tablespoons fat-free dry milk powder; enough cold water to make 1 cup
Sour cream, 1 cup	1 cup plain yogurt
Miscellaneous	
Broth, beef or chicken, canned, 1 cup	1 bouillon cube dissolved in 1 cup boiling water
Capers, 1 tablespoon	1 tablespoon chopped dill pickles or green olives
Chile paste, 1 teaspoon	¼ teaspoon hot red pepper flakes
Chili sauce, 1 cup	1 cup tomato sauce, ¼ cup brown sugar, 2 tablespoons vinegar, ¼ teaspoon ground cinnamon, dash of ground cloves, and dash of ground allspice
Gelatin, flavored, 3-ounce pkg.	1 tablespoon unflavored gelatin and 2 cups fruit juice
Ketchup, 1 cup	1 cup tomato sauce, ½ cup sugar, and 2 tablespoons vinegar (for cooking; not to be used as a condiment)
Tahini (sesame-seed paste), 1 cup	¾ cup creamy peanut butter and ¼ cup sesame oil
Vinegar, cider, 1 teaspoon	2 teaspoons lemon juice mixed with a pinch of sugar
Wasabi, 1 teaspoon	1 teaspoon horseradish or hot dry mustard
Seasonings	
Allspice, ground, 1 teaspoon	½ teaspoon ground cinnamon and ½ teaspoon ground cloves
Apple pie spice, 1 teaspoon	½ teaspoon ground cinnamon, ¼ teaspoon ground nutmeg, and ⅛ teaspoon ground cardamom
Bay leaf, 1 whole	¼ teaspoon crushed bay leaf
Chives, chopped, 1 tablespoon	1 tablespoon chopped green onion tops
Garlic, 1 clove	1 teaspoon bottled minced garlic
Ginger	
Crystallized, 1 tablespoon	⅛ teaspoon ground ginger
Fresh, grated, 1 tablespoon	⅛ teaspoon ground ginger
Herbs, fresh, 1 tablespoon	1 teaspoon dried herbs or ¼ teaspoon ground herbs (except rosemary)
Horseradish, fresh, grated, 1 tablespoon	2 tablespoons prepared horseradish
Lemongrass, 1 stalk, chopped	1 teaspoon grated lemon zest
Mint, fresh, chopped, 3 tablespoons	1 tablespoon dried spearmint or peppermint
Mustard, dried, 1 teaspoon	1 tablespoon prepared mustard
Parsley, fresh, chopped, 1 tablespoon	1 teaspoon dried parsley
Vanilla bean, 6-inch bean	1 tablespoon vanilla extract

Metric Equivalents

The information in the following charts is provided to help cooks outside the United States successfully use the recipes in this book. All equivalents are approximate.

Cooking/Oven Temperatures

	Fahrenheit	Celsius	Gas Mark
Freeze Water	32° F	0° C	
Room Temp.	68° F	20° C	
Boil Water	212° F	100° C	
Bake	325° F	160° C	3
	350° F	180° C	4
	375° F	190° C	5
	400° F	200° C	6
	425° F	220° C	7
	450° F	230° C	8
Broil			Grill

Liquid Ingredients by Volume

¼ tsp	=	1 ml				
½ tsp	=	2 ml				
1 tsp	=	5 ml				
3 tsp	=	1 tbl	=	½ fl oz	=	15 ml
2 tbls	=	⅛ cup	=	1 fl oz	=	30 ml
4 tbls	=	¼ cup	=	2 fl oz	=	60 ml
5⅓ tbls	=	⅓ cup	=	3 fl oz	=	80 ml
8 tbls	=	½ cup	=	4 fl oz	=	120 ml
10⅔ tbls	=	⅔ cup	=	5 fl oz	=	160 ml
12 tbls	=	¾ cup	=	6 fl oz	=	180 ml
16 tbls	=	1 cup	=	8 fl oz	=	240 ml
1 pt	=	2 cups	=	16 fl oz	=	480 ml
1 qt	=	4 cups	=	32 fl oz	=	960 ml
				33 fl oz	=	1000 ml = 1 l

Dry Ingredients by Weight

(To convert ounces to grams, multiply the number of ounces by 30.)

1 oz	=	¹⁄₁₆ lb	=	30 g
4 oz	=	¼ lb	=	120 g
8 oz	=	½ lb	=	240 g
12 oz	=	¾ lb	=	360 g
16 oz	=	1 lb	=	480 g

Length

(To convert inches to centimeters, multiply the number of inches by 2.5.)

1 in	=			2.5 cm		
6 in	=	½ ft	=	15 cm		
12 in	=	1 ft	=	30 cm		
36 in	=	3 ft	=	1 yd	=	90 cm
40 in	=			100 cm	=	1 m

Equivalents for Different Types of Ingredients

Standard Cup	Fine Powder (ex. flour)	Grain (ex. rice)	Granular (ex. sugar)	Liquid Solids (ex. butter)	Liquid (ex. milk)
1	140 g	150 g	190 g	200 g	240 ml
¾	105 g	113 g	143 g	150 g	180 ml
⅔	93 g	100 g	125 g	133 g	160 ml
½	70 g	75 g	95 g	100 g	120 ml
⅓	47 g	50 g	63 g	67 g	80 ml
¼	35 g	38 g	48 g	50 g	60 ml
⅛	18 g	19 g	24 g	25 g	30 ml

subject index

recipe title index